WORD 2013
FOR LAW FIRMS

Luminis Books

Check the Web for Updates

To check for updates or corrections relevant to this book, visit our updates page on the Web at www.thepaynegroup.com/downloads/word2013forlawfirms/.

How to Order

For information on quantity discounts, contact the publisher at: Luminis Books, 1950 East Greyhound Pass #18, PMB 280, Carmel, IN 46033; by phone at 317-250-9539; or via e-mail at editor@luminisbooks.com.

Include information concerning the number of books you want to purchase.

You can also purchase individual copies of the book in print or e-book format on our website: www.luminisbooks.com.

WORD 2013
FOR LAW FIRMS

PayneGroup, Inc.

Luminis Books

Published by Luminis Books
1950 East Greyhound Pass, #18, PMB 280
Carmel, Indiana, 46033, U.S.A.

Publisher: Chris Katsaropoulos
Project Manager: Debbie Abshier of Abshier House
Copy Editor & Indexer: Kelly Dobbs Henthorne of Abshier House
Interior Layout: Lissa Auciello-Brogan of Abshier House
Proofreader: Kim Heusel of Abshier House
Cover design: Joanne Riske

PUBLISHER'S NOTICE
The Publisher and Author cannot provide software support. Please contact the appropriate software manufacturer's technical support line or website for assistance. The Publisher and Author make no warranties or representations regarding the accuracy or completeness of this work and disclaim all warranties, including without limitation warranties of fitness for a particular purpose. The information contained in this guide may not be suitable for every situation, and the Publisher is not engaged in providing legal, accounting, or other professional services. Some information and links on the Internet change frequently. The Publisher is not responsible for content on third-party websites referenced in this work and does not endorse any organization or information provided on such sites. Neither the Publisher nor Author shall be liable for damages arising herefrom.

Softcover ISBN: 978-1-935462-88-0
eBook ISBN: 978-1-935462-89-7

Printed in the United States of America

10 9 8 7 6 5 4 3 2 1

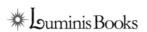

A LETTER FROM DONNA PAYNE

Here we are again, writing another Microsoft Word for Law Firms book. Our first of this title was published in March 1998, when we released *Word 97 for Law Firms.* The title went on to become a bestseller for computer books, shocking both us and many in the publishing world who had passed on the opportunity. This book, *Word 2013 for Law Firms*, is our thirteenth to date. We've continued this tradition as a direct result of the feedback we receive from people like you who have read our previous Word for Law Firms books and demand that the series continue. As Microsoft Word has changed and improved over the years, we've been able to focus on areas within the software of specific interest to the legal community. Not everyone has time to delve deeply into the software, which necessitates a book that covers all of the relevant functionality used in the creation of legal documents.

A friend and former executive at Microsoft reminded me recently that the more things change, the more they stay the same. Microsoft Word is still the leading word processing software in terms of popularity, and most law firms and legal departments have successfully made the switch. In spite of that fact, books specifically designed to address the legal professional's needs are few and far between. In our legal world, courts dictate many formatting and other document requirements, which must be adhered to without exception. Additionally, there is also a constant need to create complex, lengthy documents that also have unique formatting requirements. That is where this book differs from other books designed for the broader audience of professionals using Word 2013.

Our approach this time around was to go out to the greater community at large and ask external subject matter experts, even from competing companies, for their feedback and comments on certain features of Word 2013. In this book, you'll find inclusions from our amazing team here at PayneGroup, alongside leading industry experts including Andrea Cannavina, Barrie Hadfield, Charlene LeMaire, Clare Waller, Craig Ball, Gina Buser, Jan Berinstein, Jeffrey Roach, Dean Leung, Linda Sackett, Marcus Bluestein, Monica Bay, Norm Thomas, Peggy Weschler, Randi Mayes, Ray Zwiefelhofer, and Sherry Kappel. This is the great brain trust from which we had the great fortune to collaborate. There are many more people that we would have liked to include but alas, we wanted to keep the book to a manageable size.

It's always been PayneGroup's mission to help make the software tools available to the legal community easier to understand and use. With this goal in mind, we not only offer our Word for Law Firms publications, but training, consulting, and migration services as well. Where we see a unique software need not being addressed, we step up to the plate and create our own. For example, our Metadata Assistant was the first metadata cleaner available on the market and is now used by millions of people around the world. PayneGroup has created numerous software tools over the past two decades to assist with the creation and editing of legal documents as well as providing a number of security programs that address security and privacy concerns. We listen to what you have to say and sincerely appreciate your feedback.

Yours truly,

Donna Payne

CEO and founder of PayneGroup, Inc.

ACKNOWLEDGMENTS

In the 20 years we've been in business, and 13 books later, we have now worked with so many people that it would be impossible to thank everyone individually. Please know that we appreciate every client, some of whom have been with us from the very beginning and who are beyond loyal. A competitor once told us that they are never successful in trying to unseat us from an organization because of the loyalty that they have toward PayneGroup. You have our heartfelt gratitude.

We would also like to thank everyone who has purchased this book as well as previous versions. So many people have showed us their now dogged-eared, marked-up, sticky-note copies that they have held onto even years after the retirement of that version of software. We hope that you will find this book as helpful, and ultimately, as well used as our previous books.

Industry Experts Who Provided Comments or Quotes

We'd like to thank the experts who lent their name and thoughts for this book:

- Dean Leung, Holland & Knight LLP (www.hklaw.com)
- Monica Bay, Legal Technology News (www.lawtechnews.com)
- Craig Ball, Caig D. Ball P.C. (www.CraigBall.com)
- Peggy Weschler, ILTA (www.iltanet.org)
- Randi Mayes, ILTA (www.iltanet.org)
- Ray Zwiefelhofer, World Software Corporation (www.worldox.com)
- Marcus Bluestein, Kraft & Kennedy (www.kraftkennedy.com)
- Barrie Hadfield, Workshare (www.workshare.com)
- Charlene LeMaire, Traveling Coaches (www.travelingcoaches.com)
- Gina Buser, Traveling Coaches (www.travelingcoaches.com)
- Clare Waller, Tikit (www.tikit.com/)
- Linda Sackett, The Sackett Group (www.thesackettgroup.com)
- Norm Thomas, Litéra (www.litera.com)
- Sherry Kappel, Litéra (www.litera.com)
- Jeffrey Roach, Encoretech (www.encoretech.com)

- Andrea Cannavina, LegalTypist (www.legaltypist.com)
- Jan Berinstein, CompuSavvy (www.compusavvy.com)

International Legal Technology Association (ILTA)

The best way to describe ILTA is friends, community, educational, and beneficial. ILTA is a peer-networking organization, providing information on technology to its members to maximize the value of technology in support of the legal profession. We always look forward to the annual conference each summer as well as the other events throughout the year. Donna Payne was awarded the 2013 Vendor Thought Leader of the Year award from ILTA, and we feel very grateful to be a part of this great organization.

Many thanks to the organizers and members of ILTA, especially Randi Mayes, Peggy Weschler, Ken Hansen, Gail Persichilli, Kristy Costello, TJ Johnson, Kristi Cole, Joy Heath Rush, Robert Dubois, Michele Gossmeyer, Steve Skidmore, Janet Day, Kate Cain, Meredith Williams, Asima Macci, Shirley Crow, Kara Portwood, Michelle Spencer, and so many more. Tell a friend about ILTA: http://www.iltanet.org/default.aspx.

Special Professional Acknowledgment

Monica Bay, editor-in-chief of ALM's *Law Technology News* magazine, is a long-time supporter and advocate for news on technology that affects the practice of law. A lawyer herself, Monica works tirelessly to provide relevant and timely information to the legal community while still making the time to spotlight the achievements of others. Monica has our respect and admiration, and we are in awe of her energy.

Craig Ball is a trial lawyer, technologist, computer forensic examiner, and columnist extraordinaire. He has speaking engagements around the world and is arguably one of the most knowledgeable technical forensics experts on the planet. He's also the person to whom we bow down to as "master of all things Power-Point" for lawyers. His depth of knowledge is eclipsed only by his charm.

Charles Christian is a former practicing barrister turned independent commentator and journalist. He's our London-based friend who never fails to share honest, helpful advice on technology as well as advice on how to best extend our market into the U.K. He's been known to refer to us as seagulls, but we know it comes from his affection for our company.

Thank you also goes out to the following people for providing references and support over the years: Andy Adkins, Doug Caddell, Christy Burke, Tom Burke, Stuart Kay, Maria Luisa (Maui) Paul, Robyn Pascale, Amy Freese, Stacie Oste, Jason Tank, Mary Ann Lipkin, Zenith Murrell-Brown, Darin Fabian, Neil Pope, Jobst Elster, LaFleur, Patti O'Hara, Dennis Kennedy, JoAnna Forshee, Heather Morrow, Judi Flournoy, David Woolstencroft, Ron Poole, George Thomas, Mary Hoskins, John Sroka, Steve Sinofsky, David Michel, Peter Parsons, Sharon Nelson, John Simek, and Eugene Stein.

The list could go on and on, but there's one final person whom we want to mention here: Ross Kodner, a dear friend, colleague, and true legal expert, who passed in 2013. He was a vibrant character who has left an indelible impression on everyone he met, and he is missed.

Book Production

Last but certainly not least, this book could not be possible without the people doing all of the work behind the scenes, who often don't receive the credit they deserve. To Debbie Abshier of Abshier House who badgered us until we gave in and wrote another book. She was the first to believe in the Word for Law Firms series and has been a supporter of the book, and PayneGroup, from the very beginning. Debbie introduced us to Chris Katsaropoulos of Luminis Books, who has been incredible to work with. Chris is a published author himself and knows what it's like on both sides of the publishing process. By far, he is one of the nicest, easiest people to work with. Kelly Henthorne was a dream copy editor. She worked her magic on the editing process to make the content even better. She also put up with our ever-constant requests to make "just one more change." She's also the person who tackled the index that makes this book all the more useful. Lissa Auciello-Brogan is a pro at layout. She came up with incredible ideas that were literally out of the box and did an exceptional job with the layout of this book. Kim Heusel was proofreader extraordinaire, and thankfully caught a few typos before going to print. Finally, Joanne Riske did a remarkable job on cover design. To all of you—thank you. You made the process less painful, and at times, even fun.

ABOUT THE AUTHORS

PayneGroup, Inc., is a software training and development company specializing in working with law firms, government, and corporate legal departments. We have authored thirteen books on Microsoft software including the best-selling series, *Word 2003, Word 2002, Word 2000, and Word 97 for Law Firms* and *Excel for Law Firms.* We were an original member of the Microsoft Legal Advisory Council, and because of this, have worked with the evolution of Word and Office each step of the way. We are longtime supporters and sponsors of the International Legal and Technology Association (ILTA), a Microsoft Gold Partner, and a member of the International Association for Privacy Professionals.

Our professional services department has had the pleasure of working with thousands of people in law firms and in organizations around the world—from the United States to the Philippines, Sweden, South Africa, and all points in between. From each, we learn more about how the software is used in order to help with these books. We learn as much from our students (and clients) as they do from our teaching. If you want to take your knowledge to the next level after reading this book, we suggest that you attend our high-level Master Series: *Word 2013 for Law Firms* course.

Our products are used extensively around the globe. The famous Assistants— *Metadata, Numbering, Forms, Pleadings, Outlook Send,* and *Redact*—are the result of suggestions made by clients on what would make working with software easier. We strive for ease of use and simplified processes, and to fill the void left by other products on the market, all the while keeping the products affordable, applicable, and up to date.

The company Web address is www.thepaynegroup.com. You'll find us on Facebook at https://www.facebook.com/PayneGroup1. For more information, send an e-mail to info@thepaynegroup.com. We would love to hear from you.

PAYNEGROUP AUTHORS AND CONTRIBUTORS

At PayneGroup, we take pride in the fact that every project is a team effort, this book being no exception. The following people worked diligently on the book in some capacity, whether writing, taking hundreds of figure captures, editing, or in other ways during the extensive writing process.

Primary Writers

Donna Payne is the CEO and founder of the PayneGroup. She is a world-renowned speaker at legal and technical conferences and has moved into the keynote speaker arena. In August 2013, she received the ILTA Vendor Thought Leader of the Year award and directly after this, was featured in an article in *Law Technology News,* (profile: STEM). Donna is an author, speaker, and visionary who understands the unique needs of the industry.

Susan Horiuchi is the Vice President of Professional Services for PayneGroup. In addition to managing the professional services and training division, Susan develops client training programs and provides high-end technical training and project management services. Susan is a Microsoft Certified Trainer and has well over 20 years of experience in the legal industry and PayneGroup combined.

Annette Sanders is a Master Series for Law Firms instructor and senior trainer with PayneGroup. She frequently conducts train-the-trainer sessions on Microsoft Office, document management, PayneGroup products, and other legal-specific software to an organization's training and support personnel. Annette has more than two decades of experience in the large law firm environment providing training, support, and project management services.

Shirley Gorman is the Vice President of Client Relations for PayneGroup. She has been with PayneGroup 14 years. Prior to joining PayneGroup, Shirley had more than 20 years of experience working for a large international law firm, managing training and development services. She was also an original member of the Microsoft Legal Advisory Council.

Sue Hughes has worked in the Security Products Division of PayneGroup for the past 7 years. Prior to that, Sue worked in the IT department of a Seattle-based law firm for 13 years, which gives her unique insights into how law firms create and handle documents, as well as the pressures attorneys, staff, and IT personnel have on a daily basis. Sue is on the board of editors and is a column contributor for the *Legal Journal Newsletter*.

Tara Byers is the Vice President of Development and Product Workflow. She has been with PayneGroup for more than 16 years. She has extensive project management experience, assisting global and domestic firms with their software migrations. She is well-versed in all things Australian having just returned from a long project in Perth. Tara is a true Word expert.

Karen Walker is a senior member of the PayneGroup development team. She has been with PayneGroup 15 years. Not only is she expert at VB.Net, and the Word and Office object model, Karen has extensive database and networking experience as well. She is also one heck of a mentor. Karen has years of experience working in a large Seattle-based law firm.

Leah Matthews is also a senior member of the PayneGroup development team and has many technical certifications. Armed with her more than two decades of legal experience, she is the lead for providing our software migration service to firms moving to new versions of Office, including Office 2013.

Contributors

The following people contributed their time in some way to making this book happen.

Bryan Blackburn

Michelle Guyot

Michael Whalen

Robert Affleck

CONTENTS AT A GLANCE

CONTENTS

INTRODUCTION TO WORD 2013 FOR LAW FIRMS

The software Microsoft Word was not designed specifically for law firms. In fact, if you work in the legal industry—whether it be a law firm, the government, or corporate legal department, you might find yourself struggling with some features and functionality in order to accomplish tasks that need to be completed on a daily basis. That's why you will find this book, which is expressly written for the legal professional, a useful tool for mastering the application, finding work-arounds, and troubleshooting problems.

This book explains the new and improved features of Word 2013, and more importantly, provides information on how to successfully use Word in a legal environment. We talk about troubleshooting numbering, styles, compatibility, and yes, even pleadings. If a feature isn't used in a law firm, we save the space and tackle more useful topics.

While many legal professionals are comfortable in the world of Microsoft Word, there are still features, functionally, and, yes, workarounds that need to be discussed in a book such as this.

Word 2013 for Law Firms is our thirteenth book, and we hope you find it useful and a welcome addition to your library.

OFFICE 365 INFORMATION

This book was written primarily for those using Microsoft Office Word 2013 for Windows. That said, enough of us are now using the cloud version of the software to warrant inclusion of some Office 365 tips scattered throughout the chapters whenever features or functionality differ.

There are currently many things that you cannot do in Word using Office 365; however, since this is a cloud version, updates and new functionality are being introduced at an accelerated pace. For instance, from the time we started to write this book to the publish date, many changes have occurred; most notably, how coauthoring now works. It's safe to say as well that these enhancements will continue, and some features that do not work today will work in the future.

For this reason, this book will be useful to those who use Office 365, keeping in mind that it's written primarily for those who use the installed desktop version of Word 2013.

WHO SHOULD USE THIS BOOK

This book is written primarily for anyone who uses Microsoft Word 2013 in a legal environment, for those who work with agreements, contracts, briefs, pleadings, correspondence, and other types of legal documents. In essence, if you use Word to create, edit, or share business documents, then this book is for you. It includes information for people new to Word as well as information geared toward the more advanced, expert Word enthusiasts.

More importantly, the book has applicability for an individual working in any size organization, from the sole practitioner to the IT applications specialist in a large international law firm. And while the title identifies law firms, government and corporate legal users will see immediate parallel to the types of documents they produce. The book focuses on what we all need to accomplish—successfully using Word to create, edit, and share documents.

ACCESSING THE EXERCISE FILES ONLINE

This book provides hands-on exercises to help better familiarize yourself with each of the topics covered. You will also find additional information and the downloadable exercise files posted to our website at www.thepaynegroup.com/downloads/word2013forlawfirms/. We'll try to continually add information and value added content to that location as well, so check back regularly. We chose to make the exercise files a download rather than a CD. The reason for this decision is that many new computers, such as the ultra-books, don't come with CD-ROM drives; whereas, most people have access to the Internet to allow for new information to be shared. If you ever have problems accessing the files, please contact us directly at CustomerRelations@thepaynegroup.com, and we'll make sure you get the files you need.

HOW TO READ THIS BOOK

Each chapter in the book provides an abundance of practical, hands-on exercises. These exercises have been designed to walk you through the steps to accomplish each of the tasks needed to get the job done. If you are trying to troubleshoot a problem within a document, look for our expert sections to help resolve the issue. For the most comprehensive understanding of Word, however, we recommend that you read through all the text. We've supplemented the narrative with notes, tips, and expert sections explaining various aspects of Word's features that may not be covered in as much detail as needed if just referring to the step-by-step exercises.

You don't have to use the book in any particular order; in fact, we think that you'll find it useful again and again as a reference source as issues arise.

Conventions Used in This Book

Understanding the conventions used in this book will help you get the most out of the chapters. There are more conventions than just those that apply to Windows applications. This book has conventions of its own to make it easier to use.

Keyboard Shortcuts

Keyboard shortcuts are a combination of keys that you must press to access commands within Word 2013. Keyboard combinations are keys you must hold down simultaneously to get them to work. For example, pressing Ctrl+F is the shortcut to display the Navigation Pane. Some key combinations require pressing more than two keys. When you see a keyboard combination, you must hold down all of its keys at the same time for it to work.

Other Conventions

- **Bold Text.** Bold text has been used to indicate text you must type to complete an exercise. For example, if we ask you to name a document **clientagreement.docx**, it means to type "clientagreement.docx" (with no quotes) into the File Name box.

- **Key Conventions.** When referring to keys on the keyboard, not in Word, those keys are given the names printed on them whenever possible. The most common are Shift, Ctrl, Alt, Enter, Tab, and Spacebar. They all have initial capital letters.

Special Elements

You will see the following items used throughout this book:

TIP

This is a Tip. Tips are used to show you shortcuts and alternate methods for accomplishing tasks.

NOTE

This is a Note. Notes are used when we need to give you more information about a task or feature. We might also use Notes to help you troubleshoot mishaps.

CAUTION

This is a Caution. Cautions are used when we need to alert you to a potential problem or common misunderstanding.

EXPERT TIP

This is an Expert Tip. An Expert Tip is when we need to share information that is more advanced or considered expert level. It might be for troubleshooting or advanced functionality.

HOLLAND & KNIGHT LLP

This is an External Expert Tip. An External Expert Tip is when a leading subject matter expert, outside of PayneGroup, provides useful commentary on Word 2013 functionality.

For Addison and Cooper

GETTING AROUND WORD

Welcome to Word 2013!

Microsoft Word is one of the most invaluable tools in the legal environment, providing the means for successful creation of the legal world's most basic building block—the legal document. A solid understanding of Word basics is paramount. In this first chapter, we begin by taking a tour of the user interface and various screen components and features of the workplace in Word 2013.

WORD START SCREEN

When you first open Word, you are met with the Start screen (see Figure 1.1). In earlier versions of Word you started off with a blank document. Now you are given the option to either create a blank document, select from basic templates provided by Microsoft, search online for more Microsoft-provided templates, select from your own templates, or select from a list of recently used documents.

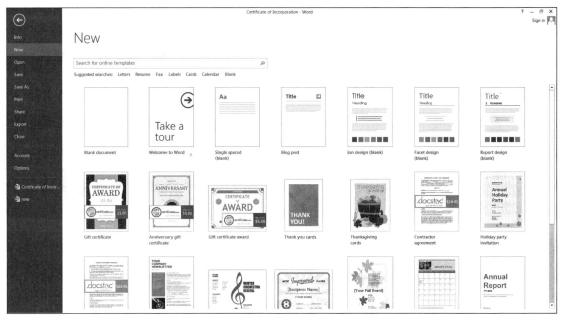

Figure 1.1   Word 2013's Start screen.

On the left side of the screen is a list of recently opened documents. The recent document list not only provides the filename, but the file location as well. The number of recent documents listed depends on your screen resolution. In a 1920x1200 screen resolution, 19 documents will display, whereas with a 1280x800 screen resolution, only 11 documents will display.

NOTE

To have Word 2013 start with the blank document as in earlier versions, you can turn off the Start screen by selecting File, Options, and from the General tab in the Start Up Options section, uncheck the Show the Start Screen When this Application Starts check box, as shown in Figure 1.2.

SIGNING INTO YOUR MICROSOFT ACCOUNT

When you open an Office 2013 application for the first time, whether it's Word, Excel, PowerPoint, or any of the other Office applications, you are prompted to sign into your Microsoft account (previously known as Windows Live ID). Many features in Office 2013 were designed to work with an online connection. In Word, not only are you able to save, open, and share files online, but you also have the ability to access services such as online dictionaries (e.g., Merriam-Webster Dictionary) or online pictures (e.g., Office.com Clip Art).

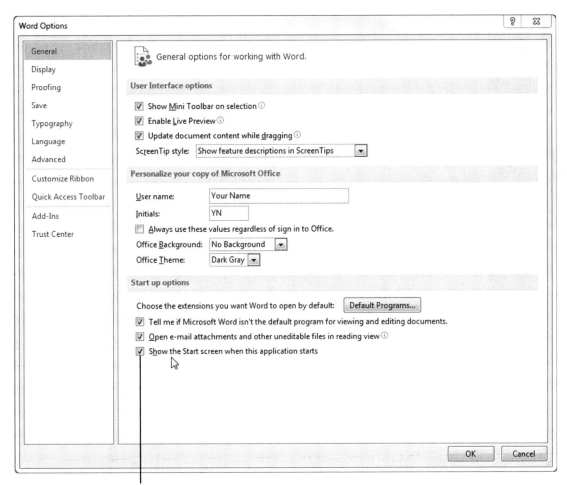

Disable Word 2013 Start screen

Figure 1.2　Disable the Word 2013 Start screen.

Any configuration changes you make to your computer, such as a desktop theme, list of recently accessed documents, pinned templates, or custom dictionaries, can all travel with you from computer to computer when you are signed into your Microsoft account.

If you opt to not sign in when prompted, you can always sign in at a later time. To sign in, simply click on Sign In in the upper-right corner of the screen or select File, Account, Sign In, as shown in Figure 1.3. After you have signed in, your account name will appear in the upper-right corner of the window.

Sign in or out

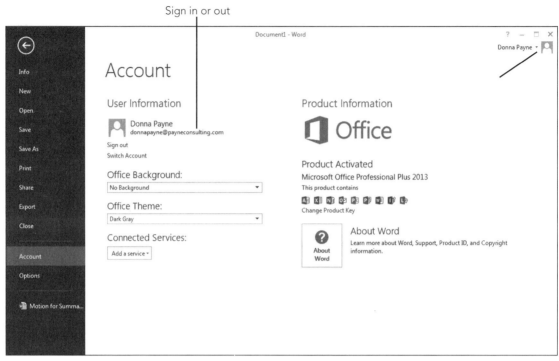

Figure 1.3 Sign in to your Microsoft Account.

NOTE

If you have a SkyDrive account set up and want to remove it from your profile, open from within Word, choose File, and then Account. Under Connected Services, find the associated SkyDrive account and click Remove, which appears to the right of each connection, and then Sign Out and Restart the computer. Removing this connection could impact other settings on your computer such as themes and backgrounds, so make sure you really want to disconnect prior to doing so.

OFFICE 365

When signing into Office 365, the first screen you will see is the Recent Documents of any files you have saved to your cloud drive. By clicking the 'See more documents in SkyDrive link', a second window will appear with the ability to Create or Upload more files. Your firm may have a custom environment that does not match this description.

OFFICE BACKGROUND AND OFFICE THEMES

In Office 2013, you can add a bit of personality to all of your Office applications with custom backgrounds and themes. Background and Themes allow you to customize the look and feel of Word with the design and background color of your choice.

To change the background color and/or theme, click on the File tab and select Account. Under User Information, click the drop-down arrow for Office Background. As you hover your mouse pointer over the selections, notice in the upper-right corner of the window how the title bar is changing. Once you find the one you like, click to select it. To change the background color, three different themes are available—White (default), Light Gray, and Dark Gray. Click the drop-down arrow for Office Theme and select from the available themes. Figure 1.4 shows how you can personalize your Office background and themes.

Figure 1.4   Personalize your Office Background and Office Theme.

NOTE

Changing your Office Background and/or Office Theme in one of the Office suite programs changes the background and/or theme in all of your Office suite programs.

Many find the default White theme to be hard on the eyes. If you are responsible for creating an image for your organization, or just want to customize the look for yourself, try Light Gray or Dark Gray.

TOURING THE WORKPLACE IN WORD

In Word 2013, the workplace has once again gone through a "look and feel" overhaul. You still see the ribbon environment with various tabs to access all of the tremendous functionality of Word; however, the workplace is much cleaner and gives more focus to what we're actually here for: the document.

Menus have been completely removed in Word 2013. The multiple menus and toolbars found in earlier versions of Word have all been replaced with ribbon tabs, commands, and two toolbars—the Quick Access Toolbar and the Mini toolbar. The following new and improved features in Word 2013 will be covered in this chapter.

- **Quick Access Toolbar.** This toolbar appears in the upper-left corner of the Word window and gets you started with three commands. You can easily customize this toolbar to add your favorite commands.

- **Tabs.** Just below the Quick Access Toolbar are nine default tabs: File, Home, Insert, Design, Page Layout, References, Mailings, Review, and View.

- **File tab and Backstage view.** The File tab essentially replaces the File menu found in earlier versions of Word. On the File tab are familiar commands such as New, Open, Save, Print, and Close. When you click the File tab, it displays what's called the Backstage view.

- **Ribbon.** The ribbon is a graphical element in the Word window that replaces menus and toolbars. The ribbon consists of organized groups of commands.

- **Contextual tabs.** Unlike the nine default tabs, contextual tabs do not show all of the time and only appear in context to what feature you are working with in Word. For example, when you access the header or footer, the Header & Footer Tools Design tab displays with options specifically for the header or footer, such as page numbering and inserting date formats—you can even set header and footer margins. When you close the header and footer, the contextual tab automatically disappears as the focus shifts away from that element.

- **Task panes.** Task panes were designed to help you work more efficiently with a number of Word's main features. Task panes are still alive and well in Word 2013 and have been added to many features that previously required a dialog box.

Word Screen Components

Everything in the Word workplace provides you with the tools needed to create and edit documents. See Table 1.1. Figure 1.5 shows the main components of the Word 2013 window.

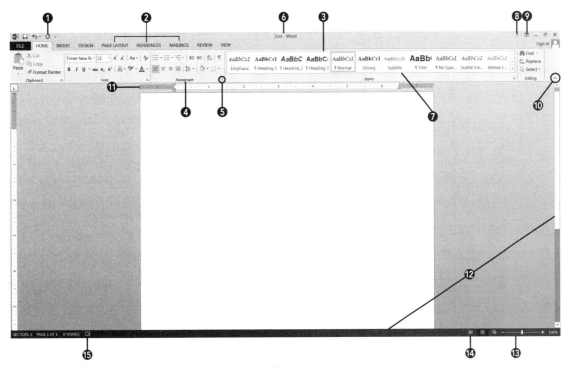

Figure 1.5   Components of the Word 2013 workplace.

Quick Access Toolbar

In earlier versions of Word, commands were found on toolbars and menus. In Word 2013, commands are found on the ribbon, the Quick Access Toolbar, the Shortcut menu, and the Mini toolbar. The Quick Access Toolbar (also known as the QAT) is customizable, allowing you to place the commands you use most often within easy reach (see Figure 1.6).

	SCREEN COMPONENT	DESCRIPTION
	TABLE 1.1—DESCRIPTION OF THE COMPONENTS OF THE WORD 2013 WORKPLACE	
1	Quick Access Toolbar	A customizable toolbar that contains your frequently used commands. It can appear above or below the ribbon.
2	Tabs	Each tab displays a ribbon with task-oriented commands specific to that tab.
3	Ribbon	The ribbon is organized using tabs for easy access to all of Word's features. It is intended to make previously buried commands more readily accessible.
4	Group	Commands are organized into logical groups on the ribbon for easy access.
5	Dialog Box Launcher	Opens a related dialog box or task pane for the group where available.
6	Title Bar	Displays the name of the program and document. If the document has not been saved, the default name will be Document(x). The title bar also shows if a document is saved in compatibility mode.
7	Gallery	Provides a collection of thumbnail designs from which to choose. Some galleries offer a live preview of the look and format for applying headers, footers, cover pages, tables, styles, and more.
8	Help	Opens the Word Help window offering online support from Microsoft.
9	Ribbon Display Options	Show Tabs and Commands is the default; alternatively, you can choose Show Tabs (without commands) or Auto-hide the Ribbon.
10	Collapse the Ribbon	Shows the tabs only. To show the ribbon again, click the Ribbon Display Options button and choose Show Tabs and Commands.
11	Horizontal Ruler	You can set and view indents and tab stops here.
12	Scroll Bar	Vertical and horizontal scroll bars allow you to quickly navigate through a document by clicking on the bar or the arrows, or dragging the scroll bar button.
13	Zoom	Click the Zoom slider located in the bottom-right portion of the status bar to set the zoom percentage for the active document.
14	Document Views	Quickly change how a document displays on-screen by clicking one of three buttons located on the status bar—Read Mode, Print Layout, or Web Layout. Outline and Draft views are found on the View tab in the Views group.
15	Status Bar	Located at the bottom of the window, the status bar displays the current state of the active document, such as the active and total number of pages, word count, whether any macros are recording, and more. Right-click on the status bar to display more options.

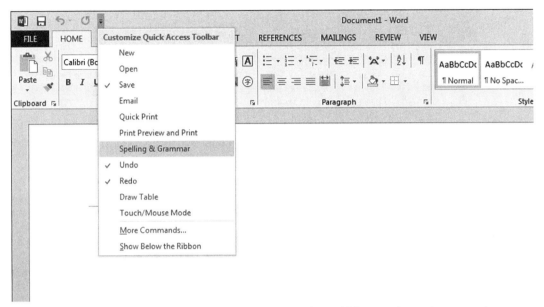

Figure 1.6   The Quick Access Toolbar can be customized to add frequently used commands.

Customize the Quick Access Toolbar

By default, the Quick Access Toolbar has only three commands—Save, Undo, and Repeat/Redo—and is located in the upper-left corner of the window. It can, however, be repositioned to appear just below the ribbon. To reposition the Quick Access Toolbar, click the down arrow at the end of the Quick Access Toolbar and select Show Below the Ribbon. Figure 1.7 shows the Quick Access Toolbar positioned below the ribbon.

Add Commands from the Ribbon

Adding commands to the Quick Access Toolbar can be accomplished in a couple of ways. The easiest way, by far, is to locate the command you want on the ribbon, right-click on the command, and then select Add to Quick Access Toolbar.

NOTE

Not only can you add commands from the ribbon to the Quick Access Toolbar, but you can also add an entire ribbon group or a dialog box launcher. Simply right-click on the group name or the dialog box launcher arrow and select Add to Quick Access Toolbar. This makes the commands available regardless of the tab that is active. Some useful groups for legal are Paragraph on the Home tab and Page Setup on the Page Layout tab. Figure 1.8 shows just how easy it is to add a command to the Quick Access Toolbar by right-clicking.

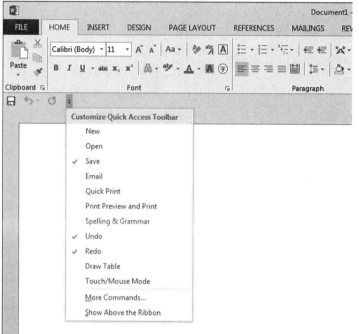

Figure 1.7

The Quick Access Toolbar can display above or below the ribbon.

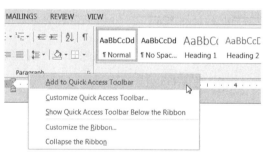

Figure 1.8 Right-click on any ribbon command to add it to the Quick Access Toolbar.

Add Commands from Customize Quick Access Toolbar

To select from a list of commonly used commands (e.g., New, Open, Save, E-mail, Quick Print, and more), click the down arrow at the end of the Quick Access Toolbar—also known as the Customize Quick Access Toolbar button—and select from the list. Each command that is on the Quick Access Toolbar will have a check mark beside it.

To select a command from the list of more than 1,700 commands available in Word, click the down arrow at the end of the Quick Access Toolbar and select More Commands. In the Choose Command From box, select All Commands, as shown in Figure 1.9. This list of commands can be filtered by the following categories: Popular Commands, Commands Not in the Ribbon, All Commands, Macros, or the ribbon tab on which the command is located.

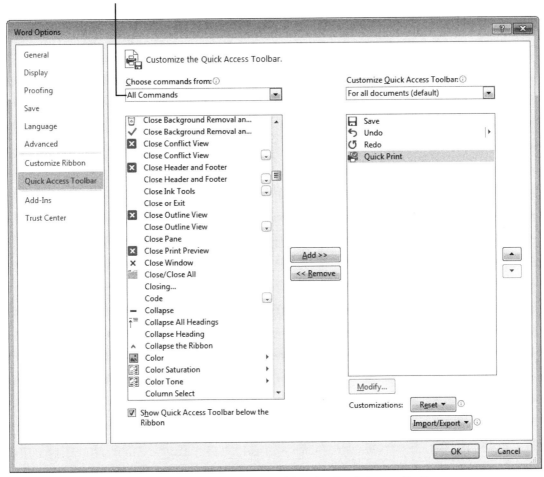

Figure 1.9 Select from hundreds of commands to add to the Quick Access Toolbar.

NOTE

When navigating to a command in the Customize Quick Access Toolbar list, you are limited to typing only the first letter of the command. After pressing the first letter of the command, you must scroll through the list using the Up and Down arrow keys.

Add a Command to the Quick Access Toolbar

1. Click Customize Quick Access Toolbar (down arrow at the end of the Quick Access Toolbar) and select More Commands.

2. Under Choose Commands From, click the drop-down list to view all of the categories. The default is Popular Commands.

3. From the Popular Commands list, select Add a Table and click Add.

4. From the Popular Commands list, select Print Preview and Print and click Add.

5. To view all of the commands available, from the Choose Commands From list, select All Commands.

6. Click on any of the commands in the list and press C to navigate to the commands beginning with the letter C.

7. Scroll down and select Close and then click Add.

8. To move the Close command to another position on the toolbar, with the Close button selected, click either the Move Up or Move Down button.

9. To remove a command, select it and click Remove.

10. Click OK to close the dialog box.

EXPERT TIP

All modifications to the Quick Access Toolbar are saved to the Word.officeUI file located by default in the following folder: C:\Users\%UserName%\AppData\ Local\Microsoft\Office.

Add a Separator

To group the commands on the Quick Access Toolbar, a vertical line known as a separator can be placed between commands. You'll find the separator at the top of the list in the Customize Quick Access Toolbar dialog box. To insert the separator, select the command you want to add a separator line after, select <Separator>, and then click Add. Adding a separator is shown in Figure 1.10.

Remove a Command

To remove a command from the Quick Access Toolbar, right-click on the command and select Remove from Quick Access Toolbar.

Reset the Quick Access Toolbar

To reset the Quick Access Toolbar to its default settings, click the Customize Quick Access Toolbar button at the right end of the Quick Access Toolbar and select More Commands. Click the Reset button and select Reset Only Quick Access Toolbar. Click Yes to confirm. Click OK to exit the Word Options dialog box and save your changes.

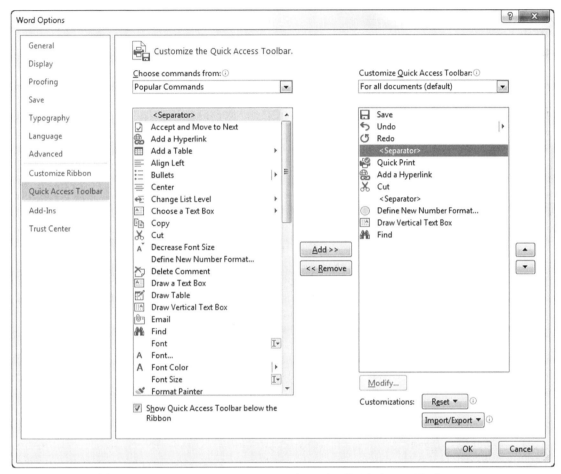

Figure 1.10   Add a separator to group your commands on the Quick Access Toolbar.

Touch/Mouse Mode

If you are working with a touch-screen device, enabling Touch Mode expands the size of the command on the ribbon, making it easier to select commands when tapping your screen.

To enable Touch Mode, you first need to add the command to your Quick Access Toolbar. Click the down arrow at the end of the Quick Access Toolbar and select Touch/Mouse Mode. This adds the Touch/Mouse Mode command to your Quick Access Toolbar. Click on the Touch/Mouse Mode command and select Touch. Notice how the commands on the ribbon are larger, making it easier to tap them with your finger. To return to Mouse Mode, click (or tap) the Touch/Mouse Mode command again and this time select Mouse. The Touch/Mouse Mode command functions as a toggle and is shown in Figure 1.11.

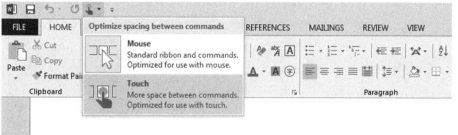

Figure 1.11 Click the Touch/Mouse Mode command to toggle from Touch to Mouse Mode.

EXPERT TIP

Copying all of the customizations you have made to your Quick Access Toolbar from one computer to another is fairly easy. There are actually two ways this can be accomplished:

- One method is to copy the file that holds the customizations from one computer to the other. By default the file is located in C:\Users\[username]\AppData\Local\Microsoft\Office and is called Word.officeUI. By default, the AppData folder is hidden. Be sure you have opted to display hidden files, folders, and drives in order to access the AppData folder.

- Another option is to export all customizations on the computer, including the Quick Access Toolbar, and then import them to another computer. Click the down arrow at the end of the Quick Access Toolbar and select More Commands. From the Customize Quick Access Toolbar tab, click the Import/Export button. Select the option to Export All Customizations and save the Word Customizations file. From the second computer, click the down arrow at the end of the Quick Access Toolbar, select More Commands, click the Import/Export button, and then select Import Customization File. Navigate to the location where you saved the Word Customizations file from the first computer, click Open, and confirm that you want to replace all existing ribbon and Quick Access Toolbar customizations.

Title Bar

At the top of the application window is the Title bar containing the icon for the application, the title of the document, and the name of the application (in this case—Word). On the far right of the Title bar are the three buttons used to minimize, restore/maximize, and close the entire Word window. New to Word 2013's Title bar are the Microsoft Word Help button and the Ribbon Display Options button. Also, just below these buttons is your Microsoft Account sign-in information.

OFFICE 365

Because you're working within a browser, be careful prior to clicking the Close button, so you don't accidentally close the browser, rather than the document.

The Ribbon

The ribbon is the mainstay of all of the Office programs. Not only will you see the ribbon interface in Word, but you will also see it in Outlook, Excel, PowerPoint, Access, InfoPath, Publisher, and OneNote. In a nutshell, the ribbon is a dynamic area devoted to commands. These commands are organized into tabs named for their functionality, and on each tab, the ribbon displays groups of task-related commands designed to give you quick and easy access to features precisely when you need them. Figure 1.12 shows the Word 2013 ribbon.

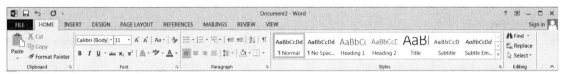

Figure 1.12   The Word 2013 ribbon.

Collapse the Ribbon

By default, the tabs and ribbon always display. However, if you prefer to have more window "real estate" so you can display more of your document, you can collapse the ribbon so that only the tabs show. To collapse the ribbon, click the Collapse the Ribbon button—it's the small caret symbol in the lower-right corner of the ribbon shown in Figure 1.13. To access any of the ribbon commands with the ribbon collapsed and only the tabs displayed, click on a tab. The ribbon will display, and you can make your selection. When finished, the ribbon goes back into hiding.

Figure 1.13

Collapsing the ribbon hides the ribbon, leaving only the tabs visible.

Collapse ribbon

TIP

Another way to collapse the ribbon is to double-click on any of the tabs, except the File tab. Double-click again on any of the tabs to expand the ribbon. You can also press Ctrl+F1 to toggle the ribbon on and off.

The Collapse Ribbon button is available in Word Web App. However, Ctrl+F1 does not control the ribbon.

OFFICE 365

Ribbon Display Options

When the ribbon is collapsed, it will only display when a tab is selected. Perhaps you would like to completely hide the tabs as well as the Status bar, or show the tabs and commands again. In the upper-right corner of the Word window, click Ribbon Display Options. There are three options available: Auto-Hide Ribbon, Show Tabs, and Show Tabs and Commands. These options are shown in Figure 1.14.

Auto-Hide Ribbon hides the ribbon, tabs, and Status bar, leaving you with only your document displaying. To access the ribbon, hover at the top of the window, and a blue band will appear. Click on the blue band, and the ribbon appears. Click away from the ribbon, and the ribbon and tabs are once again hidden.

Select Show Tabs to display just the ribbon tabs. To restore the ribbon and the tabs, select Show Tabs and Commands.

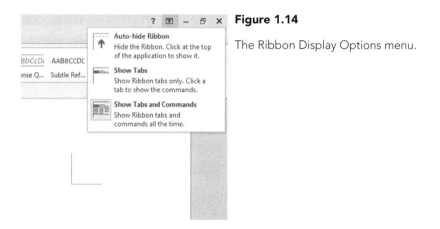

Figure 1.14

The Ribbon Display Options menu.

Groups

Commands on the ribbon are grouped together based on their functionality. Centered at the bottom of each group, you will find the name of that group, as shown in Figure 1.15. For example, on the Home tab, you will find the following groups: Clipboard, Font, Paragraph, Styles, and Editing.

Figure 1.15   Associated commands appear on the ribbon in groups.

Dialog Box Launcher

You'll notice a small arrow button in the lower-right corner of some of the groups. This button is called the Dialog Box Launcher and gives you access to the dialog box or task pane related to the group. The dialog boxes associated with the Dialog Box Launcher are very similar to the dialog boxes used in earlier versions of Word, and when making the transition from menus and toolbars to ribbons, can be very welcome. Figures 1.16 and 1.17 show the Dialog Box Launcher and resulting dialog box once it is clicked.

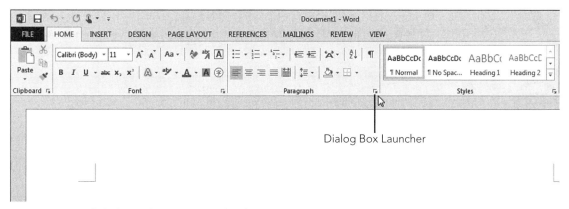

Dialog Box Launcher

Figure 1.16   Click the Dialog Box Launcher for more options.

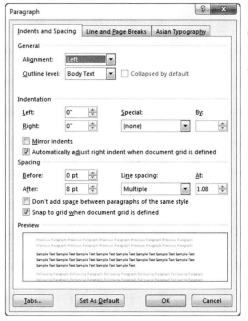

Figure 1.17

Clicking the Dialog Box Launcher in the Paragraph group opens the Paragraph dialog box.

Tabs

When you first open Word 2013, eight default tabs are across the top of the window. Each of these tabs displays a ribbon with commands relating to the subject of the tab. The tab that is selected initially is the Home tab, which contains the most basic font and paragraph formatting commands, clipboard commands, editing commands, as well as the Quick Style Gallery. The eight default tabs are Home, Insert, Design, Page Layout, References, Mailings, Review, and View.

NOTE

If you see more tabs besides the eight default tabs, you probably have a Word add-in program that creates its own separate tab. For instance, if you have a document management system, look for the tab related to that system.

EXPERT TIP

In Office 2013, tab titles display in all caps. At first glance, it appears that this cannot be changed. When you attempt to rename the default tabs, they revert to all caps. However, if you rename the tab and include a space before the name (i.e., replace Home with {space}Home), the name will display in initial caps.

Contextual Tabs

There are other tabs, 21 to be exact, that display only when needed. These tabs are called contextual tabs. For instance, when you insert a table or click inside of an existing table, the Table Tools Design and Layout tabs are displayed, as shown in Figure 1.18. Click outside of the table, and these tabs disappear; click within the table again, and they reappear. These tabs were designed to make it easier to apply task-oriented features relating specifically to that task.

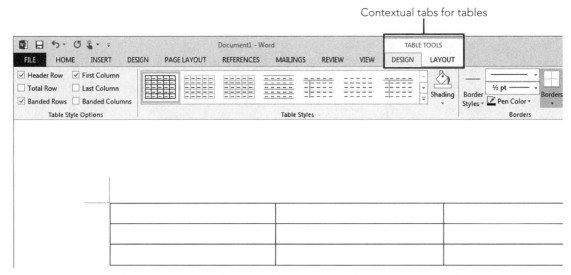

Figure 1.18 The Table Tools Design and Layout tabs are displayed when you're in a table.

The Header & Footer Tools Design tab, shown in Figure 1.19, is another great example of a contextual tab. Click within the header or footer, and the Header & Footer Tools Design tab displays, giving you easy access to commands relating to the header and footer.

Header & Footer Tools Design tab

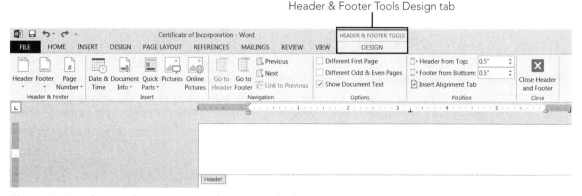

Figure 1.19   The Header & Footer Tools Design tab displays when editing the header or footer.

Following is a list of the contextual tabs available in Word 2013:

- Background Removal tab
- Blog Post tab
- Insert Blog Post tab
- Chart Tools – Design tab
- Chart Tools – Format tab
- Diagram Tools – (Compatibility Mode)
- Drawing Tools – Format tab
- Drawing Tools – Format tab (Compatibility Mode)
- Equation Tools – Design tab
- Header & Footer Tools – Design tab
- Ink Tools – Pens tab
- Outlining tab
- Organization Chart Tools – Format tab (Compatibility Mode)
- Picture Tools – Format tab
- Picture Tools – Format tab (Compatibility Mode)
- SmartArt Tools – Design tab
- SmartArt Tools – Format tab

- Table Tools – Design tab
- Table Tools – Layout tab
- Text Box Tools – Format tab (Compatibility Mode)
- WordArt Tools – Format tab (Compatibility Mode)

Developer Tab

Most people don't use the advanced development features in Word, so by default the Developer tab is hidden. If you are one of those users who develops forms, writes macros, or uses XML commands or ActiveX controls, the Developer tab is a necessity. To display the Developer tab, click the File tab, and then Options. Click Customize Ribbon and then select the Developer check box from the Main Tabs list.

Add-ins Tab

The Add-Ins tab is another tab that does not display by default. This tab will display if any COM (Component Object Model) add-ins are installed, or if any templates with toolbars from earlier versions of Word are installed.

Task Panes

Task panes provide easy access to commands and features. You'll notice several features now show up as task panes rather than as a dialog box. Some good examples are Spelling, Grammar, Dictionary, and Format Picture. These task panes and more will be discussed in greater detail when we cover features that use a task pane.

File Tab and Backstage View

The File tab essentially replaces the File menu found in earlier versions of Word. On the File tab, you will find familiar commands such as New, Open, Save, Print, and Close. When you click the File tab, it displays what is known as the Backstage view.

If you have a document open, Backstage view will default to the Info tab, which provides information about the document and options relating to the document's properties. These options include the capabilities to restrict editing of a document, check for issues relating to hidden or personal information, accessibility, compatibility, conversion of a document to the newest format, and managing versions. Figure 1.20 shows the expanded Backstage view.

Figure 1.20   Open, close, save, and print documents as well as view document properties from Backstage view.

TIP

Once in Backstage view, to return to the document all you need to do is click the arrow button in the upper-left corner of the window or press the Esc key. In Word 2013, the tabs are no longer visible from Backstage view as they were in previous versions.

OFFICE 365

While Word Web App has a Backstage view, it is limited in the available options compared to those in the installed version of Word 2013.

Print Preview and Print

In Word 2013, Print Preview and Print are now in the same window as shown in Figure 1.21. The Print tab in Backstage view not only provides options for printing, but also shows a preview of the document. To display Print Preview, select the File tab and then Print. The keyboard shortcut for Print Preview and Print is Ctrl+P.

TIP

You can add Print Preview and Print to the Quick Access Toolbar for easy access. Click the down arrow at the end of the Quick Access Toolbar and select Print Preview and Print.

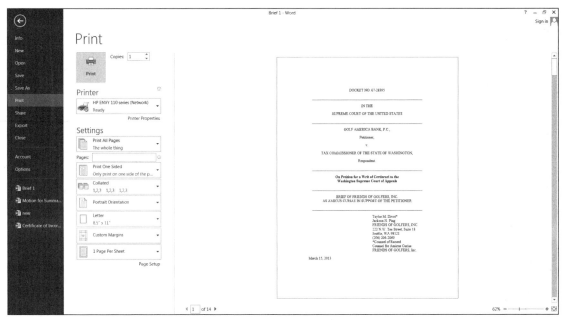

Figure 1.21 Print Preview in Word 2013 is consolidated with printing.

While in Print Preview, use the Zoom slider in the lower-right corner of the window to either zoom in to see your text better or zoom out to see page pagination. At approximately 30 percent, multiple pages will begin to display. Navigate from page to page using either the vertical scroll bar on the right or the Previous Page and Next Page buttons at the bottom of the Print Preview window.

Print the Document

The Print dialog box found in earlier versions of Word has been replaced with the Print Preview and Print window. Print options are displayed to the right of the Backstage view tabs. You can select how many copies to print, change the printer, view the printer properties, as well as set custom printer options under Settings. Click the Print button to send the document to the printer.

TIP

Add the Quick Print button to the Quick Access Toolbar to have one command to send the document directly to the printer, bypassing the Print Preview and Print window. Click the down arrow at the end of the Quick Access Toolbar and select Quick Print.

Printer Options

From the Print Preview and Print window, click on the printer to access the following options:

- **Select Printer.** Select from a list of all installed printers.

- **Add Printer.** Select this option to open the Find Printers dialog box to add another printer to the list.

- **Print to File.** Select Print to File to save the document in a print format file (*.prn).

Printer Settings

Under Settings in the Print Preview and Print window, select what pages and parts of the document you'd like to print. Select from Print All Pages, Print Selection, Print Current Page, Custom Print (prints a custom range), Document Info, List of Markup, Styles, AutoText Entries, Key Assignments, Print Markup, Only Print Odd Pages, and Only Print Even Pages. You can also opt to print on either one side of the paper or both sides of the paper and select how you want your pages collated.

NOTE

The options available for printing on both sides of the paper are determined by your printer. If automatic duplexing is available on your printer, the options for Print on Both Sides (Flip Pages on Long Edge or Flip Pages on Short Edge) will be available. If your printer does not support automatic duplex printing, you will only have the option Manually Print on Both Sides.

The rest of the options available in the Print Preview and Print window are Page Setup options. From this window, you have the ability to adjust your Page Setup options before printing without having to leave Backstage view. The available options are Orientation, Paper Size, Margins, and Pages (for printing multiple pages per sheet).

NOTE

When changing the Page Setup options from Print Preview and Print, you are only changing the settings for the current section. If your document has multiple sections and you want the changes to affect all sections, click on the Page Setup option and choose Whole Document from the Apply To list.

Status Bar

The Status bar, located at the bottom of the program window, provides important status information about the document. The Status bar can display information such as the current page and total number of pages, the number of words in the document, a check for proofing errors, whether Track Changes is turned on or off, the section number, and more. Also displayed on the Status bar are three of the View options (Read Mode, Print Layout, and Web Layout). The zoom slider and zoom percentage are also displayed at the far right of the Status bar.

The Status bar can be customized to display the options you find most helpful. Just right-click anywhere on the Status bar to display the Customize Status Bar list of options. If there is a check mark next to the option, then it will display, if active. To activate an option, all you need to do is click on it. While command options can be added to appear on the Status bar, the position of the options in the Status bar cannot be changed. Figure 1.22 shows how to customize the Status bar.

NOTE

You may notice a couple of view options missing from the Status bar in Word 2013. In earlier versions of Word, Draft and Outline views were available on the Status bar. To now access Draft and Outline views, select the View tab, and from the Views group, select Draft or Outline. Alternately, you can add these views to the Quick Access Toolbar to make them available, regardless of which tab you have active. Also missing from the Status bar is the Object Browser, which has been retired.

Figure 1.22 Customize the Status bar to show or hide additional information about the active document.

Horizontal and Vertical Scroll Bars

While dragging the button on the vertical scroll bar, Word displays ScreenTips that tell you the current page number and topic associated with that page. Figure 1.23 shows the ScreenTip on the vertical scroll bar, and Figure 1.24 displays some shortcuts for the option.

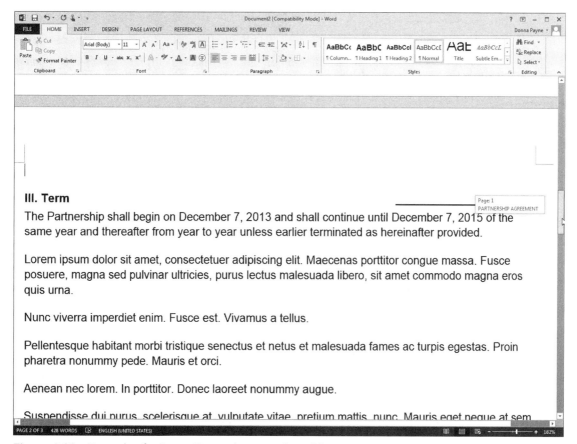

Figure 1.23   Example of a ScreenTip on the vertical scroll bar.

You can also right-click on the scroll bar button and choose from navigation options: Scroll Here, Top, Bottom, Page Up, Page Down, Scroll Up, and Scroll Down.

Figure 1.24

Shortcuts for navigating with the scroll bar and mouse.

NOTE

New to Word 2013, the vertical and horizontal scroll bars only display when you place your mouse pointer near the scroll bars. When you click back in your document and start typing, the scroll bars go into hiding.

Horizontal Ruler

You can quickly change paragraph indent settings, adjust page margins, create and modify tabs, and change the width of columns in a table using the horizontal ruler. To display or hide the horizontal ruler, click the View tab, and in the Show group, select the Ruler check box. This setting controls both the horizontal and the vertical rulers.

Vertical Ruler

The vertical ruler appears on the left side of the application pane and is only visible in Print Layout view. If the ruler is not visible, from the File tab, click Options, Advanced, and from the Display section, check the Show Vertical Ruler in Print Layout View option.

Zoom and the Zoom Slider

As mentioned previously, Zoom and the Zoom slider are displayed at the far-right end of the Status bar. To increase the zoom percentage, click the Zoom In button (plus sign). This will increment your zoom percentage by 10 percent. To zoom out and decrease your zoom percentage by 10 percent, click the Zoom Out button (minus sign). Click and drag the Zoom slider in between the Zoom In and Zoom Out buttons to quickly change the zoom percentage, as shown in Figure 1.25.

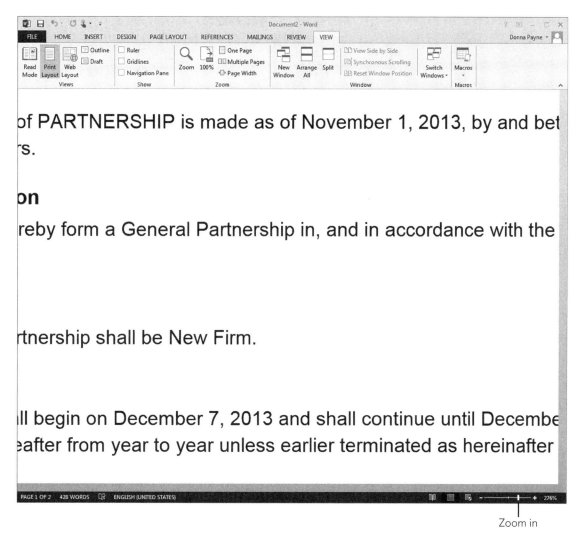

Figure 1.25 Click and drag the Zoom slider to move it to the desired zoom percentage.

To access the Zoom dialog box, click the Zoom Level button (represented as the current percentage). The Zoom dialog box gives you preset zoom options such as Zoom to Page Width, Zoom to Text Width, and more. The Zoom group on the View tab provides several options for changing the document display as well. Figure 1.26 shows changing the Zoom setting of a document.

TIP

If you use a mouse that has a wheel, you can zoom "on-the-fly" by holding the Ctrl key down while moving the mouse wheel up or down.

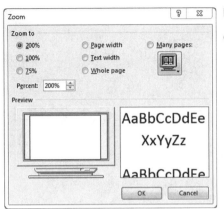

Figure 1.26

Change the zoom of the document.

ScreenTips

ScreenTips provide a means for quickly identifying commands and features in Word. As in earlier versions of Word, when you rest your mouse pointer over a command, a ScreenTip displays identifying the command and associated keyboard shortcut, if any. In Word, enhanced ScreenTips offer a larger window that displays more detailed information about the command. In Figure 1.27, there is quite a bit of help in a ScreenTip for the Show/Hide command.

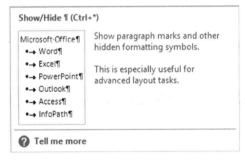

Figure 1.27

Enhanced ScreenTip for the Show/Hide command.

ScreenTips will display by default in Word 2013. To change this option, click the File tab and select Options. On the General tab, in the User Interface Options section, you can choose from three different ScreenTip style options: Show Feature Descriptions in ScreenTips (the default setting), Don't Show Feature Descriptions in ScreenTips (shows ScreenTips, but not the enhanced ScreenTips), and Don't Show ScreenTips (turns off ScreenTips altogether).

Keyboard Shortcuts

Most of the keyboard shortcuts that you used in earlier versions of Word still work. Many of the existing and new keyboard shortcuts will be discussed throughout this book. Let's first discuss what's new with shortcuts in Word 2013.

KeyTips

KeyTips are access keys that help you to quickly get to the tabs, the ribbon, and the Quick Access Toolbar without the use of your mouse. When you press the Alt key, KeyTips display represented by letters or numbers next to the tabs and the Quick Access Toolbar commands. For instance, press the Alt key to turn KeyTips on and then press H for the Home tab. KeyTips for each command will then display on the ribbon. KeyTips, as shown in Figure 1.28, are invaluable for anyone who prefers keyboard shortcut combinations instead of a mouse.

Figure 1.28   KeyTips display letters or numbers needed to execute the command.

KeyTips have replaced the accelerator keys—the underscored letter found on a menu or submenu—found in earlier versions of Word.

TIP

You can also navigate the ribbon using the Arrow and Tab keys. Tap the Alt key to activate KeyTips and then press the Right or Left Arrow to move through the ribbon tabs. Press the Down Arrow to navigate onto the ribbon. Press Tab to move through the commands and press Enter to select the command.

Stop Displaying KeyTips

If you no longer want to see the KeyTips, you can stop displaying them by either pressing Esc, or by pressing the Alt key. Think of the Alt key as a toggle for KeyTips. After you've made a KeyTip selection, you may need to press the Esc key more than once.

Legacy Keyboard Shortcuts

If you have memorized keystrokes for menus from earlier versions of Word, you may be surprised to know that they are still active (although hidden). When you press the keyboard shortcut that is used to access a menu (e.g., Alt+T to access the

Tools menu), a ScreenTip displays, confirming you are using an Office Access Key, giving you the green light to continue with the keyboard shortcut sequence. For example, Alt+T followed by an O opens the Word Options menu, just as it did in previous versions of Word.

DOCUMENT VIEWS

Word offers five views in which to display your document. You can easily switch between views using either the View options on the Status bar or from the View tab.

NOTE

To switch easily between views, click the view buttons available on the Status bar or use keystrokes: Alt+Ctrl+P for Print Layout, Alt+Ctrl+N for Draft view, and Alt+Ctrl+O for Outline view. All of the views can be found on the View tab in the Views group.

Print Layout View

Print Layout view is often the preferred view since this view shows how the document will look when it's printed. Headers and footers, footnotes and endnotes, and graphics all display in this view, making editing and formatting easy.

Web Layout View

Web Layout view shows how your document will look when opened in a web browser. Headers and footers do not display, graphics display as they would in Print Layout, and text is wrapped to fit the document window.

Draft View

Draft view is the perfect view for working with lengthy documents that require fast, simplified editing. Draft view does not display headers or footers, footnotes or endnotes, white space, or graphics, leaving little to distract you; however, it does display section breaks, which are imperative to see when working with complex documents that contain multiple sections.

By default, documents saved in Draft view will open in Print Layout view. If you prefer having documents that have been saved in Draft view open in Draft view, click the File tab, select Options, and then click Advanced. In the General section, check the option to Allow Opening a Document in Draft View.

NOTE

Draft view is often used to have a quick look at what styles have been applied in the document. With the Style Area Width displayed, the name of the style appears to the left of the paragraph. To set the Style Area Width, select File, Options, Advanced, and in the Display section, increase the width under Style Area Pane Width in Draft and Outline Views.

Outline View

Outline view displays text in an outline format, making it easy to work with headings. The Outlining tab is added in front of the Home tab with tools to help you work with the outline format. Keep in mind that many paragraph formats do not display in Outline view as they will when printed. A good example of this is if you have a paragraph that is centered, it will appear left aligned in this view.

Read Mode

Read Mode is new to Word 2013 and was designed to minimize the distractions when reading through a document. It is purely for reading, however. If you're looking to edit your document, you'll need to switch to one of the other views available in Word. Read Mode, as shown in Figure 1.29, is different from Word's Reading Layout view available in previous versions of Word.

FILE   TOOLS   VIEW   Certificate of Incorporation - Word

AMENDED AND RESTATED
CERTIFICATE OF INCORPORATION
MADISON COOPER COMPANY, INC.

MADISON COOPER Company (the "Corporation"), a corporation organized and existing under and by virtue of the General Corporation Law of the State of Washington does hereby amend the Certificate of Incorporation of the Corporation, which was originally filed on May 1, 2010, under the name MADISON COOPER Company, Inc.

ARTICLE I. The name of the Corporation is: MADISON COOPER COMPANY

ARTICLE II. The address of the registered office of the Corporation in the State of Washington is United Incorporated, 999 Third Avenue, City of Seattle, County of King, Washington 98105. The name of its registered agent at such address is United Incorporated.

ARTICLE I. The purpose of the Corporation is to engage in any lawful act or activity for which corporations may be organized under the General Corporation Law of the State of Washington as the same exists or may hereafter be amended ("Washington Law").

ARTICLE II.

Section 1. Capital Stock. (a) The total number of shares of stock which the Corporation shall have authority to issue is 430,000,000, consisting of 300,000,000 shares of Common Stock, par value $.01 per share (the "Common Stock"), and 130,000,000 shares of Preferred Stock, par value $.01 per share (the "Preferred Stock"). The Common Stock of the Corporation shall be all of one class, and shall be divided into two classes, consisting of Class A Common Stock and Class B Common Stock. The Preferred Stock may be issued in one or more series having such designations as may be fixed by the Board of Directors.

Figure 1.29   A document in Read Mode view.

You'll notice that when you open a document received as an e-mail attachment, the file will automatically open in Read Mode. Although there are many advantages to working in Read Mode, you may decide not to have it as the default view for e-mail attachments. To change this option, click the File tab and then Options. On the General tab, clear the Open E-mail Attachments and Other Uneditable Files in Reading View check box.

Using Read Mode

As the name of this view would suggest, you cannot edit the document while in Read Mode; the view is best used for reading through your document only. To view a document using Read Mode, click the View tab, and from the Views group, select Read Mode. To navigate to the next page, click the arrow button on the right side of the page. To navigate to the previous page, click the arrow button on the left side of the page. To close Read Mode, click View and then select Edit Document. You can also press the Esc key to exit the view and to allow editing to the document.

Read Mode Layout

The Read Mode layout can be changed to best suit your needs. There are several layout options on the View tab found in the upper-left corner of the screen. You can open the Navigation pane, show comments, choose from column width options, change the page color, or change the layout.

By default, the document will display on-screen with a default width and two-column format. To change the width of the columns, click the View tab, point to Column Width, and try out the available options. To view the document as it will print, click the View tab, select Layout, and then Paper Layout.

Read Mode Tools Options

Use the Read Mode Tools tab to conduct a search for text within your document by clicking Tools and then Find. With Internet access, you can conduct a Bing search on selected text. After selecting the text, click Tools and then Search with Bing.

There are several ways to open the Navigation pane in Read Mode: Select View, Navigation Pane; select Tools, Find; press Ctrl+F; or click the page number on the Status bar.

Shortcut Menu Tools

Although you cannot edit your document in Read Mode, there are several helpful features available so you can work with your document. For example, you can copy or define selected text, translate a phrase, search with Bing, insert new comments, and highlight text. This is all made easy with the shortcut menu. First, select text, then right-click and choose the command from the shortcut menu that you would like to use.

TIP

To exit Read Mode and return to editing your document, select View and then Edit Document, or press Esc. If you click the Close button (X) in the upper-right corner, you are closing the document.

Hide White Space

One advantage to working in Draft view instead of Print Layout view is the white space at the top and bottom of the page is not displayed, graphics are not displayed, and the header and footer are hidden for a less cluttered work area. An alternative to Draft view is to remain in Print Layout view and hide the white space at the top and bottom of the page, which hides the header and footer as well.

To either hide or show white space while in Print Layout view, position your mouse pointer over the area that separates the two pages. Double-click when the mouse pointer changes to two arrows.

TIP

You can also show or hide the white space by clicking Options from the File tab. Select the Display tab and under the Page Display Options section, select the Show White Space Between Pages in Print Layout View check box.

Displaying Documents

In the Windows group of the View tab, Word offers multiple ways to change the way documents are displayed.

Arrange All

The Arrange All command found in the Windows group of the View tab allows you to display all of your open documents horizontally on the screen at once.

Split Tool

The Split Tool will split the active document window into two parts allowing you to view two different areas of the same document at the same time. This can be very helpful when copying text between two parts of a large document, such as a pleading or agreement.

On the View tab, in the Windows group, click the Split button. Notice there are two sets of scroll bars—you can use them to move independently throughout the document.

To remove the split, either double-click the split line that separates the two areas of your document, or from the Windows group on the View tab, click the Remove Split command.

TIP

The shortcut key for activating the Split tool is Alt+Ctrl+S. Remove the split using the same shortcut key.

View Side By Side

To visually compare two documents vertically side by side, one click at a time, choose View Side By Side in the Window group on the View tab. Notice that as you scroll through one of the documents, you are also scrolling through the other document at the same rate. This is referred to as Synchronous Scrolling and is enabled by default. To toggle Synchronous Scrolling on and off, click the Synchronous Scrolling command in the Window group of the View tab. When you are ready to restore the documents to full size, click the View Side By Side command again.

Display Settings

There are many custom settings for each of the views available in Word 2013. Select the File tab and then select Options. The view settings are located in two places—on the Display tab and on the Advanced tab in the Display section. Both the Display and Advanced settings are displayed in Figures 1.30 and 1.31.

Getting Help

Office 2013's Help feature is extensive and includes online help as well as assistance when you are offline. If you have an Internet connection, Help will default to searching for help online, which is often more up-to-date and comprehensive.

Click the Microsoft Word Help button found in the upper-right corner of the Word window or press F1, and the Word Help window will display, as shown in Figure 1.32. Word Help contains a number of options that you can use to get the help you need. Type in your search term and press Enter to conduct your search.

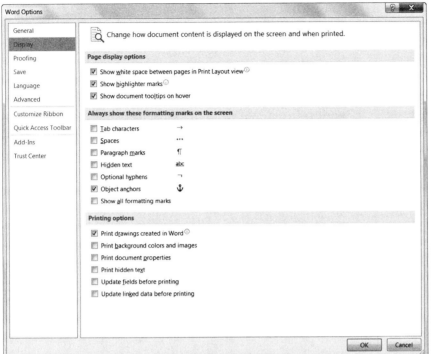

Figure 1.30

Word view settings are located in the Display section of the Word Options dialog box.

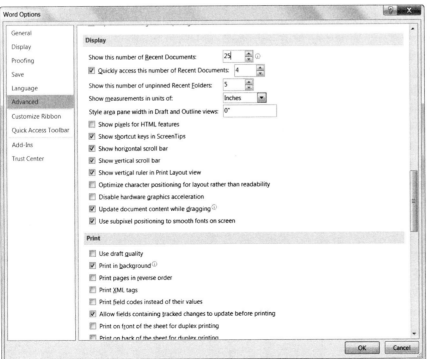

Figure 1.31

Additional Word view settings are located in the Advanced section of the Word Options dialog box.

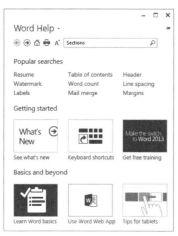

Figure 1.32

Type a keyword search or click any of the available links to get help in Word.

EXPERT TIP

If an Internet connection is available, Help will default to Word Help from Office.com and conduct your search term online. If you have not established an Internet connection and logged into your Microsoft account, the word Offline will appear in the Help window. Click the down arrow to the right of Word Help to view both of the options: Word Help from Office.com and Word Help from your Computer.

KRAFT
KENNEDY

Marcus Bluestein, Chief Technology Officer with Kraft & Kennedy, Inc., on Word 2013 and Office 365 Integration

While Microsoft Office 365 has many components, its integration with Microsoft Word 2013 is rather simple. Word 2013 can use SharePoint Online—part of the Office 365 subscription—as a repository or as a storage platform. Most Office 365 subscriptions also include web versions of the Office applications, which allows you to use programs like Word in a web browser without having to install it on your computer. This web application has the same feature set as the installed version, excluding legacy integrations, such as with document management systems. Moreover, Word 2013 has integration with SharePoint (Office 365 and on premise) built into its "open and save" dialog boxes. While this is a straightforward addition, it greatly simplifies the process of working with Word and SharePoint. Overall, the Word 2013 integration with Office 365 is an online experience. If you want to be able to work on your documents or library offline and synchronize them next time you are back online, consider leveraging SkyDrive Pro.

CREATING AND ACCESSING DOCUMENTS

Integral to the practice of law is the creation of documents—ranging from simple correspondence to complex pleadings and briefs. Although many legal documents are created from scratch, the bulk of documents are created using content from existing documents. We inherit those source documents from others within the firm, clients, opposing counsel, and from myriad other sources. While most people with Word experience know how to create new and open existing documents, Word 2013 offers more options for the creation process than ever before. This chapter contains useful information and tips for creating legal documents, as well as accessing and working with existing ones.

CREATING A NEW DOCUMENT

In Word 2013, Microsoft has added a shortcut for creating new documents; this is the Start screen where you can create a new blank document or base the document on an existing template. This screen shows by default when you start Word. You also can use keyboard shortcuts, select New from the File menu, or click New on the Quick Access Toolbar.

Many firms will have a Document Management System (DMS) and third-party or home-grown template package in place as well that can facilitate document creation.

There is no right or wrong way for creating documents—just use the method that you prefer or that is recommended at your firm.

Create a New Document

1. Click the File tab and then New. Depending on installation options, you can choose which type of document to create. The default options are shown in Figure 2.1.

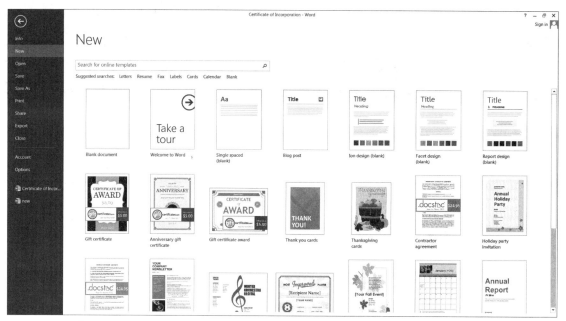

Figure 2.1 If you don't see the type of file you want to create, you can search online for templates on which to base your document. You can also access personal templates on which to base your document.

OFFICE 365

Click the SkyDrive menu (or other location your firm may have provided) and then click Create, Word document. Name the document and click Create. Or press Ctrl+N.

2. From the templates displayed, click Blank Document.

3. Press Ctrl+N to create another new, blank document.

4. Click the down arrow on the Quick Access Toolbar and click New to add this button to the toolbar.

5. Click the New button on the Quick Access Toolbar to see another method for new document creation.

6. Close all but one of the new, blank documents created.

TIP

Add the New button to the Quick Access Toolbar by clicking Customize Quick Access Toolbar (the down arrow at the end of the toolbar) and select New.

SAVING A DOCUMENT

After you've created a document, you will need to save it. Most people have horror stories of working on files for hours and then somehow closing without saving and losing the contents or edits. To avoid scenarios such as this, it's important to save, and save often.

When you first save a document, you choose a filename, set the file location where the document should be saved, and then set other options such as file protection. While Word supports filenames of up to 255 characters in length, it's best to limit it to something much shorter. Just for fun, here's what a 255-character filename looks like.

255-characters:

AbcdefghijklmnopqrstuvwxyzAbcdefghijklmnopqrstuvwxyzAbcdefghijklm-nopqrstuvwxyzAbcdefghijklmnopqrstuvwxyzAbcdefghijklmnopqrstuvwxyz-AbcdefghijklmnopqrstuvwxyzAbcdefghijklmnopqrstuvwxyzAbcdefghijklm-nopqrstuvwxyzAbcdefghijklmnopqrstuvwxyzAbcdefghijklmnopqrstu

Not only is it important to condense the filename, it's also useful to pick a name that is descriptive enough to find the document later.

NOTE

Beginning in Word 2007, files are saved with the .docx file extension. This differs from .doc as seen in Word 97-2003. The Office Open XML file format used in Word 2013 is comprised of compressed XML files, which results in a smaller file size and better stability overall. Chapter 3, "Compatibility and Conversion," goes into much greater detail on the subject of file formats as well as how to remain compatible with earlier versions of Word.

TIP

The following characters can't be used in a document name: / \ > < * ? " | : . Document names can contain numbers 0 through 9, letters, hyphens, periods, spaces, underscores, and exclamation points, however.

In the next exercise, a file is saved to your computer. If your firm uses a DMS, just save the document as you normally would using the firm's document management system's guidelines.

Save a Document to the Documents Folder

1. Click the File tab and click Save or press Ctrl+S, which is the keyboard shortcut combination for saving a file.

2. Select Computer in the middle pane and click Browse to get to the Save As dialog box. Navigate to the folder in which you want to save the file.

3. In the File Name box, type **Parties of Record**.

4. The default Save as Type is .docx. Click Save to save the document in the new file format.

5. Keep this document open for the next exercise.

TIP

You can go directly to the Save As dialog box without going to Backstage view by pressing the F12 function key on the keyboard.

If the file is being shared from the Word Web App, the standard Save icon in Word 2013 will now have a circular arrow within it. This indicates the file changes will be resolved to the SkyDrive (or other cloud storage).

OFFICE 365

Bypass Backstage View When Saving

The default behavior when you choose Save As or Open is to take you to Backstage view and not a dialog box as occurred in previous versions of Word. If you prefer to go directly to the Save As or Open dialog box, click the File tab and then Options. Click the Save tab, and in the Save documents section, check Don't Show the Backstage When Opening or Saving Files.

NOTE

Chapter 3 goes into much greater detail about saving documents, especially when it's necessary to share documents with others using earlier versions of Word.

Saving as a PDF File

Word 2013 can now open and edit most PDF files. This is a new and useful feature for legal professionals, as many of the documents that come across your desk and Inbox are PDFs.

While opening a PDF file from within Word is new, recent versions have allowed for files to be saved in PDF.

Save a Word Document as a PDF

1. Open a Word document you want to save as a PDF.

2. Click the File tab and then click Export.

3. Click the Create PDF/XPS button.

NOTE

XPS is an XML Paper Specification format designed by Microsoft as a read-only document, which opens in an XPS Viewer window. Anyone can read XPS files—just open the file, and the file displays in a separate window. The text cannot be edited, but you can copy and paste text from that file into a Word document.

4. Navigate to the location where you want to save the file.

5. Click Options to view the settings available for PDF. You can choose to save the entire document, only the page where your insertion point is located, selected text, or a range of pages. You can also choose to save the file as a PDF/A file, which is required by some courts. Click OK to close the Options dialog box.

6. Click Publish. The PDF file opens automatically in your default PDF application after it's created.

NOTE

You can also save documents as PDF files through the Save As window. When saving a document, change the Save As Type to PDF. From here you can even change your publishing options. Note that if you use this method, it is not saving the document in addition to the PDF, only the PDF.

OFFICE 365

Save the file as a PDF file through the standard File, Print method.

We're not finished with PDF documents yet. Later in this chapter, the new and exciting feature where PDF files can be opened and edited from within Word is discussed.

Applying File Protection

The nature of attorney/client relationships requires that some documents be secured with passwords, and even encryption. Other documents that might warrant protection include budgets, human resources documents, or any type of document that contains confidential or privileged information.

Word, Excel, and PowerPoint include options for protection, as shown in Figure 2.2. With the document open, click the File tab and then Info. Click the Protect Document button to see a list of options for securing the file.

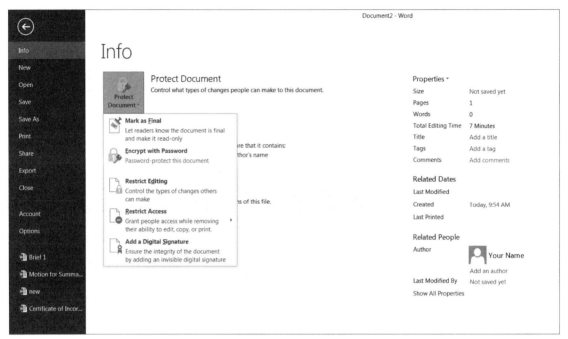

Figure 2.2 Word offers varying levels of protection for sensitive documents.

OFFICE 365

Applying File Protection is not an option in Word Web App.

Mark as Final

The option to Mark as Final is just a visual warning or message that the document should not be edited. It does not prohibit someone from doing so. A Message Bar will appear at the top of the document with the notice that the document is in final form and should not be edited. Clicking a button labeled Edit Anyway allows anyone to proceed with changes. And since there is no password protection with Mark as Final, clicking the File tab, Info toggles the protection off at any time.

Encrypt with Password

The Encrypt with Password setting displays a dialog box that prompts you to enter a password. It's imperative to remember your password since there is no recovery available from Microsoft. Passwords are case sensitive as well. Finally, the protection is only as strong as the password entered. Use longer password strings with a combination of upper- and lowercase letters, as well numbers and symbols. This will make the protection more robust and difficult to break.

Restrict Editing

At times you may need to restrict a document's content from changing and allow for only formatting changes. Or perhaps you only want content but need the format to remain unchanged due to court rules or a set of standardized styles used within the firm. In these instances, you can use the Restrict Editing functionality. When you restrict formatting, click Settings to choose which styles are permitted for use. To disable all editing, choose the Editing restrictions that, dependent on additional restriction options selected, will track all changes made by the reviewer of the file, allow only comments, or protect the document to allow for fill-in forms. The final step to restricting editing is to click Start Enforcement. Setting a password is optional, and the same rules apply—it's case sensitive, and there is no help if you forget the password.

Restrict Access

Firms with document management systems will use this software to restrict access to documents and folders. This is often used when an ethical wall needs to be imposed. If there is no document management system, you can make an ad hoc effort to accomplish this by restricting permissions via a template used within the firm, or you can add individual permissions.

Add a Digital Signature

A digital signature authenticates the document's authenticity and integrity. In order to sign a document, you will need a digital ID.

AutoSave

A section about saving documents would not be complete without talking about AutoSave. It's not a replacement for saving a document manually and often; however, if you forget to save and Word closes unexpectedly, there is a chance at least that the file can be recovered. Of course, there is no guarantee, so it should never be used in place of traditional saving methods.

The new AutoSave attempts to automatically save files in the background that have not yet been saved. For example, say you started with a blank document, drafted several pages, and didn't remember or have the opportunity to save. Then you receive an unexpected client call and close the file. Rather than clicking Save, you accidentally click Don't Save. Sound familiar? In previous versions of

Word, you wouldn't be able to get the file back; however, in Word 2013, there is at least a chance that the file can be recovered. Here's how it works.

To recover an unsaved document, from the File tab click Info, click Manage Versions, and then click Recover Unsaved Documents. The unsaved files will display the first few words that were typed in the document, followed by the word Unsaved and a random number. You will notice that the unsaved files will display in an *.asd file format.

CAUTION

If you do not see any unsaved files, then the file did not get saved, and there is nothing that can be done to get it back. That's why saving files often is imperative. You cannot fully rely on the AutoRecover or AutoSave features to do this for you, and this feature is often incompatible with document management systems.

CLOSING DOCUMENTS

The easiest part of working with a file is closing it. There are at least three separate keyboard shortcuts for closing a file, as well as through the File tab.

Closing a Document

1. The Parties of Record document should still be open from the previous exercise. If not, just open any document that you can use to close the file.

2. Click the File tab and then Close.

3. If you saved your edits before closing the document, Word automatically closes the document. If changes were made to the file since you've last saved, you'll see the message box shown in Figure 2.3.

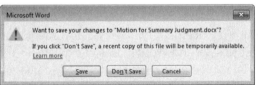

Figure 2.3

Word prompts to save if new edits were made to an existing file.

4. Click Save to save the document and have Word close the document.

Closing Document Shortcuts

The following keyboard shortcuts can be used to close documents in Word.

- Ctrl+W

- Ctrl+F4

- Alt+F4 (closes the Word application as well)

TIP

Word power users often state that they miss the ability to hold the Shift key and click File, Close, which resulted in all open documents being closed. To replicate this behavior in Word 2013, all you need to do is add the Close/Close All command to the Quick Access Toolbar and press Shift when the command is clicked. To add the command to the toolbar, right-click on the Quick Access Toolbar and choose Customize Quick Access Toolbar from the shortcut menu. Click the arrow next to Choose Commands From and select All Commands. Type C to move to the beginning of the list of commands starting with the letter C. Scroll down the list until you locate Close/Close All. Don't select Close All—this won't produce the desired result. Make sure you find the one with the / separator. Add the command to the Quick Access Toolbar and close the Word Options window to return to the document. Hold the Shift key and click the Close/Close All button. This closes all open documents, prompting you to save those that have new edits if applicable.

OFFICE 365

Choose File, Exit or click the X (Exit) button to close a file. Ctrl+W and Ctrl+F4 also close the file.

SkyDrive and the Cloud

As of the publication date for this book, Microsoft offers 7 GB of free cloud storage where you can save your files. One of the benefits to using cloud storage is the ability to access those files across multiple computers and mobile devices. This service requires a Microsoft account, such as a SkyDrive or an Outlook.com account; then you can sign into the account from within Word or another Microsoft Office application, as shown in Figure 2.4.

EXPERT TIP

In a law firm environment, you may not want client documents saved in the cloud until a cloud storage policy has been established. Office 2013 can be configured to disable the SkyDrive sign-in option using the Office Customization Tool, Group Policy Object, or by changing the registry.

If you want to change the default file location for saving documents, you can set an option to make the computer the default instead of a cloud location. Click File and then Options. Select Save and in the Save Document section, check the option to Save to Computer By Default. Click OK to accept the change and close Options.

Figure 2.4   Sign in to SkyDrive to access files from any location or computer.

EXPERT TIP

If you are an internal tools developer and want to create an additional cloud storage location for Office 2013, Microsoft has a document that may be useful. It's at http://www.microsoft.com/en-us/download/details.aspx?id=35474. The link is active as of the time of this book's release date; however, if it stops working, search for the term Integrating additional cloud storage services in Office 2013. Some third parties have created scripts for adding other cloud services such as Dropbox and Google Drive directly to Office. If you are interested in adding these or other services, a quick search online will produce instructions and download utilities; however, since they are unsupported by Microsoft, we'll leave you to explore on your own.

**KRAFT
KENNEDY**

**Marcus Bluestein, Chief Technology Officer with Kraft & Kennedy, Inc.,
on SkyDrive**
Microsoft Office 2013 includes integration with Microsoft SkyDrive for cloud storage,
a service that will operate a lot like Dropbox and other cloud-based file systems.
Microsoft offers two versions of SkyDrive. The first, widely adopted version is just
called SkyDrive and is targeted at consumers. The account is stored in Microsoft's
cloud and is associated with the user's Microsoft online account. Many of the features
you have come to expect from other services are available with this solution, including synchronization, two-factor authentication, purchasable extra space, smartphone
apps, etc.

SkyDrive Pro is for corporate users. The account is associated with a business e-mail
address, and data is stored either in Office 365 or in an on-premise installation at the
client site over SharePoint 2013. One of the distinguishing features of SkyDrive Pro is
its ability to take SharePoint libraries offline (this used to be available through
Microsoft Groove and then via Microsoft SharePoint Workspace, but both of those
products are now end-of-life). Some other SkyDrive features, like two-factor authentication, are likely to make their way into SkyDrive Pro later in 2013.

LITÉRA

Norm Thomas of Litéra and formerly with Microsoft on SkyDrive and SharePoint
Office files can be created and edited from within any SkyDrive, SkyDrive Pro, or
SharePoint library as well. To create a new Microsoft Office file, just click the Create
link, and the option to create any of these Microsoft Office files is offered:

- Word
- Excel
- PowerPoint
- OneNote
- Excel Survey (Excel worksheet with prestructured dialog box queries to create
  social networking polls and collaborative voting)

Just by double-clicking, you also can edit these types of Microsoft Office files stored
in SharePoint libraries no matter where they've been created. Users remain within a
browser and begin editing in Microsoft Office Web Apps, even if they do not have
Microsoft Office installed on their desktops or mobile devices.

If a desktop version of Microsoft Office is installed, users editing in the browser
environment of Microsoft Office Web Apps can switch to the desktop version any
time, even while in the middle of editing the document, without downloading the
document locally.

Ray Zwiefelhofer, President World Software Corporation, on Document Management Systems

A document management product has always been symbiotic with Microsoft Word and other office products. The value of a document management system for law firms is to have consistent and organized methods for quickly retrieving client content. To ensure accurate and speedy retrieval, each file must be saved with consistent validated metadata fields. The Worldox document management software intercepts the Save, Save As, and Open commands and prevents any hard drive directory access, forcing the user to fill out an appropriate "profile form," which contains validated fields, such as client, matter, document type, and other key fields to make retrieval and searching easier.

Microsoft has significantly modified the file save/open process for its latest version. What in the past decade has been one click to save or open a document, now consists of many paneled windows suggesting saving to SkyDrive or other methods. Law firms that have a DMS installed will save to its DMS only, not SkyDrive and other sources.

OPENING DOCUMENTS

Opening existing documents is easy if you have access to and know where the file was saved. If you normally save to the default Documents folder, finding and opening your documents will be relatively easy—that is until the folder starts to fill up. You may have a more organized folder structure in which to store documents on your network, and then the process of finding and opening will require a few additional steps.

NOTE

Your firm may have a document management system installed. If so, when you select the Open command, you will be using that program's search capabilities to find an existing file.

New to Word 2013, when you click the File tab and choose Open, you remain in Backstage view. The Backstage view, as shown in Figure 2.5, includes several options to open documents from various locations—files saved locally, on the network, or in the cloud.

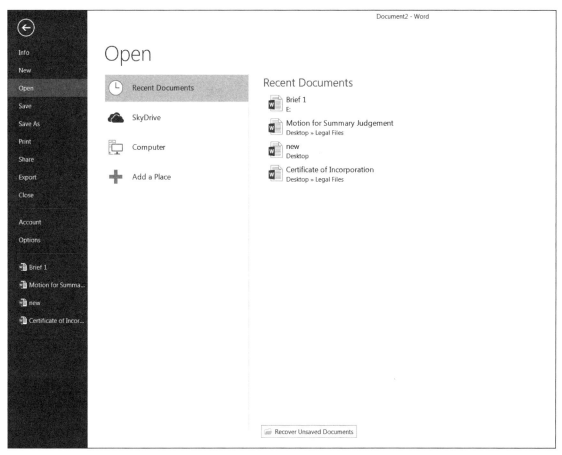

Figure 2.5   Open an existing document saved on your computer or in another location.

You'll want to navigate to where the document resides, and if it is saved on a local or network drive, you will select Computer, choose a folder from the Recent Folders list, or click Browse to navigate to the Open dialog box, as shown in Figure 2.6.

The Open dialog box contains a number of features that allow you to access one or more files. The Places bar, located on the left side of the dialog box, displays shortcuts to Favorites you have added, the Desktop, Recent Places, Libraries, Local Computer, and the Network.

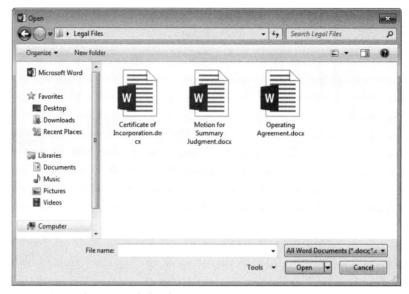

Figure 2.6   The Open dialog box.

OFFICE 365

Opening a .doc file in Word Web App automatically converts the file to a .docx file.

OFFICE 365

To open a document, click the SkyDrive menu and choose either Files or Recent Docs.

EXPERT TIP

New in Word 2013, the Backstage view displays whenever you select the Open, Save (in an unsaved document) or the Save As command. If you prefer to go directly to the Open or Save As dialog box as in previous versions of Word, click the File tab, and then Options. Click the Save tab, and in the Save documents section, check Don't Show the Backstage When Opening or Saving Files.

Recent Documents

When you choose the Open command, you will see as many as 25 recently opened documents listed. If you have a document that you want to always see on this list, you can "pin" it to the list. Hover your mouse pointer over the document and click on the Pin This Item to the List button at the far right of the document name. Notice how this moves your pinned document to the top of the list and a small pushpin icon appears to the right. To unpin the document, click again on the pushpin button.

OFFICE 365

NOTE

EXPERT TIP

Clicking the SkyDrive menu will take you to Files and Recent docs.

If you have a document management system, you may only see documents in the Recent Documents list that are saved locally or on your network.

You can change the number of documents that display in the Recent Documents list by clicking the File tab and then clicking Options. Select the Advanced tab and in the Display section, set the value for Show This Number of Recent Documents. The default is 25—you can set the value from 0 to 50.

There is an option that allows for recently opened documents to display in the left pane of Backstage view for easier access, as shown in Figure 2.7. To set this option, on the File tab, click Options. Choose Advanced, and in the Display section, check the Quickly Access this Number of Recent Documents option and set the value. You can display up to 25 documents.

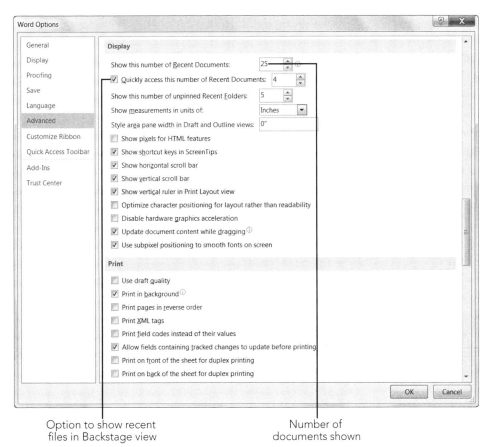

Option to show recent files in Backstage view

Number of documents shown

Figure 2.7 Quickly access recent documents in Backstage view.

CAUTION

The Quick Access option may visually appear to clutter the File tab with too many documents showing.

NOTE

As indicated in Chapter 1, "Getting Around Word," you will also see a list of recent documents when you first launch Word. The Start screen displays a list of recent documents on the left side of the screen.

Recent Folders

Similar to the recent documents list, you can now see a list of folders recently accessed. Click the File tab and select Open. When you select Computer, a list of recently accessed folders displays as well as the folder where the active document is saved, if any. Any of the recent folders can be pinned to ensure it will always appear on the list. Hover your mouse pointer over the folder name and click on the Pin This Item to the List button at the far right of the folder name. Notice how this moves your pinned folder to the top of the list and a small pushpin icon appears to the right. To unpin the folder, click again on the pushpin button.

EXPERT TIP

To set how many folders display in the Recent Folders list, click the File tab and then click Options. Select Advanced, and in the Display section, set the value for Show This Number of Unpinned Recent Folders. You can display between 0 and 20 folder locations.

EXPERT TIP

Keep in mind that displaying the recent list of files, or file locations, can reveal confidential information if displayed in a group setting during a presentation.

Open an Existing Document from the Documents Folder

1. Click the File tab and choose Open, or press the keyboard shortcut combination Ctrl+O.

2. Select Computer.

3. Select My Documents in the Recent Folders list if it is displayed or click Browse.

4. In the Documents library, double-click on the Parties of Record.docx file to open it.

5. Close the document.

File Formats Available to Open in Word

Dependent upon what was configured when Office was installed, you may have up to 18 file types from which to choose. Some of the more common file formats you will be working with are listed here.

- Word 2007-2013 Document (*.docx)
- Word 2007-2013 Macro-Enabled Document (*.docm)
- Word 97-2003 Documents (*.doc)
- All Word Templates (*.dotx, *.dotm, *.dot)
- PDF files (*.pdf)

NOTE

New in Word 2013 is the ability to open and edit PDF files. Read more about this in "Opening PDF Files in Word."

There are additional file formats available in Word, and while they may be used infrequently, it's helpful to know what's available within the application.

- XML Files (*.xml)
- All Web Pages (*.htm, *.html, *.mht, *.mhtml)
- Rich Text Format (*.rtf)
- Text Files (*.txt)
- OpenDocument Text (*.odt)
- Recover Text from Any File (*.*)
- WordPerfect 5.x (*.doc)
- WordPerfect 6.x (*.wpd, *.doc)
- Works 6–9 (*.wps)

Opening PDF Files in Word

Word can now directly open PDF files. Once the file is opened in Word, it becomes an editable document. PDF files can be opened in Word, edited, and then saved as a Word file format or back to a PDF file. This can be very useful, although the result is not always perfect.

Open a PDF File in Word

1. From within Word, click the File tab, then Open. Locate any PDF file. If you don't have one handy, you can use the instructions for saving a file as a PDF earlier in this chapter.

2. Upon opening a PDF file, a message box will display, as shown in Figure 2.8.

Figure 2.8 When opening a PDF in Word, you are reminded that the document may not look exactly like the original PDF.

3. Click OK to close the message box, and the PDF file opens in Word.

4. Review the file and note the similarities and differences between the PDF and Word versions of the file.

5. Now that the document is in Word, you are free to insert graphics, tables, and apply styles and formatting—anything that you could do with a standard Word document.

NOTE

As you gain more practice with opening PDF files in Word, you will quickly notice differences between the two files. For example, the header and footer content in the Word document no longer displays in the header and footer, but rather in the main area of the document. It's important to remember that the layout of the document can differ and not appear exactly the same as the PDF file.

Resaving the Converted PDF File

As soon as you've opened a PDF file in Word, the file is converted to Word, although the process is not yet complete since it still has the PDF file extension. You can save the file as a Word document or resave it as a PDF file. Word offers some protection for overwriting the original file. First, if you click Save, the Save

As dialog box appears instead. The file type in the Save As dialog box defaults to Word; however, you can click the down arrow next to Files of Type and change it back to PDF. It's good practice to save a copy of the file and not save over the original in the event that the formatting is off.

Opening Notifications

In Word 2013, you may open a file and notice that the file opens in Protected View, indicating that editing the file is not recommended. The Protected View message displays, as shown in Figure 2.9. You can certainly read the file, but be sure the file is from a trusted source before clicking the Enable Editing button, which fully opens the document for editing.

To access the Protected View settings, from the File tab, click Options and select Trust Center, then click the Trust Center Settings button. Click Protected View to display the options. Each option is defined in Table 2.1.

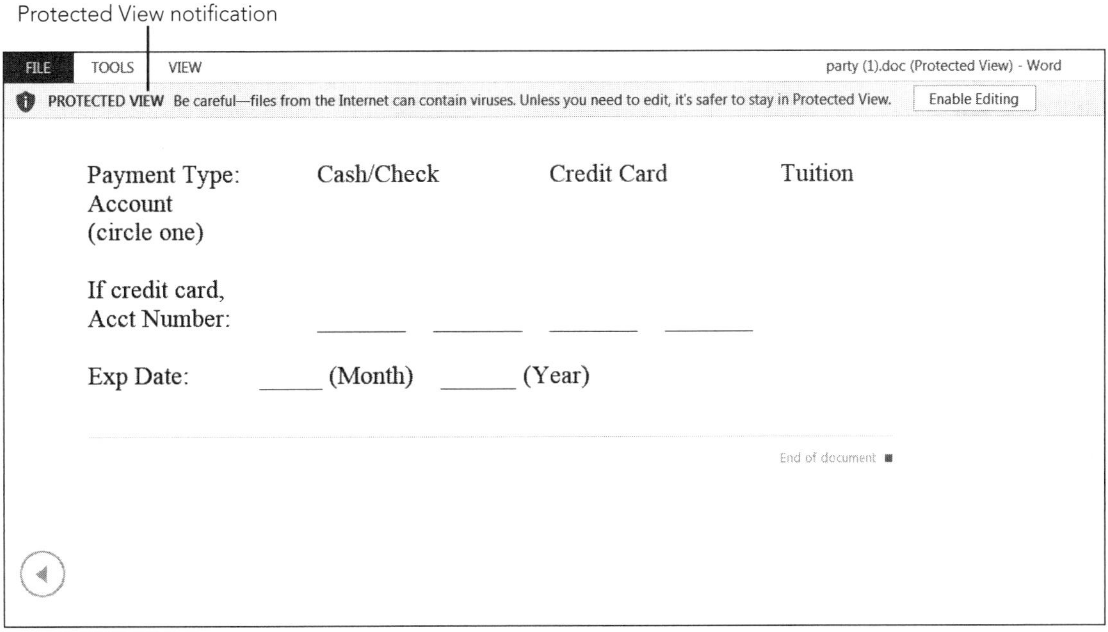

Protected View notification

FILE	TOOLS	VIEW	party (1).doc (Protected View) - Word

🛡 PROTECTED VIEW Be careful—files from the Internet can contain viruses. Unless you need to edit, it's safer to stay in Protected View. [Enable Editing]

Payment Type: Cash/Check   Credit Card   Tuition
Account
(circle one)

If credit card,
Acct Number: _____ _____   _____   _____

Exp Date: _____ (Month) _____ (Year)

End of document ■

Figure 2.9   The document displays as read only when in Protected View.

TABLE 2.1—PROTECTED VIEW SETTINGS	
SETTING	**DESCRIPTION**
Enable Protected View for files originating from the Internet	Any Word files opened directly from the Internet will open in Protected View.
Enable Protected View for files located in potentially unsafe locations	Any Word files downloaded from the Internet that reside in the Downloads folder location or other temporary Internet file location will open in Protected View.
Enable Protected View for Outlook attachments	Opening a Word attachment from an Outlook 2013 e-mail message opens in read-only mode; changes cannot be made to the original document.

The Backstage view offers additional details on a protected file. Click the File tab and then click Info. Alternatively, you can click the Protected View notification that displays above the document for more details, and it will automatically take you to the Backstage view. From here you will find more details about the document and Protected View options, as shown in Figure 2.10.

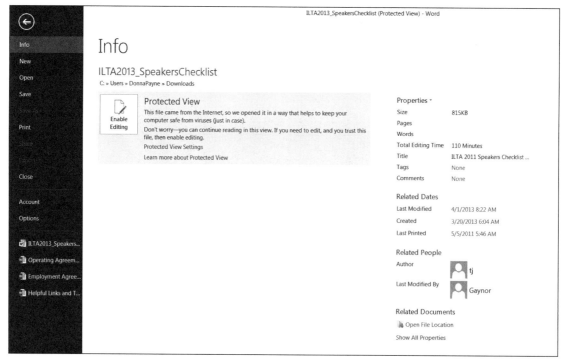

Figure 2.10 Additional details are found in Backstage view when opening a Protected View document.

EXPERT TIP

By default, when opening a Word document that is attached to an e-mail message, the Word document opens in Protected View, is read-only, and opens in the Read Mode view. There is a setting that will disable the document opening in Read Mode. Click the File tab, Options, General, and in the Start Up Options section, the option is Open E-mail Attachments and Other Uneditable Files in Reading View. If you clear the check box, the attachment will open in its original view.

EXITING WORD

There is a significant change when attempting to close any Office 2013 application—the Exit command in the Backstage view has been removed. In fact, choosing File, Exit is no longer an option. To exit out of Word 2013 completely, close all of your documents, and when you close the last document, you will automatically exit Word.

TIP

To replicate the Exit functionality that existed previously in Word, you can add the Exit command to the Quick Access Toolbar. When the command is clicked, all documents will close, and Word will close.

OFFICE 365

Click your Account Name and choose Sign out. Close any browser tabs as necessary.

COMPATIBILITY AND CONVERSION

Assuming you are either contemplating an upgrade from an earlier version of Microsoft Office to Office 2013 or you've already upgraded to the 2013 version, you'll need to be aware of issues related to compatibility and conversion when working with documents from earlier versions of Word.

All firms are now collaborating and sharing documents with others (clients, co-counsel, opposing counsel), and they may not be using the same version of Office that you are using. When sharing files, it's important to know when to keep a document in the same file format and when to convert a file to the latest file format. You'll also need to know the steps to follow in order to properly convert a document, and lastly, you'll need to know what Word 2013 features aren't available if you keep the file format in the lower version.

FILE FORMATS EXPLAINED

When saving a new Word 2013 document, you will be saving in the new Office Open XML file format. In Word, a document will have the file extension of *.docx (*.doc in previous versions of Word). This file type is mostly comprised of compressed XML files, which results in a smaller file size.

NOTE

The *.docx file format is the default format for Word 2007-2013 documents.

The default Save as Type in Word 2013 is *.docx unless the default option setting has been changed. To change the default file format, click the File tab, Options, and then Save. Select the Save Files in this Format drop-down list to view other file formats available, as shown in Figure 3.1.

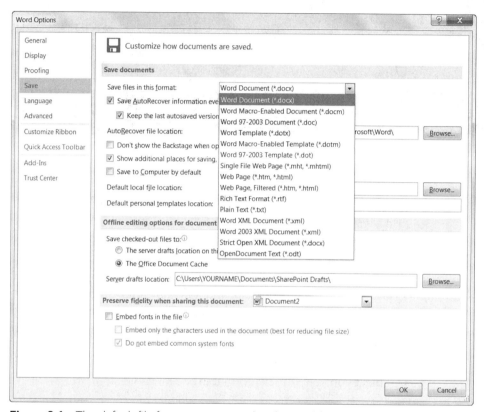

Figure 3.1   The default file format setting can be changed for all newly created documents.

COMPATIBILITY MODE

The term Compatibility Mode in Word 2013 refers to how a document, created in a version earlier than Word 2013 (this includes Word 2010 on down to Word 97), is opened in the newer version of Word. When an older version of a Word document is opened in Word 2013, you will see the term "Compatibility Mode" in the Title bar located at the top of the application window, as shown in Figure 3.2.

This is a reminder that while you can't introduce the new Word 2013 features to the document, you can still fully edit the document. This also means that your document will remain compatible with earlier versions of Word. In fact, documents created in Word 2003 or an earlier version will have a *.doc file extension. In the next section, we'll take a look at how to save a document in this format.

Figure 3.2   Compatibility Mode will display in the Title bar if the document was created with an earlier version of Word.

SAVE A DOCUMENT IN WORD 97-2003 COMPATIBLE FORMAT (COMPATIBILITY MODE)

When you are collaborating with others who are using an earlier version of Word, you'll want your document to have the same look and feel in both environments. This means that you will need to save your Word 2013 document down to the Word 97-2003 file format (*.doc). Doing this will allow you to have control over the exchange of content between the two environments that are not using the same version of Word. When the document is saved in this earlier file format, any Word 2013 features not compatible with Word 97-2003 will not be available.

Save a Document in Compatibility Mode

1. Create a new document.
2. Click the File tab and choose Save or Save As, or press Ctrl+S.
3. Navigate to a folder where you want to save the document.
4. In the File Name box, type **Compatibility Document Practice**.
5. Select Word 97-2003 Document (*.doc) from the Save as Type list and click Save.

Saving the document in the earlier format ensures that the recipient will be able to open the file without conversion. It is perfectly acceptable to keep this document in the *.doc file format as long as you are collaborating with other parties who continue to use earlier versions of Word.

Documents will automatically open in Compatibility Mode in Word 2013 when any of the following events occur:

- The file was originally saved in a file format used in previous versions of Word whether .doc or .docx (e.g., if a 2010 .docx file is opened in 2013, it will display in Compatibility Mode).

- A file was converted from Word 2013 to a Word 97-2003 file format using the Save As command.

- The Word options default file format is set to automatically save to a lower version of Word (*.doc format).

- If the document was originally created in Word 2013 and the document is opened in a lower version of Word on another computer, edited, and then saved, when the document is reopened in Word 2013, it will open in Compatibility Mode.

COMPATIBILITY PACK

A quick mention of the Compatibility Pack is necessary at this point because if you send a Word 2013 *.docx document to others using Word 2003, 2002, or 2000, they will not be able to open and edit the document without installing the Compatibility Pack. The good news is that they can go to Microsoft.com and search for the keywords *Office Compatibility Pack* to find this free download from the Microsoft website.

NOTE

The Office Compatibility Pack is for Word, Excel, and PowerPoint.

When editing a document in Word 2013 that was created in Word 97-2010, some 2013 features will be completely disabled, as shown on the ribbon in Figure 3.3, while others will be partially disabled. Disabled features will appear grayed out on the ribbon. When you hover your mouse over the grayed-out command, the Enhanced ScreenTip offers useful information and stays as a reminder that you have limited functionality in Compatibility Mode documents.

NOTE

As the ScreenTip indicates, to enable Word 2013 features, you will need to convert the document. This process will be covered in "Converting a Document" later in this chapter.

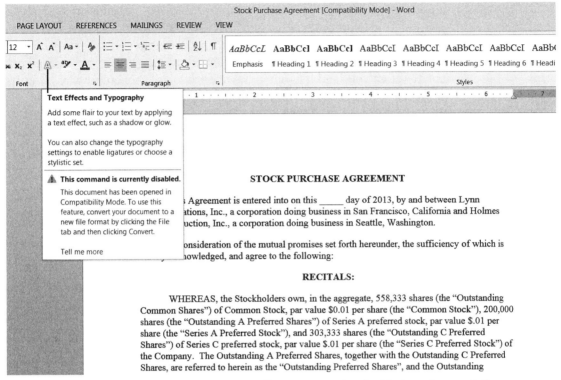

Figure 3.3   This ScreenTip shows that the Text Effects command is disabled in a Compatibility Mode document.

Table 3.1 includes a sampling of new features introduced in Word 2013. You can decide which features will be commonplace in a legal environment.

TABLE 3.1—NEW WORD 2013 FEATURES— MOST NOT FOR LEGAL	
FEATURE	**DESCRIPTION**
Web video	Insert an online video and play it directly from Word or open it in a browser.
Customized footnote columns	Have footnotes display in a 1-, 2-, 3-, or 4-column format.
Collapsed by Default headings	If the Collapsed by Default setting in the Paragraph dialog box is set, when the document is reopened, the headings will remain collapsed.
Marking comments as done	When using the comments feature in balloons, marking a comment as done will dim the comment and shrink it to one line.

It's important to remember that if any of these Word 2013 features are added to a document and that document is shared with someone using a lower version of Word, when that person opens the document some features will be completely or partially lost, and the layout of the document may change. You can check your document before you send it to someone using a lower version of Word by using the Compatibility Checker, which we discuss in the next section.

COMPATIBILITY CHECKER

Before sharing a Word 2013 document with someone else, you can check for features that are not supported by earlier versions of Word by running the Compatibility Checker. To manually run the Compatibility Checker, click the File tab, Info, Check for Issues, and then select Check Compatibility, as shown in Figure 3.4.

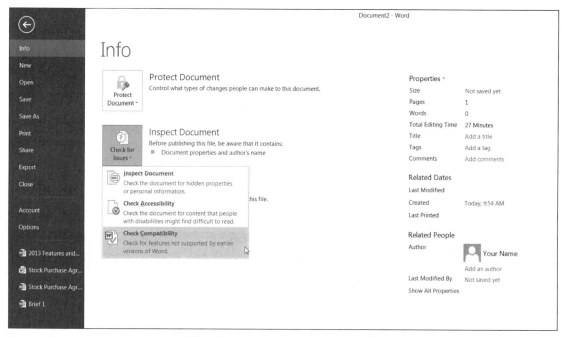

Figure 3.4 Running the Compatibility Checker manually will help to determine whether any features are not compatible with an earlier version of Word.

When you check the compatibility manually, you will notice an available option that allows you to select the versions to show. In the Microsoft Word Compatibility Checker dialog box, click Select Versions to Show. By default, all Word versions are selected. If, however, you know the version of Word the recipient of your document is using, then deselect the other versions. If you're unsure which version that person is using, keep all versions selected.

NOTE

The Select Versions to Show list always defaults back to all versions selected.

Manually Run the Compatibility Checker

1. Open a document on which you want to check compatibility.

2. Click the File tab, Info, Check for Issues, and then select Check Compatibility.

3. In the Microsoft Word Compatibility Checker dialog box, if you do not see anything listed, that means your document is fully compatible with all lower versions of Word. If you see items listed, narrow down the list by selecting the specific version of Word you want to check compatibility for from the Select Versions to Show drop-down list.

4. Click OK to close the dialog box.

The following features will be checked and reported on when the Compatibility Checker is run:

- Alignment tabs
- Alternative text in table properties
- Apps for Office
- Blocked authors
- Citations and bibliographies
- Charts
- Collapsed comments (marked as done)
- Embedded objects
- Embedded video
- Equations
- Footnotes formatted in multiple columns
- New content controls
- New numbering formats
- New shapes and text boxes
- New WordArt effects
- Office 2007 charts

- Open XML embedded objects
- OpenType features
- Previous-version WordArt
- Previous-version diagrams
- Previous-version charts
- Relative text boxes
- Repeating section content controls
- SmartArt graphics
- Text effects
- Themes
- Tracked moves
- Web video

Word's Automatic Compatibility Checker

When you save a file to the Word 97-2003 (Compatibility Mode) format, the Compatibility Checker will automatically run, scanning the file for features in the document that are not supported or that function differently in earlier versions of Word. The report displays in the Microsoft Word Compatibility Checker dialog box, as shown in Figure 3.5.

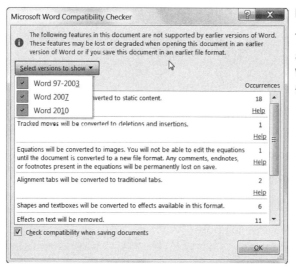

Figure 3.5

The Compatibility Checker will automatically run as soon as Word discovers you are saving a file in the *.doc format.

Editing Legacy Documents in Word 2013

If you've been working in Word for quite some time, you will have saved hundreds and possibly thousands of documents to your network or document management system, with the bulk of them probably in the *.doc file format. You can open any of these documents in Word 2013 and edit them as needed without doing anything extra. In other words, the document can remain in the *.doc file format for as long as you would like. This will be a time-saver and will work splendidly when collaborating with others who are still working in earlier versions of Word. By design, however, you won't be able to use any of the new Word 2013 features in those documents until you actually convert the file to a Word 2013 document.

When you do decide to convert a document, you could consider the *.doc file an archived file, and when it's converted to a *.docx file, you can save the new document as a new version or copy rather than overwriting the original document.

CAUTION

When a document is converted to Word 2013, the layout of the document may change. Keeping a copy of the original file may come in handy in case you need to refer to it.

What You Need to Know When Collaborating

As mentioned in the previous section, you can open and edit any earlier Word documents in Word 2013 with no problem. In fact, if you are collaborating with others outside of your firm and you are either unsure of the version of Word they are using or you know they are working in a lower version of Word, it's best to keep the document or save new documents in the lower version's file format. It's easy if the author of the originating document is in a lower version, then you don't have to do anything except edit the document and send it back and forth. When you do this, there is no conversion that takes place. Steer clear of the impulse to convert the document just because you are in Word 2013.

No Round-Tripping

The trap you want to avoid is "round-tripping" documents when collaborating with others. Round-tripping is the process of repeated conversion of a file into different file formats. Here's one example of how this works. A client sends you a Word 2003 document (*.doc), which you open and save as a Word 2013 document (*.docx). After making your edits, you send the document back to the client, and they open it and save it back down to a Word 2003 document (*.doc).

One of the biggest problems with round-tripping is that the file can become unstable. Formatting can change or be lost, and at worst, the file can become corrupt. The key take-away here is to avoid the practice of round-tripping at all cost.

Don't Convert the Document

On the other hand, we recommend when the originating author creates the document in Word 2003 and sends it to you for review and edits, you open the document, edit as needed, and then send it back to the originating author in the same *.doc file format. You do *not* want to convert the document to Word 2013.

Know Your Collaborator

The same problem can surface when you are the originating author of a Word 2013 document and you send the document to recipients who are still in Word 2003. Because they need the Compatibility Pack to open and edit the file, the same unexpected changes can happen to the document. If you know ahead of time what version of Word they are using, you can help them out by saving the file as a 97-2003 document (*.doc) and then keeping the document in that same format for the duration of the collaboration.

CONVERTING A DOCUMENT

When you've decided to convert an earlier Word version of a document to Word 2013 format, you have a choice of two methods—using the Convert button in Backstage view or using the Save As function. We've identified some pros and cons for each, as shown in Table 3.2, and we'll explain the steps to convert a document using each method.

TABLE 3.2—CONVERT VERSUS SAVE AS		
CONVERSION METHOD	**PROS**	**CONS**
Convert button	Takes fewer steps to convert	Overwrites the original file unless you save it as a new document immediately after converting; may not integrate with the document management system
Save As function	Creates a new file when converting; should integrate with the document management system with the choice to save as a new document or a new version	Takes more steps to convert

Convert a Document Using the Convert Button

If you want to convert a document, replacing the original document with the new file format, and you are not using a document management system, then you can use the Convert button method.

Convert a Document via Convert Button

1. Open the exercise file Convert This Certificate.doc available at www.the paynegroup.com/downloads/word2013forlawfirms/.

2. Click the File tab, click Info, and then select Convert. A message box displays informing you about the conversion, as shown in Figure 3.6.

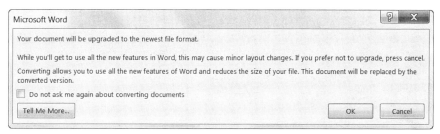

Figure 3.6   Converting a document may result in changes to the document.

3. Click OK.

4. Click Save to complete the conversion.

NOTE

Rather than replacing the original file with the newly converted file, you could save the converted file as a new document. After Step 3 in the previous exercise, click the File tab, Save As, and navigate to the location where you want to save the converted file. Note that these extra steps are easy to miss and may result in you accidentally overwriting the original. However, these steps may be available with document management systems.

Convert a Document Using the Save As Function

If you want to convert a document and create a new copy or version of the document, then use the Save As method.

NOTE

This method appears to integrate best with document management systems; however, testing in your own desktop environment is always recommended.

Convert a Document via Save As

1. Open the exercise file Convert This Certificate 2.doc available at www.the paynegroup.com/downloads/word2013forlawfirms/.

2. Click the File tab, and then choose Save As, and navigate to the location on your network where you want to save the file.

3. Select Word Document (*.docx) at the top of the Save As Type list.

4. Ensure the Maintain Compatibility With Previous Versions of Word check box is cleared (unchecked).

5. Click Save and read the message box that displays.

6. Click OK to complete the conversion.

CAUTION

Converting a file may change the layout of the document as Microsoft indicates in its message box upon conversion.

NOTE

You will want to test each conversion method in your environment to determine which method provides you with the best end results.

EXPERT TIP

Doing a bulk conversion of existing *.doc files is not necessary nor recommended. Files should be converted only on an as-needed basis. This is primarily due to the fact that earlier versions of Word files are compatible with Word 2013.

WORKING WITH IMPROPERLY CONVERTED DOCUMENTS

If you have been working in Word for years, you most likely have encountered problems related to improperly converted documents. In fact, the troubleshooting skills you've gained from this prior experience can be applied to Word 2013 documents. In general, problems exist in documents as the result of improper conversion techniques as well as improper pasting of content into Word documents.

The symptoms of a problematic document range from Word not complying with a simple command, such as restarting page numbering on an exhibit page, to a document that consistently crashes the Word application every time you edit the document. How a document becomes corrupt is buried in the document's unique history; however, some basic pasting and troubleshooting techniques can serve you well when dealing with these situations.

While proper conversion of legacy documents, including the appropriate method of pasting content into new documents, requires additional effort, that effort will pay off tenfold. It will help ensure that problems are not likely to arise in the future when working with that document or copying/pasting content from that document to others. This is critical because most lawyers use existing content when creating new documents. Proper conversion of documents helps to reduce the likelihood of unpleasant surprises when working with those documents down the road. Reapplying formatting is a small price to pay for a healthy, stable document.

BEST PRACTICE PASTING TECHNIQUES

Copying and pasting content from other documents, files, and websites into a Word document is easy. However, dependent upon the paste method used, you may be pasting in hidden formatting codes that will initiate unexpected behavior in your document, and the document may eventually become corrupt and unusable.

The best method for copying and pasting text from another document, file, or website is to use the Keep Text Only paste option. You can do this by clicking on the Paste Options button that appears below the pasted text, and choosing the Keep Text Only option. On the other hand, if you are absolutely certain that all the content in the Word document from which you are copying is "clean," and you currently do not experience much document corruption in your desktop environment, and the document did not come from outside of the firm, then you may be able to get away with using the Merge Formatting paste option. However, if there's any question in your mind, it's always good insurance to make it a standard practice to paste content into your Word document using the Keep Text Only paste option and then reapply the formatting that was lost.

NOTE

As described further in Chapter 4, "Formatting," you can now set default paste options. This means that you can change settings to have Word automatically paste in the text using Keep Text Only as the default. To review these options, click the File tab, Options, Advanced, and in the Cut, Copy, and Paste section, change the first four options as needed.

TROUBLESHOOTING A PROBLEM DOCUMENT

This chapter wouldn't be complete without talking about how to work with unruly files and how to, once and for all, properly clean up a document. If you're a savvy Word user, you've probably already experienced a plethora of problems with documents and have implemented procedures for document cleanup in order to stabilize a document to get it out the door. In fact, if you have experienced any problems in the past, you'll likely find our suggestions similar to what you currently do when tackling documents with issues.

Troubleshooting Tip #1

If you uncover a problem with a document, try doing the exact same process in a new, blank document. It's best to re-create what you're doing, rather than copy content from the problematic document and then paste into the new one. You might find that the new document works perfectly well, which is confirmation that it's not a Word application problem, but rather a document-specific issue.

Troubleshooting Tip #2

Select the entire problem document, except for the last paragraph mark of the document (leave this behind as it can still contain legacy hidden codes), copy it to the clipboard, and then paste it directly into a new, blank document. See if the problem persists. This method is a standard paste (not Keep Text Only), and therefore, you don't have to reformat the document.

Troubleshooting Tip #3

If you're finding that the problem is within a specific section of the document or within a specific header or footer, you can delete all of the section breaks within the document and reinsert them where needed. You will need to re-create the header and footer information for each section.

Troubleshooting Tip #4

Find out if the same problem exists when you open the document on another computer. You may find that there is something in your configuration that could be causing the issue with the document.

Troubleshooting Tip #5

When a document is so bad that it closes Word when trying to edit it, try opening the document using Open and Repair. This well-known feature repairs damaged documents and can be found in the Open dialog box and by selecting Open and Repair from the drop-down list next to the Open button, as shown in Figure 3.7. If any repairs were made when opening the document, a Show Repairs dialog box will display.

NOTE

Open and Repair is also available in Excel and PowerPoint, and some document management systems integrate this feature into its Open dialog box.

EXPERT TIP

New in Word 2013, if the document is a *.docx, Open and Repair will automatically open the document in a new, blank document.

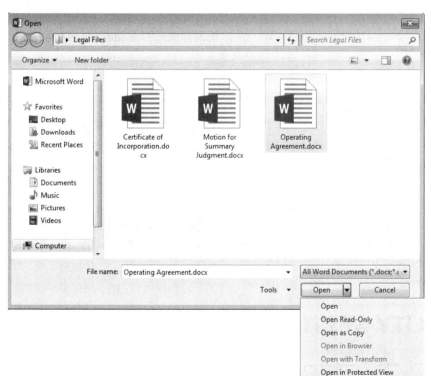

Figure 3.7 If a document is behaving strangely or you suspect corruption, use Open and Repair.

Troubleshooting Tip #6

To completely clean a problem document will take more time, but it will save hours of frustration later on—especially if the document will be used frequently or the document acts as a precedent and other documents will be created based on it. Select the entire document minus the last paragraph mark, copy it to the clipboard, create a new, blank document, and then paste the text using the Keep Text Only command from the Paste Options button. Using this method, you'll need to reapply styles and formatting to the document, as well as re-create headers, footers, and footnotes. This technique only transfers text from the main document area without any of the formatting.

Troubleshooting Tip #7

Insert the document into a new, blank document that is preferably from a standard template containing firm styles for the reformatting of text. Click the Insert tab, and in the Text group, click the arrow next to Object and choose Text from File. Navigate to the suspect document and then click Insert. This method is especially helpful with documents that will not open in Word.

Troubleshooting Tip #8

Saving the document to the Word XML Document (.xml) or Rich Text Format (.rtf) and back to .docx will sometimes correct the problems. In the Backstage view, choose Save As and choose either the .xml or .rtf file format. Save and close the file. Now reopen the file and save it in the .docx file format. When you close and reopen the file, see if the issues persist.

Any of the preceding methods will require that you give your document a good once over to be sure the page numbering, headers and footers, and section breaks are still properly in place.

COMPATIBILITY SETTINGS

Text, line spacing, page layout, and tables are a few of the compatibility settings that are noticeably selected when viewing documents created in an earlier version of Word. Compatibility settings were designed to allow the document to display in Word 2013 similarly to the version in which it was created. If you open an older Word document, and click the File tab, Options, Advanced, and scroll to the bottom under Compatibility Options for: (it will list your document's name), next to the Lay Out This Document as if Created in option, you will see the version in which the file was created.

NOTE

Occasionally you will see "Custom" showing for the document. This means that when the document was created, one or more additional compatibility options were selected, or the document was created in a format that is not available in the list.

EXPERT TIP

In the WordPerfect to Word conversion days, when WordPerfect showed in the list and the entire firm had already migrated to Microsoft Office, it meant that the WordPerfect file was opened directly into Word and saved as a Word document. This is an example of an improper conversion method, typically resulting in document instability.

Check Compatibility on a Document

1. Open an older, existing document from your document management system or network drive.

2. Click the File tab, click Options, and then click Advanced.

3. Under Compatibility Options for: (it will list your document's name), next to the Lay Out This Document as if Created in option, you will see the version in which the file was created.

4. Click Cancel to return to the document.

CAUTION

As a standard practice, you never want to change (select or deselect) any of the compatibility options because (1) it can result in an improper layout of your document, giving undesired results; (2) the setting can change to Custom and you will lose the original indicator reflecting what version of Word the document was originally created in; and (3) these settings travel with the document, so anyone else checking the compatibility settings will no longer see the original settings.

NOTE

When a document has been converted to the latest file format using the methods described in the "Converting a Document" section in this chapter, Word will automatically change the compatibility settings to Microsoft Word 2013.

WORD 2013 COMPATIBILITY SETTINGS

Unlike earlier versions of Word, when a new document is created in Word 2013 or has been converted to Word 2013, there are only seven layout options available and no compatibility options display by default, as shown in Figure 3.8.

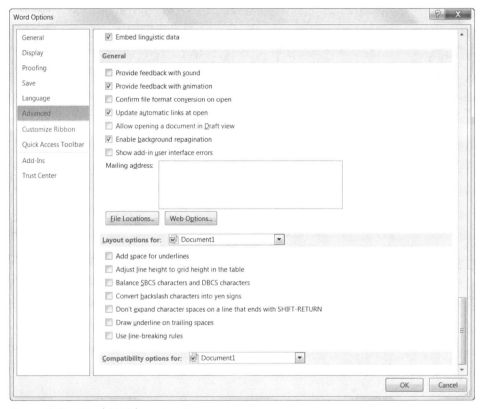

Figure 3.8 Word 2013 layout options.

EXPERT TIP

If you are in charge of creating templates for the firm and have had to set certain compatibility settings within the templates, such as with line-numbered pleading templates, you will find that you no longer have these same options available in Word 2013. In this case, your only two options available are to re-create the pleading templates in Word 2013 without any compatibility settings or to create the pleading templates in Word 2010 with the compatibility settings. Unfortunately, if the latter is used, whenever someone creates a document based on the template, by default it will save to the latest file format, consequently changing the compatibility settings of the document to Word 2013 and resulting in an unintended change in the layout of the document.

LITÉRA

Sherry Kappel of Litéra on Conversion and Compatibility

1. **Compatibility or Capability.** If a document will be edited across many different versions of Office/Word, [Compatibility Mode]—keeping it at the 97-2003 .doc level—is a best practice. If your document requires use of advanced functionality—embedding of Excel charts, video or graphics, for example—make the complete leap to the 2013 .docx format. And once you do, don't look back.

2. **When you must convert, don't Convert.** Too often, the Convert button is seen as a quick means to a meaningful end. It's not. You are far better off selecting all content in the document (minus the paragraph marker at the end), copying the selection, then creating a new document into which you relocate the copied content, as described in the next step.

3. **Consider your source and Paste accordingly.** When relocating an entire document's worth of content from one document to another: Does it contain tables? numbering? custom styles? field codes? sections? graphics? footnotes? If so, a Paste using the Keep Text Only option deletes these elements from your result. If that's your desire—and you have an extra day to put it all back together again—Keep Text Only is the proper choice for that document. It won't be the proper choice in other circumstances.

4. Don't make yourself or your collaborators dizzy: never round-trip. Never.

5. I know this is a Word book, but *never* Convert a PowerPoint presentation file. Start over. Always.

FORMATTING

After you have typed the textual content of your document, the majority of the work from that point forward involves adding visual effects, or formatting, to make your documents more visually appealing or to comply with formatting requirements established by court systems. You can either apply formatting as you type, or type your text first and then go back and format it later. This chapter addresses two types of formatting—character and paragraph. In addition to these two formatting features, this chapter also covers different methods to reveal the formatting as well as document themes.

FORMATTING AND LEGAL DOCUMENTS

Proper formatting is the crux of working with legal documents. As a general rule, no other documents require the precise settings that legal documents require—particularly those documents that are filed with courts. By focusing on the proper formatting of legal documents, you will not only save yourself time in creating visually appealing documents, but you will also ensure that documents filed with court systems will not be rejected for noncompliance with court-regulated formatting requirements.

OFFICE 365

Because legal documents are so formatting intensive, always keep in mind that Word Web App is best used for text editing while in a cloud environment. Although you can apply some formats in the Web App, many of the formats you need will only be found in the installed version of Microsoft Office Word.

UNDERSTANDING THE HIERARCHY OF FORMATTING

The formatting functionality in Microsoft Word is based on a three-tier hierarchy of character, paragraph, and section settings, each offering easy-to-use features for modifying the format of a document. We will look at all of these types of formatting starting with character formatting.

Character Formatting

Character formatting is the most basic type of formatting. You can apply character formatting to single or multiple characters or symbols. Character formatting can be used to apply font formats, such as bold, underline, and italics.

OFFICE 365

When applying character formatting to selected text, note that Word Web App deselects text after the formatting has been applied. Be sure to reselect the text prior to applying the next character format.

Paragraph Formatting

Paragraph formatting is applied to the entire paragraph and not just to selected characters. Paragraph formatting includes paragraph attributes such as centered, right, or justified text alignment, line spacing, spacing between paragraphs, tab stop settings, indentations from the left and right margins, borders and shading, bullets, paragraph numbering, and much more.

NOTE

There is no such thing as line formatting in Word. You can apply character formatting to all of the characters in one line, but you cannot apply paragraph formats to one line within a paragraph without affecting the entire paragraph.

Section Formatting

The most comprehensive part of the hierarchical structure related to formatting is section formatting. Section formatting affects the entire section and is used to set options such as margins, page orientation (landscape or portrait), line numbers, headers, footers, and more. See Chapter 6, "Page Setup and Layout," for more information on section formatting.

Since legal documents are typically chockfull of section breaks, it's important to understand how section break formatting works.

Section breaks cannot be added, deleted, or otherwise edited in the Word Web App.

Differentiating Between Character and Paragraph Formatting

A paragraph is defined as any amount of text, a graphic, objects (such as equations and charts), or other items that are followed by a paragraph mark. Paragraph formats affect the appearance of the entire paragraph, not just specific lines or words within a paragraph.

Characters are letters, numerals, symbols, punctuation marks, and spaces. Character formats can be defined as any formatting that can be applied to an individual character without affecting the rest of the paragraph.

Identifying Which Character Formats Have Been Applied

Word provides a WYSIWYG (What You See Is What You Get) display that shows text on the screen reflective of the formatting applied. Bold text shows up in bold, italics appear italicized, and so forth. There are times when a more precise method of determining the formatting may be desired. Character formats can be identified using the Reveal Formatting task pane.

The Reveal Formatting task pane is a useful tool for troubleshooting errant formatting. More on the Reveal Formatting task pane can be found in "Reveal Formatting" later in this chapter.

True WYSISYG is only available when the view is changed to Reading View. The only other view is Editing view.

APPLYING AND RECOGNIZING CHARACTER FORMATTING

The application of character formatting is simply a matter of selecting the desired text and choosing the desired format. After the text is selected, formatting can be applied using a variety of methods—selecting commands located in the Font group on the Home tab, selecting options from the Font dialog box, clicking commands on the Mini toolbar, or by using keyboard shortcuts.

The Character on the Left Controls Formatting

Any character, including spaces, can contain character formatting. If no characters are selected and bold formatting is applied, the next characters typed will be bold. If a character is underlined and the insertion point is placed to the immediate right of that character, any subsequent typing is underlined.

Using the Mini Toolbar

The Mini toolbar, shown in Figure 4.1, is a small semitransparent toolbar that appears whenever text is selected. Hover your mouse pointer over the Mini toolbar, and it will remain visible. Hover away from the toolbar or begin another task, and the Mini toolbar disappears. The Mini toolbar is also accessible when you right-click.

By default, the Mini toolbar is made up of a combination of 13 font and paragraph formatting commands: Font, Font Size, Increase Font Size, Decrease Font Size, Format Painter, Styles, Bold, Italic, Underline, Text Highlight Color, Font Color, Bullets, and Numbering.

Some of the buttons on the Mini toolbar, however, are contextual—the buttons on the right of the toolbar can change depending on the surrounding text (see Figure 4.2). For instance, if you right-click on a word, the commands on the Mini toolbar are the default commands listed previously. If you are in a table and right-click, the Styles button is replaced with Insert and Delete commands for the table.

The Mini toolbar also displays when right-clicking to display the shortcut menu.

To turn off the Mini toolbar when text is selected, from the File tab, click Options. Click General, and under User Interface Options, clear the Show Mini Toolbar on Selection check box.

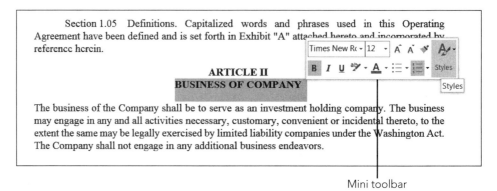

Figure 4.1 The Mini toolbar offers both font and paragraph formatting options.

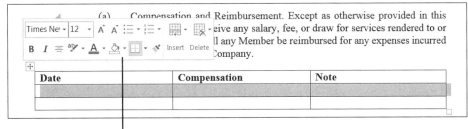

The Mini toolbar changes
based on what is active.

Figure 4.2   The Mini toolbar buttons can change depending on where your cursor is located.

The Mini toolbar cannot be customized.

NOTE

Word Web App does not provide the ability to turn off the Mini toolbar.

OFFICE 365

Apply Formatting from the Ribbon

The Home ribbon, shown in Figure 4.3, includes the most frequently used commands in Word. The ribbon contains font and paragraph formatting as well as cut, copy, and paste options, styles, and other editing commands.

To apply character formatting, select the text and then click the desired command in the Font group located on the Home tab. To access the Font dialog box for additional options, click the dialog box launcher in the bottom-right corner of the Font group.

Figure 4.3   Apply common font formats from the Home ribbon.

Apply Character Formats from the Ribbon

1. Create a blank new document.

2. Type **=rand()** and press Enter.

3. Select the word "powerful" in the first paragraph.

4. Click the Home tab, and in the Font group, click Bold, and then click Underline.

5. Click the down arrow next to the Underline button in the Font group and select Double Underline.

6. Click Underline in the Font group to remove the underlining.

7. Click the Clear All Formatting button in the Font group to clear the formatting.

Change Case

Change Case allows you to change text from lowercase to uppercase and from uppercase to lowercase and more. On the Home tab, in the Font group, click Change Case and select the desired capitalization (see Figure 4.4).

TIP

Press Shift+F3 to toggle between lowercase, capitalize each word, and uppercase.

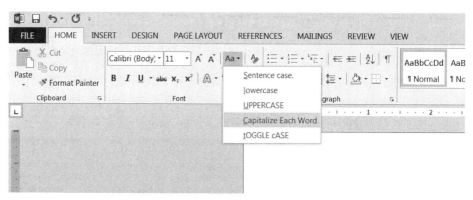

Figure 4.4   Select an option to change the case.

Highlighting Text

Highlighting in Word is the electronic equivalent of using a highlighter pen to call attention to an area of the document. Highlighting is not categorized as a character format, although it can be considered a character attribute.

Highlighting Text

1. Create a blank new document and type **This text has yellow highlighting. And this text has green.**

2. On the Home tab, click the arrow next to the Text Highlight Color button in the Font group.

3. Click to select Yellow.

4. Notice the cursor looks like a highlighter pen. Select "This text has yellow highlighting." by dragging the cursor across the text.

5. The text should now appear with yellow highlighting.

6. On the File tab, click Options, and then click Display. Clear the Show Highlighter Marks check box and click OK.

7. The previously highlighted text no longer displays the highlighting.

8. Select the word "green" and click the arrow next to the Text Highlight Color button and choose Green. Notice that the original yellow highlighting displays now. The Show Highlighter Marks option in Word Options is now checked.

9. Select all of the text, right-click in the selection, and from the Mini toolbar, click the down arrow next to Text Highlight Color and then choose No Color to remove the highlighting.

EXPERT TIP

The Show Highlighter Marks option found in the Display section of the Word Options dialog box controls both the display and printing of highlighting.

TIP

To quickly remove highlighting in a document, use the Find and Replace feature to find highlighting and remove it.

CAUTION

Some people mistakenly think that using either highlighting or shading is a way to redact text and information in documents. This is not the case. Within a Microsoft Word document, anyone can remove that formatting to reveal the underlying text. Additionally, after a Word file is converted to a PDF file, that PDF text can be copied and pasted into a text editor, such as Microsoft Notepad. At that point, all formatting is removed and the underlying text is revealed. Always use a true redaction tool such as PayneGroup's Redact Assistant or other third-party software for redaction.

Using Shortcut Keys to Format

Most production-oriented typists prefer to use shortcut keys rather than using the mouse to apply formatting. It is possible to apply character formatting for some of the most commonly used shortcut keys listed in Table 4.1.

TABLE 4.1—SHORTCUT KEYS TO APPLY CHARACTER FORMATTING TO SELECTED TEXT			
COMMONLY USED SHORTCUT KEYS			
Bold	Ctrl+B	Small Caps	Ctrl+Shift+K
Italic	Ctrl+I	Next larger font size	Ctrl+Shift+>
Underline	Ctrl+U	Next smaller font size	Ctrl+Shift+<
ALL CAPS	Ctrl+Shift+A	Change Case	Shift+F3

Using the Font Dialog Box

The Font dialog box, shown in Figure 4.5, is opened by clicking the dialog box launcher in the Font group located on the Home tab. The Font dialog box is the primary location of character formats. It offers the ability to change the Font, Font Size, Underline, Color, and add effects such as All Caps.

TIP

Press Ctrl+D to open the Font dialog box.

Figure 4.5

Use the Font dialog box to apply character formatting.

Word Web App does not provide a Font dialog box.

Text Effects and Typography

You may want to place emphasis on selected words within your document. Word 2013 has an array of formatting choices you can apply. Click the Text Effects button in the Font dialog box to open the Format Text Effects dialog box, as shown in Figure 4.6.

Figure 4.6

You can make the text stand out by adding effects to characters.

You can also quickly access Text Effects on the ribbon. In the Font group on the Home tab, click the Text Effects and Typography button, as shown in Figure 4.7.

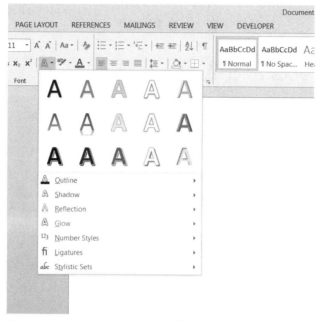

Figure 4.7 Quickly apply text effects from the ribbon.

Character Spacing

The Advanced tab of the Font dialog box includes settings for Character Spacing and OpenType features. Character Spacing applies a character attribute that affects the position of characters in relation to one another. These options are Scale, Spacing, Position, and Kerning.

Some legal documents, such as Agreements, may have titles with spaces between the letters for added emphasis. Rather than using the space character to achieve the desired effect, consider using Word's Character Spacing feature.

OpenType Features

Available in both Word 2013 and Publisher 2013 is the ability to apply professional typographical features, such as ligatures and stylistic sets that work with many OpenType fonts. These features are available in the Font dialog box, Advanced tab, in the OpenType Features section.

The OpenType features available will depend on the OpenType font being used in the active document.

NOTE

REVEAL FORMATTING

Press Shift+F1, and the Reveal Formatting task pane displays showing the formatting applied at the insertion point or the selected area within a document. As shown in Figure 4.8, the Reveal Formatting task pane is divided into three sections—Font, Paragraph, and Section. If the document contains tables or numbered lists, additional sections will appear in the task pane. Each section reveals the formatting associated with the insertion point or the selected area of the Word document.

OFFICE 365

The Reveal Formatting task pane is not available in Word Web App.

The Reveal Formatting task pane appears on the right side of the document window and can be closed by clicking the close button in the upper-right corner of the task pane or by pressing Shift+F1 again.

The Font section of the Reveal Formatting task pane displays the font style, size, and other character attributes for selected words, phrases, or paragraphs. You can even open the Font dialog box to make formatting changes to selected text by clicking the Font hyperlink.

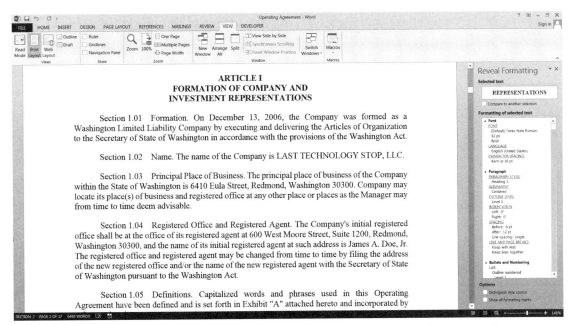

Figure 4.8   Use the Reveal Formatting task pane to quickly view or change the formatting of selected text or sections of a document.

The Paragraph section displays formatting for the paragraph where the insertion point is located. This can include paragraph style, alignment, indents, spacing, text flow options, tabs, and more.

The Section portion displays margins, page layout, section formatting, and paper size.

TIP

Click any of the blue hyperlinks within each section to open the corresponding dialog box.

Use Reveal Formatting to Apply Character Formatting

You can use the Reveal Formatting task pane to display and apply character formatting to selected text.

Apply Formatting Using the Reveal Formatting Task Pane

1. In a new, blank document, type **Johannesen v. Johnson, et al.** and select the text.

2. Press Shift+F1 to open the Reveal Formatting task pane. Notice the font name and size appear under Font.

3. Click the blue hyperlink in the Font section of the Reveal Formatting task pane to open the Font dialog box.

4. Select All Caps.

5. Change the Font to Arial, Font Style to Bold, and Size to 14.

6. Click OK.

7. Look under Font in the Reveal Formatting task pane. Notice that each of the attributes you applied is now visible. A new section called Effects has also been added.

8. Close the Reveal Formatting task pane by clicking the Close button in the upper-right corner of the task pane.

Apply and Clear Formatting Options

The Reveal Formatting task pane offers a quick method to detect and apply formatting of surrounding text to the selection, or to clear formatting altogether.

If the active cursor is within a word or several words are selected, the Selected Text box attempts to display the active word or the first few words of the selected text. If no text is selected, the preview displays the words Sample Text.

When you place your mouse over the Preview box, a down arrow appears with three options:

- **Select All Text With Similar Formatting.** Selects all text in the document with the same font and paragraph formatting.

- **Apply Formatting of Surrounding Text.** Detects and formats selected text to match the formatting of the text to the left of the first character in the selection.

- **Clear Formatting.** Strips direct character and paragraph formatting and then resets the selected text to Normal style.

NOTE

You can also clear formatting by clicking Clear All Formatting located in the Font group on the Home tab.

TIP

To remove direct character formatting, press Ctrl+Spacebar, or press Ctrl+Q to remove direct paragraph formatting. These two shortcuts are important to remember when troubleshooting formatting in a document.

DOCUMENT THEMES

While Document Themes are not as commonly used in legal documents as other types of formatting, it's still a good idea to understand what they are and how they work in the event that you encounter them from an ambitious template designer.

The first command found on the Design tab is Themes. This feature allows you to format an entire document quickly. A document theme is a collection of formatting choices that can affect colors, fonts, and effects (e.g., lines and fill effects) within a document (see Figure 4.9).

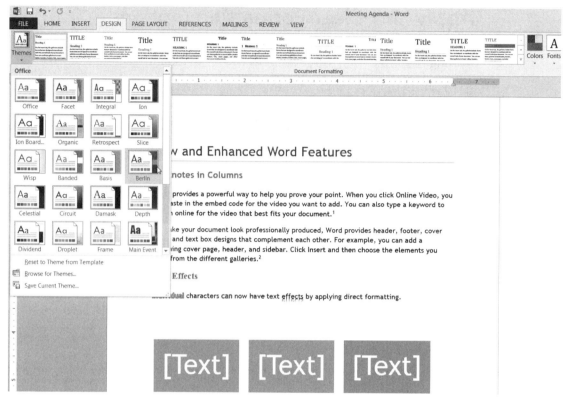

Figure 4.9 Hover your mouse over a theme to see a live preview of changes.

In a new Word document, the default theme is the Office theme. That means that there are certain colors, fonts, and effects associated with the Office theme that control how the document is formatted. When you change one theme to another, it can also change the colors, fonts, and effects throughout the document.

Apply a Theme

1. Open the exercise file Themes and Effects.docx.
2. Click the Design tab, and in the Document Formatting group, click Themes.
3. Hover your mouse over several of the built-in themes and watch the formatting of your document change.
4. Click to apply a different theme.
5. Keep this document open for the next exercise.

Theme Fonts

The theme fonts control the heading and body text fonts in a document. The current theme applied defines which font is used for both the headings and body of the document. You can essentially change an entire document's font by selecting a different theme font.

To change the theme fonts in the document, click the Design tab, and in the Document Formatting group, click Fonts. Choose from more than 20 different theme font sets.

NOTE

As your mouse rests over each theme font selection, the document shows a live preview of the font changes without applying the changes.

The new theme fonts applied will globally change the heading and body text fonts throughout the document. This is done instantly because the heading and body text fonts are designed to inherit the changes made when a new theme is applied. This is apparent when viewing the Font dialog box, as shown in Figure 4.10.

In the Font dialog box, the +Body and +Headings found at the top of the Font list are what allow the body and heading fonts to change in the document when a new theme font set (or document theme) is applied.

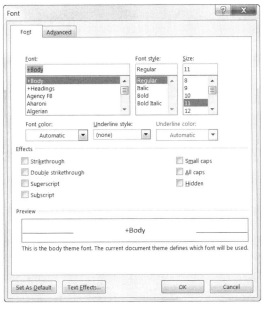

Figure 4.10

Word is designed to inherit the body and heading fonts from the new theme fonts or document theme applied.

Apply Theme Fonts

The default font for standard body text paragraphs in a default Word document based on the Normal template is Calibri. The headings, if applied in a document, are set to Calibri Light. The reason for this is because the Office theme fonts are defined as Calibri for +Body and Calibri Light for +Heading.

Apply a Theme Font

1. The exercise file Themes and Effects.docx should still be open from the previous exercise.

2. Click the Design tab, and in the Document Formatting group, click Fonts.

3. Rest your mouse pointer over the theme fonts to see a live preview of the font changes. Select the Arial-Times New Roman theme font. Note the themes are not in alphabetical order.

Edit or Delete Theme Fonts

You may need to modify or even delete theme fonts you no longer need. To do so, right-click the custom theme font and choose either Edit or Delete.

Theme Colors

Theme colors control the text and background colors in a document. There are four text and background colors, six accent colors, and two hyperlink colors. You can change an entire document's text and background color formatting by simply selecting a different theme color.

To change the theme colors in the document, click the Design tab, and then click Colors in the Document Formatting group.

EXPERT TIP

If you don't want the built-in themes to display in the Themes gallery, Microsoft recommends that you move the theme files into another folder. The reason Microsoft doesn't recommend deleting the built-in themes is because the only way to get those themes back is to reinstall Office.

WHERE IS PARAGRAPH FORMATTING INFORMATION STORED?

All paragraph formatting information is stored in the paragraph mark/pilcrow (¶), which is located at the end of the paragraph. Every paragraph has a paragraph mark. If a paragraph mark is deleted, the paragraph that was below the deleted paragraph mark merges with the above paragraph and inherits that formatting.

New Paragraphs Keep the Formatting of the Preceding Paragraph

When Enter is pressed to start a new paragraph, Word carries over the preceding paragraph's formatting to the new paragraph. After a paragraph is formatted, subsequent paragraphs created after the original paragraph retain the original's formatting until it is changed.

When you delete a paragraph mark, the paragraph formatting from the previous paragraph takes precedence in the combined paragraphs. The same holds true when backspacing over a paragraph mark. No matter how you delete the paragraph mark, the formatting above wins.

Using a Manual Line Break

There are times when a line break is desired within a paragraph. Pressing the Enter key creates a new paragraph, but pressing Shift+ Enter creates a manual line break instead of a new paragraph. This line break is also known as a line feed, a soft return, or a text-wrapping break. Insert a manual line break when you want to force text onto the next line, but don't want a new paragraph, as shown in the document title in Figure 4.11.

You can achieve the same results by clicking the Page Layout tab, click Breaks in the Page Setup group, and then select Text Wrapping.

Figure 4.11   Manual line breaks are used to create a new line within a paragraph.

How to Apply Paragraph Formats

To apply paragraph formatting you can place your insertion point anywhere within the paragraph and then choose the desired format. Select multiple paragraphs to apply formatting to all the paragraphs simultaneously. Formatting can be applied by using the commands in the Paragraph group of the Home tab, within the Paragraph dialog box, by clicking the commands on the Mini toolbar, or by using shortcuts keys.

Apply Formatting from the Ribbon

To apply paragraph formatting, place the insertion point within the paragraph (or select multiple paragraphs) and click the desired command in the Paragraph group of the Home tab (see Figure 4.12). To access the Paragraph dialog box for additional options, click the dialog box launcher in the lower-right corner of the Paragraph group.

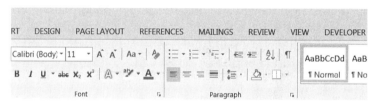

Figure 4.12 Apply common paragraph formats from the Home ribbon.

Apply Formats from the Ribbon

1. Create a new document.

2. Type text as a title at the top of the page and then center it by clicking the Home tab and clicking Center from the Paragraph group.

3. Place your insertion point at the end of the title and press Shift+Enter to insert a line break and type your name.

4. With your insertion point still in the title, click Line and Paragraph Spacing in the Paragraph group, and then click Add Space After Paragraph.

5. In the Paragraph group, toggle on Show/Hide if it is not on.

6. Type a paragraph under the title and name.

7. Set a 0.5-inch first-line indent by clicking the Paragraph dialog box launcher on the Home tab, and on the Indents and Spacing tab of the Paragraph dialog box, select First Line from the Special drop-down list. The By box will automatically register 0.5".

8. Click OK.

Using the Paragraph Dialog Box

Additional paragraph formatting options can be found in the Paragraph dialog box, shown in Figure 4.13. Click the Paragraph dialog box launcher in the lower-right corner of the Paragraph group to view these options.

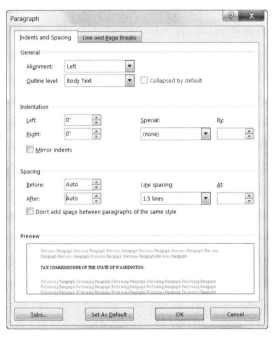

Figure 4.13

Set alignment, outline level, indentation, paragraph and line spacing, and tabs from the Paragraph dialog box.

Paragraph Alignment

There are four alignment options from which to choose: left, center, right, and justify. Using the commands on the ribbon in the Paragraph group will apply these settings. You can only apply one alignment to a paragraph.

Keyboard Shortcuts for Alignment

You can use keyboard shortcuts to quickly apply paragraph alignment. Table 4.2 lists the four keyboard shortcuts for paragraph alignment.

TABLE 4.2—KEYBOARD SHORTCUTS TO APPLY PARAGRAPH ALIGNMENT	
ALIGNMENT COMMAND	**KEYBOARD SHORTCUT**
Left	Ctrl+L
Center	Ctrl+E
Right	Ctrl+R
Justify	Ctrl+J

OUTLINE LEVEL

Although this topic will be covered more in depth in Chapter 11, "Complex Documents," an overview of this paragraph level format is discussed here.

Outline Level allows you to impose a hierarchy in the document that can be used with the Navigation pane, in Outline view, and is helpful when generating a Table of Contents (see Figure 4.14).

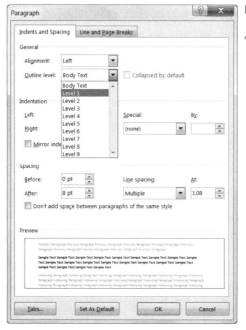

Figure 4.14

Assign paragraphs an outline level.

Any text that is formatted with an outline level of Body Text will not display in the Navigation pane and will not be included in the Table of Contents. Any text that is formatted with an outline level (or Heading Style) 1 through 9 will display in the Navigation pane and can be included in the Table of Contents.

Assigning an outline level is a good way to change the hierarchy of a paragraph without changing its format.

Collapse and Expand Outline Levels

New to Word 2013 is the ability to collapse heading or outline levels that have an outline level 1 through 9 assigned. You can collapse or expand these top-level paragraphs whether it is a heading style or just a direct paragraph format.

Collapse and Expand Outline Levels

1. Open the exercise file Operating Agreement.docx available for download at www.thepaynegroup.com/downloads/word2013forlawfirms/.

2. Navigate to ARTICLE I on page 1 and hover your mouse over that paragraph. You will see a gray triangle, as shown in Figure 4.15.

Figure 4.15   An expanded heading shows all subparagraph numbering.

3. Click the gray triangle to collapse the heading and its subparagraph numbering, as shown in Figure 4.16. This collapses only the ARTICLE I group.

4. Right-click the heading text beneath ARTICLE I, and from the shortcut menu, select Expand/Collapse and then select Collapse All Headings.

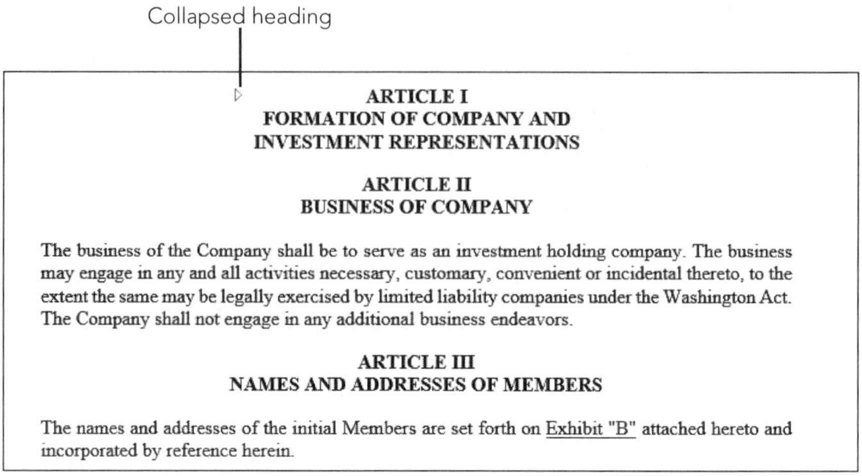

Collapsed heading

ARTICLE I
FORMATION OF COMPANY AND
INVESTMENT REPRESENTATIONS

ARTICLE II
BUSINESS OF COMPANY

The business of the Company shall be to serve as an investment holding company. The business may engage in any and all activities necessary, customary, convenient or incidental thereto, to the extent the same may be legally exercised by limited liability companies under the Washington Act. The Company shall not engage in any additional business endeavors.

ARTICLE III
NAMES AND ADDRESSES OF MEMBERS

The names and addresses of the initial Members are set forth on Exhibit "B" attached hereto and incorporated by reference herein.

Figure 4.16   A collapsed heading hides the subparagraph numbering.

5. Right-click the heading text beneath any ARTICLE paragraph, and from the shortcut menu, select Expand/Collapse, and then select Expand All Headings.

6. Click in the ARTICLE I paragraph again, and from the Home tab, in the Paragraph group, click the dialog box launcher. Next to Outline Level, check Collapsed by Default. This provides the same result as Step 3.

NOTE

The expanded or collapsed heading is a file setting, so the next person who opens the file in Word 2013 will have the same setting.

EXPERT TIP

The collapsed heading setting is not backward compatible to Word 2010 and earlier versions. For those not using Word 2013, all headings will display as expanded by default when the document is opened.

OFFICE 365

While headings are displayed properly in Word Web App, Collapse and Expand Headings is not available.

Disable Collapsed Headings

Collapsed headings could be considered hidden text, so if you prefer not to open documents with headings collapsed, you can set an option to automatically expand headings when a document is opened. From the File tab, click Options, click Advanced, and in the Show Document Content section, select the Expand All Headings When Opening a Document check box.

This option is a user setting, not a document setting, so changing this option does not affect the file. If a heading is collapsed, then it will remain collapsed for all Word 2013 users unless they enable the Expand All Headings When Opening a Document option.

Also, since the setting expands collapsed headings when a file is opened, it's still possible to copy a collapsed heading into another document and not realize that some of the information may be hidden.

SETTING INDENTS

Legal documents make heavy use of numbered paragraphs. All numbered paragraphs are based on Microsoft Word's indents. A solid working knowledge of indents will help to understand how the numbered paragraphs have been formatted.

Word has five types of indents: left, right, hanging, first line, and mirror. Each indent is described here:

- **Left Indent.** Determines the distance of all lines within a paragraph from the left margin.

- **Right Indent.** Determines the distance of all lines within a paragraph from the right margin.

- **First Line Indent.** Indents only the first line of text within a paragraph.

- **Hanging Indent.** Indents every line of text within a paragraph, except the first line.

- **Mirror Indent.** Choose from Inside or Outside and all lines within a paragraph indents on the left or right margins, respectively, but alternates the indent to the opposite margin on the next page.

There are four ways to set indents:

- Clicking the Indent buttons in the Paragraph group of the Home tab.
- Dragging the indent markers on the ruler.
- Using the Paragraph dialog box.
- Using shortcut keys for left and hanging indents.

Using the Ruler

There are four indent markers on the ruler (see Figure 4.17) that control the First Line, Hanging, Left, and Right Indents. The first line of the paragraph in the figure displays how text indents only on the first line while the rest of the paragraph follows the Left Indent. The Right Indent marker forces the paragraph away from the right margin.

The First Line Indent is controlled by the downward-pointing triangle; the Hanging Indent is controlled by the upward-pointing triangle; and the Left Indent is controlled by the small gray box below the triangles. The Right Indent is controlled by the upward-pointing triangle on the right edge of the ruler.

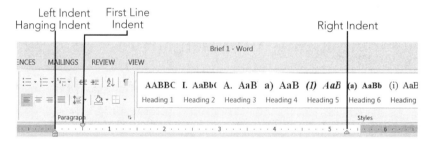

Figure 4.17 Setting indents on the ruler can be difficult for new users and takes some practice.

Use the Ruler to Set an Indent

1. With any open document, place your mouse (without clicking) over the triangle that represents the First Line Indent on the ruler until you see the ScreenTip.

2. Click and drag the First Line Indent marker to the 1-inch position on the ruler.

3. Release the mouse. The indent has changed.

4. Hold the Alt key and move the First Line Indent marker to the 0.5-inch position.

NOTE

Holding the Alt key while dragging displays the measurement as you drag.

NOTE

You can also set First Line Indents and Left Indents on the ruler without dragging. You click in the paragraph that you want to indent. Next, click the Tab setting button at the far left of the horizontal ruler until it changes to a First Line Indent marker. Click on the horizontal ruler at 1 inch, and then click again on the horizontal ruler at 0.5 inch.

Using the Paragraph Dialog Box to Set Indents

On the Home tab, click the dialog box launcher in the Paragraph group to open the Paragraph dialog box. On the Indents and Spacing tab, you'll find the Indentation section. In this section, the Left and Right Indents can be changed by either typing in a specific measurement or by using the up and down arrows to set the measurement. To set a First Line or Hanging Indent, click the down arrow under Special and set a specific measurement for the indent.

Keyboard Shortcuts for Setting Indents

Try using some of the keyboard shortcuts in Table 4.3 when working with indents.

TABLE 4.3—USE SHORTCUT KEYS TO SET INDENTS	
INDENT	**KEYBOARD SHORTCUT**
Increase the Left Indent	Ctrl+M
Reduce the Left Indent	Ctrl+Shift+M
Create/Increase the Hanging Indent	Ctrl+T
Reduce the Hanging Indent	Ctrl+Shift+T

NOTE

Left and Right Indents can also be set on the Page Layout tab, in the Paragraph group.

Set Indents

1. Create a new, blank document.

2. Type **=rand()** and press Enter. This creates five paragraphs with generic text.

3. Format the first paragraph with a First Line Indent of 0.5 inch.

4. Format the second paragraph with a Hanging Indent of 2 inches.

5. Format the third paragraph with a 1-inch Left Indent and a 1-inch Right Indent (double indent).

Double Indents

In order to create a double indent, you need to set the Left and the Right Indents in the paragraph. This formatting is frequently used for quotes in pleadings and briefs or for a legal description in a real estate document.

TIP

You can also set indents from the Page Layout tab, in the Paragraph group. Set Left and Right Indents or click the Paragraph dialog box launcher for more options.

NOTE

Indents can be set automatically with an AutoCorrect option setting called Set Left- and First-Indent with Tabs and Backspaces, which is an AutoFormat As You Type option. If this option is enabled, when you press Tab in the first position of the first line, a First Line Indent will be set. To set a Left Indent, click in the first position of any line except the first line and press Tab.

PARAGRAPH SPACING

Paragraph spacing is the amount of space between paragraphs. When you press Enter and begin typing the following paragraph, you will see what paragraph spacing has been set. This is not to be confused with the line spacing setting, which is the amount of space between each line within a paragraph. Line spacing is discussed later in this chapter.

Spacing Before and After determines the distance between paragraphs. A Spacing After setting of 8 points creates 8 points of white space following the paragraph. This is the Word user's alternative to placing an extra return between paragraphs.

Use Spacing After

1. If you don't have the previous file open, create a document with several paragraphs of text.

2. Select all of the standard text paragraphs in the document, and on the Home tab, click the Line and Paragraph Spacing button in the Paragraph group and choose Add Space After Paragraph. This command adds space after the paragraph. If space already exists, the option becomes Remove Space After Paragraph.

NOTE

Alternatively, clicking the Paragraph dialog box launcher and changing the Spacing After to 12 pt is another way to add space after the paragraph.

NOTE

To remove the Space After setting to selected paragraphs, click the Line Spacing button in the Paragraph group and select Remove Space After Paragraph.

TIP

Pressing Ctrl+0 (zero) toggles on and off 12 points of Space Before, which can be very helpful when working with pleadings that have line numbering.

LINE SPACING

Line spacing determines the amount of vertical space between lines of text within a paragraph. This can be changed in the Indents and Spacing tab of the Paragraph dialog box, by clicking the Line Spacing button in the Paragraph group of the Home tab, or by using shortcut keys.

The concept of single and double spacing within paragraphs is a familiar one, but Word provides even more precise control over line spacing. The settings available for line spacing are Single, 1.5 Lines, Double, At Least, Exactly, and Multiple.

NOTE

The default line spacing in Word 2013 is set to 1.08 Multiple line spacing. See Chapter 7, "Styles," for more information on the default settings for the Normal style.

Single, 1.5 Lines, and Double

All three of these choices set the line spacing for each line to accommodate the largest font on that line. For example, in a single-spaced paragraph with a font size of 10 points, the line spacing would be a little more than 10 points—the actual size of the characters plus a small amount of extra space (also known as leading, which is pronounced "ledding"). In that same example, 1.5 line spacing would be about 15 points, and Double would be about 20 points. The amount of extra space varies depending on the font used.

NOTE

Leading, a typography term, was used in the days of hand-typesetting when strips of lead were used to increase the vertical distance between lines.

TIP

The keyboard shortcuts for line spacing are

Ctrl+1—Single Spacing

Ctrl+2—Double Spacing

Ctrl+5—1.5 Spacing

At Least

At Least sets a minimum line spacing that Word can adjust in order to accommodate a larger font size or graphic that would not otherwise fit within the specified spacing. This setting requires that a specific measurement be set.

Exactly

Exactly sets a fixed line spacing that Word does not automatically adjust. If portions of characters or graphics appear to be cropped, increase the spacing measurement. This option makes all lines evenly spaced. This setting requires that a specific measurement be set.

CAUTION

You may notice a graphic, chart, or other object in a Word document that appears to be cropped. If exact line spacing is used, only a small portion of the inserted graphic, chart, or other object will display. To resolve this issue, click within the paragraph and check the line spacing to determine if this is the cause of the problem.

Multiple

Multiple allows line spacing to be increased or decreased by any percentage. For example, setting Multiple line spacing to a measurement of 1.2 will increase the space by 20 percent. Setting line spacing to a multiple of 0.8 will decrease the space by 20 percent. Setting the line spacing to a multiple of two is the equivalent of setting the line spacing to Double. In the At box, type or select the line spacing desired.

Line Spacing and Pleadings

Pleadings have historically relied on the Word Option "Suppress extra line spacing at the top of page." This feature has been removed in Office 2013. Be sure to work with an experienced Word 2013 template developer who knows about changes in the software and how it will affect legacy documents so your text continues to line up with the pleading paper's numbered lines.

TAB STOPS—SETTING AND CLEARING

By default, tab stops are preset at 0.5-inch intervals from the left margin. Pressing the Tab key moves the insertion point to the next tab stop in the current paragraph. Instead of pressing Tab multiple times to reach a desired location, set a new tab stop and press Tab once. Setting a manual tab stop removes all default tab stops located to the left of it. Word provides the ability to create Left, Centered, Right, Decimal, and Bar tabs, as shown in Figure 4.18.

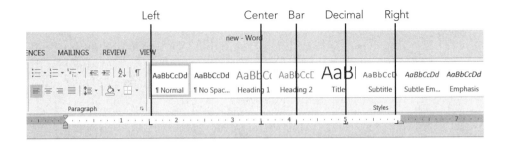

Attorney	Firm	Practice Group	Hours	Status
Jane Smith	Landers Forrest	Litigation	47.00	Complete
Everett Jones	Mission Marks	Corporate	88.25	Pending
Randall Lewis	Lewis Jones	Corporate	61.50	Complete

Figure 4.18 Setting tab stops using the ruler is efficient, but does not allow you to set tab leaders.

Setting Tabs Using the Ruler

Tabs can be set using the ruler, first by selecting the type of tab needed and then clicking within the ruler at the desired tab location. To select a specific tab alignment, click the Tab Alignment button located on the left side of the ruler until the desired type of tab is showing. After a tab type is selected, click the position on the ruler where that type of tab should be set.

The Bar tab is used to insert a vertical line at a specific point in the document. If you insert multiple paragraphs using the Bar tab, you will get a long vertical line through those paragraphs.

NOTE

If you do not see the horizontal ruler, click the View tab, and in the Show group, check Ruler. It's also important to note that the ruler will not display when working in Read Mode or Outline view.

Set Tabs Using the Horizontal Ruler

1. Create a blank new document.

2. Click the Tab Alignment button until the Center Tab displays. Click the horizontal ruler at 1.5 inches to set the tab.

3. Click the Tab Alignment button until the Decimal Tab displays. Click the horizontal ruler at 3 inches to set the tab.

4. Click the Tab Alignment button until the Left Tab displays. Click the horizontal ruler at 4 inches to set the tab.

5. Click the Tab Alignment button until the Right Tab displays. Click the horizontal ruler at 6 inches to set the tab.

6. Press the Tab key and type **NAME**.

7. Press the Tab key and type **HEIGHT**.

8. Press the Tab key and type **CITY**.

9. Press the Tab key, type **MONTH,** and press Enter.

10. Press the Tab key and type your name.

11. Press the Tab key and type your height (in decimal format).

12. Press the Tab key and type your city of birth.

13. Press the Tab key and type the month you were born.

NOTE

You can remove tabs by clicking and dragging the tab marker off the horizontal ruler. To affect several paragraphs at the same time, first select the paragraphs, and then remove the tabs.

Using the Tabs Dialog Box

Tabs can also be set using the Tabs dialog box. This dialog box is accessible by clicking the Home tab, clicking the Paragraph dialog box launcher in the Paragraph group, and then clicking Tabs. In addition to setting tabs, the Tabs dialog box provides the ability to alter the default tab stops as well as set tab leaders.

To remove a single tab, select the tab from the list under Tab Stop Position and click Clear. Clicking Clear All clears all user-defined tabs in the selected paragraphs. Clear All sets the tabs back to the default tab stop position of every 0.5 inch.

Adding Tab Leaders

Setting a tab leader fills the space before a tab stop with dotted, dashed, or solid lines. Leaders can be set when the tab is created using the Tabs dialog box, or by selecting an existing tab stop from the list, selecting the desired leader, and clicking Set.

Following are some tab leader examples:

Dotted..with a tab stop at 3 inches.

Dashed ----------------------- with a tab stop at 3 inches.

Solid_____with a tab stop at 3 inches.

EXPERT TIP

You may find documents that have a series of periods, hyphens, or underscores in it to create the effect of a dotted, dashed, or solid leader. Do not rule this out when troubleshooting tab alignment problems.

Inserting Tab Leaders

1. Create a blank new document.
2. Click the Home tab, click the dialog box launcher in the Paragraph group, and then click the Tabs button.
3. In the Tab Stop Position box, type **6**.
4. Under Alignment, choose Right.
5. Under Leader, choose 2 (dotted).
6. Click Set and notice that the new tab is added to the list.
7. Click OK. The new tab is now on the horizontal ruler.
8. Type **NAME**, and press the Tab key to move to the right tab.
9. Type **EXTENSION** and press Enter.
10. Type a short list of names and extensions using the setup from the exercise.

NOTE

It's important to remember that when using the Tabs dialog box to modify tabs, you must select the tab you want to change from the list first before making the change.

EXPERT TIP

Users may report that when they press the Tab key, their indents are changed instead. Remember that the reason for this is that the option Set Left- and First-Indent with Tabs and Backspaces has probably been set (File tab, Options, Proofing, AutoCorrect Options button, AutoFormat As You Type tab).

Alignment Tabs

Alignment tabs offer options for setting tab stops that align relative to the margin or left indent, and automatically adjust if the orientation, margins, or paper size changes. The feature is found in the Position group on the Header & Footer Tools Design tab. See Chapter 6, "Page Setup and Layout," for detailed information on Alignment tabs.

CONTROLLING TEXT FLOW

The Line and Page Breaks tab of the Paragraph dialog box includes Widow/Orphan Control, Keep Lines Together, Keep with Next, Page Break Before, Suppress Line Numbers, Don't Hyphenate, and Textbox paragraph formatting options. Understanding what each feature does and knowing how to apply them is extremely important when it comes to formatting and troubleshooting documents. The Line and Page Breaks tab in the Paragraph dialog box is shown in Figure 4.19.

Figure 4.19

Control text flow using options on the Line and Page Breaks tab.

You will want to control the text flow to avoid awkward transitions between elements on your page, such as the separation of the heading from the paragraph that follows the heading. This will also control small amounts of text being abandoned at the bottom or top of a page from subsequent pages.

Widow/Orphan Control

Widow/Orphan control prevents Word from placing the last line of a paragraph by itself at the top of a page (widow), or the first line of a paragraph by itself at the bottom of a page (orphan). This setting is on as a default in Word.

NOTE

Widow/Orphan control should be turned off if the text must be aligned with line numbers, such as in a pleading.

Keep With Next

The Keep With Next option prevents a page break between one paragraph and the following paragraph. Keep With Next is often applied to headings to prevent them from remaining at the bottom of the page by themselves, as shown in Figure 4.20.

CAUTION

Keep With Next can force a large amount of text to move as a unit. If you see a large amount of white space at the bottom of a page, look to see if Keep With Next has been applied to multiple paragraphs.

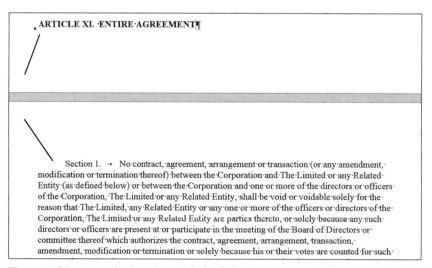

Figure 4.20   Keep the heading with the following paragraph for proper text flow.

Keep Lines Together

The Keep Lines Together setting prevents a page break within a paragraph. If you have several lines of a paragraph that are split between two pages, applying Keep

Lines Together moves the entire paragraph to the next page. An example would be a signature block that you want to keep together, as shown in Figure 4.21.

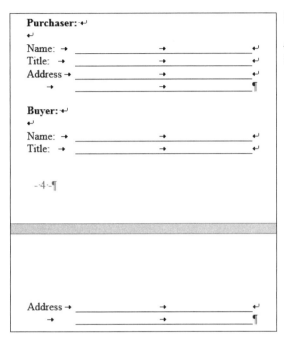

Figure 4.21

Apply Keep Lines Together to the Buyer's signature.

CAUTION

Because Keep Lines Together forces the entire paragraph to move as a unit to the next page, it can cause the bottom margin of the preceding page to appear unusually large. For instance, a 14-line paragraph formatted with Keep Lines Together will jump entirely to the next page, even if only one of its lines is forced onto the next page. This leaves a 13-line gap at the bottom of the preceding page.

Page Break Before

The Page Break Before setting forces Word to insert a page break before a paragraph. This page break will look exactly like a soft or automatic page break, so users may not be aware that formatting is causing the page break.

Paragraph Position Marks

If Show/Hide is turned on and nonprinting characters are displayed, any paragraph formatted with Keep Lines Together, Keep With Next, or Page Break Before will display a black nonprinting square to the left of the paragraph, as shown in Figure 4.22.

TIP

If a user is experiencing unexpected behavior with the flow of paragraphs, you can easily display nonprinting characters and look for Paragraph Position Marks. Double-click on the black square to display the Line and Page Breaks tab of the Paragraph dialog box.

CAUTION

An inherent danger with several of the text flow options described previously is that since they are all paragraph attributes, they can easily propagate in your document, especially if Show/Hide is turned off and the Paragraph Position Marks are not visible. For example, after applying Keep With Next to a paragraph, pressing Enter creates a new paragraph also formatted with this setting.

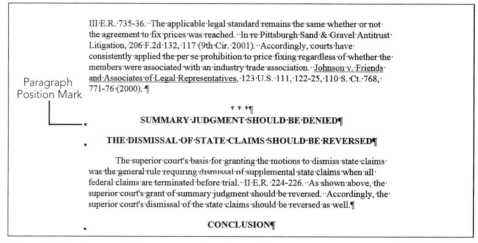

Figure 4.22 Paragraph Position Marks indicate that Keep with Next, Keep Lines Together, or Page Break Before is set.

Suppress Line Numbers

Line numbering is considered page layout formatting, but it can be suppressed for designated paragraphs. Suppress Line Numbers keeps line numbers from appearing next to lines of selected paragraphs in sections of a document that have line numbering. Word omits suppressed lines from the numbering sequence. For more information on Line Numbers, see Chapter 6, "Page Setup and Layout."

Don't Hyphenate

If your document has hyphenation in it, you can exclude paragraphs from hyphenation by selecting Don't Hyphenate on the Line and Page Breaks tab of the Paragraph dialog box. For more information on Hyphenation, see Chapter 6 , "Page Setup and Layout."

Text Box Options

When a text box is selected, you can define formatting options for how tightly text is wrapped within the text box. This setting can also affect the position of the text box slightly. Select the text box and specify tight wrap for First and Last Line, First Line Only, or Last Line.

USING FORMAT PAINTER

The Format Painter button found on the Mini toolbar and in the Clipboard group on the Home tab, makes it possible to copy character or paragraph formatting from one location to another. This is useful if complex character or paragraph formatting has been applied and re-creating it would take considerable time.

Copy Paragraph Formatting

Paragraph formatting is copied by placing your insertion point in the desired paragraph that contains the formatting you want to copy, clicking the Format Painter button, and then clicking the destination paragraph to paste the formatting.

Double-clicking the Format Painter button locks the feature to the "on" position so that any paragraphs that are clicked receive the same copied formatting, until the Format Painter button is clicked again and turned off. Pressing the Esc key will also turn off the Format Painter.

Using Format Painter to Copy Paragraph Formatting

1. Open the exercise file List.docx available for download at www.thepaynegroup.com/downloads/word2013forlawfirms/.

2. Click in the paragraph with the word File.

3. Click on the Bullets button in the Paragraph group on the Home tab to apply bullet formatting.

4. With your insertion point in the bulleted paragraph, double-click the For-mat Painter button in the Clipboard group on the Home tab. Notice your cursor now resembles a small paintbrush.

5. Click several of the other paragraphs.

6. Press Esc to turn the Format Painter off or click the Format Painter button again to turn it off.

NOTE

The Format Painter can be found on the Mini toolbar as well as in the Clipboard group on the Home tab.

Copy Character Formatting

To copy character formatting, click on text containing the desired formatting, click the Format Painter button, and then select the destination text to paste the for-matting. Again, multiple instances can be "painted" with the desired formatting by double-clicking the Format Painter button. Any text selected receives the cop-ied formatting until the Format Painter is turned off.

Keyboard Shortcuts for Using Format Painter

If you prefer keyboard shortcuts, you can get the same result using a shortcut key rather than clicking the Format Painter button with the mouse (see Table 4.4).

TABLE 4.4—USE KEYBOARD SHORTCUTS TO COPY AND PASTE FORMATTING	
COMMAND	**KEYBOARD SHORTCUT**
Copy Formatting	Ctrl+Shift+C
Paste Formatting	Ctrl+Shift+V

OFFICE 365

Word Web App does not provide the Format Painter.

PRODUCTIVITY TOOLS

Working in the legal industry can pose demands on time, so finding tools that promote efficiency that can be incorporated into daily work is essential. Word 2013 has a variety of these built-in productivity tools designed to enhance the work performed in Word. There are tools designed to help you paste text with certainty and to effectively navigate and search for terms and objects in a document. You can find and insert legal symbols, proof the document from one task pane, and insert frequently used clauses or signature blocks where needed to systematically build a document.

CUT, COPY, AND PASTE

Moving and copying text from the same, or a separate, document utilizes these frequently used commands: Cut, Copy, and Paste. These commands can be applied from the ribbon or by using keyboard shortcuts.

From the Ribbon

You can cut, copy, and paste as well as preview the paste directly from the ribbon, as shown in Figure 5.1. Select the text, and on the Home tab in the Clipboard group, choose the appropriate command. The Cut command will remove the selected text and add it to the Office Clipboard, whereas Copy will add the selected text to the Office Clipboard, but will not remove the selected text from its original location.

Figure 5.1 Use the Cut, Copy, and Paste commands.

NOTE

The Office Clipboard is found on the Home tab, in the Clipboard group, by clicking the dialog box launcher. The task pane will open on the left side of the Word window by default. As in earlier versions of Word, when the Clipboard task pane is open, it will add each individual item that you cut or copied. The task pane can hold up to 24 pieces of information and is available to paste the individual items into any document (or other Office application) until the last Office application is closed and it empties the Office Clipboard.

After you've cut or copied text, in the Clipboard group on the Home tab, click the upper half of the Paste command to paste the text where your insertion point is located.

NOTE

Each time you use the Paste command in Word, the Paste Options button displays, as shown in Figure 5.2. Depending on what information has been cut or copied, the Paste Options button will display different options. When information is pasted from different applications, such as Excel or PowerPoint, additional paste options will be available.

OFFICE 365

Your browser window may only allow you to cut, copy, and paste via the keyboard shortcuts: Ctrl+X, Ctrl+C, and Ctrl+V. Contact your network administrator for access to the browser's Clipboard if you prefer to use the buttons or right-click methods.

Paste Preview

Let's say you copied text from another document and are not sure how it will look when pasted into the current document. Rather than pasting it and then clicking Undo to remove it, Paste Preview will help you make the decision by showing you how the text will look before you paste it into your document. Once you've decided which one you want, click to paste it at your cursor location.

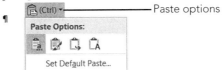

(A) → The·Corporation·will·pay·any·and·all·documentary,·stamp·
or·similar·issue·or·transfer·taxes·payable·in·respect·of·the·issue·or·delivery·of·shares·of·one·class·
of·Common·Stock·on·the·conversion·of·shares·of·the·other·class·of·Common·Stock·pursuant·to·
this·paragraph·(d)(5);·provided,·however,·that·the·Corporation·shall·not·be·required·to·pay·any·
tax·which·may·be·payable·in·respect·of·any·registration·of·transfer·involved·in·the·issue·or·
delivery·of·shares·of·one·class·of·Common·Stock·in·a·name·other·than·that·of·the·registered·
holder·of·the·other·class·of·Common·Stock·converted,·and·no·such·issue·or·delivery·shall·be·
made·unless·and·until·the·person·requesting·such·issue·has·paid·to·the·Corporation·the·amount·of·
any·such·tax·or·has·established,·to·the·satisfaction·of·the·Corporation,·that·such·tax·has·been·
paid.·¶

¶ —————————————— Paste options

Figure 5.2   Choose the paste option that works best.

To access Paste Preview, after you've copied text, place your insertion point in the
document where you want to paste the text, and then on the Home tab, in the
Clipboard group, click the lower half of the Paste command. Hover the mouse
over each of the icons under Paste Options and notice the formatting changes.
Click the icon with the desired formatting results to paste it into the document.

TIP

You can also see the paste options by right-clicking in the document where you want
to paste the text and hover the mouse over each of the Paste Option icons for a preview of the text before making your selection.

Keyboard Shortcuts

The keystroke commands for Cut, Copy, and Paste are Ctrl+X, Ctrl+C, and Ctrl+V,
respectively.

TIP

There are keyboard shortcuts associated with the Paste Options button as well. To
apply the Keep Text Only option, after you've pasted the text, press the Ctrl key to
access the Paste Options button and then press T. Hover over each of the icons to
discover the keystroke for each option—the letter will display within the parentheses.

To disable the Paste Options button, from the File tab, choose Options. Click Advanced and then under the Cut, Copy, and Paste section, clear the Show Paste Options Button When Content is Pasted check box. If you disable the Paste Options button, you can still access the Paste Options by clicking the lower half of the Paste button in the Clipboard group on the Home tab.

Default Paste Options

Set pasting behavior preferences so that Word automatically pastes text into the document with your preferred default. From the File tab, click Options and then click Advanced. View the four options in the Cut, Copy, and Paste section, as shown in Figure 5.3. You can also access these settings by selecting Set Default Paste from the Paste Options button. There are default settings you can define when pasting within the same document, between documents, and from other programs.

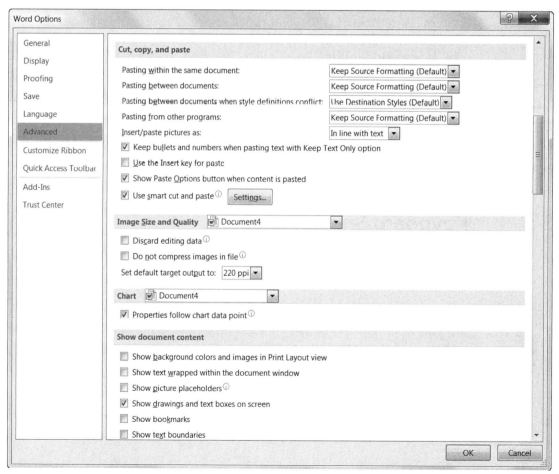

Figure 5.3 Control how text is being pasted into a document from Word or other programs.

NAVIGATION PANE

The Navigation pane incorporates three functions, all of which will be useful when working with legal documents. You can conduct a search that includes text or specific properties, such as footnotes or comments. Likewise, you can browse just the headings in the document or show just the pages of the document. You may notice that the Headings tab in the Navigation pane resembles the Document Map feature found in earlier versions of Word.

To access the Navigation pane, press Ctrl+F or click Find in the Editing group on the Home tab. It will automatically open the Navigation pane on the left side, as shown in Figure 5.4. As you begin typing the keyword(s) to search by, Word promptly begins to highlight areas throughout the document that meet the search criteria.

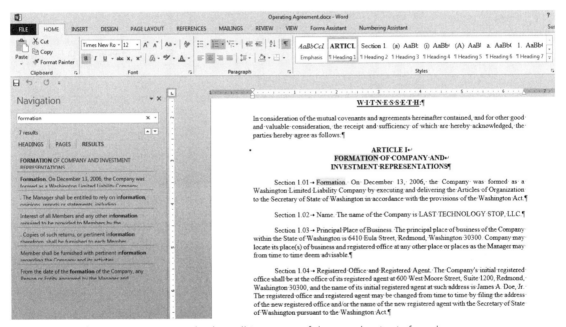

Figure 5.4   The Navigation pane displays all instances of the search criteria found.

In addition to the highlighted text in the document, any matches found will display under Results in the Navigation pane. Each instance will have the search criteria in bold formatting and will display in the order in which it appears in the document. Clicking on a match displayed in the Results pane will take you to that area of the document with the keyword(s) selected. When you edit the document, it pauses the search and clears the Results pane. To show the results again, click the Next Search Result button (the downward-pointing arrow in the Navigation pane) to go to the next instance of the keyword(s) in the document or click the Previous Search Result button (the upward-pointing arrow in the Navigation pane) to go to the previous instance of the keyword(s).

After conducting a search, click Headings in the Navigation pane and notice the highlighted heading(s), indicating in which heading the search criteria is located. Also try clicking Pages in the Navigation pane and notice that it displays only the page(s) in which the search criteria is found.

TIP

Conduct a Keyword Search Using the Navigation Pane

1. Create a blank new document.

2. Type **=rand()** and press Enter.

3. In the Editing group on the Home tab, click Find or press Ctrl+F to open the Navigation pane.

4. In the Search Document box, type **theme**. Notice the search begins as soon as you start typing.

5. In the Navigation pane, click on the second match found from the Results list and notice the word is selected in the document.

6. In the Navigation pane, click the Next Search Result button (the downward-pointing arrow) to go to the next instance of the keyword.

7. Place your insertion point in the document before the word theme that is selected, type **firm**, and press the Spacebar. Notice the Results pane no longer displays the search results. Click the Next Search Result button twice to go to the next instance of the keyword and continue the search.

Clicking Page Number on the Status bar will open and close the Navigation pane.

TIP

Browse Headings

When editing legal documents that use heading styles, those headings will appear in the Navigation pane. Click Headings at the top of the Navigation pane to display the headings and any subheadings in the document. Click on a heading to go to that location in the document. In addition to browsing headings, there are additional options such as promote and demote headings, insert or remove headings, move a heading including its subheadings by dragging and dropping to a different location, and print just a single heading and its contents. All of these options are available directly from the Navigation pane, as shown in Figure 5.5.

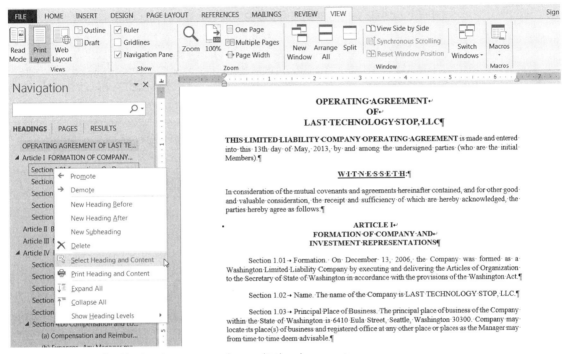

Figure 5.5 Use the Navigation pane tools to edit the document.

Use the Navigation Pane

1. Open the exercise file Operating Agreement.docx from www.thepaynegroup. com/downloads/word2013forlawfirms/.

2. On the View tab, in the Show group, select the Navigation Pane check box.

3. At the top of the Navigation pane, select Headings.

4. Click any of the headings in the Navigation pane to move to those locations within the document.

5. Click the black arrow next to Article IV Rights and Duties of Manager to collapse the heading. Notice the arrow changed to white, which indicates a collapsed heading. Click the white arrow to expand the heading.

6. Click to select Article V Rights and Obligations of Members. Notice this heading has four subheadings under it. Click and drag the Article V heading and drop it between Article III Names and Addresses of Members and Article IV Rights and Duties of Manager. Release the mouse when you see the blue horizontal line where you want to drop the moved text. Notice the paragraphs renumber automatically, and the text has been moved in the document.

NOTE

When heading styles are in use, numbered paragraphs will automatically adjust when a numbered paragraph using a heading style is moved. Likewise, if a heading style is deleted, the subsequent heading styles, if applicable, will renumber accordingly. This is one of the benefits to using heading styles in legal documents. Learn more about styles and numbering in Chapter 7, "Styles," and Chapter 8, "Bullets and Numbering."

7. Under Article VI Meetings of Members; Consent, Section 6.01 Meetings of Members, right-click (f) Unanimous Consent and choose Promote. Notice how the paragraph automatically numbers. The document has been updated as well.

8. Repeat step 5 to promote paragraph (a) Procedure for Consent.

9. Right-click Article VI Meetings of Members; Consent and choose New Heading After. Press Shift+Enter to insert a line break and type **ADDI-TIONAL MEMBERS**. Press Enter and type: **From the date of the formation of the Company, any Person or Entity approved by the Manager and Members representing a Majority Interest may become a Member of this Company**.

10. To close the Navigation pane, click the Close button in the upper-right corner of the Navigation pane.

11. Keep this document open for the next exercise.

NOTE

If the Navigation pane is open and you open other documents or create a new document, the Navigation pane will also remain open with the other documents.

FIND AND REPLACE

When editing lengthy documents, it frequently requires finding specific text and inserting manual edits. Occasionally you'll need to find and globally replace text throughout the document. The Find feature allows you to locate one or more instances of text or objects. The Replace command adds the ability to replace the text or formatting that is found with something else. Word combines the Find, Replace, and Go To commands, making them available in the same dialog box.

An example of using the Find and Replace feature is to find the word "contract" and replace it with "agreement." To open the Find and Replace dialog box, press Ctrl+H, or in the Editing group on the Home tab, click Replace.

TABLE 5.1—COMMON KEYBOARD SHORTCUTS	
KEYBOARD SHORTCUT	**RESULT**
Ctrl+F	Opens the Navigation pane and selects the Results tab.
Ctrl+H	Activates the Find and Replace dialog box and selects the Replace tab.
Ctrl+G or F5	Activates the Find and Replace dialog box and selects the Go To tab.

Find and Replace Text

1. The Operating Agreement.docx exercise file should still be open from the previous exercise.

2. Press Ctrl+Home to go to the top of the document. This Operating Agreement indicates the company is incorporated as a limited liability company (LLC), but it should be a limited liability partnership (LLP).

3. Press Ctrl+H to open the Find and Replace dialog box, as shown in Figure 5.6.

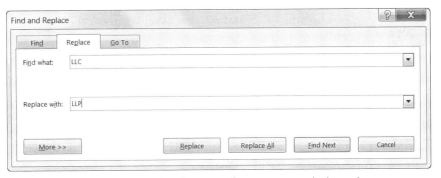

Figure 5.6 You can find and replace text, formatting, symbols, and more.

4. In the Find What box, type **LLC** and press Tab.

5. In the Replace With box, type **LLP**.

6. Click the Find Next button. Notice it stops on and selects "LLC."

7. Click Replace. Notice it automatically moves to and selects the next instance of "LLC."

8. Click Replace. Continue finding and replacing the remaining instances.

9. A message box will display when Word has finished searching the document. Click OK and keep the Find and Replace dialog box open.

10. In the Find What box, type **liability company** and press Tab.

11. In the Replace with box, type **liability partnership**.

12. Click the Find Next button. Notice it stops on and selects "LIABILITY COMPANY."

13. Click Replace. Notice it automatically moves to and selects "Liability Company."

14. Click Replace. Continue finding and replacing the remaining instances.

15. Click OK to close the Searching has finished message box. Click Close to close the Find and Replace dialog box.

TIP

It's a good rule of thumb to use all lowercase when finding and replacing text because Word will stop on all instances of the word or words, automatically applying the initial capitalization or all capitals if it exists in the original text.

CAUTION

Using Replace rather than Replace All allows you to review each occurrence of the text before replacing it with the new text. Replace All will globally change all instances in the document.

Search Options

If you do not find what you're looking for when conducting a standard search, you can narrow a search by using the search options available in the Find and Replace dialog box. Open the Find and Replace dialog box and click the More button to expand the Search Options, as shown in Figure 5.7. Each of the search options is described here.

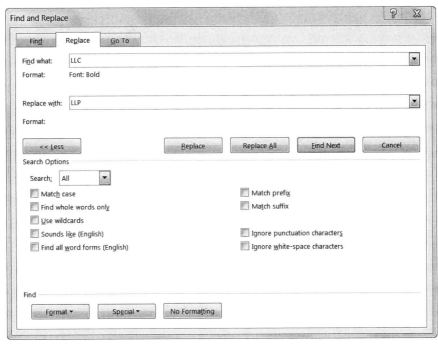

Figure 5.7   Narrow the search by selecting one or more search options.

Match Case

As you conduct a search in Word, when you type the text in all lowercase, the search process will stop on all instances of the word regardless of its case. For example, search for "company" and it will stop on "COMPANY," "Company," and "company." If you are replacing "company" with "corporation," Word will replace the word in the same case it was originally. Therefore, "COMPANY" becomes "CORPORATION," and "Company" becomes "Corporation," and so forth.

To narrow the search to only stop on a specific case, select the Match Case search option. Word will only stop on the text when it matches the specific case that is typed in the Find What box. Using the preceding example, if you search for "COMPANY" and select the Match Case search option, it will only stop on "COMPANY," not on "Company" or "company."

Whole Words Only

Many words are contained within other words, so when you conduct a search, it may find too many matches. For example, the word "he" is found in the words "the," "there," "she," etc. To ensure Word only finds the exact word you are looking for, select Whole Words Only.

Wildcards

Operators and expressions can be used when finding or replacing text. Within the context of a pattern search, an operator is a symbol that holds a position for a combination of characters. To use this feature, you must check the Use Wildcards option under Search Options in the Find and Replace dialog box.

The first example of a wildcard search is "b?t," which finds any three-letter word that starts with "b" and ends with "t" such as "but," "bat," and "bit." A more complex example is "[Tt]i*de," which finds all words that include a capital or lowercase "t" followed by the lowercase letter "i" and any number of characters that precede the letters "de." Examples of words that would be found include "Tide," "tide," and "tirade," but not "TIDE" because of the case of the letters. Any combination of characters can precede or follow the pattern combinations.

NOTE

Searching by using wildcards is always case sensitive.

The available wildcards in Word include the options under the Find column, as shown in Table 5.2.

TABLE 5.2—USE WILDCARDS TO EXPAND YOUR SEARCH		
FIND	**OPERATOR**	**EXAMPLE**
Single character	?	c?t finds cat or cot
Any string of characters	*	W*d finds Word and World
One specified character	[ ]	W[io]n finds win and won
Single character in a range	[-]	[f-m]ight finds fight, light, and might, but does not find eight, night, and right
Single character except that inside the brackets	[!]	M[!a]st finds mist and most but not mast
End of a word	>	(et)>finds bet, but not better
Beginning of a word	<	<(reg) finds register but not preregister
One or more occurrences of the previous character or expression	@	Se@t finds set and seat
From n to m occurrences of the previous character or expression	{n,m}	10{1,3} finds 10, 100, 1000
At least n occurrences of the previous character or expression	{n,}	Re{1,}d finds red and reed
Exactly n occurrences of the previous character or expression	{n}	Re{2}d finds reed but not red

Sounds Like

This setting locates words that sound alike, but are spelled differently. Selecting the Sounds Like (English) option and searching for "there" would find "there," "their," and "three" (yes, the number 3 spelled out does not *sound* at all like there and their). A search for the word "heir" would find "heir," "hair," and "hare," but not "air."

Variations of the Same Word

Another feature of Word is the ability to find variations of the same word. For instance, if you want to find all instances of the word "run," you could use Find All Word Forms to locate "run," "ran," and "running," although the letter combinations are not the same. Other aspects of this search feature involve handling possessive and case-sensitive scenarios.

TIP

Note that Word does not recommend doing a Replace All when you are using Find All Word Forms. If you try to do so, Word will display a warning that Replace All is not recommended. You then can cancel the process.

Match Prefix and Suffix

Sometimes it is necessary to further narrow a search when you have multiple variations of the same word. For example, you may have a document that uses the term "view" quite liberally, such as "preview," "viewer," "viewing," and so on. Let's say you want to narrow the search to only stop on the latter two terms, but not stop on the word "preview." When Match Prefix is enabled, Word looks for and recognizes text as a prefix only if it appears at the beginning of the word. Likewise, if you choose Match Suffix, it only finds words that appear at the end of the word. You'll try out the Match Prefix option in the next exercise.

Use the Match Prefix Search Option

1. Create a blank new document and type the following text with a paragraph mark in between each: **review**, **reviewing**, **reviewer**, **previews**.

2. On the Home tab, in the Editing group, click the drop-down arrow next to Find and choose Advanced Find.

3. In the Find What box, type **review**.

4. Click the More button to expand the Search Options.

5. Select the Match Prefix check box.

NOTE

6. Click Special at the bottom of the dialog box and choose Any Letter.

    Learn more about using special characters later in this section.

7. Click Reading Highlight and select Highlight All.

8. Notice the words that are highlighted. To clear the highlighting, click Reading Highlight and then choose Clear Highlighting.

You can use the Match Suffix search option when you want to find the text that is at the end of the word.

TIP

If you wanted to replace some of the found terms with something else, you could use the Find Next button to stop on each term, then select the Replace tab to enter the Replace With text, and click Replace as needed.

Ignore Punctuation Characters

Have you ever searched for a word and wasn't sure if it had punctuation in the middle of it or not? In earlier versions of Word you had to conduct two searches—one with punctuation, then one without punctuation. For example, you may want to search for the proper use of the word "its" and you may have two variations of the word—"its" and "it's"—throughout the document. In the Find and Replace dialog box, in the Find What box, type "its" and then check Ignore Punctuation Characters under Search Options. Each time you click Find Next, it will stop on both "its" and "it's."

NOTE

The punctuation characters Word will ignore are left and right single quotation marks, left and right double quotation marks, apostrophe, hyphen, comma, period, and exclamation point.

Ignore White Space Characters

With multiple people editing a document, you may find that certain terms may be spelled differently throughout the document, even though it may be just a hyphen or a space. For example, you might find various instances of the word "firm-wide," such as "firm wide" and "firmwide." To clear this up and to make this term consistent throughout the document, you could do one Find and Replace and check Ignore White Space Characters. Using this method will stop on both "firm wide" and "firmwide," and then you can replace it with "firm-wide" from the Replace tab.

NOTE

White space characters include single or multiple instances of the following: space, tab, space symbol (character code 0020), zero width joiner symbol (character code 200D), zero width nonjoiner symbol (character code 200C), and four-per-em space symbol (character code 2005). Surprisingly, the nonbreaking space is not considered a white space character.

Format

The Format button at the bottom of the Find and Replace dialog box offers options to search for and replace formatting alone or in combination with text and other symbols. Format choices include character formatting such as bold and italic, paragraph formatting such as line spacing or justification, tab stops, styles, and more.

Having styles properly applied in legal documents is a must. You can learn more about this in Chapter 6, "Styles." A quick way to restyle a document is to use the Find and Replace function to find a specific style and replace it with another specified style. For example, if there are a lot of Normal styles applied throughout the document, you may want to replace them with the firm's standard Body Text style.

Find and Replace Styles

1. With any open document, press Ctrl+H to open the Find and Replace dialog box.

2. In the Find What box, click Format, and then choose Style.

3. In the Find Style dialog box, select the Normal style and click OK.

4. In the Replace With box, click Format, and then choose Style.

5. In the Find Style dialog box, select the Body Text style and click OK.

6. Click Replace All to run the operation on the entire document.

7. Click OK and close the Find and Replace dialog box.

TIP

The Find and Replace dialog box retains anything you added or selected in the Find What and Replace With boxes during the active Word session, including typed text, formatting, and any search options selected. To clear the formatting, click in the Find What box and click the No Formatting button and do the same for the Replace With box to clear all formatting searches.

Special Characters

There are certain legal documents that use special characters frequently. Some of the common special characters you're familiar with when working on legal documents are the paragraph symbol, section symbol, and copyright symbol, just to name a few. With Word you can find special characters in addition to text, then replace them with other special characters and text. Let's say you have an agreement that refers to "Section 2.1(a)" and other numbered sections throughout the document, and then you realize that rather than have "Section" spelled out, you want the section symbol (§) in its place.

Find and Replace Special Characters

1. Create a blank new document.

2. Type **Section 2.1(a)** and press Enter.

3. Type **Section 3.4(c)**.

4. Press Ctrl+H to open the Find and Replace dialog box.

5. In the Find What box, type **Section** and press Tab.

6. In the Replace With box, click Special, and then choose § Section Character.

7. Click Replace All.

8. Click OK on the message box that tells you how many replacements were made. Close the Find and Replace dialog box.

NOTE

There are 22 choices on the Special button when you have your insertion point in the Find What box as shown in Figure 5.8. There are only 15 choices on the Special button when you have your insertion point in the Replace With box.

TIP

Sometimes corruption can be found in the header and footer layer of a Word document, and these documents typically have multiple sections. Bringing the document down to a single section and then rebuilding the document by reinserting each required section where appropriate is a good way to possibly remove corruption that was residing within one of the sections.

To do this, conduct a Find and Replace All by finding Section Break on the Special button, and then replacing with the Caret Character (or other unique symbol that is not used in the document). Next, conduct another Find and Replace All by finding Caret Character on the Special button, and then replace with Section Break on the Special button. Now test to see whether the same corruption problem exists in the header or footer.

See Chapter 3, "Compatibility and Conversion," for more tips on troubleshooting problem documents.

Figure 5.8   Find and replace special characters.

EXPERT TIP

Table 5.3 displays codes that can be used for a Find and Replace, but are not listed on the Special button.

TABLE 5.3—CODES NOT FOUND ON THE SPECIAL BUTTON IN THE FIND AND REPLACE DIALOG BOX	
CODE	WHAT IS FOUND
^a	Comment (balloons must be off; looks for comment reference)
^19	Opening field brace (when field codes are visible)
^12	Page or section (when replacing, inserts a page break)
^0nnn	ANSI (4 digit) characters, where nnn is the character code
^nnn	ASCII (3 digit) characters, where nnn is the character code
^Unnnn	Unicode (4 digit) characters, where nnnn is the character code
^21	Closing field brace (when field codes are visible)

AutoFormat As You Type

Word's AutoFormat As You Type features offer a variety of formatting replacements while typing. Many of these save you the time of having to go back and properly format text.

The most helpful features are described in the following list:

- "Straight quotes" with "smart quotes." Replaces the generic vertical quotation mark with "curly quotes," which have been considered good typography for the past few decades.

- Ordinals (1st) with superscript. Replaces 1st with 1st, 2nd with 2nd, etc.

- Fractions (1/2) with fraction character (½). Applies superscript to many fractions.

- Hyphens (--) with dash (—). Replaces two hyphens with the em dash.

- Internet and network paths with hyperlinks. When typing a URL or website, Word will automatically apply the hyperlink to the text.

NOTE

The *Bold* and _italic_ with real formatting feature is actually a legacy feature that goes way back to earlier word processors, where the asterisk and underlines allowed a typist to apply bold and italic while formatting.

However, when working with legal documents, particularly those that need to be filed with the courts, the last thing you want is Word to start making formatting decisions for you. While this may be acceptable for nonlegal documents, legal documents have a whole set of formatting rules unto themselves. When these AutoFormat As You Type features are left on, you will find that Word automatically applies styles, bullets, tables, and other formatting while you're typing.

Take a look at these options by going to the File tab, Options, Proofing, AutoCorrect Options, and review the AutoFormat As You Type tab. Following is a list of some of the features that are commonly turned off when working with legal documents.

AutoFormat As You Type:

Apply As You Type section

- Automatic Bulleted Lists
- Border Lines
- Built-in Heading Styles
- Automatic Numbered Lists
- Tables

Automatically As You Type section

- Define Styles Based on Your Formatting

NOTE

The AutoFormat tab is not to be confused with the AutoFormat As You Type tab. The AutoFormat tab works only with the AutoFormat Now command that does not display on the ribbon by default. You would have to add the AutoFormat Now command to the Quick Access Toolbar and then click the command and the AutoFormat dialog box will display. When you click OK, Word will automatically reformat the document based on the options set on the AutoFormat tab.

SPELLING AND GRAMMAR

When using the Spelling Checker, it can reduce the number of errors that might otherwise show up in your documents. Some spelling corrections occur automatically as you type, while others require you to manually run the Spell Check process. The Grammar Checker is similar in that it will look for grammatically incorrect sentences and offer corrective suggestions, but it will not automatically make the corrections for you.

Spelling and Grammar Options

Before running a spelling or grammar check, it's important to know the options available when Word identifies a spelling or grammar error so that you know what to expect. Take a look at the options by going to the File tab, Options, Proofing, as shown in Figure 5.9.

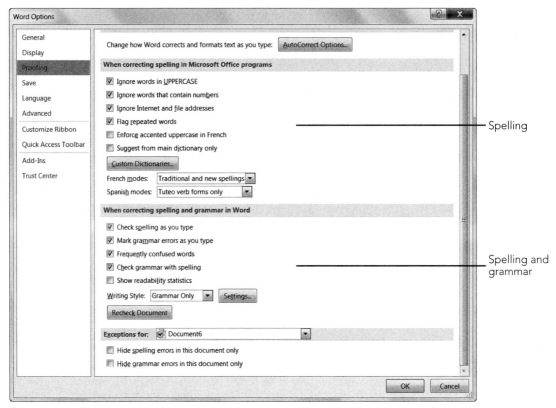

Figure 5.9 The spelling and grammar options determine how and if spelling and grammar checking takes place.

NOTE

Your firm may already have preselected the spelling and grammar checking options, which may be different from the default options shown in Figure 5.9.

Each of the spelling and grammar options is described in the following list:

- **Ignore Words in UPPERCASE.** When this option is selected, the spelling checker does not detect words that are 100 percent uppercase.

- **Ignore Words that Contain Numbers.** Check this, and the spelling checker will not detect words that include numbers.

- **Ignore Internet and File Addresses.** Check this option to have Word skip Internet, e-mail, and file addresses during a spell check.

- **Flag Repeated Words.** Duplicate words adjacent to each other will be flagged.

- **Enforce Accented Uppercase in French.** Missing accent marks in French uppercase words will be flagged.

- **Suggest from Main Dictionary Only.** Suggests spelling corrections from the main dictionary only and not from any custom dictionaries you may have installed on your computer. Make sure to clear this option if you have a custom dictionary (legal, medical, or engineering) and want to use it together with the main dictionary during spell checking.

- **Custom Dictionaries.** Word has a built-in dictionary, but you will want to add familiar words to a custom dictionary of your own. This would include your name, the firm name, unusual street names, and possibly some legal and technical terms. Some firms have created a custom dictionary that includes a list of all attorney and paralegal names to reduce the instance of Word stopping on each name referenced in the document. Of course, someone would need to be in charge of maintaining this custom dictionary.

CAUTION

If you accidentally clicked the Add button on a word while running the spelling checker, the misspelled word will be added to the custom dictionary. You will need to remove the unwanted word from the custom dictionary, or it will be skipped the next time you run the spelling checker. For detailed information, see the "Edit the Custom Dictionary" section of this chapter.

- **French Modes**

  - **Traditional and New Spellings.** Words from both the new and traditional French spelling dictionaries are suggested for misspelled words.

  - **Traditional Spelling.** Use French spelling rules that predate the spelling reform of 1990. Suggests words from the traditional spelling dictionary.

  - **New Spelling.** Words from the French new spelling dictionary are suggested for misspelled words.

- **Spanish Modes**

  - **Tuteo Verb Forms Only.** The Spanish spelling checker recognizes only tuteo verb forms.

  - **Tuteo and Voseo Verb Forms.** The Spanish spelling checker recognizes both tuteo and voseo verb forms.

  - **Voseo Verb Forms Only.** The Spanish spelling checker recognizes only voseo verb forms.

- **Check Spelling as You Type.** Enables automatic spell checking. Errors are flagged in the document with a red wavy line under the detected spelling error. To see possible suggestions, right-click the marked word.

- **Mark Grammar Errors as You Type.** Enables automatic grammar checking. Errors are flagged in the document with a blue wavy line under detected grammar errors. Right-click the marked text to see possible suggestions.

- **Frequently Confused Words.** Flags a mistaken or misused word within a sentence.

- **Check Grammar with Spelling.** To check grammar when a spell check is run, select this option. If this option is checked, the Show Readability Statistics option will become available.

- **Show Readability Statistics.** Readability statistics provide information such as the number of words, characters, paragraphs, and sentences in the document. Word also calculates the average number of sentences per paragraph, words per sentence, characters per word, and more.

- **Writing Style.** Set various rules used by the grammar checker.

- **Hide Spelling Errors in this Document.** This option hides the red wavy line under detected spelling errors. You can select a specific document from the Exceptions For list or select All New Documents. Running the spelling checker will still detect spelling errors.

- **Hide Grammatical Errors in this Document.** Turns off the blue wavy lines that reflect detected grammatical errors. You can select a specific document from the Exceptions For list or select All New Documents.

NOTE

The grammar checking feature encompasses two default writing styles—Grammar Only and Grammar & Style. Each style allows you to select the grammar checking options that will work best for your documents. To choose a specific writing style, on the File tab, click Options, and then select Proofing. Select a Writing Style from the drop-down list and click Settings to set specific options, as shown in Figure 5.10.

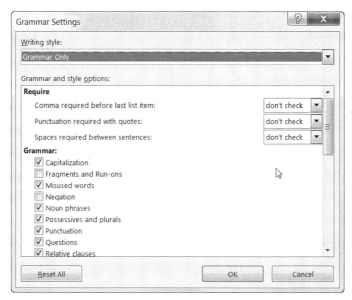

Figure 5.10

Fine-tuning some of the available options can make grammar checking a more useful tool for certain legal documents.

Check Spelling and Grammar As You Type

When the Check Spelling and Check Grammar As You Type options are enabled, the document will automatically be marked when Word detects a misspelling with a red wavy underline or grammatically incorrect sentence with a blue wavy underline. Rather than check for spelling and grammar errors as you are typing, you may prefer to wait until the document is finished before initiating a manual spelling and grammar check.

Correct Spelling and Grammar Errors As You Type

1. Create a blank new document.

NOTE

This exercise assumes you enabled the options Check Spelling As You Type, Mark Grammar Errors As You Type, and Frequently Confused Words on the Proofing tab in the Word Options dialog box.

2. Type **Grantor desires to provide an trust fund to be used primaraly for the education and benfit of Joseph Cooper and is subject to the terms and conditions set fourth herein.**

3. Right-click each of the flagged words that have the blue and red wavy underline and choose the correct replacement word.

Check Spelling and Grammar Manually

When you've finished editing or drafting a document, you'll want to manually run the Spelling Checker, and if preferred, run the Grammar Checker at the same time.

NOTE

If you want to run the Grammar Checker with the Spelling Checker, enable the Check Grammar with Spelling option on the Proofing tab in the Word Options dialog box.

You can run the Spelling and Grammar Checkers by doing one of the following:

- Press F7 on the keyboard.

- Click the Spelling & Grammar button in the Proofing group on the Review tab.

- Click the Spelling and Grammar Check icon on the Status bar, as shown in Figure 5.11.

Indicates spelling errors

Figure 5.11

An X on the book icon indicates there are proofing errors found in the document; a check mark indicates no proofing errors were found.

Spelling and Grammar Task Pane

When you initiate the Spelling and Grammar Checker and Word finds a proofing error, a Spelling or Grammar task pane will open on the right side of the window, as shown in Figure 5.12. Depending on your spelling and grammar settings, a misspelled word can appear in the document as selected (with gray shading) and with a red wavy underline. A grammar error can appear with the sentence selected (with gray shading) and with a blue wavy underline.

Figure 5.12

Correct a flagged error using the Spelling and Grammar task panes.

The Spelling task pane will have the following options available:

- **Ignore.** Skips the word once.

- **Ignore All.** Skips the same word in the entire document.

- **Add.** Creates an entry in the custom dictionary.

- **Change.** Fix the error by using one of Word's suggestions. If the error is in the document multiple times, use Change All.

- **Change All.** Fix the same error in the entire document by using one of Word's suggestions.

- **Speaker Icon.** Click to hear an audio playback of the word.

- **Definition.** The bottom of the task pane defines the word.

Depending on the error Word found, the Grammar task pane will have the following options available:

- **Ignore.** Ignores the suggestion once.
- **Change.** Fix the error by selecting one of Word's suggestions and clicking Change.
- **Explanation.** The bottom of the task pane will either explain what grammar error occurred (e.g., "A" or "An") or a definition of the suggested word with a speaker icon allowing for an audio playback of the suggestions.

NOTE

When you initiate a manual spelling or grammar check, Word works downward in the document from where your insertion point is located. When it reaches the end of the document, it will continue back up to the top of the document until the spelling and grammar check has finished.

AutoCorrect

In addition to the spell checking features we've already examined, you can further eliminate the possibility of spelling errors through the use of AutoCorrect. Auto-Correct is a feature that automatically corrects spelling errors as you type. Word already has a long list of default AutoCorrect entries for commonly misspelled words, and you can also create your own. For example, let's say you consistently misspell the word "affidavit" as "affadavit"—no problem, you can create an Auto-Correct entry that will automatically recognize the misspelled word and replace it with the correct spelling.

From the File tab, choose Options, select Proofing, and then click the AutoCorrect Options button. Select the AutoCorrect tab and create your own AutoCorrect entries, as shown in Figure 5.13.

CAUTION

Word will automatically correct more misspellings than you find on the AutoCorrect list if the option Automatically Use Suggestions from the Spelling Checker is selected. On the AutoCorrect tab, clear this option to better handle automatic corrections.

NOTE

In earlier versions of Word, right-clicking on a misspelled word allowed you to add to the AutoCorrect list as an option on the shortcut menu. This option is no longer available in Word 2013.

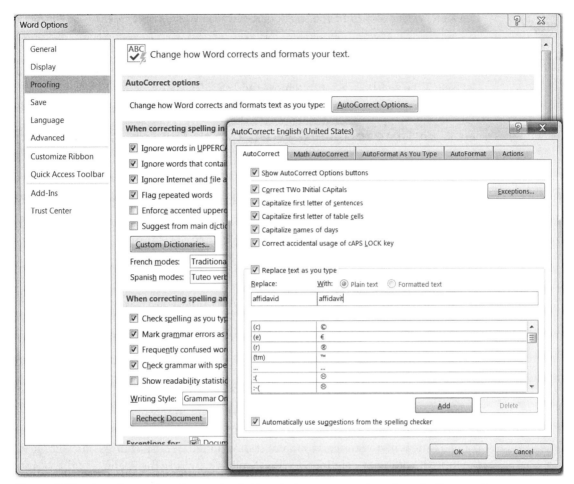

Figure 5.13   AutoCorrect is a time-saving feature that you can use to automatically correct misspelled words.

Add Words to the Custom Dictionary

The standard dictionary built into Word is comprised of thousands of commonly used words and terms that provide the basis for the spelling checker to accurately proof the text in your documents. However, during the spell checking process, Word may not recognize some words, such as names, addresses, and so forth. You have the option to add unrecognized words that Word detects as misspelled into the custom dictionary. When prompted with misspelling suggestions, you can click Add To Dictionary, and those words will no longer be flagged as misspelled.

CAUTION

Be careful what you add to your dictionary because you will no longer be prompted to spell check that word! Should you mistakenly add a word to your custom dictionary, you can edit the dictionary and remove the word. On the File tab, click Options, Proofing, Custom Dictionaries. In the Custom Dictionaries dialog box, click Edit Word List, select the word you want to remove, and click Delete.

Add an Unrecognized Word to the Custom Dictionary

1. Create a blank new document.

2. Type **Lewiston, Elden, & Kumasaka LLP** and press Enter twice. Notice that Elden and Kumasaka are flagged as being misspelled (if you have the option Check Spelling as You Type enabled).

3. Right-click Elden and choose Add To Dictionary.

4. Press F7 to run the Spelling Checker. The Spelling task pane opens with a suggested spelling. Click Add. The next time you type these names, they will not be marked as misspelled.

Edit the Custom Dictionary

Whether you have added words to your Custom Dictionary over a period of time, or you have been designated as the Custom Dictionary administrator, there may come a time when you need to make some changes. Those changes may come in the form of adding or deleting words as well as changing the spelling of the words. The Edit Dictionary feature does not allow you to edit words, so you will need to delete and then add the word back to the Custom Dictionary.

Edit the Custom Dictionary

1. Click the File tab, Options, Proofing, and click the Custom Dictionaries button.

2. Select the dictionary to be edited.

3. Click Edit Word List.

4. Add or Delete the words to the Custom Dictionary.

5. Click OK three times.

The custom dictionary file (Custom.dic) is located in the following directory: C:\Users\%UserName%\AppData\Roaming\Microsoft\UProof.

As a result, any words that are added to the custom dictionary will apply to only the user who added them. These spelling additions do not travel with the file.

Reset the Spelling Checker

Everyone knows the benefits of using the Spelling Checker, but not everyone knows the benefits of resetting the Spelling Checker. Imagine a document's spelling was checked by co-counsel and sent to you for revision. When you check the spelling, you may not find any errors because you did not type any new misspellings. However, you will want to reset the Spelling Checker, which will reset any words that co-counsel could have designated to be ignored. Yes, misspellings can be ignored!

Reset the Spelling Checker

1. Open a document where the spelling has already been checked.

2. On the File tab, click Options, and then select Proofing.

3. In the When Correcting Spelling and Grammar in Word section, click the Recheck Document button.

4. Click Yes to reset the Spelling and Grammar Checker and then click OK to close the Word Options dialog box.

5. Press F7 to run the Spelling Checker again.

You may be looking for a command to add to the Quick Access Toolbar that resets the spelling checker. The Spelling Recheck Document command found in the All Commands list does not reset words that have been flagged with the Ignore All option. It will, however, reset words flagged with Ignore. Even macro recording the steps to reset the Spelling Checker does not reset any words where Ignore All was selected. Running a manual reset or having a programmer create this routine are the only current solutions.

DICTIONARY AND APPS FOR OFFICE

One of the newest features available in Office 2013 is the Apps for Office. Similar to downloading an app on a smartphone, you can download an app that integrates with Office 2013, whether it's a dictionary that would be widely used within Word or an exchange rate app that may help you with calculations in Excel.

NOTE

Downloads may be blocked at your firm.

To download a dictionary, from the Review tab, in the Proofing group, click the Define button, or right-click a word in your document and select Define. The Dictionaries task pane will open if no dictionaries have been installed, as shown in Figure 5.14.

Figure 5.14

The Dictionaries task pane displays to install an online dictionary.

Define a Word

1. Open an existing document.

2. Right-click on a word and choose Define.

3. The Dictionary task pane opens, providing a definition for the selected word.

4. If there is a See More link below the definitions, click it to see additional information including a thesaurus and the word used in sample sentences.

5. Double-click another word in the document to define it. The Dictionary task pane automatically inserts the word into the task pane and provides the definition.

PROOFING LANGUAGE

Office 2013 supports the ability to type, edit, and proof in multiple languages. The default proofing and editing language is determined at the time Office 2013 is installed and configured. You can change language settings from within Office. From the Review tab, in the Language group, click Language, and then click Language Preferences. Select a language from the Add Additional Editing Languages list and click Add, as shown in Figure 5.15.

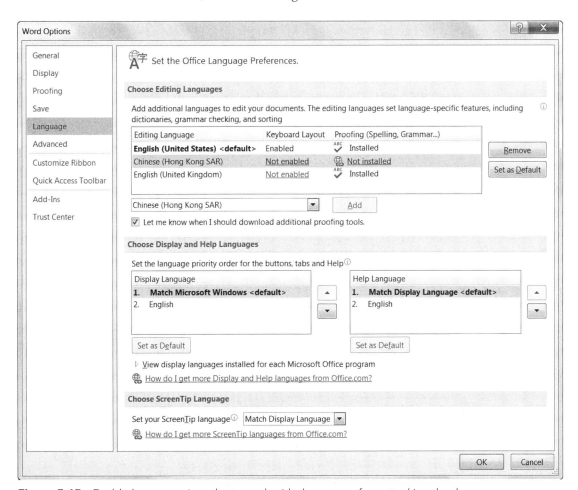

Figure 5.15   Enable languages in order to work with documents formatted in other languages.

NOTE

After adding a language, the Keyboard Layout column will display "Not Enabled" if the keyboard needs to be enabled. The Proofing column will indicate if the proofing tools are installed. If it displays a "Not Installed" link, click the link to go to Office.com's Office 2013 Language Options. Select the language you want to enable, and the Language Pack will either be a free download or for purchase. On the for purchase Language

Packs, you will see a note indicating that if you purchased an Office 365 subscription, it can be used to install Office in different languages rather than buying a Language Pack.

After installing an additional language, you will still have only one default language for new documents. When using multiple languages in a single document, you will want to tell Word which language proofing tools should be used by paragraph. For example, if the first paragraph is in English (US) and the second paragraph is in Spanish (Mexico), you'll want to select the second paragraph and apply proofing tools for that language. From the Review tab, in the Language group, click Language, and then click Set Proofing Language. Select Spanish (Mexico) and click OK.

EXPERT TIP

If a document has several paragraphs that consist of two different languages, you may want to create a style that references the language so that when the style is applied to a paragraph, the language is automatically set. All other paragraphs will be the default language. Learn more about creating styles in Chapter 7, "Styles."

CAUTION

In the Language dialog box, the default option Detect Language Automatically will change the language setting of an individual paragraph if it finds a word in the paragraph that is similar to a word in another language, such as French. This will cause Word's spelling checker to enable the affected paragraph with an incorrect proofing language. For best results, you will want to clear this check box.

THESAURUS

The Thesaurus is a built-in tool that allows you to search for words that have similar and opposite meanings. The Thesaurus task pane is shown in Figure 5.16. There are several ways to open the Thesaurus task pane:

- Click in a word and press Shift+F7.
- Right-click a word, choose Synonyms and then Thesaurus.
- On the Review tab, in the Proofing group, click Thesaurus.

TIP

Swap out the original word by right-clicking a word, choose Synonyms, Thesaurus, and then choose one of the suggestions. Your original word will be replaced with your selection.

Figure 5.16

A list of alternate words is displayed in the Thesaurus task pane.

TRANSLATION

Imagine receiving a document that was partially or entirely written in a different language and you needed something to help with the translation. Word can translate selected words or phrases and even an entire document. The translation options are Translate Document, Translate Selected Text, and Mini Translator.

The Translate Selected Text and Mini Translator features are designed to work with single words or short phrases, not complete sentences or whole documents.

Choose Translation Language

Before using the Translate Document feature or the Mini Translator feature, you'll want to set your translation language preferences for each. On the Review tab, in the Language group, click Translate, and then Choose Translation Language. The Translation Language Options dialog box displays, as shown in Figure 5.17. It's okay if you miss this step since Word will automatically take you there the first time you try to use the Translate Document or Mini Translator feature.

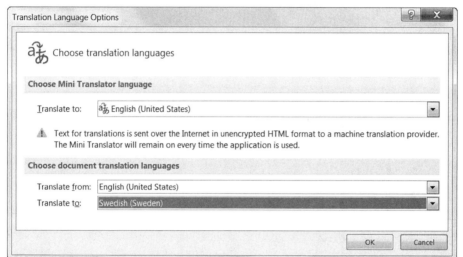

Figure 5.17

Set the Mini Translator language for ScreenTip translation and set the language for the document translation service.

NOTE

As indicated in the Translation Language Options dialog box, the text is sent over the Internet in unencrypted HTML format to a machine translation provider. Due to the unsecure nature of this service, law firms may opt out of using this service.

Translate Document

When you choose to translate the entire document, the active document will be translated by the Microsoft Translator service by way of the web. From the Review tab, in the Language group, click Translate, and then click Translate Document. You will be prompted to confirm sending the document before the document is sent to the translator service. Once you send the document for translation, you can select from a number of languages, as shown in Figure 5.18.

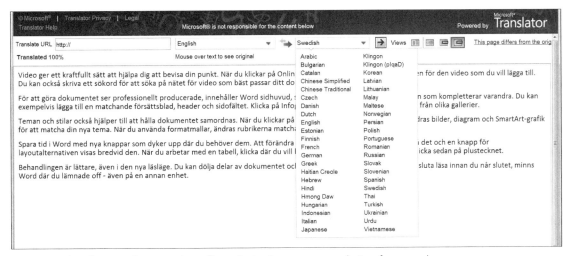

Figure 5.18   The translator service offers whole document translation for many languages.

The translator service will automatically display the entire document in the language you preselected. Hover your mouse over a sentence to see a tooltip display with the sentence in the original language. If you would like to see both languages side by side or top and bottom, to the right of Views, click Side by Side or Top/ Bottom for a different display of the original and translated documents.

Translate Selected Text

Perhaps you receive a document where the language is in English (US) and a small portion of the document is in a different language. You can translate one word at a time, multiple words, or an entire sentence. Select the text you want to translate, and from the Review tab, in the Language group, click Translate, and then click Translate Selected Text. The Research task pane opens on the right, as shown in Figure 5.19.

TIP

You can also right-click on selected text, and then choose Translate from the shortcut menu. The Research task pane will automatically update with the selected text and translate it into the language you've previously chosen.

Figure 5.19

The Research task pane translates the selected text.

Mini Translator

Translate, as you go by using the Mini Translator. When enabled, hover your mouse over a word in your document and the Online Bilingual Dictionary dimly appears above the focused word and displays a translation. To enable the Mini Translator, on the Review tab, in the Language group, click Translate, and then click Mini Translator, as shown in Figure 5.20.

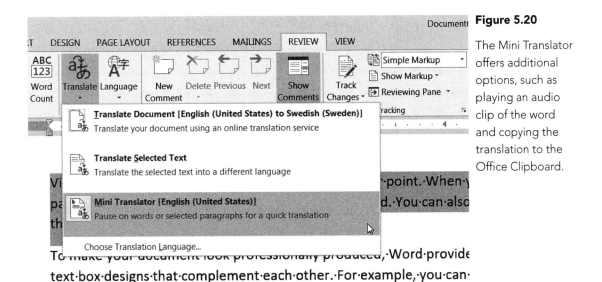

Figure 5.20

The Mini Translator offers additional options, such as playing an audio clip of the word and copying the translation to the Office Clipboard.

From the Online Bilingual Dictionary ScreenTip, you can open the Research task pane, copy the information displayed to the clipboard, play an audio pronunciation of the word, and get help and updates—all in one place. When you are finished using the Mini Translator, toggle it off by going to the Review tab, and in the Language group, click Translate, and then click Mini Translator.

WORD COUNT

Certain court briefs may limit the maximum number of words that can be used in a document. The Word Count feature not only counts the number of words in a document, but it also keeps statistical information, such as number of pages, characters, paragraphs, and lines. To initiate a word count, on the Review tab, in the Proofing group, click Word Count. The Word Count dialog box shows the number of words in the document, and you can choose whether to include textboxes, footnotes, and endnotes, as shown in Figure 5.21. You can also initiate a Word Count on selected text. The statistics displayed will be for just the selected text area.

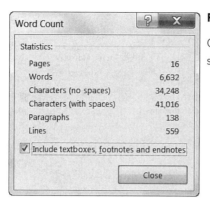

Figure 5.21

Count the number of words in a document or in a selection.

TIP

When Word Count is enabled on the Status bar, it keeps a running tally of the total number of words in the active document. For access to more details, you can click Word Count on the Status bar, and it will open the Word Count dialog box.

LEGAL SYMBOLS

Legal documents often require the use of special legal symbols or characters. Symbols or special characters can be inserted using several methods: the Symbol dialog box, keyboard shortcuts, recently used symbol list, and AutoCorrect.

Using the Symbol Dialog Box to Insert Symbols

The Symbol dialog box offers two tabs—Symbols and Special Characters. From the Insert tab, in the Symbols group, click Symbol, and then click More Symbols. The Symbols tab lists the entire set of characters for each of the symbol fonts installed on your computer, including normal text. This tab displays the actual characters as they will appear in your document. Select a symbol and click Insert, or double-click the symbol to insert it into your document.

NOTE

Any symbol inserted from the Symbols tab is automatically added to the recently used symbols list.

Select the Special Characters tab to review commonly used characters and symbols, such as Nonbreaking Hyphen, Nonbreaking Space, Copyright, Registered, Trademark, Section, and Paragraph. Select a symbol and click Insert, or double-click a symbol to insert it into your document. Notice that some of the symbols already have keyboard shortcuts assigned to them.

TIP

You can create a new keyboard shortcut for any symbol by selecting the symbol or character and then clicking Shortcut Key to assign a new keyboard shortcut. Using the keyboard, type a preferred set of combined keys, and if the keyboard combination is available, Currently Assigned To will indicate "[unassigned]." Click Assign to assign the keyboard combination to the symbol. Be sure to not assign a keyboard shortcut that already exists.

Using the Recently Used Symbols List

Word lists 20 of the most recently used symbols when you click the Symbol command on the Insert tab, as shown in Figure 5.22. If you inserted a handful of symbols into your legal documents, then you are certain to find them at the top of the recently used symbols list. The next time you want to insert a symbol from that list, place your insertion point where you want to insert the symbol and select the symbol from the list.

Keyboard Shortcuts for Legal Symbols

Some of the common keyboard shortcuts used to insert symbols into legal documents are listed in Table 5.4.

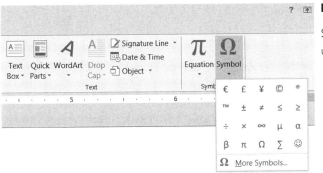

Figure 5.22

Select from the 20 recently used symbols.

TABLE 5.4—KEYBOARD SHORTCUTS FOR SYMBOLS AND CHARACTERS USED IN LEGAL DOCUMENTS		
SYMBOL/CHARACTER	**SAMPLE**	**KEYBOARD SHORTCUT**
Copyright	©	Alt+Ctrl+C
Double closing quote	"	Ctrl+',"
Double opening quote	"	Ctrl+`,"
Ellipsis	…	Alt+Ctrl+. (period)
Em dash	—	Alt+Ctrl+Num Lock+–
En dash	–	Ctrl+Num Lock+–
Euro	€	Alt+Ctrl+E
Nonbreaking Hyphen	-	Ctrl+Shift+Hyphen
Nonbreaking Space	°	Ctrl+Shift+Space
Registered	®	Alt+Ctrl+R
Single closing quote	'	Ctrl+','
Single opening quote	'	Ctrl+`,`
Trademark	™	Alt+Ctrl+T

NOTE

The keyboard shortcuts that include Num Lock indicates that the Num Lock key on the number pad of the keyboard must be enabled. It is not necessary to press this key again if it is already enabled. Also, the comma indicates a separation of two characters that should be pressed. The comma does not need to be typed in these instances.

Create a Keyboard Shortcut for a Symbol

1. Create a blank new document.

2. On the Insert tab, click Symbol, and then select More Symbols.

3. Select the Special Characters tab.

4. Select the Section symbol (§) and click Shortcut Key.

5. Press Alt+Shift+S in the Press New Shortcut Key box.

6. Click Assign if the keyboard shortcut isn't assigned to any other command.

7. Close both dialog boxes and try out your new keyboard shortcut.

NOTE

Shortcut key combinations include a combination of Ctrl, Alt, Shift, and a letter or other character on the keyboard. If the keyboard shortcut is already assigned, it will be noted after you type in the new shortcut key combination. If the notation indicates that it is unassigned, the key combination you entered will work. One exception is the KeyTip assigned to the tabs in Word will not indicate it is already assigned (e.g., Alt+F displays as unassigned, but it is the keyboard shortcut to access the File tab).

EXPERT TIP

Custom keyboard shortcut assignments are stored in the Normal.dotm. If keyboard shortcuts are needed for the entire firm, review Chapter 10, "Creating and Distributing Templates," to learn how this is set up and the ideal place to store these shortcuts for all users.

BUILDING BLOCKS

If you've made use of the AutoText feature in earlier versions of Word, you are really going to enjoy using building blocks. Based on the AutoText concept of saving and reusing frequently used text, tables, and graphics, using building blocks provides a new way to save information in a user-specified gallery so it can be reused in any Word document.

Word 2013 comes with many predefined building blocks, including headers, footers, cover pages, page numbering, tables, text boxes, watermarks, and more.

To access the Building Blocks Organizer to preview Word's built-in building blocks, click the Insert tab, in the Text group, click Quick Parts, and then select Building Blocks Organizer, as shown in Figure 5.23.

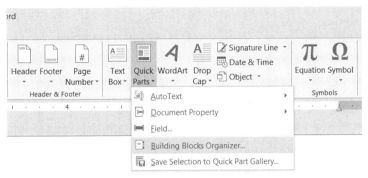

Figure 5.23

Preview, edit, delete, and insert building blocks using the Building Blocks Organizer.

Create a New Building Block

If you find that you are typing the same text over and over again, or you purposely look for certain documents that have text in it that you repeatedly copy, you may find that creating a building block entry is more efficient. Once a building block entry is created, you can use it as often as you want in any new or existing document.

Create a Building Block

1. Create a blank new document.

2. Type the name of your firm.

3. Press Enter and type the firm's address.

4. Press Enter and type the city, state, and ZIP code.

5. Select all of the text you just typed.

6. Click the Insert tab, and in the Text group, click Quick Parts, and select Save Selection to Quick Parts Gallery.

7. In the Create New Building Block dialog box (shown in Figure 5.24), type **FirmAddress** in the Name box and type **Firm name and address** in the Description box.

8. Click OK. You will insert the building block in the next exercise.

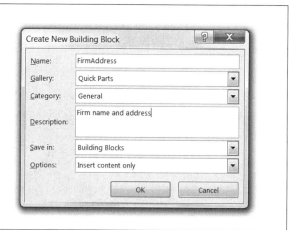

Figure 5.24 Save time by creating a building block for office locations, frequently used phrases, or signature blocks.

NOTE

Read on to learn about creating a category to organize building blocks and using different galleries in which to store them.

EXPERT TIP

When you save a building block, it gets saved in the Building Blocks.dotx file. Although you do have the option to change the save location to the Normal.dotm file, the default is the Building Blocks.dotx file, which will only contain building block entries. Alternatively, the Normal template stores other types of information, such as user-created keyboard shortcuts.

By default, building blocks are saved to

c:\Users\[username]\AppData\Roaming\Microsoft\Document Building Blocks\1033\15.

In the event the computer needs to be replaced, it is always a good idea to have a backup of the Building Blocks.dotx file stored in a safe location, such as on a server.

Insert a Building Block

A building block can be inserted into a document in a variety of ways. Just place your insertion point where you want to insert the building block entry and use one of the following options:

- Navigate to the Quick Parts gallery (or other gallery the building block was saved in), and click the building block to insert.

- Type the name of the building block and press F3.

- Navigate to the Quick Parts gallery (or other gallery the building block was saved in), right-click the building block, and choose one of the insertion options.

- Click the Insert tab, click Quick Parts in the Text group, and then click Building Blocks Organizer. Find the desired Building Block and click Insert.

If you've completed the Create a Building Block exercise, you are now ready to insert it into your document. Try the next exercise to insert a building block.

Insert a Building Block

1. Create a blank new document.

2. On the Insert tab, in the Text group, click Quick Parts to view the newly created entry. Click on the entry to insert it into your document.

3. Insert the entry again by typing **Firm** and pressing F3.

Redefine a Building Block

There will be times when the language of an existing building block entry changes and you'll want to redefine it. To redefine a building block entry, you just need to edit the text as necessary and re-create the entry.

Redefine a Building Block

1. Create a blank new document.

2. On the Insert tab, in the Text group, click Quick Parts, and click to insert the entry.

3. Edit the text as necessary.

4. Select the text, and on the Insert tab, in the Text Group, click Quick Parts, and then click Save Selection to Quick Part Gallery.

5. In the Name box, enter the same name you gave it when you originally created it and click OK.

6. A message box displays asking if you want to redefine the building block entry. Click Yes.

TIP

If you don't remember the name of the building block entry, open the Building Blocks Organizer (Insert tab, Quick Parts, Building Blocks Organizer), find and make note of the building block name, then click the Insert button to insert it into your document. You can now modify it as needed and re-create the building block with the same field criteria.

Edit the Properties of a Building Block

After you've created a building block entry, you may decide later that you want to change the name, gallery, category, description, and more by editing the properties of a building block. Open the Building Blocks Organizer, select the building block, click Edit Properties, and the Modify Building Block dialog box displays, as shown in Figure 5.25.

You can also access the Modify Building Block dialog box by right-clicking the building block entry in the gallery and choosing Edit Properties.

Building Block Galleries

When creating a building block, Word provides the initial choice of 34 building block galleries in which to save the entry. When an individual gallery is selected, it provides a preview of the entry as well as the category, name, and description of the entry. The galleries available on the ribbon are listed in Table 5.5. The galleries offered help you to organize your building blocks in logical places. After reviewing all of these galleries, you may start thinking about which galleries you may want to use.

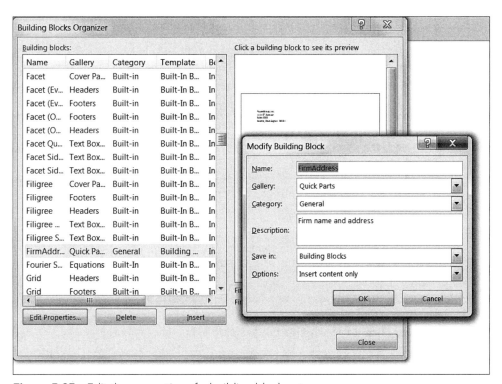

Figure 5.25   Edit the properties of a building block entry.

TABLE 5.5—LIST OF BUILDING BLOCK GALLERY LOCATIONS

GALLERY	LOCATION
AutoText	Insert>Quick Parts
Bibliography	References>Bibliography
Cover Page	Insert>Cover Page
Equation	Insert>Equation
Footer	Insert>Footer
Header	Insert>Header
Page Number (Current Position)	Insert>Page Number, Current Position
Page Number (Bottom of Page)	Insert>Page Number, Bottom of Page
Page Number (Page Margins)	Insert>Page Number, Page Margins
Page Number (Top of Page)	Insert>Page Number, Top of Page
Quick Parts	Insert>Quick Parts
Table of Contents	References>Table of Contents
Tables	Insert>Table, Quick Tables
Text Box	Insert>Text Box
Watermark	Design>Watermark

EXPERT TIP

There are 19 other building block galleries that are not on the ribbon. These can be accessed in the All Commands list when customizing the ribbon. See Chapter 10, "Creating and Distributing Templates," for using custom building block galleries.

There are certain galleries that will insert a building block in a specific area of the document. For example, inserting a building block from the Footer gallery will automatically insert the building block into the footer of the document without requiring you to navigate to the footer area first.

Use Building Blocks from the Gallery

Although there are more than 250 predefined building blocks in Word 2013, most of your building blocks will probably need to be created in order to meet the firm or your department standards. Some of the built-in building blocks may get you started in the right direction.

Insert a Building Block from the Footer Gallery

1. Create a blank new document.

2. Click the Insert tab and then click Footer from the Header & Footer group.

3. Scroll through the list and view the different built-in Footer building blocks and click to insert one of them.

4. Click Close Header and Footer to return to the document.

NOTE

Many of the header and footer built-in building blocks are designed to adapt to a different page orientation, paper size, and margins, so manual adjustments are not necessary if any of these page layout settings change when inserting a building block from these galleries.

Save a Building Block to a Gallery

You may find it easier to save a building block in a gallery other than the Quick Parts gallery. A few benefits to storing a building block in a different gallery is that the gallery name makes it easy to locate, and the preview in that location is easy to identify before you insert it. For example, you may not know what name you gave the building block, but you know the building block is inserted into the header of the document. Click the Insert tab and click Header to view the building blocks stored in the Header gallery.

To save a building block to a specific gallery, first select the text (graphic, text box, or table), navigate to and click the appropriate gallery into which you want to save the building block, and then click Save Selection to the [gallery name] Gallery.

Quick Parts Gallery

If you create a new building block using the Quick Parts command, the entry is saved in the Quick Parts gallery. To view the Quick Parts gallery, click Quick Parts on the Insert tab to view a list of the building blocks you created. This list includes a preview to help you to choose which building block to insert. Hover your mouse over the entry preview to see a description of the building block and click to insert it into your document.

TIP

If you are unsure what you named a building block or find that the building block you created is not showing in a particular gallery, you may want to go directly to the Building Blocks Organizer to view the entire collection of building blocks and sort the list by gallery.

Building Block Category

To organize building blocks within a gallery, you can define a category to group building blocks together. You'll want to name the category something that best describes the type of document the building block would be used in or even name the section of the document to which the building blocks would apply (e.g., Office

Addresses or Signature Blocks). Categories are flexible because you can create your own system of organization.

Create a Building Block Category

1. Open an existing document that has blocks of text you would like to save.

2. Select the first block of text.

3. Click the Insert tab, click Quick Parts, and then click Save Selection to Quick Part Gallery.

4. Type a name in the Name box.

5. Select Create New Category from the Category drop-down list.

6. In the Create New Category dialog box, type a name in the Name box and click OK.

7. Select the second block of text and repeat steps 3 and 4.

8. Select the category you created earlier from the Category drop-down list.

9. Click OK.

10. Create a blank new document and insert the building blocks from the new category.

TIP

Add one space, underscore, or other character in the Category name box before typing the category name. This places the category at the top of the list in the gallery.

Saving Entries to the Template

Every time you exit Word you'll be prompted to save the new entries you created or modified during that session of Word to the Building Blocks.dotx file, as shown in Figure 5.26. It's important that you click Save to ensure all the new or changed entries are available the next time you start Word.

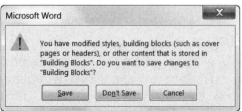

Figure 5.26

Save the new building block entries to the template.

If you created several building block entries and Word crashed before you had a chance to properly close Word and save the entries to the template, you will lose all of the new entries.

CAUTION

Delete a Building Block Entry

The entire collection of building blocks is located in the Building Blocks Organizer. You may find that you no longer use some of the building block entries and need to clean up or delete some of those entries. To start this process, you'll need to go to the Building Blocks Organizer.

Delete a Building Block Entry

1. Click the Insert tab, click Quick Parts, and then click Building Blocks Organizer.

2. If you remember the name of the entry, begin typing the name or scroll through the list of entries and select the entry you want to delete.

3. Click Delete, click Yes to confirm the deletion, and then click Close to close the dialog box.

You can also delete a building block entry by going to the gallery it is saved in, right-clicking the entry, and choosing Organize and Delete, as shown in Figure 5.27. The Building Blocks Organizer will open with the entry selected. Click Delete and confirm the deletion.

TIP

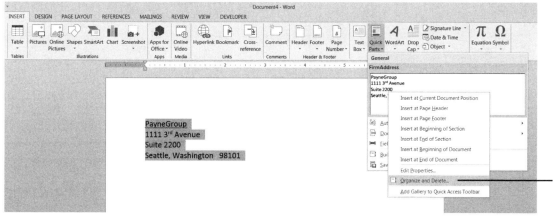

Figure 5.27   Delete a building block from the Quick Parts gallery.

OFFICE 365

Office 365 as a Productivity Tool

Perhaps one of the biggest productivity tools for Office 2013 and Office 365 is having the ability to access and share documents from anywhere in the world. If a file is saved to your SkyDrive folder or SharePoint, you can access them and so can others within your firm if they have permission to do so. When a file is edited, they are editing the original copy, without having to make a duplicate.

When others edit your document, you will see what areas they are working on and every time the file is saved, the edits are saved with it and displayed to everyone who is collaborating on the file.

EXPERT TIP

Microsoft Surface as a Productivity Tool

If you use a Surface tablet device, you can view and edit documents through a mobile version of Microsoft Office. Imagine being on an airplane, accessing and making changes to a document, and then saving and sending the file when you land. Now that's a productivity tool. There are two versions of Surface at the time of this writing. The first is Surface RT which is a scaled-down version compared to Surface Pro, which to some may be more like a desktop replacement. Both models support Microsoft Office and will allow you to view and edit Word documents.

PAGE SETUP AND LAYOUT

As anyone who has worked in a law firm knows, great importance is placed on the structure and layout of documents. The reason for this is two-fold: establishment of a standard look and feel with similar types of documents for corporate branding purposes and adherence to court and other administrative filing formatting requirements.

Additionally, you can find yourself working on a wide variety of legal documents ranging from simple correspondence with different first-page headers to complex multi-section documents consisting of a cover page, table of contents, table of authorities, followed by 20 pages of document text—all containing different page numbering formats. Without a doubt, the latter type of complex document can push a word processing program to its limits. Next to basic formatting and style techniques, understanding how to work with page setup and layout is critical for legal users.

PAGE SETUP

With the creation of legal documents, multiple page setup decisions need to be made on a regular basis—including the setting of margins, paper size, and page orientation. These settings can be found on the Page Layout tab as well as by clicking the Page Setup dialog box launcher. To quickly access some of the Page Setup options on the ribbon, click the Page Layout tab, and in the Page Setup group, select from the options available, as shown in Figure 6.1.

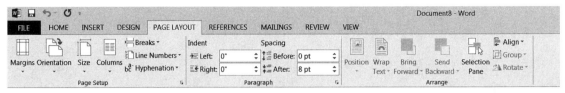

Figure 6.1 You can set margins, orientation, and much more directly from the ribbon.

Margins

On the Page Layout tab in the Page Setup group, click Margins to view a listing of six preset margin settings, as shown in Figure 6.2. Click Custom Margins to access the Page Setup dialog box for additional options. After making a change to the margins in the Page Setup dialog box, a new Last Custom Setting option will appear at the top of the Margins list.

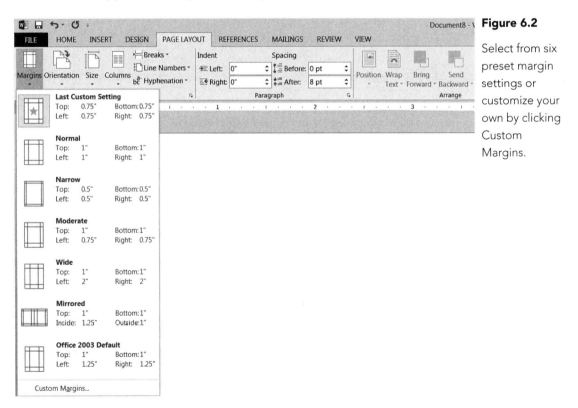

Figure 6.2

Select from six preset margin settings or customize your own by clicking Custom Margins.

NOTE

The preset margin settings apply only to the section where your insertion point is located. If your document has multiple sections, you can apply the same margin settings to the entire document by clicking Custom Margins and selecting Whole Document from the Apply To list.

TIP

If custom margins have been set in the Page Setup dialog box, the Last Custom Setting will display at the top of the list in the Margins button. This setting will stick even after Word has closed and reopened. This feature is a time-saver when working with multiple documents that require the same margin settings.

Custom Margins

By default, Word sets the top, bottom, left, and right margins at 1 inch. To make specific changes to the margins, from the Page Layout tab in the Page Setup group, click Margins, and then select Custom Margins. The Page Setup dialog box will display with the Margins tab selected. The settings on the Margins tab are shown in Table 6.1.

TABLE 6.1—MARGIN SETTINGS	
SETTING	**DESCRIPTION**
Top	Distance between top of the page and top of the first line on the page.
Bottom	Distance between bottom of page and bottom of the last line on the page.
Left/Right	Distance between left/right edge of page and left/right end of each line with no left indent. Used when printing single-sided pages. When you select the Mirror Margins check box, the name of this option changes to Inside/Outside.
Gutter	Amount of extra space to add to the margin to allow for binding. The extra space is added to the left or top side of all pages depending on the Gutter Position. If Mirror Margins is selected, the gutter position will not be available and the extra space will be applied to the inside margin.
Orientation	Select from either Portrait or Landscape. When you change the orientation of a page, Word transfers the Top and Bottom margin measurements to the Left and Right margin measurements, and vice versa.
Multiple Pages	There are four options to choose from: • **Normal.** Selected by default, this is the page layout used for most documents and is a standard single page. • **Mirror Margins.** Creates margins on left and right pages that mirror each other with equal margins. Used for duplex printing (on both sides of the paper) such as with books or manuals. • **2 Pages Per Sheet.** Prints two pages on one sheet of paper. This is useful for creating folded place cards or handouts. • **Book Fold.** Use to create a folded booklet. Word prints two pages on one side of the paper and automatically sets the page orientation to landscape. When selecting this option, choose the number of pages to print per booklet in Sheets Per Booklet drop-down list.

continued

TABLE 6.1—*CONTINUED*	
SETTING	**DESCRIPTION**
Apply To	Select what part of the document to apply the changes to within the document. The choices include the following: **Whole Document.** Any changes made in the Page Setup dialog box affect the entire document. **Selected Section(s).** Changes would be applied to the current section(s) selected. (This option only appears in a document with more than one section.) **This Point Forward.** Changes only affect the rest of the document, starting with the place where the insertion point is located. *Be careful!* Choosing this option in the middle of a document can create a section break, which may lead to unintended consequences.
Default	Changes default margin settings. Word saves new settings in the attached template and overwrites old settings. Whenever you base a document on that template, Word uses the new settings.

CAUTION

Be careful not to set any margin less than .25 inch as text may get cut off when printing. While custom margins will display accurately on-screen, they may not print properly if the margin is less than .25 inch.

TIP

Margins can be set by dragging the margin boundaries located on the horizontal ruler or vertical ruler while in Print Layout view. When the mouse pointer becomes a double-headed arrow and displays the margin tooltip, drag the margin boundaries to change the margin. Additionally, holding down the Alt key as you drag the margin boundary will display the exact measurement of the margin.

Page Orientation

The page orientation in Word is set to portrait by default; however, documents may contain a combination of portrait and landscape sections. To set the page orientation, select the Page Layout tab in the Page Setup group and then choose either Portrait or Landscape, as shown in Figure 6.3. Changing the orientation using this method will apply this orientation attribute only to the section where your cursor is located. If you want to change the page orientation for an entire document that has multiple sections, click the Page Setup dialog box launcher on the Page Layout tab, select either Portrait or Landscape under Orientation, and then select Whole Document from the Apply To list.

Paper Size

The default paper size in the U.S. English version of Word is 8.5 by 11 inches. If the paper size needs to be changed, this change is generally made within the firm's templates. However, if you need to change the paper size on-the-fly, from the Page Layout tab in the Page Setup group, click Size and choose from a list of various paper sizes, as shown in Figure 6.4.

Word 2013 provides many paper sizes from which to choose. Click the Size button in the Page Setup group and click More Paper Sizes for additional choices.

Paper Tab

Additional page settings are available in the Page Setup dialog box. The Paper tab includes options for choosing paper type, size, and even paper source for printers with more than one paper tray. Print options, which are your default print settings, can also be set from this location. To access these settings from the Page Layout tab, click the Page Setup dialog box launcher and then select the Paper tab.

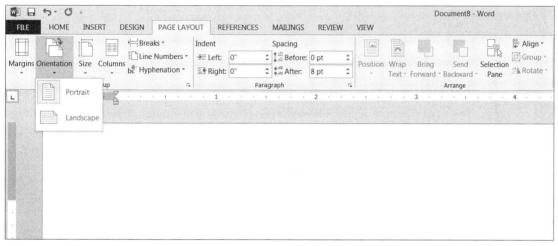

Figure 6.3   Change the page orientation to Portrait or Landscape layout.

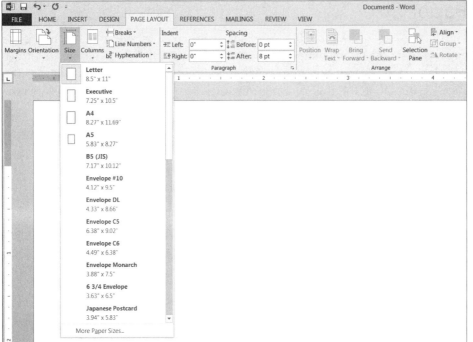

Figure 6.4

The paper size is typically set in the template.

Layout Tab

The last tab in the Page Setup dialog box is the Layout tab. This tab includes options for applying different types of section and column breaks, creating specific types of headers and footers, setting vertical alignment, and applying line numbering and borders to your documents. Some of the features found in this section of the Page Setup dialog box are discussed at length later in this chapter—for now, each of the settings is described in Table 6.2.

NOTE

Understanding the Vertical Alignment feature is a huge time-saver. Utilizing this feature, and in particular the Center option, eliminates the hassle of trying to center text vertically on the page by using Hard Returns or Spacing Before and After. Text will always remain centered on the page as you edit, add, or remove text.

TABLE 6.2—SETTINGS ON THE LAYOUT TAB

SETTING	DESCRIPTION
Section Start	When section or column breaks are inserted, the following list denotes the type of break and the location where Word starts the new section: • **Continuous.** Immediately follows the previous section without inserting a page break. • **New Column.** Moves existing text within a section to the top of the next column. • **New Page.** A new section starts at the top of the next page. • **Even Page.** A new section starts on the next even-numbered page. • **Odd Page.** A new section starts on the next odd-numbered page.
Suppress Endnotes	Prevents endnotes from being printed at the end of the current section. Word will print the current section's endnotes in the next section, preceding the endnotes in that section. This option is available only when you have specified that endnotes be placed at the end of sections.
Different Odd And Even	Specify if you want a different header or footer for even-numbered pages and a different header or footer for odd-numbered pages. This option affects the entire document, regardless of the number of sections.
Different First Page	Specify if you want a different header or footer on the first page of a document (or section) that is different from the header or footer used in the rest of the document (or section).
From Edge	Specify the distance between the edge of the page and the header or footer.
Vertical Alignment	Choose how text is distributed between the top and bottom margin: • **Top.** Aligns the top line with the top margin. • **Center.** Centers paragraphs between the top and bottom margins. • **Justified.** Expands the space between paragraphs to align the top line with the top margin and the bottom line with the bottom margin. • **Bottom.** Aligns the bottom line with the bottom margin.
Line Numbers	Set line-numbering options. This is often used for legal documents to assign sequential numbering to each line on a page. This is not the line numbering option used in pleadings.
Borders	This button accesses the Borders and Shading dialog box with the Page Border tab selected. Apply a page border to an entire document or to specific areas within a section of a document.

Line Numbering

Some legal documents, such as patent applications, require line numbering to appear in the left margin in documents, depending on filing requirements. The line numbering options are accessed by clicking Line Numbers in the Page Setup group on the Page Layout tab. Choose from four options, as shown in Figure 6.5, or select Line Numbering Options to access the Layout tab of the Page Setup dialog box.

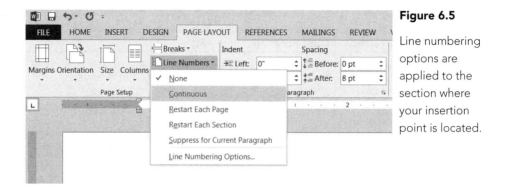

Figure 6.5

Line numbering options are applied to the section where your insertion point is located.

In the Page Setup dialog box, at the bottom portion of the Layout tab, select Line Numbers and choose the options required for your document. The Line Numbers dialog box includes options for setting the starting line number, setting the distance of the numbers from the text, and setting the intervals by which to count. You can also have the line numbering restart at the beginning of each new page, restart numbering at each new section, or have it continue to number sequentially throughout the entire document.

NOTE

This line numbering feature is not meant for use with the line numbered pleading paper required in certain courts in the Western United States. The line numbering for pleadings will be located in the header layer of the document and can have 26, 28, or more lines per page depending on the jurisdiction. See Chapter 11, "Complex Documents," for more information on creating a pleading.

Page and Section Breaks

A legal document can be broken into several parts and can contain a combination of different types of breaks. Some breaks are inserted automatically when text fills up the page; others need to be inserted manually. The following is a list of some of the more common breaks found in legal documents:

- **Soft Page Break.** This type of break is automatically created when you type enough text on one page and the text flows onto the next page.

- **Hard Page Break.** You insert this type of break manually whenever you want to start a new page, but continue to work within the same section.

- **Next Page Section Break.** You insert this type of break manually to start both a new page and a new section. This is generally used when the new section has a different header or footer, or a different page setup, such as changing the page orientation from portrait to landscape for an exhibit page.

NOTE

Hard page breaks are used sparingly in documents because the pagination controls, such as Keep With Next and Keep Lines Together, are generally used to control the flow of text onto the next page so that paragraphs and lines are not split across a page. To learn more about controlling pagination, refer to Chapter 4, "Formatting."

There are other breaks that are used infrequently in legal documents, but you may from time to time rely on one or more of these:

- **Column Break.** When working with multiple columns, it forces the text to break to the top of the next column.

- **Text Wrapping Break.** This is used to wrap text around a table or other object. Text wrapping and position of the table or object in relation to the text is generally set in the table or object properties.

- **Continuous Section Break.** Creates a section break without creating a new page so you can have multiple sections on the same page. You will see these types of breaks if you selected text in the middle of a document and applied a multi-column, newspaper-style format. The section breaks would appear above and below the multi-column formatted text.

- **Even Page Section Break.** Creates a section break at the beginning of the next even-numbered page in a document. This could be used where all of the chapter titles begin on an even-numbered page.

- **Odd Page Section Break.** Creates a section break at the beginning of the next odd-numbered page. This could be used in a document where all of the chapter titles begin on an odd-numbered page. This is similar to how a book is set up.

TIP

Insert a column break by pressing Ctrl+Shift+Enter.

CAUTION

When using Odd or Even Page Section Breaks, Word will insert a blank page as needed to get to the next odd or even page. These blank pages will not display on-screen; however, you will see the blank page in Print Preview and when printing.

Insert a Hard Page Break

Occasionally, you may want to start at the top of the next page even though there is still room for additional text on the current page. For example, at the end of the document you may have an appendix or index that needs to be on its own page. You can insert a hard page break to create a new page in the same section. Place your insertion point at the beginning of the paragraph that will start on the next page, and from the Page Layout tab, click Breaks, and choose the appropriate break, as shown in Figure 6.6.

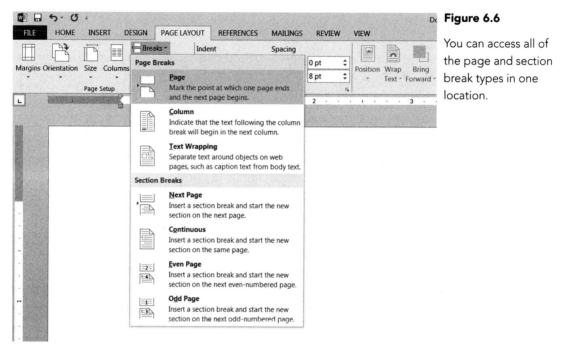

Figure 6.6

You can access all of the page and section break types in one location.

TIP

Press Ctrl+Enter to quickly insert a hard page break.

Insert Page Breaks

1. Create a blank new document.

2. Save the document as **My Breaks.docx.**

3. Click the View tab, and then in the Views group, click Draft.

4. Type **=rand(20)** and press Enter.

5. Notice the soft page break.

6. Go to the beginning of the second paragraph on page two and press Ctrl+Enter to insert a page break. Notice the difference between the soft and hard page breaks.

7. Switch to Print Layout view to see how page breaks are displayed.

8. Switch back to Draft view.

9. Double-click the Page Break to select the Page Break and the paragraph mark directly after it and press Delete on the keyboard to delete the page break. If you don't see the words Page Break, you may need to turn on the display of nonprinting characters by clicking Show/Hide on the Home tab, in the Paragraph group.

10. Save the document and keep it open for the next exercise.

Section Breaks

A section break allows you to apply different page layout formatting to different parts of a document. The section break can be identified in several views, but is easiest to find in Draft view. The section break consists of a double-dotted line, as shown in Figure 6.7. In Draft view, it extends from one side of the page to the other.

When you are ready to create a new section in a document, on the Page Layout tab click Breaks and specify the type of section break that you want to insert. After you've added a section break, there's a double-dotted line with the words "Section Break" that appear in your document when Show/Hide is enabled. You can see Section Breaks best when in Draft view, although you can see them in other views, except for Read Mode. A section break indicates where new formatting begins in the document.

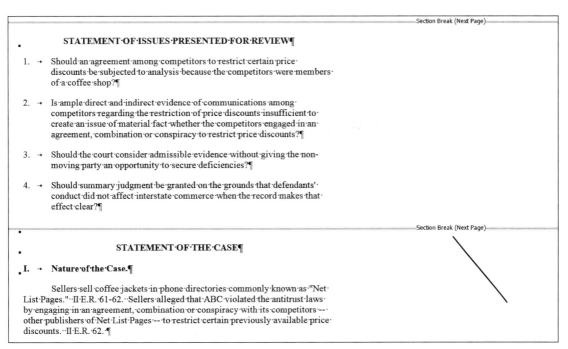

Figure 6.7   You can view the section break more clearly in Draft view.

Insert Section Breaks

1. Your document from the last exercise, My Breaks.docx, should still be open.

2. At the top of the document, type **TITLE PAGE** and press Enter.

3. Click the Page Layout tab and then click Breaks in the Page Setup group.

4. Under Section Breaks, select Next Page.

5. Press Ctrl+End to go to the end of your document.

6. Repeat steps 3 and 4 to insert another Next Page Section Break.

7. Leave this document open for the next exercise.

TIP

You can verify which section you are in by looking at the Status bar. Press Ctrl+End to move to the end of the document and notice how the section number on the Status bar changes in a document with multiple sections. If you are not seeing the section information on the Status bar, right-click the Status bar and choose Section.

CAUTION

To remove or delete a Section Break, place your insertion point on the break itself and press the Delete key. The section above the deleted break will inherit all the section formatting from the section below. If you want to just change the type of break for an existing section, don't delete the section and reinsert it, simply click in the section to be modified and display the Page Setup dialog box. Use the Section Start option on the Layout tab to change the section break type.

TIP

When troubleshooting complex documents, it is useful to know where section breaks have been inserted. Press the function key F5 and choose Section from the Go to What list. By clicking the Next button, Word will take you to the beginning of each section.

Change Formatting in a Specific Section

As discussed previously, as the complexity of the document increases, you may need to break the document into sections and set individual attributes for each section. In the preceding exercise, you created a document with multiple sections. In the next exercise, you will adjust margins and change paper orientation in one of the sections of your document.

Change Page Formats in a Section

1. Your document from the previous exercise, My Breaks.docx, should still be open.

2. Press Ctrl+End to move to the end of your document. You should be in Section 3.

3. Click the Page Layout tab, click Orientation in the Page Setup group, and choose Landscape.

NOTE

By default, the orientation change only applies to the section in which your insertion point is located. To change the orientation for the entire document, click the Page Setup dialog box launcher on the Page Layout tab, click the Margins tab, select the orientation, and then in the Apply To list, select Whole Document.

4. The last page should now be in landscape orientation, while the rest of the document is in portrait orientation.

5. Press Ctrl+Home to go to the top of the document.

6. Click the Page Setup dialog box launcher and select the Layout tab.

7. Select Center from the Vertical Alignment drop-down list.

8. Be sure that the Apply To box has This Section selected.

9. Click OK. Your "TITLE PAGE" text should now be vertically centered on the page.

Headers and Footers

The header and footer appear at the top and bottom of every document, and depending on what is required, they can contain information such as graphics or firm logos, page numbers, document ID, or date. After this information is inserted, it will automatically repeat throughout the document, or alternatively, you can set it up to vary from section to section.

Access the Header and Footer

There are multiple ways to access the header and footer, and the options may change depending on which view you are in. When in Print Layout view, the quickest way to get into the header or footer is to double-click in the header or footer area.

TIP

In Print Layout view, you can right-click in the header or footer area, and then select Edit Header or Edit Footer, as shown in Figure 6.8.

If you are working in Draft view, you will need to access the header or footer from the ribbon. On the Insert tab in the Header & Footer group, click Header or Footer and a gallery displays with built-in header and footer formats. Near the bottom of the gallery, click Edit Header or Edit Footer to access the header or footer.

NOTE

The gallery connected to the header and footer commands are building block galleries. These galleries offer the ability to insert, save, and remove header and footer formats. Learn more about building blocks in Chapter 5, "Productivity Tools."

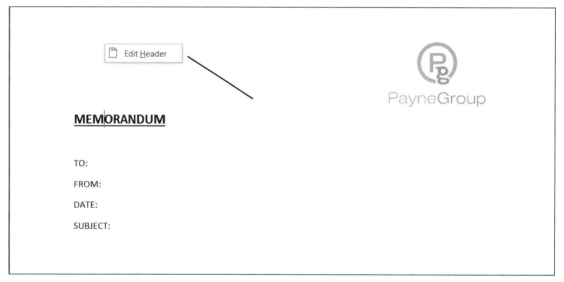

Figure 6.8   Access the header quickly by right-clicking in the header area.

Header & Footer Tools Design Tab

Word automatically displays the Header & Footer Tools Design tab when working in either the header or footer of the document. Use the ribbon to quickly add the page number, date, current time, or to switch between the header and footer in the document. A nonprinting dashed line separates the header and footer areas from the main body of the document. To quickly go back to the main body of the document, double-click in the text area of the main document or click the Close Header and Footer button on the ribbon.

The groups available on the ribbon include Header & Footer, Insert, Navigation, Options, Position, and Close, as shown in Figure 6.9.

Figure 6.9 Everything you need for the header and footer is found on the ribbon.

The following list provides an explanation of each command found on the ribbon, moving from left to right.

- **Header.** Contains a gallery of header designs for one-click insertion and options to edit, remove, and save a custom header.

- **Footer.** Contains a gallery of footer designs for one-click insertion and options to edit, remove, and save a custom footer.

- **Page Number.** Provides a gallery of options for Top of Page, Bottom of Page, Page Margins, and Current Position. You can also access the Page Number Format dialog box and the Remove Page Numbers option.

- **Date & Time.** Opens the Date and Time dialog box with a list of available date formats that can be inserted as an updating field or as text.

- **Document Info.** Provides a list of several document property fields you can insert such as Author, Filename, FilePath, and Document Title.

- **Quick Parts.** This same gallery is found on the Insert tab and includes custom building block entries to insert directly into the header or footer. This also contains options for inserting document properties and fields, provides access to the Building Blocks Organizer, and has an option to save a building block entry into the gallery.

- **Pictures.** Opens the Insert Picture dialog box.

- **Online Pictures.** Search for and insert Office.com Clip Art or Bing Image pictures.

- **Go to Header.** Switches to the header when currently in the footer.

- **Go to Footer.** Switches to the footer when currently in the header.

- **Previous Section.** Moves to the previous header or footer in the document.

- **Next Section.** Moves to the next header or footer in the document.

NOTE

The Previous Section and Next Section commands do not always move to the previous or next section of a document. Depending on the setup of the document, the user could move from a section's First Page Header to the same section header when the Different First Page option is selected, or from an Odd Page Header to an Even Page Header when that option is selected.

- **Link to Previous.** Keep or break the link between headers and footers in a previous section.

- **Different First Page.** Insert a header or footer on the first page that is different from the rest of the pages within the section.

- **Different Odd & Even Pages.** Insert a header or footer on odd-numbered pages that is different from the even-numbered pages in the document.

- **Show Document Text.** Works as a toggle to either show or hide the text of the main document while working in the header and footer layer.

- **Header from Top.** Sets the header margin and measures the distance from the top of the page.

- **Footer from Bottom.** Sets the footer margin and measures the distance from the bottom of the page.

- **Insert Alignment Tab.** Set a tab setting that is relative to the margin or left indent that will automatically adjust if the margin or page orientation changes.

- **Close Header and Footer.** Closes the header and footer layer and returns to the main document with the Home tab selected.

Now that we've discussed the various options available on the ribbon, let's take a look at how to use some of these options in a letter that requires a firm logo in the header as well as how to navigate to the footer to insert text.

Insert Content into Header and Footer

1. Open the exercise file Business Letter.docx found at www.thepaynegroup. com/downloads/word2013forlawfirms/.

2. On the Insert tab, click Header in the Header & Footer group and click Edit Header.

3. Press Ctrl+R to align to the right margin.

4. On the Header & Footer Tools Design tab in the Insert group, click Pictures. Navigate to the Sample Pictures folder in the Pictures Library (or navigate to the folder where your firm logo is located), select a picture, and click Insert.

5. Depending on the size of the original picture, you may notice the graphic is too large for the header. On the Picture Tools Format tab in the Size group at the end of the ribbon, click in the Height box and type **1**, and then press Enter. Notice the Width adjusts proportionally.

NOTE

For more exciting details on what you can do with graphics, see Chapter 14, "Graphics."

6. Click the Header & Footer Tools Design tab to reactivate it, and in the Navigation group, click Go To Footer.

7. Type **DRAFT FOR DISCUSSION ONLY**.

8. Click Close Header and Footer.

9. Keep this document open for the next exercise.

Insert Page Numbering

Compared to earlier versions of Word, there are more options for inserting page numbers into a document. You can view these options from the Header & Footer Tools Design tab in the Header & Footer group by clicking Page Number. You will see four Building Block galleries of page numbering choices. Those options are Top of Page, Bottom of Page, Page Margins, and Current Position, as shown in Figure 6.10.

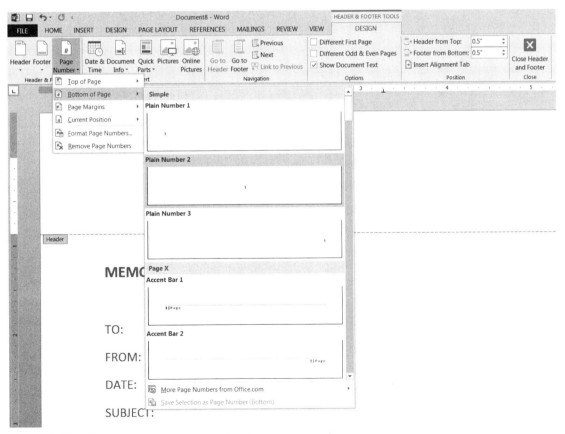

Figure 6.10 Choose where you want to insert the page number.

To insert the Page field code at your cursor location (as was done in earlier versions of Word), click Page Number, select Current Position, and then choose Plain Number from the gallery.

Format Page Number

There are times when you need to change the format of a page number in your document. For example, you may have a table of contents and would like page numbering to be in lowercase Roman numeral format. As long as your document is divided into sections, you can apply different page number formatting in each section of your document.

To change the format of a page number and restart the page numbering, on the Header & Footer Tools Design tab, click Page Number, and then click Format Page Numbers. The Page Number Format dialog box will display, as shown in Figure 6.11.

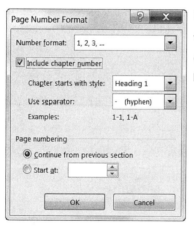

Figure 6.11

You can change page number formatting, add the chapter number using applied styles, and restart page numbering all in one place.

Different First Page

In certain documents, you may want the information on the first page of a header or footer to be different than the subsequent header and footer pages of the same section. In Word, use the Different First Page option to achieve this result. When Different First Page is enabled, you are able to create a header and footer on the first page that is different than the header and footer content on subsequent pages within the same section. For instance, in a business letter you may want the firm logo in the header of the first page, but have subsequent headers contain the date and page numbering only. A sample of a letter header is shown in Figure 6.12.

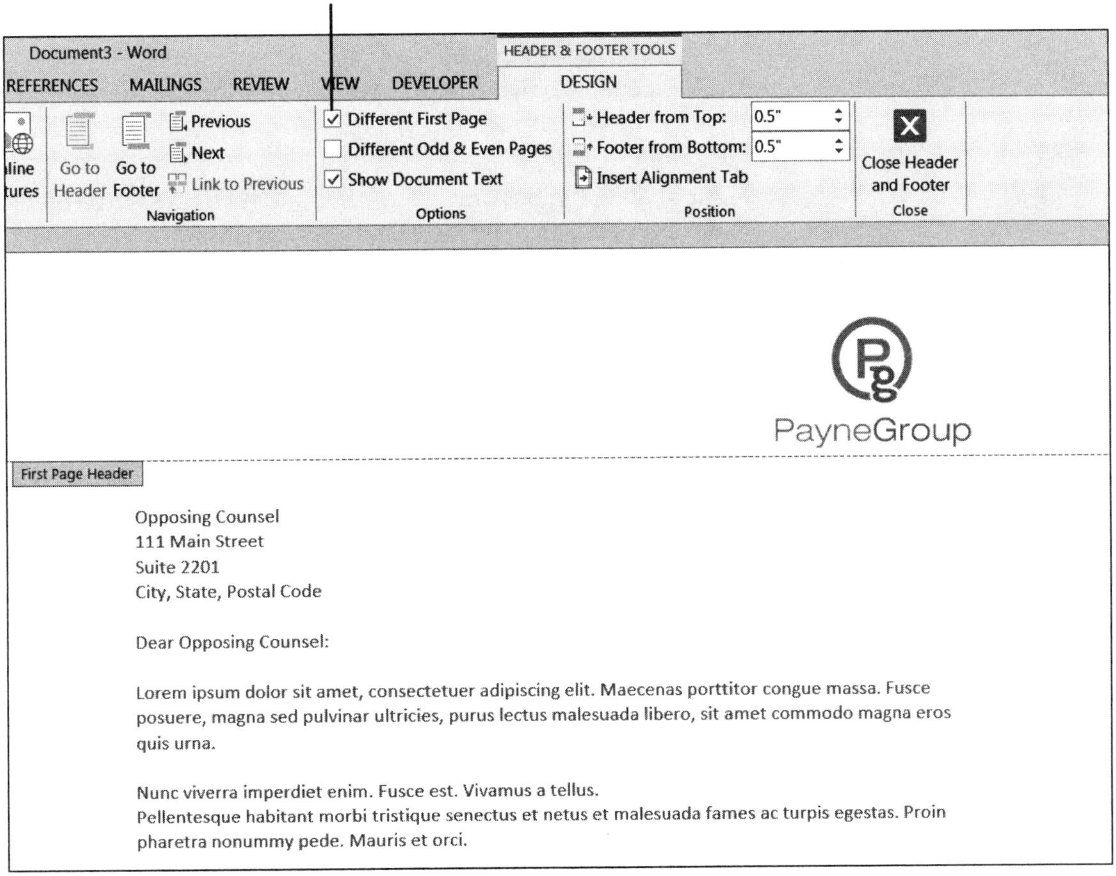

Figure 6.12   It's common for letter templates to be set up with the Different First Page setting enabled.

Insert Page Numbering and Use Different First Page

1. The document from the previous exercise should still be open.

2. Double-click the header area of the document to quickly access the header of the letter.

3. Click the graphic to select it and press Ctrl+X to cut the graphic onto the clipboard.

4. In the Options group on the Header & Footer Tools Design tab, select the Different First Page check box. Notice the First Page Header notation below the header. Press Ctrl+V to paste the graphic into the header.

5. Press Ctrl+R to right align the graphic in the First Page Header section.

6. Click Close Header and Footer.

NOTE

Since this letter is a single page, in order to access the next page header, you will need to create a second page.

7. Press Ctrl+End to go to the bottom of the letter and then press Ctrl+Enter to insert a page break.

8. Double-click the header area of the second page to access the header.

9. Press Ctrl+L to prepare the page number to be left aligned.

10. Type **Page** and press the Spacebar. In the Header & Footer group on the Header & Footer Tools Design tab, click Page Number, point to Current Position, and then click Plain Number.

NOTE

Learn more about setting up a letter template in Chapter 10, "Creating and Distributing Templates."

Alignment Tabs

The Alignment Tab is a little known, yet powerful, feature that is useful in documents where you know there's a possibility that the margins, paper size, or the page orientation will change. For example, let's say a document originated in the New York office with the standard 8.5-by-11-inch paper size format. It is then sent to the London office for review and finalization. When the person in the London office changes the paper size to its standard format (the A4 paper size of 8.27 by 11.69 inches), the alignment tabs used in the document will automatically adjust to match the new paper size.

Alignment tabs can be set relative to the margin or left indent and can be found in the Position group on the Header & Footer Tools Design tab.

Use Alignment Tabs

1. Create a blank new document.

2. Right-click in the header area and select Edit Header.

3. At the left margin, type **Left** and press Tab.

4. At the centered tab stop, type **Centered** and press Tab.

5. At the right tab stop, type **Right**. Notice the text is properly aligned to the existing tab stops.

6. Click the Page Layout tab, click Orientation in the Page Setup group, and then select Landscape.

7. If needed, decrease your zoom percentage in order to see the entire page. Notice that the text is still aligned with the tab stops as if it were still in portrait orientation.

8. Now, let's see the difference it makes with Alignment tabs. Delete everything in the header except for the word Left.

9. With your insertion point at the end of the word Left, click the Header & Footer Tools Design tab, and then click Insert Alignment Tab from the Position group. The Alignment Tab dialog box displays, as shown in Figure 6.13.

Figure 6.13

Set an alignment tab to place a tab relative to the margin or indent.

10. Under Alignment, select Center, select Margin from the Align Relative To list, and then click OK.

11. Notice the insertion point moves to the center of the document. Type **Centered**.

12. Click Insert Alignment Tab from the Position group on the Header & Footer Tools Design tab.

13. Under Alignment, select Right, select Margin from the Align Relative To list, and then click OK.

14. Type **Right**. Notice the alignment tabs do not use the tab stops that are visible on the ruler. Now, we'll switch the orientation again to see how the alignment tabs adjust.

15. Click the Page Layout tab, click Orientation in the Page Setup group, and then click Portrait.

16. Notice the text is properly aligned left, centered, and right.

17. On the Page Layout tab, click Margins in the Page Setup group, and then click Narrow. Notice how the tabs automatically adjust to match the margin changes.

NOTE

It's difficult to differentiate between an alignment tab and a traditional tab because the nonprinting character (right arrow) is the same for both. Even using the Reveal Formatting task pane (Shift+F1) does not indicate that alignment tabs have been set.

TIP

Legal documents are often shared between attorney and client, as well as co-counsel or opposing counsel. If you're going to share your document, use the Compatibility Checker to see if alignment tabs have been used in the document. From the File tab, click Info, Check for Issues, Check Compatibility. If alignment tabs have been used in the document, you'll see a notation under Summary that the alignment tabs will be converted to traditional tabs.

Watermarks

Common watermarks used in legal documents are the words CONFIDENTIAL or DRAFT, as shown in Figure 6.14. A watermark is inserted into the header layer behind the text of the main document and displays in a large, light-colored gray font. The placement and size of the watermark can be changed by editing the watermark. Any custom text can be added to a watermark, and a picture watermark can even be used.

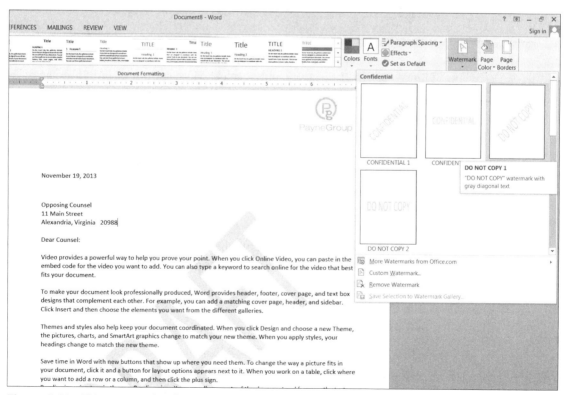

Figure 6.14   This watermark indicates the document is not in final form.

To insert a watermark, click the Design tab, and in the Page Background group, click Watermark. You can select a built-in watermark from the gallery, as shown in Figure 6.15, or you can create your own custom watermark. From this same gallery, you can remove an applied watermark from the document or save a custom watermark to use in other documents.

Figure 6.15

Choose a built-in watermark.

Insert, Edit, and Remove Watermarks

1. Create a blank new document, type **=rand(20)**, and press Enter.

2. Click the Design tab, and from the Page Background group, click Watermark. Click on one of the built-in watermarks to apply it to your document.

TIP

If you're having trouble seeing the watermark on the screen, press Ctrl+P to view the watermark in Print Preview. Press the Esc key to return to the document.

3. Click Watermark again. This time select Remove Watermark.

4. To create a custom watermark, click Watermark, then Custom Watermark. The Printed Watermark dialog box displays.

5. Select Text Watermark, and in the Text field, type **your firm name**.

6. Select Times New Roman from the Font drop-down list and click OK.

7. Right-click in the Header area and select Edit Header.

8. Double-click on the watermark to select it, and the WordArt Tools Format tab appears offering tools for working with the watermark.

TIP

Selecting a watermark is not the same a selecting text. Hover your mouse over the watermark until your mouse pointer shows the black four-headed arrow and then double-click.

9.   From the WordArt Tools Format tab in the Text group, click Edit Text. Change the firm's name to the firm's initials and click OK.

10.   In the Text group, click Spacing, and then select Loose.

11.   Double-click the document area (away from the watermark, header, and footer) to return to the main body of the document.

TIP

The Remove Watermark command will remove the watermark from all sections in a multi-section document.

EXPERT TIP

If you have the Different First Page option selected in a document and you want to add the watermark to all pages, do not apply it from the Watermark gallery. This method only inserts the watermark on the first page *or* all subsequent pages within the section, depending on where your insertion point is located when you insert the watermark. Instead, click Watermark, choose Custom Watermark, choose Text Watermark, and type the watermark text next to Text. This method will insert the watermark on all pages.

STYLES

A style is a set of formatting properties that have been saved and named so that the same formatting can be quickly applied elsewhere. If you need to create a lengthy agreement or pleading in which each heading needs to be numbered, centered, bold, and underlined, applying each of these formatting attributes would take a considerable amount of time if you manually applied it to each heading. A better alternative is to save that set of formatting properties as a style and then apply that style to all those headings throughout the document. Modifying the style's formatting automatically updates any text with that same style applied.

When you learn to use and master styles, you will leverage the power of Word and dramatically increase your efficiency!

WHY USE STYLES?

Many legal documents require precise formatting to meet court-specified rules. If these rules are not adhered to, you run the risk of documents being rejected by the courts. Even for documents not being filed with a court, it's useful to have consistent formatting in order to create a standardized look. Many firms consider this standardized look for their documents as part of their corporate branding. With styles, consistent and precise formatting is easy to apply and modify.

Document editing is just one benefit to using styles. The list of benefits includes:

- **Document Sharing.** Using styles when multiple people are editing the document takes all of the guesswork out of formatting.

- **Court Rules.** Styles can build essential court-required formatting into the document so that all users can confidently create court documents quickly.

- **Branding through Consistency.** Firms spend a tremendous amount of time and energy on branding an image. When a firm creates its own styles based on its branding, documents become recognizable through their consistent formatting.

- **Table of Contents.** Table of Contents is designed to work with styles. TOCs are easily created and updated when using styles.

- **Navigation.** A combination of styles and using Word's Navigation pane provides one-click access to headings and subheadings used throughout the document.

TYPES OF STYLES

There are five types of styles in Word: character, paragraph, linked, table, and list styles.

- *Character styles* can be applied to individual characters or words. Apply character style attributes using commands from the Font group on the Home tab.

- *Paragraph styles* can include both font and paragraph formatting. When you apply a paragraph style, the formatting is applied to the entire paragraph. A good example is a title or heading style.

- *Linked styles* contain both character and paragraph formatting. Apply linked styles to the entire paragraph or to selected text. When you apply a linked style to selected text, only the character formatting will be applied.

- *Table styles* apply border, shading, alignment, and character formats to entire tables or portions of a table.

- *List styles* apply outline number or bullet formats to lists.

NORMAL STYLE

The Normal style is present in any discussion regarding Word styles and is often referred to as the "mother of all styles." Simply put, every style, at some level, is based on the Normal style.

By default, when you first open a blank document, the beginning paragraph has the Normal style applied. Most of the built-in styles provided by Microsoft are based on Normal. This means that those built-in styles inherit all of the formats of the Normal style, plus the additional formats unique to that built-in style.

NOTE

If the style description displays +Headings or +Body, this means that the styles will inherit the font attributes from the Document Theme and will change if the Document Theme is changed.

IDENTIFY STYLES IN A DOCUMENT

There are a number of ways to identify the styles that exist in a Word document. You can add the Style command to the Quick Access Toolbar, view styles using the Style gallery found in the Styles group on the Home tab, and access styles from the Apply Styles task pane or from the Styles task pane. To display the names of linked or paragraph styles in the document window, view the document in Draft or Outline view with the Style Area pane showing. All of these methods are discussed in the following sections.

Add the Style Command to the Quick Access Toolbar

You might find it helpful to add the Style command to the Quick Access Toolbar in order to quickly view the style applied at the cursor position, as shown in Figure 7.1. To do this, on the File tab, click Options, and then Quick Access Toolbar. In the Choose Commands From list, select Popular Commands. Select Style from the list, and then click Add. Click OK to close the Word Options dialog box.

The Style command displays the style name at the cursor position and includes a drop-down arrow that, when clicked, shows a list of styles available in the current document, as shown in Figure 7.2.

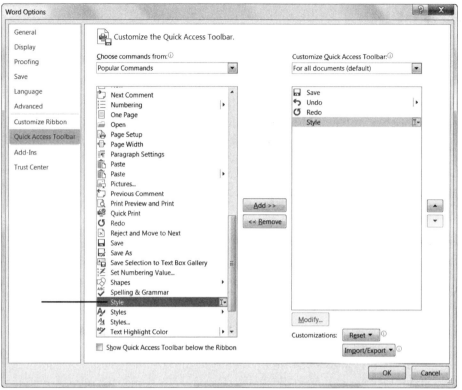

Figure 7.1

Add the Style command to the Quick Access Toolbar to view and/or apply styles in your document.

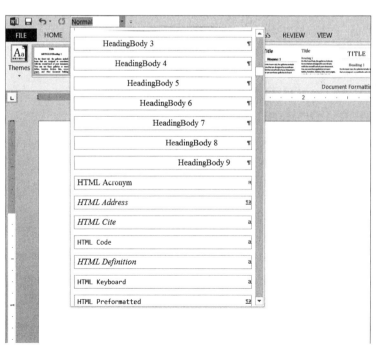

Figure 7.2

Click the down-arrow on the Style command added to the Quick Access Toolbar to see a list of styles.

Style Gallery

Located on the Home tab, in the Styles group, the Style gallery displays a row of styles, along with a preview of the style formatting. Click the down arrow to the right of the gallery to display the next row of styles, or click the More button to view the entire Style gallery. See the Style gallery in Figure 7.3.

NOTE

Table and List styles do not display in the Style gallery.

Move between
More ——— rows

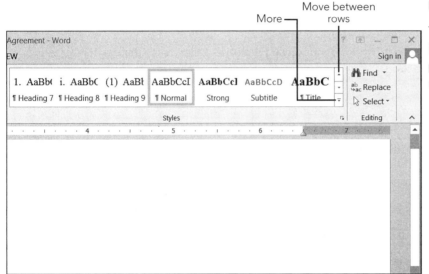

Figure 7.3

The Styles group on the Home tab allows you to preview, apply, and modify styles.

Hover your mouse over a style in the Style gallery and you will see a live preview of the style in your document.

Use Live Preview from the Style Gallery

1. Create a blank new document.

2. Type **rand()** and press Enter to insert random text in the document.

3. Place your insertion point in the first paragraph.

4. In the Styles group on the Home tab, place your mouse over the Heading 1 style, and then place your mouse over the Title style. Notice how the formatting changes each time your selection changes.

5. Click the More button next to the Style gallery to display the entire gallery of styles, and even preview a few more styles.

6. Click in the document to close the expanded gallery.

7. Keep this document open for the next exercise.

NOTE

The style is not applied until you click on the style.

By default, Word's preset list of 16 recommended styles displays in the Style gallery. You can, however, add or remove styles as needed.

NOTE

For detailed instructions on modifying the Style gallery, see Chapter 10, "Creating and Distributing Templates."

Mini Toolbar

The Styles command is also found on the Mini toolbar. Right-click in your document and from the Mini toolbar, click Styles. The same styles listed in the Style gallery will display.

Apply Styles Task Pane

The Apply Styles task pane makes it easy to apply, reapply, and modify styles in a document. To open the Apply Styles task pane, click the More button to the right of the Style gallery on the Home tab and select Apply Styles. You can also open the task pane by pressing Ctrl+Shift+S. Figure 7.4 shows the Apply Styles task pane.

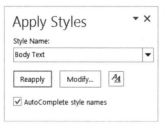

Figure 7.4

The Apply Styles task pane makes it easy to apply, reapply, and modify styles.

NOTE

Reposition the Apply Styles task pane by clicking on the title (Apply Styles) and then dragging.

Styles Task Pane

In the Styles task pane, you can view the list of styles filtered by those that are applied in the current document, user-defined styles, or all styles. The Styles task pane allows you to apply, modify, create, and manage styles.

To open the Styles task pane, click the Styles dialog box launcher in the Styles group on the Home tab or press Alt+Ctrl+Shift+S. With the Show Preview box checked, the list of styles will display a preview of the styles, making it easy to identify some of the style's formatting such as the font, font size, indents, alignment, and other font and paragraph attributes. The Styles task pane is shown in Figure 7.5.

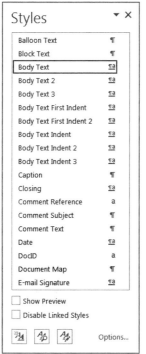

Figure 7.5

Open the Styles task pane to apply, modify, create, and manage styles.

For additional menu choices, hover over a style in the Styles task pane and then click the drop-down arrow to the right of the style when it appears. Or, right-click the style and the same menu choices appear, as shown in Figure 7.6.

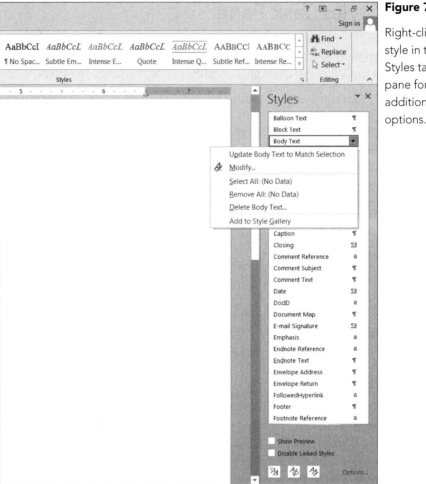

Figure 7.6

Right-click on a style in the Styles task pane for additional options.

TIP

Hover the mouse over a style in the Styles task pane, and a ScreenTip displays with detailed information about the style (see Figure 7.7).

TIP

By turning on the Reveal Formatting task pane (Shift+F1), the type of style, style name, and style properties are identified for the text where your insertion point is located.

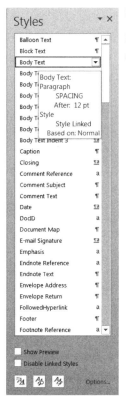

Figure 7.7

Hover over a style in the Styles task pane to view information about the style.

Style Pane Options

Click Options at the bottom of the Styles task pane to access the Style Pane Options dialog box, as shown in Figure 7.8. The Style Pane Options dialog box provides options that allow you greater control over what styles and formatting are displayed in the Styles task pane as well as how they are sorted within that pane.

Figure 7.8

Style Pane Options help you fine-tune what styles display in the task pane.

Select Styles to Show

In the Select Styles to Show list, the following choices are available:

- **Recommended.** This default option displays Word's preset list of 16 styles.

- **In Use.** Lists just the styles applied in the document.

- **In Current Document.** Lists the styles available in the current document.

- **All Styles.** Lists all the custom styles in the document as well as Word's built-in styles.

Select How List is Sorted

Click the drop-down arrow next to Select How List is Sorted and choose from the following options:

- **As Recommended.** This default option sorts the list according to Word's preset design with what Microsoft defines as the most commonly used styles listed at the top.

- **Alphabetical.** Sorts the styles in alphabetical order.

- **Font.** Groups the styles together by font.

- **Based On.** Lists the styles in order of the style on which they are based.

- **By Type.** Groups the styles by style type and then in alphabetical order.

Additional Options

In addition to having the styles display in the Styles task pane, there are more options to allow font, paragraph, as well as bullet and numbering formatting to appear in the task pane. In the Styles task pane, click Options, and three choices appear under Select Formatting to Show as Styles:

- **Paragraph Level Formatting.** Allows any direct paragraph formatting applied in the document to show in the Styles task pane.

- **Font Formatting.** Allows any direct font formatting applied in the document to show in the Styles task pane.

- **Bullet and Numbering Formatting.** Allows any bullets and numbering formatting schemes applied in the document to show in the Styles task pane.

In the Style Pane Options dialog box, there are two options under Select How Built-in Names are Shown:

- **Show Next Heading When Previous Level is Used.** The only heading styles that display in the Styles task pane by default are Heading 1 and Heading 2. Heading 3 will display in the task pane once Heading 2 is applied in the document. Once Heading 3 is applied in the document, then Heading 4 will become visible in the task pane, and so on.

- **Hide Built-in Name When Alternate Name Exists.** If a style is renamed with an alias (e.g., Body Text, BT), only the alias name displays in the Styles task pane. In this example, only BT would display.

  When you make any selections in the Style Pane Options dialog box, you can choose to have the settings apply to the active document by selecting the Only in this Document option. Alternatively, you can have the settings apply to new documents based on the active template (the template you used to create the document) by selecting the New Documents Based on this Template option.

NOTE

To save Style Pane Options settings to the template, you must have rights to modify the template.

Display Style Names in the Document Window

Sometimes it's useful to see what style is applied to more than one paragraph at a time. In the next exercise, you will display style names in the left margin of the document window when in Draft or Outline view. You do this by enabling the Style Area pane.

Enable the Style Area Pane

1. Create a new blank document.

2. Type **rand()** and press Enter to insert random text in the document.

3. Click the View tab, and in the Views group, select Draft.

4. Click the File tab, select Options, and then Advanced.

5. In the Display section, type **1** in the Style Area Pane Width in Draft and Outline Views box.

6. Click OK to close the Word Options dialog box.

7. To change the width of the Style Area pane, click and drag the style area border line.

NOTE

Once you enable the Style Area pane, it will display for all documents when in Draft or Outline view.

APPLY STYLES

To apply a style, select the text you want to apply the style to and then indicate what style should be applied. There are multiple ways to apply a style. Detailed descriptions of these options are found in the following section. When applying a style, choose from the following methods:

- From the Style command (when added to the Quick Access Toolbar)
- From the Style gallery
- From the Mini toolbar
- From the Apply Styles task pane
- From the Styles task pane
- From the Style dialog box (in Draft view, double-click on any style in the Style Area pane)
- Apply keyboard shortcuts assigned to specific styles

NOTE

When applying a paragraph or linked style to a single paragraph, it's not necessary to select the entire paragraph—just place your insertion point anywhere in the paragraph and apply the style.

OFFICE 365

Microsoft Word Web App provides styles from which to choose; however, styles cannot be created or modified in the cloud version.

Apply Styles

1. Create a blank new document.

2. Type **Title**.

3. In the Styles group on the Home tab, click the More button to the right of the Style gallery.

4. Select the Title style to apply it to the paragraph.

5. Press Enter and type **Subtitle**.

6. Click the dialog box launcher from the Styles group on the Home tab to open the Styles task pane.

7. Select the Subtitle style, press Enter, and then close the Styles task pane.

8. Type **Another Subtitle** and press Enter again.

9. Click the More button to the right of the Style gallery and select Apply Styles (see Figure 7.4).

TIP

You can also open the Apply Styles task pane by pressing Ctrl+Shift+S.

10. Type **Body Text** and click Apply.

11. Type **=rand(2)** and press Enter to insert random text.

12. Right-click in the Title paragraph at the top of the document. Select Styles from the Mini toolbar and then select Heading 1.

13. Click in the Subtitle paragraph and press Alt+Ctrl+2 to apply the Heading 2 style.

14. Click in the Another Subtitle paragraph and press F4 to repeat the last action (apply Heading 2).

EXPERT TIP

If you select text that doesn't include any paragraph marks before applying a linked style (a style that contains both font and paragraph formatting), you will apply only the character attributes of the style. The paragraph's style will not change.

To prevent this, you can disable linked styles. From the Styles group on the Home tab, click the dialog box launcher to open the Styles task pane and select the Disable Linked Styles check box, as shown in Figure 7.9.

NOTE

To apply a style to text that already has a style applied, just apply the new style to that text. It is not necessary to clear the existing style's formatting first.

If you do need to clear all formatting from text—including the style—use the Clear All Formatting command found on the Home tab, in the Font group. Clear Formatting can also be found by clicking the More button to right of the Style gallery or clicking Clear All at the top of the Styles task pane.

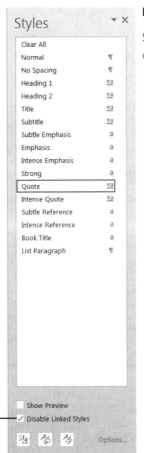

Figure 7.9

Select Disable Linked Styles to prevent applying only the character formatting of a linked style.

Keyboard Shortcuts

Built-in Heading 1, Heading 2, and Heading 3 styles have default shortcut keys assigned: Alt+Ctrl+1, Alt+Ctrl+2, and Alt+Ctrl+3, respectively. Table 7.1 lists built-in, style-related keyboard shortcuts.

OFFICE 365

The keyboard shortcuts and task panes mentioned in Table 7.1 are not available in the Office 365 cloud version of Word.

TABLE 7.1—USE KEYBOARD SHORTCUTS TO QUICKLY APPLY STYLES	
KEYBOARD SHORTCUT	**DESCRIPTION**
Alt+Ctrl+1	Applies Heading 1
Alt+Ctrl+2	Applies Heading 2
Alt+Ctrl+3	Applies Heading 3
Ctrl+Shift+L	Applies List Bullet
Ctrl+Shift+N	Applies Normal
Ctrl+Shift+S	Activates the Apply Styles task pane
Alt+Ctrl+Shift+S	Activates the Styles task pane

Create Keyboard Shortcuts for Styles

To create your own keyboard shortcuts for applying the styles you use most often, follow the steps in the next exercise. The keyboard shortcut you create for a style is saved with the document only and will not be available in new or other existing documents.

Assign a Keyboard Shortcut to a Style

1. Create a blank new document.

2. Type **=rand()** and press Enter to insert random text in the document.

3. Press Ctrl+A to select all of the text.

4. Press Ctrl+Shift+S to open the Apply Styles task pane.

5. Type **Body Text** and click Modify.

6. In the Modify Style dialog box, click Format and then select Shortcut Key.

7. In the Customize Keyboard dialog box, in the Press New Shortcut Key box, press Alt+B.

8. Click Assign.

9. Click Close and then click OK.

TIP

Make sure Word is not already using the key combination you choose. Check the notation next to Currently Assigned To and if [unassigned] displays, you can use this key combination without fear of overwriting an existing keyboard shortcut.

Be careful when assigning keyboard shortcuts using the Alt key plus a single letter or number. The letters F, H, N, G, P, S, M, R, W, and X are reserved for the main tabs in Word, and depending on the number of commands added to the Quick Access Toolbar, several numbers will be reserved. When assigning the keyboard shortcut, the Currently Assigned To section will still display [unassigned], and you may accidentally overwrite an existing shortcut.

Word includes options that will automatically apply a style to specific types of inserted text. It is recommended that these options be turned off in order to prevent Word from potentially applying the wrong style to specific types of formats.

On the File tab, click Options, Proofing, and then select AutoCorrect Options. On the AutoFormat As You Type tab, these options are found in the Apply As You Type section:

- **Built-In Heading Styles.** This feature will apply Heading 1 through 9 to paragraphs formatted with similar formats.
- **Define Styles Based On Your Formatting.** As you are formatting text, Word applies a style automatically—without you doing anything other than applying formatting.

MODIFY EXISTING STYLES

The beauty of styles is being able to quickly modify formatting without having to visit each paragraph in the document where that style is applied. By applying styles to all of the paragraphs in the document, when global edits need to be made to the styles, all you need to do is modify those styles.

There are basically two ways to modify a style: by example or using the Modify Style dialog box.

Modify a Style by Example

Modifying a style by example is probably the quickest way to make changes to a style. First, you apply the formatting changes to the text on which the style has been applied, and then you just update the style to include those changes. Right-click on the style from either the Style gallery, the Styles task pane, or the Mini toolbar Styles command, and select Update [style] to Match Selection.

Modify a Style by Example

1. Create a blank new document.

2. Type **=rand()** and press Enter to insert random text in the document.

3. Press Ctrl+A to select all text in the document.

4. Click the More button to the right of the Style gallery on the Home tab and then click on the Quote style.

5. Click in the first paragraph and then click the Align Left command from the Paragraph group on the Home tab.

6. Click the More button to the right of the Style gallery on the Home tab, right-click Quote, and then select Update Quote to Match Selection, as shown in Figure 7.10.

7. Keep this document open for the next exercise.

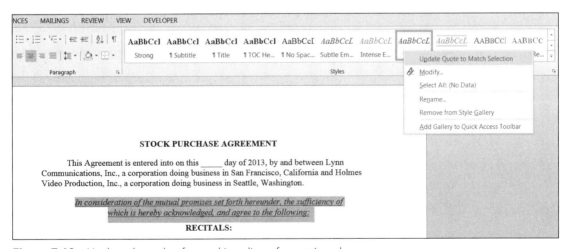

Figure 7.10 Update the style after making direct formatting changes.

TIP

You can also access the Update [style] to Match Selection option by clicking on the down arrow next to the style name in the Styles task pane.

NOTE

Since all styles do not display in the Style gallery, modifying a style by example may need to be accomplished using another method.

NOTE

When selecting Update [style] to Match Selection, make sure the insertion point does not contain any formatting you don't want to be part of the style. For instance, if the insertion point is in text that is bold when you update the style, bold will become part of the style definition.

Modify a Style Using the Modify Style Dialog Box

The Modify Style dialog box can be accessed from the Style gallery, the Styles task pane, the Mini toolbar Styles command, the Apply Styles task pane, and through the Style dialog box. To access the Modify Style dialog box from the Style gallery or the Styles task pane, right-click on the style and click Modify. To access the Modify Style dialog box from the Apply Styles task pane and the Style dialog box, click the Modify button.

Modify a Style Using the Modify Style Dialog Box

1. The document from the previous exercise should still be open.

2. Click in the first paragraph.

3. Press Alt+Shift+S to open the Apply Styles task pane.

4. Click Modify to open the Modify Style dialog box, as shown in Figure 7.11.

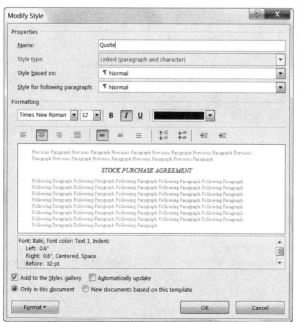

Figure 7.11

The Modify Style dialog box provides several formatting options all in one place.

5. In the Formatting section of the Modify Style dialog box, click Bold.

6. Click Format and choose Paragraph to open the Paragraph dialog box.

7. On the Indents and Spacing tab in the Spacing section, set the spacing Before to 0 pt and the spacing After to 12 pt, and then click OK twice.

Don't Add Space Between Paragraphs

When making a list, you often want to have no space separating each of the items, but still have space following the last item. This, of course, can be accomplished through manual edits by changing the spacing After setting for each item; however, to automate this process, just use the Don't Add Space Between Paragraphs of the same style option when modifying the style.

Open the Modify Style dialog box, click Format and then Paragraph. Add spacing After and then select the Don't Add Space Between Paragraphs of the Same Style check box.

Automatically Update a Style

At first glance, the Automatically Update option appears to be a great timesaving feature. When you select this option, formatting changes you make to text will automatically be added to the applied style—no need to update the style to match the selection. However, it also takes away the ability to apply "direct formatting" to specific text. For instance, if you have several paragraphs with the Body Text style applied and you want the text in one of those paragraphs to be formatted as bold, as soon as you apply Bold to the text, the style will automatically update to be defined as Bold and all of the text in the document with the Body Text style applied will become bold.

By default, Table of Contents styles (TOC 1–TOC 9) and Index styles (Index 1–Index 9) are set to automatically update based on direct formatting edits. Since these styles are not used throughout the document, having them automatically update makes it easy to modify the formatting without unexpected consequences.

NOTE   When you modify a style, the changes will only apply to the current document. However, you can add the change to the template from which the document was created, so any new documents created from that same template will contain the updated style. In the Modify Style dialog box, select the New Documents Based on this Template option.

For more information on creating and managing templates, see Chapter 10, "Creating and Distributing Templates."

EXPERT TIP

If a style changes unexpectedly, one of the first troubleshooting techniques is to see if it's been set to automatically update. To do this, go to the Home tab, and locate the style in the Styles group. Right-click on the style listed in the Style gallery and choose Modify. Ensure that Automatically Update is not enabled at the bottom of the Modify Style dialog box. Another reason for the unexpected change is when a style is based on another style that has changed; or perhaps if a new template was attached, the styles from that template could have automatically inserted. Knowing how to troubleshoot styles will help you solve these unexpected formatting scenarios.

STYLE SETS

A Style Set is a collection of styles that, when applied, updates the document with the style definitions contained in the Style Set. Style Sets are found on the Design tab in the Document Formatting group. Click the down arrow to view the next row of Style Sets in the Style Set gallery or click the More button to open the entire gallery. Keep in mind that the style definitions in the Style Set will replace existing style definitions in the document.

Save a Style Set

You can customize your own Style Set and save it for future use. Modify the styles in a document as needed, and on the Design tab in the Document Formatting group, to the right of the gallery, click the More button, and then choose Save as a New Style Set.

NOTE

If you'd like a style to be part of the Style Set, be sure it's in the Style gallery. Saving a Style Set captures only the style definitions of those styles found in the Style gallery.

Delete a Style Set

To delete a custom Style Set, click the Design tab, and in the Document Formatting group, right-click the Style Set listed under Custom and select Delete from the shortcut menu.

CREATE A NEW STYLE

On occasion, you may need to create a custom style. When you create a style, formatting at the insertion point will become part of the style definition. At any point during the creation of the style, you have the option to modify the style's formatting using the standard formatting dialog boxes.

Create a Style by Example

The fastest way to create a new style is to format text exactly how you want the style formatting defined. Select the option to create the style and give it a name.

Create a Style by Example

1. Create a blank new document.

2. Press Ctrl+Shift+N to apply the Normal style to the paragraph.

3. Type **My Title** and click the Center command in the Paragraph group on the Home tab to center the paragraph text.

4. Select the typed text and press Ctrl+I to italicize the text.

5. Click the Paragraph dialog box launcher from the Home tab, click the Line and Page Breaks tab, and select the Keep With Next option.

6. Click OK to close the Paragraph dialog box.

7. Click the More button to the right of the Style gallery on the Home tab and select Create a Style.

8. In the Name box, type **My Title Style**.

9. Click OK.

TIP

To create a new style, you can also right-click the formatted text selection, click Styles on the Mini toolbar, and then choose Create a Style, or you can click the New Style button at the bottom of the Styles task pane.

Style Properties

When creating a style, click the Modify button in the Create New Style from Formatting dialog box to access more advanced options or to add more formatting to your style, as shown in Figure 7.12. More options are available when creating a style (see Figure 7.13).

Figure 7.12

During style creation, click Modify to access more options.

Figure 7.13

There are several options available when creating a style.

Style Type

When creating a style by example, the Style Type will default to Linked. However, when you click Modify, you can change the Style Type. If you did not click Modify, the Linked Style Type cannot be changed once the style is created. For more information on style types, see the "Types of Styles" section in this chapter.

Style Based On

A style inherits the formatting of the style on which it is based. To simplify this "chain of command," most styles are based on the Normal style. You can set Normal style as the base style by, either applying Normal style to the paragraph you are using as an example when creating the style, or you can select Normal from the Style Based On drop-down list from the Create New Style from Formatting (or Modify Style) dialog box.

Here is an example of how a style inherits formatting: Unless your firm has custom templates in place, Word's Normal style is defined as Calibri (Body) 11 pt. A new style is created and Style Based On is defined as Normal. The new style will reflect Calibri (Body) 11 pt (assuming no other font is defined in the new style). Change the Normal style's font to Arial 12 pt, and the new style will reflect, or inherit, the Arial 12 pt font attributes.

Style for Following Paragraph

The Style for Following Paragraph option determines the style that is applied when Enter is pressed. By default, when a new style is created, the Style for the Following Paragraph will be the same as the style itself. This feature can be changed to make document creation easier. For instance, if you always have a generic paragraph follow a title, you can define your Title style to be followed by the Body Text style. Apply the Title style first, type your title text, and when you press Enter, the style of the following paragraph will be Body Text.

RENAME STYLES

At times you may need to rename a user-defined style in a document. To do this, from either the Style gallery or the Styles task pane, right-click on the style and click Modify. Change the name and then click OK.

Keep in mind that changes made to styles, by default, pertain to the current document only. To make global changes to styles, see Chapter 10, "Creating and Distributing Templates."

Cut, Copy, and Paste Styles between Documents

The easiest way to transfer a linked or paragraph style between documents is to copy a paragraph mark that has the style applied to it in the first document, and then paste that paragraph mark into the second document. The drawback to this copy/paste method is that if the copied style already exists in the second document, the style's attributes from the first document are not pasted.

EXPERT TIP

When copying/pasting text between two documents in which the style applied exists in both documents and the formatting doesn't match, the text will be pasted in Normal style with the formatting applied as direct formatting. To update the style in the target document with the same formatting copied from the source document, click in the pasted text, right-click on the style you want to update, and select Update [style] to Match Selection.

TIP

When multiple people work on a document and one is not as fluent with styles as the other, you may find that direct formatting has been applied to text. For instance, Heading 1 in most instances in a document might be 14 pt and bold; however, in a few instances it appears centered and underlined as well. The most likely cause is that direct formatting has been applied: to the text. In the Styles task pane or Style gallery, right-click on the Heading 1 style and choose Select All [number of Heading 1 styles in document] Instances. Then, to quickly remove direct character formatting, press Ctrl+Spacebar. To remove paragraph formatting, press Ctrl+Q.

OFFICE 365

Text with a style applied that has been copied from an installed copy of Microsoft Word and pasted to the Word Web App document will be converted to Normal, if the style is not one of the standard Web App styles. Therefore, when pasting a standard Word style to the Web App, the style will be pasted; however, the formatting may be different.

Styles can also be copied between documents and templates using the Organizer, described in the following section.

The Organizer

The Organizer, shown in Figure 7.14, is a good way to copy multiple styles between documents and templates. It's also a quick way to delete or rename existing styles.

TIP

To select multiple contiguous styles, select the first style, hold the Shift key and click the last style you want to select. To select nonadjacent items, hold the Ctrl key as you click each style name.

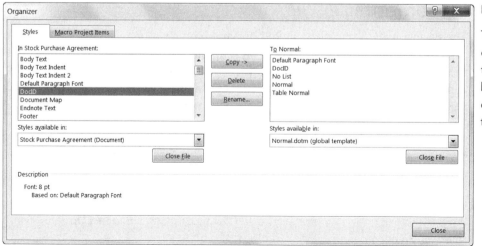

Figure 7.14

The Organizer can be used to copy styles between documents or templates.

Copying Styles Using the Organizer

1. Create a new blank document.

2. Open the Styles task pane (Alt+Ctrl+Shift+S).

3. Click Manage Styles at the bottom of the task pane.

4. In the Manage Styles dialog box, click Import/Export. The list on the left displays the styles used in the active document. Styles used in the Normal template are on the right.

5. On the right, just below Styles Available in Normal.dotm (global template), click Close File, and then click Open File.

6. Select the exercise file My Template.dotx (downloaded from www.thepayne group.com/downloads/word2013forlawfirms/) and click Open.

7. From the In My Template.dotx list, select the Title and Heading 1 styles and click Copy.

8. If prompted, click Yes to All to overwrite the existing style entries.

9. Click Close.

NOTE

More in-depth options for managing styles are covered in Chapter 10, "Creating and Distributing Templates."

TRAVELING COACHES

Char LeMaire, Chief Learning Officer and Principal of Traveling Coaches, on Favorite Style Tips

If the document formatting is consistent, you can quickly get styles applied to the document by following these steps:

1. Turn on the Styles task pane and check to see if the styles that should be applied are part of the document. If your firm uses a well-designed Normal template, they should be there. If not, you may need to copy, create, or modify the styles you will use into the document first.

2. Click in the first paragraph that needs to have a style applied. Often you'll see several paragraphs that should all be styled the same, such as the ones that have a first-line indent, spacing after, and left or full justification.

3. From the Editing group, click the Select drop-down list and choose Select Text with Similar Formatting. All the paragraphs in the entire document that have that same direct formatting applied are selected.

4. From the Styles task pane, click on the style you want to apply to the paragraphs. All the selected paragraphs now have that style applied.
5. Move to the next paragraph that you see in the document that needs to have a style applied and repeat steps 3 and 4.

Try this the next time you are challenged with a poorly formatted document and a looming deadline. You'll save yourself time and frustration.

BULLETS AND NUMBERING

Almost every legal document contains some type of bulleted or numbered list. Adding bullets to a document can help make it more interesting and readable, while numbering helps organize your thoughts in a logical order. Whether you're creating a contract, agreement, pleading, or other type of document, a combination of basic numbered lists and multilevel outline lists can help organize the content of your document. Understanding how to use the numbering tools available in Word will help you to create consistently formatted documents and will allow you to make changes to those documents more quickly. Needless to say, mastering numbering is an absolute necessity for legal professionals.

This chapter covers the following bullets and numbering features:

- Working with different types of bullets
- Creating simple numbered lists
- Working with complex outline numbering
- Understanding how styles and numbering work together
- Using list styles
- Using third-party numbering solutions

BULLETS AND NUMBERING OVERVIEW

A bullet is a graphical element that appears to the left of text and is designed to draw attention to the text that follows. Bullets can be square, round, arrow-shaped, check boxes, basically any symbol you like; you can even use your firm logo as a bullet.

Numbered lists can have different types of numeric formats such as Arabic, Roman, and alphanumeric; they can also be formatted with different fonts and font sizes. While numbered lists typically are numbered consecutively, the numbering can be restarted at contiguous or noncontiguous locations within the document.

Both bullets and numbering can be applied to existing text by selecting the text or list of items and then turning on the bullets or numbering feature. To start a bulleted or numbered list from scratch, apply either the bullets or the numbering feature and start typing. Word offers a number of methods for applying bullets or numbering:

- Click either the Bullets or Numbering command from the Paragraph group on the Home tab.

- Click the down arrow to the right of the Bullets command or the Numbering command from the Paragraph group on the Home tab and select from the available libraries.

- Apply a built-in bulleted or numbered style (i.e., List Bullet, List Number).

- Type one of the characters Word recognizes to convert to a bullet, or the first number of your list, followed by a space or tab, and let AutoFormat As You Type convert the text into automatic bullets or numbering.

- Use a keyboard shortcut.

Bullets and numbering can be removed from text by clicking either the Bullets or the Numbering command on the Home tab to toggle the feature off, or by pressing Enter twice.

ACCESS THE BULLETS AND NUMBERING LIBRARIES

The Bullets and Numbering commands on the ribbon provide only one format for each bullet and number. Clicking the down arrow next to the Bullets or Numbering commands offers a thumbnail library of several predefined bullets and numbering formats from which to choose. Rest your mouse pointer over any of the bullet or numbering formats in the gallery to see a live preview of the format. The Bullet and Numbering libraries also will keep track of any recently used bullets or numbering as well as the bullets or numbering used in any open documents.

BULLETS, SIMPLE NUMBERING, AND STYLES

Some built-in styles are designed to work with bullets and simple numbering, specifically the List Paragraph, the List Bullet, and List Number styles.

List Paragraph Style

By default, if the Normal style is applied to the active paragraph when you apply bullets or numbering, the List Paragraph style is applied, and the bullets or numbering is applied as direct formatting. If the style applied to the active paragraph is any style other than Normal, the paragraph will stay in that style and bullets, or numbering, will be applied as direct formatting. To apply bullets or numbering that are built into the style and do not include direct formatting, see the Bullets and Numbering Styles section.

EXPERT TIP

The List Paragraph style contains certain font and paragraph formats, but does not include formatting for the bullet or number. That's why you'll notice that the same List Paragraph style is applied to both the bullet and number.

Bullets and Numbering Styles

Word has several built-in bulleted and numbered styles that can be applied to lists: List Bullet and List Bullet 2 through List Bullet 5 for bullets and List Number and List Number 2 through List Number 5 for simple numbering. To view these styles, click the Styles dialog box launcher in the Styles group on the Home tab, and the Styles task pane opens (see Figure 8.1). In the bottom-right corner of the Styles task pane, click Options, and the Style Pane Options dialog box opens. In the Select Styles to Show list, choose All Styles. Select Alphabetical from the Select How List is Sorted list and then click OK. Scroll through the styles list and locate the List Bullet and List Number styles. Click any List Bullet or List Number style to apply the style to selected paragraphs.

See Chapter 7, "Styles," for more information about styles.

The List Bullet and List Number styles have the bullets or numbering built into the style.

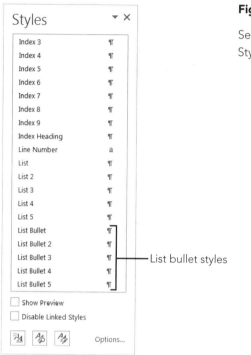

Figure 8.1

Select and apply a List Bullet style from the Styles task pane.

BULLETED LISTS

Bulleted lists can be applied to your text through a variety of methods. The Bullet library, accessed by clicking the down arrow to the right of the Bullets command found on the Home tab in the Paragraph group, has seven preset bulleted lists from which to choose (see Figure 8.2). Click the desired bullet or click Define New Bullet to define a new bullet character and format.

NOTE

Any bullets selected during the current Word session also will be available under the Recently Used Bullets list. The Document Bullets list will also display any bullets in use in any open documents.

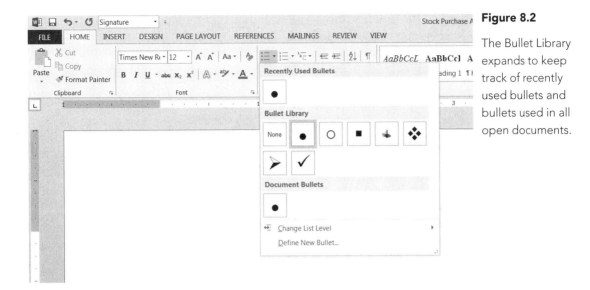

Figure 8.2

The Bullet Library expands to keep track of recently used bullets and bullets used in all open documents.

Apply a Bulleted List

To apply a bulleted list using the ribbon, from the Paragraph group on the Home tab, click Bullets. To apply a different bullet type, click the down arrow to the right of the Bullets button to select from available bullet formats.

Apply Bullets Using the Ribbon

1. Create a new blank document.

2. Type **Loan Agreement** and press Enter. Type **Table of Contents** and press Enter. Type **Exhibit 1** and press Enter. Type **Exhibit 2** and press Enter. Type **Exhibit 3**.

3. Press Ctrl+A to select all the text, and from the Paragraph group on the Home tab, click Bullets.

4. After Exhibit 3, press Enter and type **Index**. When you are in a bulleted list and press Enter, the paragraph formatting that contains the bullet continues to the next paragraph.

5. Select all of the list items, and from the Paragraph group on the Home tab, click the down arrow next to the Bullets command. Hover your mouse pointer over each of the bullets in the library to see a preview of how the bullets will look in the document.

6. Select a different bullet to apply to your list.

7. Click the down arrow next to the Bullets command. A Recently Used Bullets group and a Document Bullets group have been created.

8. Close the document without saving.

NOTE

The Recently Used Bullets will reset after closing Word.

The Bullet Library remembers all bullets applied and displays when Word reopens.

The Document Bullets list displays bullets used in all currently open documents and will reset after closing Word.

Apply Bullets Using a List Bullet Style

1. Create a new blank document.

2. Type **Estate Planning** and press Enter. Type **Bankruptcy** and press Enter. Type **Finance** and press Enter. Type **Securities**.

3. Press Ctrl+A to select the list.

4. Click the Styles dialog box launcher in the Styles group on the Home tab to open the Styles task pane.

5. In the bottom-right corner of the Styles task pane, click Options.

6. In the Select Styles to Show list, select All Styles. Select Alphabetical from the Select How List is Sorted list and click OK.

7. Click List Bullet 3 to apply the style to the list.

8. Close the Styles task pane.

9. Close the document without saving.

TIP

The keyboard shortcut to apply the List Bullet style is Ctrl+Shift+L.

Apply Bullets Using AutoFormat As You Type

1. Create a new blank document.

2. Select the File tab, Options, Proofing, and then click AutoCorrect Options.

3. Select the AutoFormat As You Type tab, and under the Apply As You Type section, check the Automatic Bulleted Lists check box and click OK twice.

4. Type an asterisk (*) and press Tab. A bullet is automatically applied to the paragraph.

5. Close the document without saving.

Table 8.1 includes the AutoFormat As You Type characters to type, along with their corresponding bullet, when creating a bulleted list.

TABLE 8.1—APPLY A BULLETED LIST USING AUTOFORMAT AS YOU TYPE	
TYPE THIS	**SYMBOL/BULLET**
*	•
-	-
--	■
>	➢
->	➔
=>	⇨

Turn Off a Bulleted List

Bullets are just as easy to turn off as they are to turn on. If bullets were applied using the ribbon, use any of the following methods to toggle off the Bullets feature:

- Click Bullets on the Home tab in the Paragraph group.

- Press Enter twice at the end of a bulleted list.

- Press Backspace at the end of a bulleted list.

The quickest way to turn off a bulleted list is to press Enter twice. The first time you press Enter, it gives you the bullet. The second time you press Enter, it turns off the bullet and returns you to the margin in a new paragraph.

Pressing Enter followed by Backspace will remove the bullet and change the indent to line up with the bulleted text above. Press Backspace again, and the indents change to line up with the bullet above. If the original bullet applied had an indent, you may be able to press Backspace one more time, and the indents will change to wrap text back to the margin.

NOTE

If pressing Backspace does not adjust the indents, then the option to Set Left- and First-indent with Tabs and Backspaces is not activated (File tab, Options, Proofing, AutoCorrect Options, AutoFormat As You Type).

If bullets were applied by using one of the List Bullet styles, the method for turning off the bullet is to select a different style for the paragraph. Even though pressing Enter twice will turn off the bulleted list, the List Bullet style is still applied. Typically when a bulleted list is complete and you press Enter, you should apply the Body Text style or another style to the paragraph.

Define a Custom Bullet

You may want to customize a bulleted list with a new bullet symbol not found in the Bullet Library. In the Paragraph group on the Home tab, click the down arrow next to Bullets and choose Define New Bullet.

In the Define New Bullet dialog box, you can change the bullet using the Symbol, Picture, or Font buttons (see Figure 8.3). Change the bullet character and the preview updates automatically.

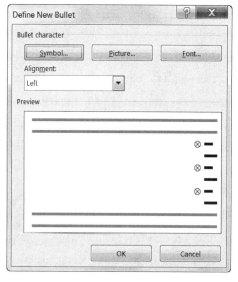

Figure 8.3

Click the Symbol button to choose a symbol from the available system fonts.

Define a Custom Bullet Using a Symbol

1. Create a new blank document.

2. In the Paragraph group on the Home tab, click the down arrow next to the Bullets command.

3. Select Define New Bullet.

4. From the Define New Bullet dialog box, click Symbol.

5. Select any symbol and click OK.

6. Click OK again.

7. From the Home tab, in the Paragraph group, click the down arrow to the right of Bullets. The new symbol appears in the Recently Used Bullets, the Bullet Library, and the Document Bullets lists.

8. Close the document without saving.

NOTE

The newly created bullet appears in the Recently Used Bullets list, the Bullet Library, and the Document Bullets list. After Word is closed and reopened, although the Recently Used Bullets list and the Document Bullets list will be reset, you will find the custom bullet in the Bullet Library.

LEGALTYPIST, INC.

Andrea Cannavina, CEO of LegalTypist, Inc., www.legaltypist.com, on Paragraph Numbering in Word

I am a big user of lists, and I love bulleted lists; however, I don't always want to use the small dot used as the default for my bullets. Word allows you to customize your bullet lists by picking a symbol or picture.

Click the drop-down arrow next to the bullet list button and select Define New Bullet. Click on Symbol and a dialog box pops up, indicating which symbols are available for the current font. Different fonts have different symbols—so click through until you find the one you want, select—and voilá, your bullet list now has the new symbol.

You can even color your bullets! Go back to Define New Bullet and select the Font button. From there you can choose a color to be applied to your bullets.

Changing things up, even little things, like customizing the bullet in a list, can bring the visual interest needed to capture the attention of your readers.

Adjust List Indents

By default, bulleted lists are indented .25 inch from the left margin and set with a .25-inch hanging indent. To change the indents, right-click on the bullet you want to change and choose Adjust List Indents from the shortcut menu.

The Adjust List Indents dialog box allows you to make changes to the relative position of both the bullets and text, change what follows the bullet, and set the tab stop position. The Adjust List Indents dialog box, as shown in Figure 8.4, has the following options:

- **Bullet Position.** Specifies the distance between the margin and the bullet. Type a position in the Bullet Position box or click the arrows to increase or decrease the distance of the bullet from the margin.

- **Text Indent.** Text Indent sets the hanging indent.

- **Follow Number With.** Specifies what follows the bullet. Choose from Tab character, Space, or Nothing. Tab character is the default.

- **Add Tab Stop At.** Set the position of the tab stop when Tab Character is selected from the Follow Number With list.

Figure 8.4

Set the indents and tab stop for a bulleted list.

TIP

Quickly change the bullet and text position by clicking on any bullet and then dragging it to the right or left. When you release the mouse button, the entire bulleted list will move. This method will also update the Adjust List Indents dialog box with the new position settings.

SIMPLE NUMBERED LISTS

The most basic type of numbered list is 1, 2, 3 or A, B, C. Any one of the following methods will begin a numbered list:

- Click the Numbering button in the Paragraph group on the Home tab.

- Click the down arrow next to the Numbering button in the Paragraph group on the Home tab to view the Numbering Library. Click to apply a numbered list.

- Type the character representing the basic number or letter followed by a period or closed parenthesis, press Tab, and allow AutoCorrect's AutoFormat As You Type to convert the text to a numbered list.

Numbered lists can have different numeric formats (e.g., Arabic, Roman, alphanumeric) as well as specific size and font choices. They also can be restarted at contiguous or noncontiguous locations within the document.

Apply a Simple Numbered List

A simple numbered list can be created easily by clicking the Numbering button located in the Paragraph group on the Home tab. To choose from a gallery of preset numbered lists, click the down arrow next to the Numbering button to view the available choices, as shown in Figure 8.5. After a numbering format has been applied to a document, it will display in the Recently Used Number Formats list. The Document Number Formats list will display all number formats used in any open documents.

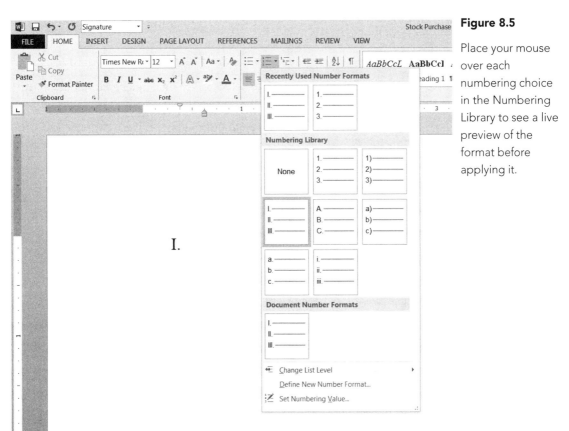

Figure 8.5

Place your mouse over each numbering choice in the Numbering Library to see a live preview of the format before applying it.

The Recently Used Number Formats list will reset after closing Word.

The Numbering Library remembers all number formats applied and displays when Word reopens.

The Document Number Formats list displays number formats used in all open documents and will reset after closing Word.

Apply a Simple Numbered List Using a List Number Style

1. Create a new blank document.

2. From the Paragraph group on the Home tab, click Numbering.

3. Type **Formation** and press Enter. Type **Name** and press Enter. Type **Principal Place of Business**.

4. Press Ctrl+A to select the entire list.

5. Click the Styles dialog box launcher in the Styles group on the Home tab to open the Styles task pane.

6. In the bottom right corner of the Styles task pane, click Options.

7. In the Select Styles to Show list, select All Styles. Select Alphabetical from the Select How List is Sorted list and click OK.

8. Click List Number to apply the style to the list.

9. Close the Styles task pane.

10. Close the document without saving.

Apply a Simple Numbered List Using AutoFormat As You Type

1. Create a new blank document.

2. Select the File tab, Options, Proofing, and then click AutoCorrect Options.

3. Select the AutoFormat As You Type tab, and under the Apply As You Type section, select the Automatic Numbered Lists check box and click OK twice.

4. Type a **1** followed by a period and press Tab. A number is automatically applied to the paragraph. Type **first item** and press Enter. The next sequential number displays.

5. Select and delete the entire list. Try starting an automatic numbered list by typing an **A** followed by a closed parenthesis and press Tab.

6. Close the document without saving.

Turn Off a Numbered List

The quickest method to turn off a simple numbered list is to press Enter twice. The first time you press Enter, it gives you the next sequential number. The second time you press Enter, it turns off the numbering and returns you to the margin in a new paragraph.

Pressing Enter followed by Backspace will remove the numbering and change the indent to line up with the numbered text above. Press Backspace again, and the indents change to line up with the number above. If the original number you applied had an indent, you may be able to press Backspace one more time, and the indents change to wrap text back to the margin.

NOTE

If pressing Backspace as indicated does not adjust the indents, then the option to Set Left- and First-indent with Tabs and Backspaces is not activated (File tab, Options, Proofing, AutoCorrect Options, AutoFormat As You Type).

The Numbering button on the Home tab, Paragraph group, also acts as a toggle. Clicking Numbering once will turn numbering on; clicking it again will turn numbering off.

If numbering was applied by using one of the List Number styles, the method for turning off the numbering is to select a different style for the paragraph. Even though pressing Enter twice will turn off the numbered list, the List Number style is still applied. Typically when a numbered list is complete and you press Enter, you should apply the Body Text style or something similar.

Customize a Numbered List

To create a number format not found in the Numbering Library, click the down arrow to the right of the Numbering button on the Home tab in the Paragraph group. Select Define New Number Format, and from the Define New Number Format dialog box, change the number style, the font, the number format, or specify the alignment of the number (see Figure 8.6).

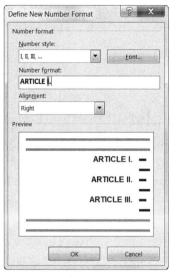

Figure 8.6

The font, format, style, and position of a number can all be modified through the Define New Number Format dialog box.

In the Number Format box of the Define New Number Format dialog box, you can add text before and after the number. For example, you may want to include parentheses around the number or add the word Article or Section before the number. The number will appear with gray shading in the Number Format box.

TIP

If the number is accidentally deleted from the Number Format box, just click the down arrow in the Number Style box and select the number format to reinsert it.

Customize a Simple Numbered List

1. Create a new blank document.

2. In the Paragraph group on the Home tab, click the Numbering down arrow and select Define New Number Format.

3. Click Font to open the Font dialog box. Set the Font and Font Style to Times New Roman and Bold, set the Size to 12, and click OK to return to the Define New Number Format dialog box.

4. From the Number Style drop-down list, select I, II, III and click OK.

5. Type **Initial Meeting** and press Enter. Type **Conflicts Check** and press Enter. Type **New Matter Process**.

6. Right-click the number and choose Adjust List Indents from the shortcut menu.

7. In the Adjust List Indents dialog box, set the Number Position to 0.5", set the Text Indent to 0", and leave the Follow Number With set to Tab Character.

8. Click OK to apply the customizations to the numbered list.

9. Close the document without saving.

Restart and Continue a Simple Numbered List

Many legal documents contain a combination of numbered and unnumbered lists. Numbered lists often begin, end, and restart at different points in the document. Word makes it easy to control what number is used, anywhere and anytime, within the document.

Restart and Continue a Simple Numbered List

1. Create a new blank document.

2. In the Paragraph group on the Home tab, click the Numbering down arrow and select the list you created in the previous exercise or select the I. II. III. list from the Numbering Library.

3. Type **Formation** and press Enter. Type **Name** and press Enter. Type **Principal Place of Business** and press Enter twice.

4. Type **Rights and Duties** and press Enter.

5. Click the Numbering button in the Paragraph group on the Home tab. Notice numbering automatically restarts at I.

6. Type **Management** and press Enter. Type **Tenure** and press Enter. Type **Tax Management** and press Enter twice.

7. Right-click the number in the Management paragraph and select Continue Numbering to join the numbering with the list above.

8. Right-click the Management paragraph again and select Restart at I.

9. Leave the document open for the next exercise.

EXPERT TIP

To access the shortcut menu for numbering, right-clicking precisely on the automatic number always displays the restart and continue commands on the shortcut menu. Right-clicking anywhere else within the numbered paragraph provides a shortcut menu with different options.

The Format Painter on the Home tab, Clipboard group, can be used in conjunction with numbering to continue a list. Click within a paragraph that has the correct numbering applied, and then click Format Painter once. Click the text where the next consecutive number should appear, and the Format Painter will apply the numbering to that paragraph.

Adjust List Indents

By default, simple numbered lists are indented .25 inch from the left margin and set with a .25-inch hanging indent. To change the indents, right-click on the number you want to change and select Adjust List Indents.

The Adjust List Indents dialog box allows you to make changes to the relative position of both the numbers and text, change what follows the number, and set the tab stop position. The Adjust List Indents dialog box, as shown in Figure 8.7, has the following options:

- **Number Position.** Specifies the distance between the margin and the number. Type a position in the Number Position box or click the arrows to increase or decrease the distance between the margin and the number.

- **Text Indent.** Specifies the position of the tab stop. The Text Indent sets the hanging indent.

- **Follow Number With.** Specifies what follows the number. Choose from Tab character, Space, or Nothing. Tab character is the default.

- **Add Tab Stop At.** Set the position of the tab stop when Tab Character is selected from the Follow Number With list.

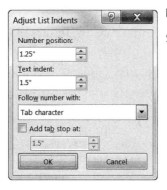

Figure 8.7

Set the indents and tab stop for a simple numbered list.

Adjust List Indents in a Simple Numbered List

1. The file from the previous exercise should still be open.

2. Right-click the number in the Management paragraph and select Adjust List Indents.

3. In the Adjust List Indents dialog box, change Number Position to 0", change Text Indent to .5", and click OK.

4. Close the document without saving.

TIP

Quickly change the number and text position by clicking on any number and dragging it to the right or left. When you release the mouse button, the entire numbered list has moved. This method will also update the Adjust List Indents dialog box with the new position settings.

MULTILEVEL LISTS

A simple numbered list is often sufficient for an agenda or memo, but documents such as briefs and agreements generally require more complex paragraph numbering. The Multilevel List feature in Word provides this functionality. The Multilevel List command is found in the Paragraph group on the Home tab. Click to select a list from the library and start applying outline numbering to your document.

There are two types of multilevel lists found in Word—those that are linked to styles and those that are not. This section examines both options.

NOTE

To make the most of Word's numbering capabilities, legal documents that require multilevel numbering work best when linked to styles. Linking multilevel numbering to styles provides greater flexibility for applying formatting options, editing, inserting cross-references, and generating a table of contents.

Apply Multilevel Numbering

The Multilevel List Library offers several outline numbering schemes from which to choose. The first three lists are not linked to Heading styles and the last four are linked to Heading styles, as shown in Figure 8.8.

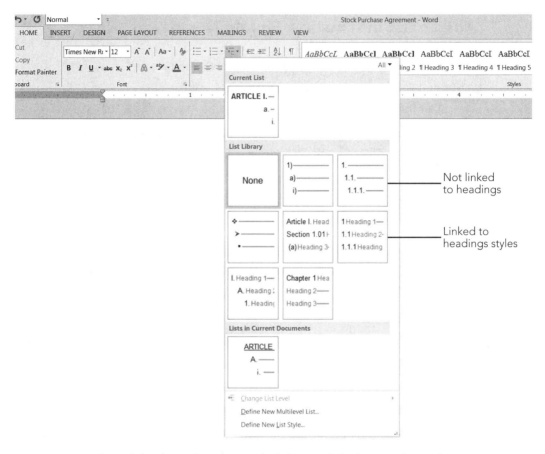

Figure 8.8 In the Multilevel List Library, note which lists are linked to Heading styles.

To apply a multilevel list, in the Paragraph group on the Home tab, click Multilevel List and select one of the lists in the List Library.

Apply Multilevel Numbering Using the Ribbon

1. Create a new blank document.

2. In the Paragraph group on the Home tab, click Multilevel List.

3. As you hover over each numbering list in the List Library, a larger preview showing all nine levels of that list displays.

4. Click to select the first outline numbered list in the gallery.

5. Type some text after the number and press Enter. A new number at the same level appears.

One thing you might not expect is that after applying multilevel numbering, the simple Numbering button is highlighted in the Paragraph group, within the Home tab. This can cause problems when sharing documents with someone who clicks first and explores what formatting is actually applied after the fact.

6. Change the numbering to the second level by pressing Tab. Type some text after the number and press Enter. A new number at the same level appears.

7. Change the numbering to the third level by pressing Tab. Type some text after the number and press Enter. A new number at the same level appears.

8. Press Enter again (or Shift+Tab) and the level promotes to the second level.

9. Press Enter again (or Shift+Tab) and the level promotes to the first level.

10. Close the document without saving.

NOTE

The Increase Indent and Decrease Indent buttons in the Paragraph group on the Home tab also will demote and promote the levels.

EXPERT TIP

If pressing Tab, Shift+Tab, or the Enter key does not adjust the numbering levels, then the option Set Left- And First-Indent With Tabs And Backspaces is not enabled (File tab, Options, Proofing, AutoCorrect Options, AutoFormat As You Type).

TIP

Alt+Shift+Left Arrow and Alt+Shift+Right Arrow will also change outline levels.

Customize a Multilevel List

To customize a multilevel list, click the Multilevel List button in the Paragraph group on the Home tab and then choose Define New Multilevel List. You also can right-click on any number in your list and select Adjust List Indents.

The following exercise will show you how to customize a multilevel list to look like the example in Figure 8.9, starting with one of Word's built-in multilevel numbering lists.

NOTE

In a multilevel list, right-clicking on a number and selecting Adjust List Indents opens the Define New Multilevel List dialog box.

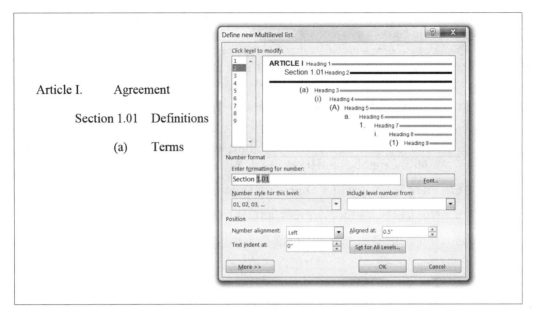

Article I.   Agreement

     Section 1.01   Definitions

          (a)   Terms

Figure 8.9 Example of a customized multilevel list.

Customize a Multilevel List

1. Create a new blank document.

2. Click the Home tab, and in the Paragraph group, click Multilevel List.

3. Select the 1., 1.1, 1.1.1 numbering list in the gallery. The first number is applied to the document.

4. Click Multilevel List again and select Define New Multilevel List (see Figure 8.10).

5. Click the More button in the lower-left corner of the New Multilevel List dialog box to view all available options. In the Click Level to Modify list, Level 1 should already be selected.

6. Click before the number in the Enter Formatting For Number box, type **ARTICLE**, and press the Spacebar.

TIP

The shaded number in the Enter Formatting For Number box is a field code. This field code is what makes the number increment each time a new number is applied. If you inadvertently delete the field code, to reinsert it, click the down arrow in the Number Style for this Level box and select the number style.

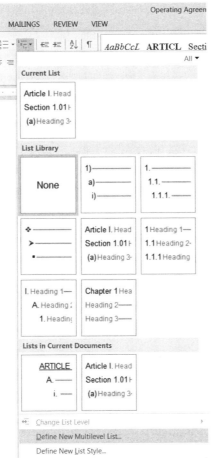

Figure 8.10

Modify the multilevel numbering for all nine levels by selecting Define New Multilevel List.

7. From the Number Style for this Level drop-down list, select I, II, III.

8. In the Text Indent At box, type **0** (zero) to have the text wrap back to the left margin.

9. From the Follow Number With drop-down list, select Space.

NOTE

Follow Number With determines which type of spacing separates the number and following text. Choose from Tab, Space, or Nothing. The default for most outlines is Tab. Choose Nothing if you want to center the number between the margins.

TIP

If you want two spaces to follow the number, type two spaces after the number in the Enter Formatting For Number box and set Follow Number With to Nothing.

10. To change the second level, select 2 from the Click Level to Modify list.

11. Select the Legal Style Numbering check box.

NOTE

When an uppercase Roman number from a previous level is used in the next level, activating Legal Style Numbering will display the number as Arabic instead of Roman. In this example, I.1 changes to 1.1.

CAUTION

Selecting the Legal Style Numbering option will cause the Number Style box to become unavailable. To make changes to Number Style, deselect Legal Style Numbering, make the edits, and then reselect Legal Style Numbering.

12. In the Aligned At box, type **.5"** to set the number one-half inch from the left margin.

13. In the Text Indent At box, type **1"**. This creates one-half inch of space between the number and text.

14. To change the third level, select 3 from the Click Level to Modify list.

15. Select the Legal Style Numbering check box.

16. Set Aligned At to **1"**.

17. Set Text Indent At to **1.5"**.

18. Click OK to apply your changes. Insert a couple of numbered paragraphs.

19. Close the document without saving.

TIP

You can also access the Define New Multilevel List dialog box by right-clicking on any existing number and choosing Adjust List Indents.

CAUTION

Always modify the multilevel list using the Define New Multilevel List dialog box. Be careful not to click the Numbering button on the ribbon to change the number to a different level. You may get inconsistent results when using this method.

Center Text Under the Number

Oftentimes you'll want to center a multilevel list number over a title. Here is an example:

Article I.
Introduction

Centering the number is fairly straightforward; however, when you press Enter after the number, the number disappears. As you have seen before, pressing Enter is an option to turn off numbering. To create the preceding example, rather than pressing Enter after the number, press Shift+Enter and type the title text.

TIP

If the number appears to be off-center, right-click on the number and select Adjust List Indents. In the Define New Multilevel List dialog box, make sure Numbering Alignment is set to Left, the Aligned At and Text Indent At are set to 0 (zero), and the follow Number With is set to Nothing. Center alignment for the entire paragraph (including the number and title text) is set by pressing Ctrl+E or by clicking Center in the Paragraph group on the Home tab.

Link Styles to a Multilevel List

The recommended method for applying a multilevel list in legal documents is by linking each numbered level to a corresponding style. The most common example of this is to link Word's nine built-in Heading styles (Heading 1 through Heading 9) to the nine levels in a multilevel list. You can also link user-defined styles to a multilevel list.

Using a multilevel list that is linked to styles allows you to simultaneously apply formatting to both the number and the text in any paragraph where the style or numbering has been applied. For example, you set up a multilevel list with Level 1 formatted as Article I. If you link that number to a style, you can format the text of the paragraph to include font size 14 pt, bold, centered, or any other formatting. Using this combination of numbering levels and styles will save you a tremendous amount of time otherwise spent formatting each element separately. Linking numbering to styles also makes inserting cross-references and generating a table of contents much easier.

As shown in Figure 8.11, four of the seven multilevel list schemes are linked to Heading styles by default.

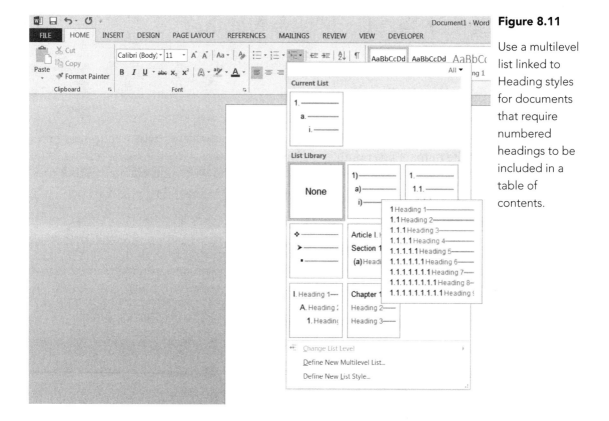

Figure 8.11

Use a multilevel list linked to Heading styles for documents that require numbered headings to be included in a table of contents.

Apply a Multilevel List Linked to Heading Styles

1. Create a new blank document.

2. In the Paragraph group of the Home tab, click Multilevel List.

3. Select the I., A., 1. multilevel list. Note this list is linked to Heading styles. The first number is applied to the document.

NOTE

You can tell which multilevel lists are linked to styles by the word Heading displayed in the preview next to the number.

4. Type **Common Stock** and press Enter.

5. Press Alt+Ctrl+2 to apply the Heading 2 style, which is linked to the second numbering level in the outline.

6. Type **Issuance and Consideration** and press Enter.

7. From the Styles group on the Home tab, click Heading 1 and type **Preferred Stock**.

8. Close the document without saving.

When working with a multilevel list linked to heading styles, you have the benefit of using the Navigation pane because the headings will automatically display. From the View tab, in the Show group, check Navigation Pane. This is a time-saver when working with large documents.

Link User-Defined Styles to a Multilevel List

Once you've had a chance to work with styles, you may want to create your own customized styles and link them to a multilevel list. As shown in Figure 8.12, the Define New Multilevel List dialog box includes the Link Level To Style list that allows you to link specific numbering levels to any user-defined styles you have created.

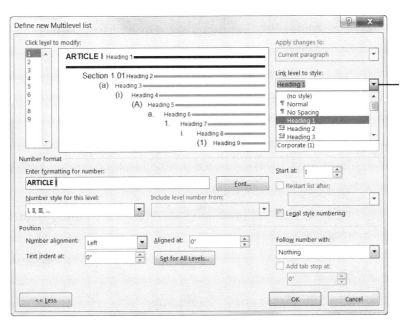

Figure 8.12

Use the Link Level To Style option to link your own styles with a multilevel numbering scheme.

A style can be linked to only one level in the multilevel list. If you have a style linked to a level and then try to link that same style to another level, the first level will show (No Style) in the Link Level To Style box.

Numbering within a Paragraph

Not only can numbering be added to the entire paragraph, as seen with adding a simple or multilevel list, but you can also sequentially number items within the same paragraph using the ListNum field. Here is an example:

The following items are required for the meeting: 1) agenda, 2) employee manuals, 3) training manuals, and 4) access cards.

For more information on Fields, see Chapter 10, "Creating and Distributing Templates."

NOTE

Simple numbered lists, multilevel lists, and ListNum fields can all be cross-referenced in your document. For more information on cross-referencing, see Chapter 11, "Complex Documents."

Insert Numbering within a Paragraph

1. Create a new blank document.

2. Type **The following items are required for the meeting:** and press the Spacebar.

3. Click the Insert tab, and from the Text group, click Quick Parts and then select Field.

4. Select ListNum, click OK, and press the Spacebar.

5. Type **agenda,** and press the Spacebar.

6. Press Alt+Ctrl+L to insert a second ListNum field and press the Spacebar.

7. Type **employee manuals,** and press the Spacebar.

8. Press Alt+Ctrl+L, press the Spacebar, type **training manuals, and**. Press the Spacebar.

9. Press Alt+Ctrl+L, press the Spacebar, and type **access cards** followed by a period.

10. Close the document without saving.

TIP

As an alternative to using the shortcut keys to insert multiple ListNum fields, simply select the first number created by the ListNum field, copy it, and then paste it to insert the fields as needed in the document.

EXPERT TIP

You can add ListNum fields in paragraphs that already contain a heading style with an automatic number. After applying the heading style, followed by the heading text, insert the ListNum field using any method, and Word will automatically insert the next level number as a field. To promote the ListNum field to the previous level, select the field and press Alt+Shift+Left Arrow. To demote the ListNum field to the next level, press Alt+Shift+Right Arrow.

List Styles

A list style is a multilevel list with nine levels and, when applied, the level one number inserts at your cursor location. You can demote and promote the levels the same as with other multilevel lists; however, list styles are not linked to heading styles by default, and it would take some work linking each of the nine levels to the proper headings. To use a list style, you must first create a new list style from the Home tab, in the Paragraph group, click Multilevel List, and then select Define New List Style.

Create a New List Style

To create a new list style, in the Paragraph group of the Home tab, click Multilevel List and select Define New List Style. From the Define New List Style dialog box, specify the formatting you want for each level of numbering.

NOTE

You can also create a list style from the Styles task pane. Click New Style to open the New Style dialog box. From Style Type, select List. Choose the formats for your list style and click OK.

Create a New List Style

1. Create a new blank document.

2. In the Paragraph group of the Home tab, click Multilevel List and select Define New List Style.

3. From the Define New List Style dialog box, as shown in Figure 8.13, type **Agreement** in the Name box.

4. From the Apply Formatting To list, select a level and specify the font, font size, indentation, and number style. Do this for each level.

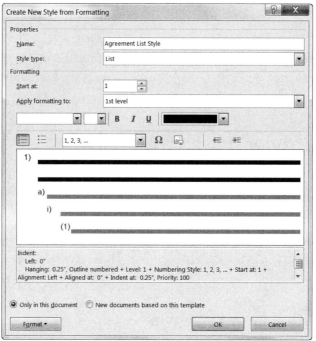

Figure 8.13

List styles can be named, customized, and saved for use in other documents.

NOTE

If you don't specify otherwise, Word will use the font type and size from the document's Normal style.

TIP

To access the Font dialog box for more font formatting options, click the Format button and select Font.

NOTE

To create a custom bulleted list style, follow the same steps as the numbered list. In the Define New List Style dialog box, select Bullets and then customize each level's formatting.

5. Select New Documents Based on This Template to make this list style available in all documents using the attached template.

6. Click OK to close the dialog box.

8. Word automatically applies the first level to the active paragraph. Type some text and press Enter.

7. In the Paragraph group of the Home tab, click Multilevel List, and notice a new List Styles section has been created. Hover your mouse over the new list style to see the name of the style display.

NOTE

Use the Tab key to demote the level and the Shift+Tab keys to promote the level.

TIP

To delete a custom list style, click the dialog box launcher in the Styles group on the Home tab to open the Styles task pane. From the Styles task pane, click the Manage Styles button. From the Edit tab, select the list style and click Delete. This only deletes the list style from the active document. To delete a list style from a template, open the template and delete the list style using the same method.

TROUBLESHOOTING: WHEN A SIMPLE NUMBERED LIST WANTS TO BE A MULTILEVEL LIST

Some numbered lists get started as just a short list of items, but quickly can become what looks like a multilevel list. These types of lists are difficult to work with because they appear to be multilevel lists, but instead they are multiple simple numbered lists.

To reproduce this type of numbering scheme, from the Paragraph group on the Home tab, click Numbering to start a simple numbered list. Type some text and press Enter. You now have two first-level numbered paragraphs. Press Tab, and the numbering level will change to the second level.

At first glance, this appears to be a multilevel list. However, when you right-click in either of the numbered paragraphs and select Adjust List Indents, the Adjust List Indents dialog box opens, as shown in Figure 8.14. This is the dialog box that you see when modifying the indents for a simple numbered list. If you were in a multilevel list, right-clicking on the numbered paragraph and selecting Adjust List Indents would produce the Define New Multilevel List dialog box, as shown in Figure 8.15.

Now position your insertion point in either of the numbered paragraphs, and from the Paragraph group on the Home tab, click Multilevel List. Select Define New Multilevel List, and the Define New Multilevel List dialog box will open. Click OK to close the Define New Multilevel List dialog box. This step transforms the simple numbered list to the multilevel list that displays in the dialog box. Right-click again on either of the numbered paragraphs in your list and select Adjust List Indents. This time, the Define New Multilevel List dialog box opens.

It is recommended that if you are creating a multilevel list, begin by using the Multilevel List command on the Home tab's Paragraph group rather than the Numbering command. However, if you inherit a document that looks like it started off as a simple numbered list, then you know that it is possible to transform it into a multilevel list, as described previously. For an even more robust method of working with a multilevel list, link the numbered list to styles, as described in the section, "Link Styles to a Multilevel List."

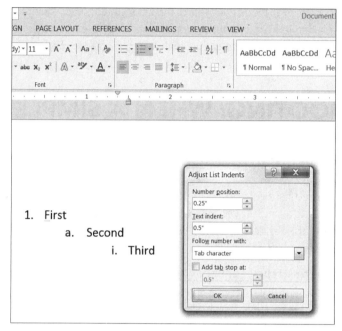

Figure 8.14

Right-click in a simple numbered paragraph and select Adjust List Indents.

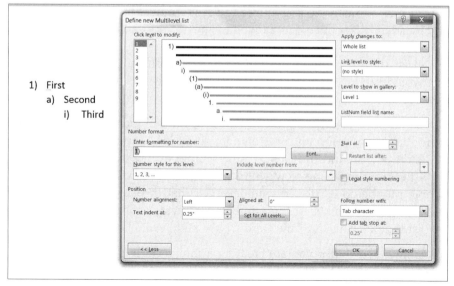

Figure 8.15

Right-click in a multilevel numbered paragraph and select Adjust List Indents.

TABLES IN LEGAL DOCUMENTS

Tables are a key ingredient in almost all documents, and legal documents are no exception. Not only do they help organize large amounts of data, they also are helpful when creating pleading captions, signature blocks, pleading indices, and much more. Tables can include calculations and are useful when you need to parse and align information, as well as sort the data in a logical manner. The best thing about tables in Word is that they are just as easy to modify as they are to create.

This chapter covers how to create, modify, and style your tables in your legal documents.

TABLE OVERVIEW

A table can be defined as a structural container for information. It is comprised of rows and columns that intersect to form cells. The smallest table that you can create is one row, one column—or in other words, a one-cell table. The maximum number of columns in a Word table is 63. The maximum number of rows is 32,767. This adds up to a lot of information that can be placed into every table in your document; 2,064,321 cells per table to be exact.

TIP

If you need more than this, you can use Microsoft Excel. The maximum number of columns in Excel 2013 is 16,384. The maximum number of rows is 1,048,576. This gives you up to 17,179,869,184 cells on every worksheet. And, if you need more than even Excel offers, consider a database such as Access or SQL.

Within each cell, you can include text, numbers, graphics, or even tables nested inside of other tables. Figure 9.1 shows the basic parts and structure of a table, and Table 9.1 provides a description of each table element.

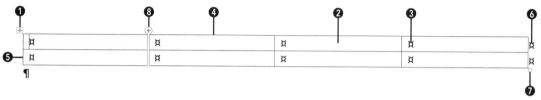

Figure 9.1 The basic elements of a table.

TABLE 9.1—ELEMENTS OF A TABLE		
	TERM	**DESCRIPTION**
1	Table Move Handle	The table move handle is available when you are working in either Print Layout or Web Layout view. When you click within a table, the move handle appears in the upper-left corner at the top of the table. Click on it and drag to a new location on the page to relocate the table.
2	Cell	A cell is formed at the intersection of a row and column. Text, graphics, or other tables can be inserted into a table cell.
3	End-of-Cell Marker	The end-of-cell markers store cell formatting and appear within every cell. These symbols appear on-screen only; they do not print. They display only when hidden characters are visible on-screen by clicking the Show/Hide command in the Paragraph group on the Home tab or by pressing Ctrl+Shift+*.
4	Column	A column is a vertical collection of cells within a table.
5	Row	A row is a horizontal collection of cells within a table.
6	End-of-Row Marker	At the end of each row is an end-of-row marker. This marker stores the row's formatting attributes.
7	Table Resize Handle	The table resize handle allows you to change the size of a table by clicking and dragging. It appears in the lower-right corner of the table when the table is active and in all views except Read Mode. Click and drag when the pointer becomes a diagonal double arrow to change the size of a table.
8	Insert Control	New in Word 2013, the insert control appears when the cursor is positioned between two rows or between two columns. Click the plus sign to insert a new row or a new column.

NOTE

To see the end-of-cell and end-of-row markers, you need to turn on the display of nonprinting characters on-screen. By showing the hidden formatting symbols, you can often troubleshoot errant behavior in your table. For instance, if the formatting in a cell is bold, but shouldn't be, the bold formatting could be stored in the end-of-cell marker, so selecting the end-of-cell marker and then turning off bold removes the bold format from the contents of the cell. Another troublesome culprit stored in the end-of-cell marker is bullets and numbering. To display nonprinting characters, click Show/Hide within the Paragraph group on the Home tab, or press Ctrl+Shift+*.

CREATE A TABLE

There are at least eight ways to create a table. Some of these methods are fun, but some are impractical as well. For instance, you can type a combination of spaces and plus signs in conjunction with Word's AutoFormat As You Type feature to create a table. Another less commonly used method would be to simply draw your table. However, most people prefer to use the Table command on the Insert tab to create new tables.

Drag to Create a Table

If your table is small, such as used in a signature block, and the table is no larger than 10 columns by 8 rows, you can use the Table Grid method. This offers a live preview of the table showing how it would appear in the document, before you even release the mouse. On the Insert tab, click Table in the Tables group. Hover your mouse over the number of rows and columns you want, as shown in Figure 9.2, and then click to insert the table.

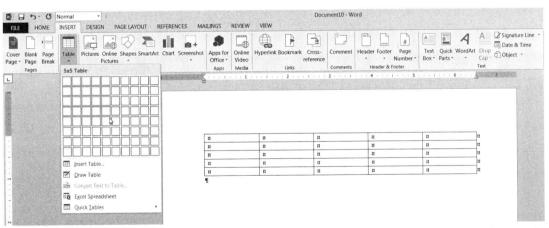

Figure 9.2   Drag your mouse over the grid to select the number of rows and columns needed for the table.

NOTE

When you hover your mouse over the grid, a live preview shows you how the table would look if it were added to the document. If you are not seeing the Live Preview, the preview option may be turned off. To activate Live Preview select File, Options, and from the General tab, choose Enable Live Preview and click OK.

TIP

While using a mouse is typically the easiest way to create a table using the table grid method, you also can use keyboard shortcuts. Press the Alt key and note the keyboard shortcut for the Insert tab (the default is N). Press the N key and then press the T key. This expands the table command. Use the arrow keys on the keyboard to indicate the number of rows and columns for the table and press Enter. If you change your mind about creating the table, just press Esc instead of Enter.

Create a Table with the Table Grid

1. Create a new blank document.

2. In the Tables group on the Insert tab, click Table.

3. Place the mouse pointer over the grid and drag down 3 rows and to the right 2 columns and then click the mouse button to create a 3-row, 2-column table.

4. Press Ctrl+A to select the entire table and press Delete.

5. Leave this document open for the next exercise.

Larger and More Complex Tables

To create a table larger than ten columns and eight rows, or to set additional table options such as Fixed Column Width, AutoFit to Contents or AutoFit to Window use the Insert Table dialog box.

To access the Insert Table dialog box, click Table from the Insert tab and choose Insert Table. The Insert Table dialog box, which is shown in Figure 9.3, is a straightforward way to create new tables or for saving default dimensions for future tables.

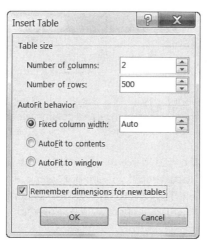

Figure 9.3

Use Insert Table to create larger tables and set options.

Create a Table from within a Dialog Box

1. The file from the previous exercise should still be open.

2. Choose Table from the Insert tab and select Insert Table.

3. In the Number of Columns box, type **2**. The maximum number of columns is 63.

4. In the Number of Rows box, type **500**. The maximum is 32,767.

5. Click OK to insert the table.

6. Press Ctrl+A to select the contents of the entire document and press Delete to remove the newly created table.

7. Choose Table from the Insert tab and select Insert Table.

8. In the Number of Columns box, type **2**.

9. In the Number of Rows box, type **10**.

10. Change the Fixed Column Width to 2". This specifies that both columns will be 2 inches wide.

11. Click OK to insert the table.

12. Close the document without saving.

Fixed Column Width

The Fixed Column Width option in the Insert Table dialog box allows you to limit columns to a specific width. If you enter content that doesn't fit in a cell that has a defined column width, the information will wrap and make the row taller. Select Auto to allow Word to create a table that has equal column widths that fit within your current margins based on the number of columns specified in the dialog box, or click the arrows to increment a tenth of an inch at a time.

EXPERT TIP

If you specify a column width, Word will do its best to respect the dimension; however, it's not always guaranteed. For instance, if you specify a column width of 1" and then type *honorificabulotudinitatipus* (meaning of honor), or any other extremely long word, the column will expand to accommodate that word. The reason this occurs is that there is no place to break the text to fit within the 1" width definition.

AutoFit to Contents

The AutoFit to Contents option automatically expands the width of the columns to accommodate text as it is typed. This is useful if the columns do not have to be fixed at a specific width dimension and you want the table to accommodate the largest width needed. If no text is input into the cell, then AutoFit to Contents will shrink the table until text is added.

AutoFit to Window

The AutoFit to Window option resizes your table automatically as the window size changes, so the table is sized to the current margin definitions. This option is most commonly used when re-creating tables for web pages.

NOTE

You can access the AutoFit command options when creating tables as well as when editing existing tables. To specify or change AutoFit parameters for an existing table, click within the table, and in the Cell Size group on the Layout tab, click AutoFit.

Remember Dimensions for New Tables

If you frequently create the same table structure, you can check the option Remember Dimensions for New Tables. Granted the options for table size and AutoFit behavior don't take much time to set; however, it's still helpful to set the default settings to eliminate repetitive steps. For instance, let's say your job requires you to create numerous pleading index tables that contain the same number of columns and parameters. You can set your defaults for all new tables to match the requirements for the pleading index by enabling the Remember Dimensions for New Tables setting. Even better, if your tables are always similar, you may want to streamline the creation process by setting up the table as a Quick Table.

CREATE A TABLE USING QUICK TABLES

Word Quick Tables provides an efficient method for the creation of common table types that include specific formatting. You will find Quick Tables on the Insert tab, under Table, as shown in Figure 9.4. These tables are actually stored in the Tables building block gallery. When you point to Quick Tables, you'll see a list of built-in table formats that include:

- Calendars (four built-in calendar formats)
- Double Table
- Matrix
- Tabular List
- With Subheads (two built-in subheading formats)

Quick Tables come with predefined formatting as well as sample data as place-holders for your content. Quick Tables range from simple tables to complex.

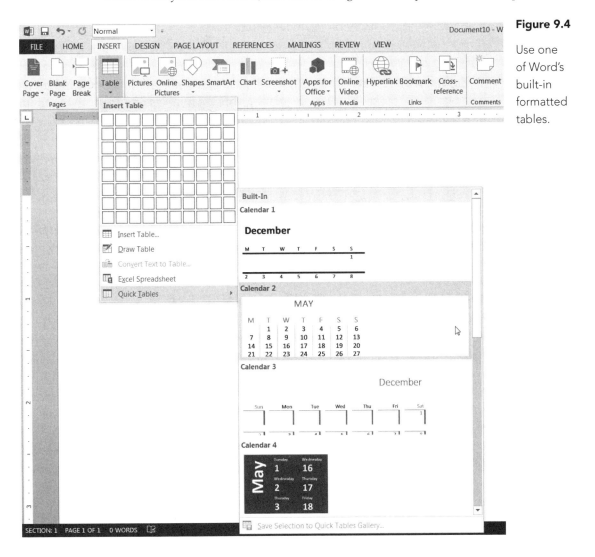

Figure 9.4

Use one of Word's built-in formatted tables.

Create a Table Using Quick Tables

1. Create a new blank document.

2. Choose Table from the Insert tab and select Quick Tables. The submenu displays with a list of built-in entries.

3. Click on the second one in the list, Calendar 2. A calendar created in a table is inserted into the document.

4. Press Ctrl+Z to undo and remove the table.

5. Insert the Matrix or Tabular Quick Table.

6. Close the document without saving.

While you may not use Word's built-in Quick Tables often, don't discount the feature because the real power is in creating your own tables and then saving them as a Quick Table to reuse later.

Save and Insert a Custom Quick Table

You can create, save, and reuse your own Quick Tables to make this feature more useful when adding tables to legal documents. You will find it comes in handy when creating client, administrative, or organizational tables that are specific to the type of work you do.

Create, Save, and Insert a Custom Quick Table

1. Create a new blank document.

2. Choose Table from the Insert tab and select Quick Tables. The submenu displays with a list of built-in entries.

3. Click on the second one in the list, Tabular List. A two-column table is inserted into the document.

4. Replace the text in the first row, first column with **Steps for Utility Patent**.

5. In the first row, second column, type **Activity**.

6. In the first column of the second row, type **Step 1,** and then in the second column, type **Perform Patent Search**.

7. In the first column of the third row, type **Step 2**. In the second column, type **Utility**. This is the type of patent you are filing.

8. In the first column of the fourth row, type **Step 3**. In the second column, type **U.S.** This is the location and filing strategy for the application.

9. In the first column of the fifth row, type **Step 4**. In the second column, type **Prepare for electronic filing**.

10. Click on the table move handle, found in the top-left corner, to select the entire table. The handle appears when you are within a table and working in either Print Layout or Web Layout view.

11. Choose Table from the Insert tab, select Quick Tables, and then choose Save Selection to Quick Tables Gallery. The Create New Building Block dialog box displays.

12. In the Name box, type **Patent Filing Steps**.

13. Accept the other defaults and click OK.

14. Create a blank new document.

15. Choose Table from the Insert tab, select Quick Tables, and then scroll to the bottom of the list. You will see the building block you saved under the General category.

16. Click on the Patent Filing Steps entry to insert it into the document.

17. Close the document, including any exercise documents that might still be open, without saving.

NOTE

The Quick Table created in the preceding exercise is probably one you'll not want to keep. You can delete it quickly by choosing Insert, Quick Table, right-clicking on the unwanted custom table, and choosing Organize and Delete from the shortcut menu. When the Building Blocks Organizer dialog box displays, the building block is selected. Just click Delete to remove the Quick Table building block and click Yes to confirm the deletion.

Draw a Table

Another method for creating a table is to draw the table in your document and then use the Design and Layout Table Options to format and organize the table. This option is useful if you prefer to visually create a table and format as you go. Figure 9.5 shows the Draw Table command.

When you select Draw Table, your cursor changes to a pencil used to draw the table, add rows or columns, draw diagonal lines, split cells, and even insert nested tables (tables inside of other tables). As you drag the mouse, take a quick look at the ruler to see the exact dimensions for the table. When you are finished drawing the table, click the Draw Table command on the Table Tools Design tab (Draw Borders group) to turn off the Draw Table feature. This command acts as a toggle. The Esc key will also turn off Draw Table.

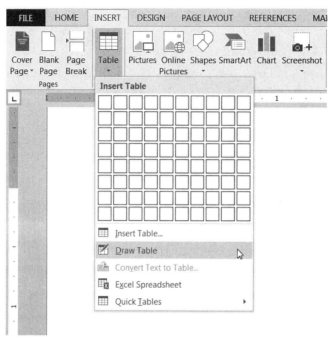

Figure 9.5

Draw a table and then use the Table Tools Design and Layout tabs to format and change the layout of the table.

Draw a Table

1. Create a new blank document.

2. Choose Table from the Insert tab and select Draw Table.

3. Click in the upper-left corner of the window where the table will begin and drag down and to the right to draw a rectangle approximately 4 inches long by 2 inches deep.

4. Draw a vertical line down the center of the cell to divide the table into two cells.

5. Draw more lines to separate the table even further, creating rows and columns.

6. Draw a diagonal line within a cell.

7. In the Borders group of the Table Tools Design tab, click the Borders down arrow and choose Draw Table to toggle off drawing mode. Alternatively, you can just press Esc.

8. Close the document without saving.

Convert Text to a Table

If information exists elsewhere, it's wasted effort to retype it. Instead, you quickly can convert text to a table, or a table to text. You can simply select existing text in your document and then convert it into a table by choosing Table from the Table group on the Insert tab and selecting Convert Text to Table to finish the conversion process.

After you select the text and go into the Convert Text to Table dialog box, Word will try to determine what character is separating the columns—whether it is a paragraph, comma, or tab. You also can designate the character separating the text so Word will know where to insert the column boundaries. The separator, also known as the delimiter, used must be consistent in order for Word to know how to parse the data into table cells.

Convert Existing Text to a Table

1. Create a new blank document, type your first name, press Tab, and then type your last name.

2. Press Enter and type another first name, press Tab, and type a last name. As you can see, Tab characters are being used to separate the data for the columns, and each record or row in this case is identified by pressing Enter and moving to a new line.

3. Select the entire list beginning with the first name through all other names in the list.

4. Click Table in the Tables group on the Insert tab and choose Convert Text to Table. The Convert Text to Table dialog box appears, as shown in Figure 9.6.

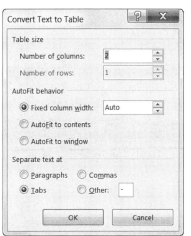

Figure 9.6

Convert existing text into a table.

5. Notice that the Number of Columns and Number of Rows have automatically been prefilled. Also notice that Tabs is automatically selected as the delimiter under Separate Text At. Click OK. The text is converted into a two-column table.

6. To convert the table back to text, click within the table, and on the Table Tools Layout tab, in the Data group, click Convert to Text. Click OK to confirm table-to-text conversion.

7. Close the document without saving.

EXPERT TIP

If you need to manipulate existing data prior to using it in Word, you may want to consider using a program such as Microsoft Excel. For instance, let's say you have a list of attorneys at your firm and you need to place each attorney's name (first, middle if applicable, and last) in adjoining, but separate, cells rather than having the attorney's full name in one cell. Within Excel, you can select the cells that contain the names, select the Data tab, and in the Data Tools group, click Text to Columns. Accept the default options if the text is separated by a space, or follow the instructions within the dialog box to work with and parse your data, before copying the results and pasting them into a Word table.

Create a Table from Excel Data

If information exists in another application, such as Microsoft Excel, before retyping it in Word, you can attempt to copy and paste it into Word and see how well it translates.

Open the other application, select the range of data, and then copy it. Return to Word and paste the information into the document.

NOTE

When you copy data from Excel and paste it into Word, you will see additional options on the Paste Options button below the pasted data. If this button does not appear, the feature may need to be enabled by choosing Options from the File tab. On the Advanced tab, in the Cut, Copy and Paste section of the dialog box, check the box next to Show Paste Options Button When Content is Pasted and click OK. An example of the Paste Options button is shown in Figure 9.7.

Title	First Name	Last Name	Company
Mr.	Joshua	Snug	ABC Industries
Ms.	Kathryn	Bug	DEF Company
Ms.	Natalie	Rug	GHI LLP

Figure 9.7

The Paste Options button provides directives for how content should be pasted and changes to show available options based on what is being pasted.

When you choose Keep Source Formatting, the pasted information will appear as it did in Microsoft Excel. Use Destination Styles will apply your default table format to the information. The difference between Link & Keep Source formatting and Link & Use Destination Styles is that they both establish a link to the original spreadsheet where the data exists; however, when the information is pasted into the Word table, a Word table format is applied. When using the link options, if the information is updated in the Excel worksheet, a change is made to the underlying Word document to reflect that change. The remaining options include Paste as Picture, where the table data converts to a picture, and Keep Text Only, which strips out the formatting and typically inserts a tab between values.

CAUTION

When information copied and pasted from another program maintains a link to the original source, there is a risk of accidental disclosure through metadata. For more information on metadata, see Chapter 12, "Collaboration."

NOTE

In general, you cannot use the linking feature between two separate files saved in the document management system.

EXPERT TIP

If you're curious what the Excel information will look like if pasted into a Word document or want to see which paste options are available when pasting the information in Word, rather than simply pasting the information, in the Clipboard group on the Home tab, click the down arrow beneath Paste. Hover over each paste option to see how the information will appear in the document—all without having to paste.

Create a Table by Inserting an Excel Spreadsheet

Let's face it, when it comes to calculations and mathematical functions, Word tables don't come close to the capabilities available in Excel. Fortunately, it's easy to insert (embed) a spreadsheet in a document, which brings all of Excel's power directly into Word. Click the Table button on the Insert tab and select the option to insert an Excel Spreadsheet. This is useful for those times when you want to utilize the full power of Microsoft Excel formulas, functions, and sorting capabilities, but want to present the information in a Word document.

When you insert an Excel spreadsheet into a Word document, you are creating an OLE object, which stands for Object Linking and Embedding. Double-click on the Excel object in the Word document to activate the object and display Excel's tabs and ribbon. Click outside of the Excel object (into the Word document itself), and the focus changes to display Word's tabs and ribbon functionality.

CAUTION

Be careful when embedding an Excel worksheet into a Word document as all worksheet tabs are visible even though only one tab displays in the Word document. If you have confidential information on another tab, anyone with access to the Word document can expose the other worksheet tabs by double-clicking the table and selecting one of the other tabs.

EXPERT TIP

Besides simple mathematical equations and formulas in Word, you'll find Excel to be much more powerful for crunching numbers or even performing basic calculations. For instance, in Word, you might resort to creating bookmarks to sum totals from different tables or areas in the document, or to add noncontiguous cell values. Fortunately, this is much easier to accomplish in Excel. Because Excel has an assigned cell address for each cell (e.g., A1, C2, Z22), you can use any cell address in your calculations. Excel also updates formula changes automatically unlike calculations in Word tables.

Another compelling reason to use Excel for some of your tables is to take advantage of Excel's powerful features, such as Flash Fill. Flash Fill looks for similar patterns and tries to fill in data based on the placement in relation to other data, including its format. Overall, the beauty of being able to embed an Excel spreadsheet directly into a Word document demonstrates how well Microsoft Office applications work together.

Create a Table with AutoFormat As You Type

Just for fun, because it's not practical to create tables in this manner when working on legal documents, you can use AutoFormat As You Type to create tables. Word recognizes combinations of plus signs (+) and hyphens (-), or spaces (using the Spacebar) to quickly create a one-row table with one or more columns. In an empty paragraph, type plus signs where the columns should begin and end and hyphens for the number of spaces in between. Once you press Enter, the table is created.

To access the AutoFormat as You Type options, select Options from the File tab, select Proofing, and then click AutoCorrect Options. On the AutoFormat As You Type tab, select or clear the Tables option, depending on the behavior you want to set.

Most people working in the legal industry tend to pick and choose which Auto-Format as You Type behavior they want enabled. This Tables option doesn't typically cause any problems, but it's up to the individual's preference whether or not to keep it enabled. While this option is enabled by default, your firm may have disabled some of the AutoFormat as You Type options when it deployed Microsoft Office.

NESTED TABLES

Tables can be nested within other tables. This feature comes in handy when one cell of a larger table requires more complex information and formatting than a single cell area can accommodate. That said, you may be more likely to see people nesting tables by accident rather than on purpose.

To nest a table, just click inside of a cell and follow any of the methods previously discussed for inserting a table. For instance, within a table cell, click Table from the Insert tab and Insert table. The newly created table is inserted into the active cell. If you've ever seen a Matryoshka doll, which is a doll nested inside another, and repeats with each doll getting smaller, it's the same concept.

NOTE

Unless you are a Word expert, try to use nested tables sparingly. They can be difficult to maintain, and if you share documents, chances are others won't know how to properly work with them.

TABLE NAVIGATION AND TRICKS

While Word 2013 is more visual than ever, making it easier to use, there are a number of helpful keyboard shortcuts for navigating a table. Table 9.2 lists keyboard shortcuts for working with tables.

TABLE 9.2—TABLE NAVIGATION KEYBOARD SHORTCUTS

PRESS THIS	TO DO THIS
Tab	Move to the next cell.
Shift+Tab	Move to the preceding cell.
Alt+Home	Move to the first cell in a row.
Alt+End	Move to the last cell in a row.
Alt+Page Up	Move to the first cell in a column.
Alt+Page Down	Move to the last cell in a column.
Shift+Left Arrow or Right Arrow	Select character by character in the current cell and then select the entire adjacent cell.
Shift+Up Arrow or Down Arrow	Select text line by line in the current cell and then select the entire adjacent cell.
F8, Up Arrow or Down Arrow	Select the current cell and the cell above or below. (Press the Esc key to end the selection.)
F8, Left Arrow or Right Arrow	Select the characters in the current cell and then all adjacent cells. (Press the Esc key to end the selection.)
Alt+5 (numeric keypad)	Select the entire table. (The Num Lock key must be turned off.)
Shift+End	Selects the current table cell. Continue to repeat this key combination to continue selecting cells, rows, and columns in the table.
Alt+Shift+Up Arrow	Move selected row up one position.
Alt+Shift+Down Arrow	Move selected row down one position.
Shift+Delete	If an entire column is selected, pressing this combination will delete the entire column. If a row is selected, it will delete the entire active row as well.
Ctrl+Tab	Inserts a tab character in the active cell.
Tab	If you are in the last cell of a table, pressing Tab adds a new row to the table.

EXPERT TIP

If you want to add text above a table that starts at the beginning of the document, press Ctrl+Home to move your insertion point to the top of the document and within the first cell of the table and then press Enter. This inserts a paragraph mark above the table where you can add a heading, title, or introductory text before the table.

You can also add indents and set tabs in table cells. Just remember to set each tab using the ruler or Tabs dialog box, and when you are within the cell, press Ctrl+Tab to move to the tab stop in the active cell.

WORKING WITH THE ENTIRE TABLE

Tables sit on top of the document layer, and as such, can be moved or manipulated similarly to a graphic object. A table move handle appears when you work in Print Layout or Web Layout view and click within the table. This handle allows you to drag the table to a new location in the document. The table move handle also provides a quick and easy way to select the entire table. The move handle, as shown in Figure 9.8, is located at the top-left corner of the table.

Move handle

Title	First Name	Last Name	Company
Mr.	Joshua	Snug	ABC Industries
Ms.	Kathryn	Bug	DEF Company
Ms.	Natalie	Rug	GHI LLP

Figure 9.8

The move handle is a tool designed for repositioning a table.

To move the table, click within the table, and then click and drag the move handle. Release the mouse button to relocate the table.

EXPERT TIP

Once you drag a table using the move handle, the table's layout changes to floating, and the text is set to wrap around the table. If this causes problems within your document, you can turn off the text wrapping. The most notable indication is that the header row does not repeat and that is because the table was probably inadvertently moved. From the Tables group on the Table Tools Layout tab, click Properties. On the Table tab, under Text Wrapping, select None.

Table Tools Design Tab

After a table is created, you can type text, insert graphics, or insert another table within the table cells. Word makes this easier with the consolidated table tools.

When your cursor is located within a table, the table is considered active. This also activates the Table Tools Design and Layout tabs. These tabs are contextual, meaning they are active only when the cursor is located within a table. These two tabs include all of the option settings, formatting and styles, and table properties that you need to work with tables. The Design tab is shown in Figure 9.9, and its options are described in Table 9.3.

Figure 9.9   When a table is active, the Table Tools contextual tabs display.

TIP

In Word 2013, the Draw Table and Eraser tools have been relocated to the Layout tab. The functionality is the same, it's just the location that has changed. The Draw Table command is still found under Borders, as in the previous version of Word.

The Design tab includes commands for formatting tables. Table 9.3 lists each command as well as a description of its function.

TABLE 9.3—DESCRIPTIONS OF COMMANDS ON THE TABLE TOOLS DESIGN TAB	
COMMAND	**DESCRIPTION**
Header Row	Displays special formatting for the first row in a table.
Total Row	Displays special formatting for the last row in a table.
Banded Rows	Shading is applied to alternate rows. This is common in accounting paper and to any table that requires different formatting for alternating rows.
First Column	Displays special formatting for the first column in a table.
Last Column	Displays special formatting for the last column in a table.
Banded Columns	Shading is applied to alternating columns.
Table Styles	Choose from existing table styles to format the entire table. Click the More button in the Table Styles group to display the full gallery of table styles or to create, clear, or modify a style.
Shading	Apply shading in the selected or active cells. Click the drop-down arrows to select a color or to specify No Color.
Border Styles	Select a preset border from the Theme Borders list. Click Border Sampler to copy the formats of an existing border and then use the Border Painter to paste the border formatting. This feature is new in Word 2013.
Line Style	Select a border line style from the drop-down list.
Line Weight	Specify the thickness of the border line.
Pen Color	Specify a color for the border.
Borders	Displays a drop-down menu with all the border formatting options available for tables, including View Gridlines.
Border Painter	Choose a border style, line style, line weight, and/or pen color, and then use the Border Painter to apply to specific borders. This feature is new in Word 2013.

Table Styles

Table styles allow you to change the format of your table quickly by applying pre-designed formatting. Table styles are similar to other types of styles in their application; you find the appropriate style and apply it. You also can modify it or create an entirely new style based on it.

Similar to working with normal styles, direct formatting also can be applied on top of the table style, which at times can create confusion. Fortunately, you can right-click on a table style in the gallery and choose to apply the style and clear direct formatting, if necessary. This option strips out the direct formatting, applying the original table style before any direct formatting was applied.

Built-In Table Styles

Word shows a sampling of table styles in the Table Styles gallery located on the Table Tools Design tab. When your insertion point is in a table, you can hover with the mouse over the table styles to see a live preview of how each style will affect the look of your table in the document. If you apply the table style, you apply to the table the formatting attributes that are stored in the style. To view more table styles, click the More button (downward-pointing arrow) to the right of the Table Styles gallery, as shown in Figure 9.10.

Figure 9.10 Expand the More button in the Table Style gallery to show all available table styles.

Apply Styles to a Table

1. Create a new blank document and insert a new 2-column, 3-row table. Add some text in the first row as a header row. Click within the table to activate it, if necessary.

2. With your cursor inside the table, click on the Table Tools Design tab and hover your mouse (without clicking) over several of the styles that appear in the Table Styles gallery. Notice how your table formatting changes to match each style without applying it.

3. In the Table Styles gallery, click the first down-pointing arrow to display the next row of available table styles. You can use up or down arrows to keep the gallery small and still see the live preview.

4. In the Table Styles gallery, click the More button to display all style choices. Using the More button is a great way to see all available styles at one time.

5. In the display of all table styles, in the second row of styles located in the Grid Tables category, click on the style called Grid Table 3–Accent 1 (second column).

6. Keep this document open for the next exercise.

Modify Table Styles

If a style is close to what you want but still not perfect, you can apply the style and then modify it to fine-tune the format. The style can be modified by clicking the More button in the Table Styles group and selecting Modify Table Style, or you can right-click on the style and choose Modify Table Style, as shown in Figure 9.11. Either option displays the Modify Style dialog box where you can make changes.

Figure 9.11

A quick way to modify the style is to right-click on the style and choose Modify Table Style.

Modifying a Table Style

1. The exercise from the previous exercise should still be open.

2. Click the More button in the Table Styles group and choose Modify Table Style from the drop-down list.

3. Click Cancel.

4. Right-click on the applied table style (Grid Table 3–Accent 1) in the Table Styles gallery and choose Modify Table Style from the shortcut menu. This also displays the Modify Style dialog box, as shown in Figure 9.12.

5. Click the drop-down arrow next to Apply Formatting To and select Header Row.

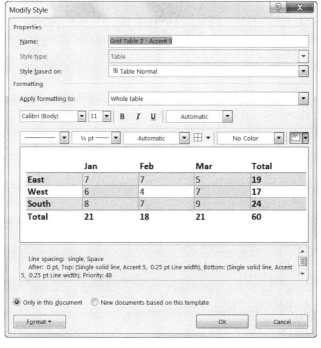

Figure 9.12

Modify the formatting of a table style through the Modify Style dialog box.

6. Click the Italic button on the dialog box and change the text alignment to Align Center. This applies italic formatting to your header row and centers the text, but only in the header row.

7. In the Apply Formatting To drop-down list, select Whole Table.

8. Change the font to Arial, 16 point.

9. Click the Format button to review the other options that can be modified for the applied style.

10. Click OK to modify the style and close the dialog box.

11. Close the document without saving.

Shortcut Menu

You may have noticed that you can right-click on a style and then choose to modify it from the shortcut menu. You also can apply or clear formatting, create or delete styles, or set the default. The shortcut menu provides easy access to many aspects of styles.

Using the Shortcut Menu to Work with Styles

1. Create a new blank document and insert a table with four columns and four rows.

2. In the first column of the first row, type **Name**, press Tab, and type **Location**. Press Tab and type **RSVP**, and then press Tab and type **Notes**.

3. Select the first row of the table and apply Bold, Italic, and Center formats.

4. Select the Table Tools Design tab and right-click on any style listed in the Table Styles gallery. Choose Apply (and Clear Formatting). Note that this option does not clear the italic and center formatting; however, the bold format has been removed.

5. Press Ctrl+Z to undo.

6. Right-click on another table style and choose Apply and Maintain Formatting. Note that this does not maintain all of the formatting—especially with respect to bold format.

7. Right-click on the same table style again, but this time choose Set As Default. You can set the table style as your default for all new tables created. Figure 9.13 shows how to set table style defaults. This option is more powerful than the similarly worded option for creating tables because more formatting is saved and retained as the default table style.

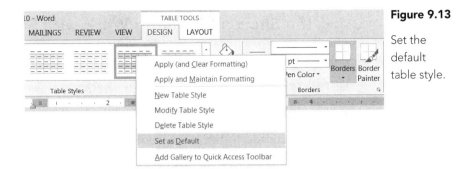

Figure 9.13

Set the default table style.

8. Click Cancel to close the dialog box without changing the default table style.

9. Close the document without saving.

NOTE

When you set a table style as a default, you have a choice to make it the default for the active document only or for all documents based on the attached template. Either choice will automatically apply the new default table style using any table insertion methods.

Create a Table Style

It's one thing to apply a predefined style that Microsoft has created for you and another thing to create your own. Keep in mind that the real power of this feature resides in the ability to create your own table styles to streamline the formatting process when working with tables. Table styles allow you to specify and tweak how a table should appear with respect to borders, shading, table properties, and other formatting. After a table style is created, it can be applied to other tables in the same document or to tables in other documents, which results in consistent-looking tables throughout all documents for corporate branding purposes.

Not only can you control the overall table format, you can set specific formats for a header or end row, certain columns, and even for individual cells.

NOTE

As is true with List styles, table styles cannot be created by example and do not show in the Styles task pane.

Using the Shortcut Menu to Work with Styles

1. Create a new blank document.

2. Press the keyboard shortcut Alt+Ctrl+Shift+S to open the Styles task pane.

3. Click the New Style button located at the bottom of the Styles task pane.

4. Type **Pleading Index** in the Name field.

5. From the Style Type drop-down list, select Table. Figure 9.14 shows the dialog box used for creating a style based on formatting.

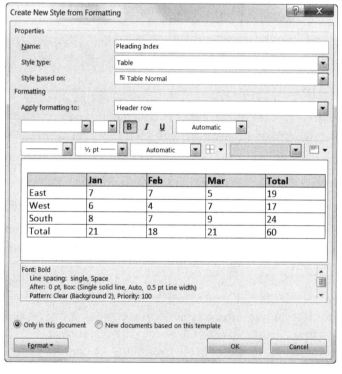

Figure 9.14

Apply font, color, borders, alignment, and other formatting to your table style.

6. Select a double-line format from the Line Style drop-down list.

7. Click the drop-down arrow next to the Borders button and choose Outside Borders to apply the double-line format to the outside border only.

8. Select the single-line format from the Line Style drop-down list.

9. Choose Inside Borders from the Borders list.

10. In the Apply Formatting To section, select Header Row from the list.

11. Click Bold, and from the Fill Color drop-down list, select a light-gray fill color.

12. Click the Format button and choose Table Properties. The Table Properties dialog box opens, as shown in Figure 9.15.

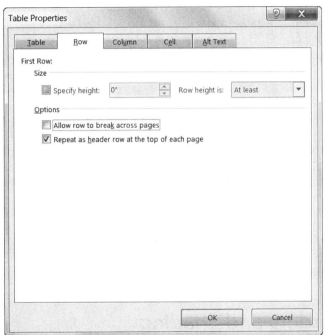

Figure 9.15

The Table Properties dialog box allows you to set properties for the table, row, column, or cell.

13. On the Row tab, select Repeat as Header Row at the Top of Each Page and click OK.

14. Select New Documents Based on this Template to save this style in the attached template and click OK.

15. Open the Apply Styles task pane (Ctrl+Shift+S), begin typing **Pleading Index** until the name appears, and then press Enter to apply. The Insert Table dialog box displays, as shown in Figure 9.16.

Figure 9.16

After applying a table style, choose the table size by entering the values in the Insert Table dialog box.

16. In the Number of Columns box, type **2**. In the Number of Rows box, type **20**.

17. Click OK. The table is inserted into the document with the properties of the Pleading Index style.

18. Close the document without saving.

NOTE

To apply the new table style to an existing table, on the Table Tools Design tab, in the Table Styles group, click the More button to the right of the gallery, and under Custom, select the new table style.

Borders and Shading

The Table Tools Design tab includes options to set table borders and shading; in fact, there are five unique commands on the ribbon that affect borders and shading. They are Shading, Borders, Line Style, Line Weight, and Pen Color.

Border Styles and Border Painter

The default border will have a single-line style, with a one-half point border width, and Automatic is set as the color. In the Borders group on the Table Tools Design tab, click the lower half of the Border Styles split button and select a different border style with various changes in line style, width, and color, as shown in Figure 9.17.

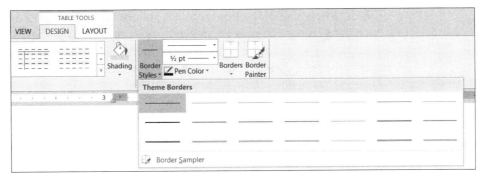

Figure 9.17   Choose from a selection of Border styles.

As soon as you select a border style, the Border Painter button becomes available, as shown in Figure 9.18, and your cursor changes to a pen. Click a border to apply the selected border style.

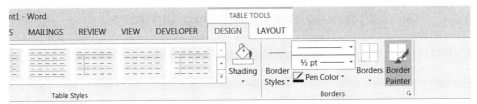

Figure 9.18   The Border Painter will apply the border formats to selected borders.

After you select a border style, you can add formats in addition to or in place of the border style by making changes to the line style, width, or color, all of which are found in the Borders group on the Table Tools Design tab.

When you use the Border Painter to apply the formatting to selected borders, click the lower half of the Border Styles split button and notice the Recently Used Borders section has been created.

NOTE

If you're familiar with the Format Painter tool available in the Clipboard group on the Home tab, you might be aware that double-clicking the button keeps the feature enabled so formats can be applied to multiple items until you turn off the feature. This is not the case with Border Painter. When the Border Painter is enabled, it stays active until you turn the feature off. There is no need to double-click.

Click the lower half of the Border Styles split button, choose Border Sampler, and notice your cursor changes to an eyedropper, as shown in Figure 9.19. Click the border that you would like to copy the formatting from. Now, click another border to paste that formatting to, as shown in Figure 9.19. Continue to paste the border formatting, as needed.

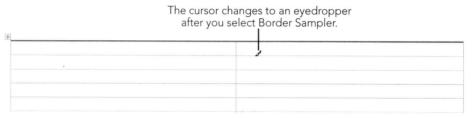

The cursor changes to an eyedropper
after you select Border Sampler.

Figure 9.19 Paste the border formatting.

Set Borders and Shading Options

1. Create a new blank document and insert a 4-column, 10-row table.

2. In the Borders group on the Table Tools Design tab, click the lower half of the Border Styles button and choose Single Solid Line 1½ Pt. Notice that your mouse changes to a pen.

3. Click all of the border lines within the first row to paste the border style.

4. In the Borders group on the Table Tools Design tab, click Border Painter to toggle off the painting mode.

5. Select the first row of the table, and in the Table Styles group on the Table Tools Design tab, click the lower half of the Shading split button and choose one of the gray-shaded colors.

6. Select the last row of the table, and in the Table Styles group on the Table Tools Design tab, click the upper half of the Shading split button. This is the same color selected in the previous step.

7. In the Borders group on the Table Tools Design tab, click the lower half of the Border Styles button and choose Border Sampler. Notice your mouse changes to an eyedropper.

8. Click one of the borders in the first row that you applied in Step 2. Notice that your mouse changes to a pen.

9. Click and drag across the top border of the entire last row.

10. In the Borders group, click the Border Painter button to toggle off painting.

11. Click in a cell that contains shading. In the Table Styles group, click the lower half of the Shading split button and choose No Color.

12. In the Borders group, click the lower half of the Borders button. This displays a list of border options including View Gridlines and Borders and Shading, which displays the Borders and Shading dialog box.

13. In the Borders group, click the Pen Color drop-down arrow and choose a color. Notice that your mouse changes to a pen and that the line style and width remain unchanged.

14. Click a border line to apply a new color to the border line. Press Esc to toggle off the Border Painter button.

15. Keep this document open for the next exercise.

TABLE TOOLS LAYOUT TAB

The Layout tab is shown in Figure 9.20, and its options are described in Table 9.4.

Figure 9.20   When a table is active, the Table Tools Layout tab displays.

Selecting Table Elements

You probably find it easy to use the mouse to select parts of a table; however, some people who are less comfortable with tables, or even using a mouse, may find it easier to use the Select command. On the Table Tools Layout tab, click Select in the Table group.

TABLE 9.4—DESCRIPTION OF COMMANDS ON THE TABLE TOOLS LAYOUT TAB

COMMAND	DESCRIPTION
Select	Click to select the cell, column, row, or table.
View Gridlines	Toggle on or off gridlines that surround the table. Unlike borders, gridlines are not designed to print.
Properties	Displays the Table Properties dialog box.
Draw Table	Changes the cursor to enable drawing border lines in a table by clicking and dragging the mouse. Draw horizontal borders for rows and vertical borders for columns.
Eraser	Erases border lines from the table.
Delete	Click to delete cells, columns, rows, or table.
Insert Above	Inserts a new row above the active row.
Insert Below	Inserts a new row below the active row.
Insert Left	Inserts a new column to the left of the active column.
Insert Right	Inserts a new column to the right of the active column.
Merge Cells	Merges any selected cells into one cell.
Split Cells	Splits the selected cells into multiple new cells.
Split Table	Divides the table into two separate tables.
AutoFit	Controls how text is resized into columns. Choose from AutoFit Contents, AutoFit Window, or Fixed Column Width.
Height	Specifies the row height for the active cells/rows.
Width	Specifies the column width for the active cells/columns.
Distribute Rows	Applies the same row height to selected rows.
Distribute Columns	Applies the same column width to selected columns.
Alignment Buttons (9)	These nine buttons apply vertical and horizontal alignment of text within the selected cells.
Text Direction	Changes the direction of the text within the selected cells.
Cell Margins	Displays a subset of the Table Options dialog box where you can change the size and control options related to cell formatting.
Sort	Displays the Sort dialog box where you can sort information in the table.
Repeat Header Rows	Repeats the header row(s) at the beginning of each new page of the continuous table.
Convert to Text	Converts a table to text.
Formula	Displays the Formula dialog box where you can build a formula with mathematical or logic equations.

View Gridlines

Gridlines show the table structure; in other words, where the rows and columns meet as well as the outline of the table. Their purpose is to assist with alignment. Gridlines are not borders, and they do not print by default. The View Gridlines command in the Table group toggles gridlines on and off.

Sometimes people may confuse gridlines with borders. If you see what looks like table borders on the screen, but they do not print, you are probably viewing gridlines.

Table Properties

Before the ribbon was introduced, most post-creation table formatting took place in the Table Properties dialog box. The Properties command displays the Table Properties dialog box where you can fine-tune settings for the table, controlling cell, row, column, and table properties all in one location.

Table Tab

The Table tab of the Table Properties dialog box includes options for Size, Alignment, Text Wrapping, Positioning, Borders and Shading, and Options.

- **Preferred Width**. Specify the exact size of the table. This is useful if the entire table needs to be no greater or no smaller than a specific size. Your preferred width can be measured in unit measurements of either inches or percentages.

NOTE

If you know approximately how much of the page should be occupied by the table, you can use a percentage as the Preferred Width. For instance, if you specify 50 percent, the table will occupy approximately one-half of the page, regardless of whether the page orientation or margins change. This can be a real time-saver when working with documents that require a specific layout, such as a form.

- **Alignment**. Set the alignment for the table (not the text in the table) here. Figure 9.21 shows different table alignments applied. You also can specify an indent for the table in this section.

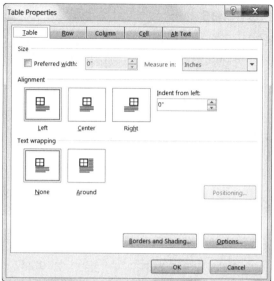

Figure 9.21

Example of left, right, and centered table alignment.

- **Text Wrapping**. This setting allows you to control text position in relation to the table. The Around option enables text wrapping around the table.

- **Positioning**. Specify the table position relative to the column, margin, or page (see Figure 9.22). This also allows you to specify the distance from the surrounding text.

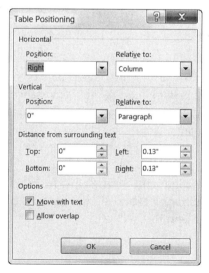

Figure 9.22

The Table Positioning dialog box.

- **Borders and Shading**. Displays the Borders and Shading dialog box.

- **Options**. Displays the Table Options dialog box where you can set options such as the default cell margins, cell padding, or space between cells in the table, and to Automatically Resize to Fit Contents. The Table Options dialog box is shown in Figure 9.23.

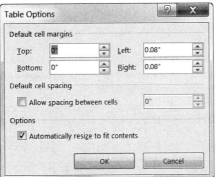

Figure 9.23

Adjust table options in this dialog box.

- **Cell Spacing**. By default, table cells are directly adjacent to one another. If you need extra space (sometimes called padding) between cells, you can adjust the cell spacing.

- **Automatically Resize to Fit Contents**. Resize the table when text is entered that is greater than the width of the column.

Row Tab

The Row tab of the Table Properties dialog box includes options for Size, Alignment, Text Wrapping, Positioning, Borders and Shading, and Options. This tab is shown in Figure 9.24.

- **Specify Height**. Specify the exact height of the row. It's important to note that if you set your row height to an exact number and this number is less than what is necessary to display the contents, information can be cut off or not appear at all in the row.

- **Allow Row to Break Across Pages**. If you have a large amount of information in one cell/row, the row may split across two pages. The default for Word tables is to allow rows to break across pages.

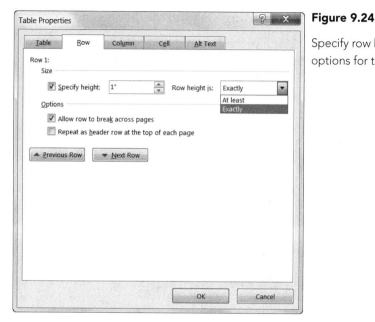

Figure 9.24

Specify row height and other options for the row.

NOTE

To prevent text in a row at the bottom of the page from splitting onto the next page, select the entire table, and on the Layout tab, click Properties, Row tab, and uncheck the Allow Rows To Break Across Pages option. If you add new rows to the table after clearing this option, the new rows will also have this formatting applied.

- **Repeat as Header Row at the Top of Each Page**. If your table includes a header and the table spans more than a single page, you can set header rows to repeat at the top of subsequent pages.

NOTE

You can select more than one row as a heading, but you must include the first row of the table in the heading selection.

CAUTION

If you insert a manual page break (Ctrl+Enter) in a table, Word does not repeat the header row because the single table is split into two tables.

Column Tab

The Column tab of the Table Properties dialog box includes only one option, allowing you to specify the width of the column.

Cell Tab

The Cell tab of the Table Properties dialog box includes options for Size and Vertical Alignment. There is also an Options button, which displays the Cell Options dialog box where you can set different cell margins and choose to wrap text in the cell and/or fit the text to the size of the cell.

Alt Text Tab

Introduced in Word 2010, the Alt Text tab provides a place to input a title and description. Alternative text will display when the table is loading on a web page. Search engines also use the alternative text to find web pages and to assist people with visual or cognitive impairments.

Select, View Gridlines, and Set Table Properties

1. The document from the previous exercise should still be open. Click in any cell within the table.

2. In the Table group on the Table Tools Layout tab, click Properties and select the Table tab.

3. Set the Preferred Width to 3" and click OK.

4. Redisplay the Table Properties dialog box and change the Preferred Width to 5" and click OK. Note that when you change this option, the table size changes.

5. Right-click on the table and choose Table Properties from the shortcut menu. Select the Table tab, if necessary.

6. Under Alignment, select Center and click OK.

7. Now add some text above and below the table to see that the table is centered from the surrounding text.

8. Redisplay the Table Properties dialog box and select the Table tab.

9. Set Text Wrapping to Around. Click the Positioning button and the Table Positioning dialog box opens, allowing you to set the distance and position of the table to the text.

10. Under Distance From Surrounding Text, change the Top, Bottom, Left, and Right values to .15" and click OK.

11. On the Table tab, click Options.

12. Select Allow Spacing Between Cells and type **.2"** and then click OK.

13.   Click OK again to close the Table Properties dialog box.

14.   Close the document without saving.

If you set Text Wrapping for the table, you will not be able to select the row using the Selection bar. This is the result of Word treating the table as a floating graphic.

Draw Table

In the Draw group of the Table Tools Layout tab, click Draw Table, and the cursor changes to a pencil allowing you to draw border lines on an existing table or to draw a new table.

Eraser

In the Draw group of the Table Tools Layout tab, click Eraser and then click a border line to quickly merge two cells.

Deleting Table Components

If you need to delete part of the structure of the table—or even the table itself, just click in the area that should be removed and use the Delete command in the Rows & Columns group of the Table Tools Layout tab. Options include Delete Cells, Delete Columns, Delete Rows, and Delete Table.

While it does require quite a few key combinations, you can delete elements of the table or the table itself by pressing a combination of shortcut keys. For instance, press Alt+J, L, D, R to delete the active row.

Inserting Rows and Columns

The Rows & Columns group on the Table Tools Layout tab includes options to insert rows and columns. You can choose to insert the row above or below the active row(s), and the column to the left or right of the active column(s).

Inserting Rows and Columns Using the Insert Control

Click the Insert Control, which appears when you hover your insertion point to the left of two existing rows or just above two existing columns. Click the plus sign to insert a new row or column into your table.

Delete and Insert Options Using the Mini Toolbar

New in Word 2013, right-click within the table and choose either the Insert or the Delete command from the Mini toolbar (see Figure 9.25). You will notice the Mini toolbar offers the same options as the Table Tools Layout tab.

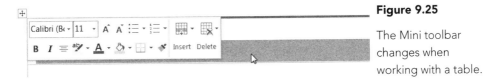

Figure 9.25

The Mini toolbar changes when working with a table.

TIP

You can right-click within a table and find the Insert and Delete commands as well as Border Styles (see Figure 9.26).

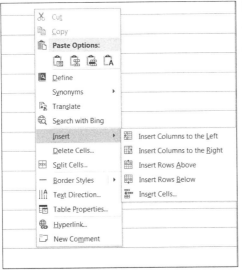

Figure 9.26

The shortcut menu offers many table commands.

Resizing Rows and Columns

There are four ways to change the row height or column width of a table:

- Drag the border of the table.
- Drag the row or column marker on the ruler.
- Click the Layout tab, choose Properties, and then select Row or Column.
- Double-click the column boundary on the right side to expand the column to AutoFit the longest string of text in the cell.

CAUTION

A common problem in Word is accidentally selecting a single cell and then attempting to adjust the column width. The settings applied affect only the selected cell, which probably will not yield the desired result. When this happens, press Ctrl+Z to undo the column resize and then deselect the cell before making the adjustment.

Merge and Split

You also can use the Merge group on the Table Tools Layout tab to modify the structure of the table (see Figure 9.27). When two or more cells are selected and you click Merge Cells, the active cells are merged into one.

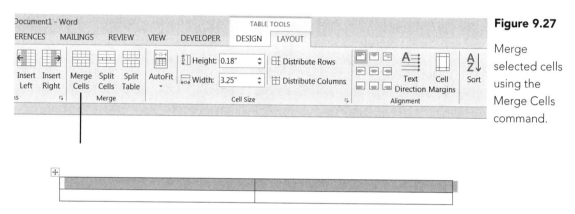

Figure 9.27

Merge selected cells using the Merge Cells command.

The Split Cells option, when clicked, displays the Split Cells dialog box (see Figure 9.28). You can specify how many columns and rows should be created from the single cell in this location.

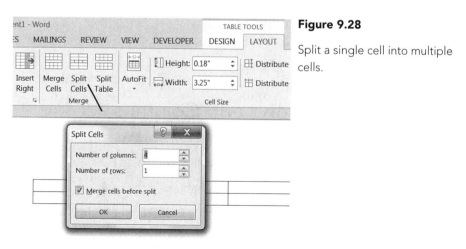

Figure 9.28

Split a single cell into multiple cells.

Split Table

The Split Table command in the Merge group of the Table Tools Layout tab, when clicked, performs two actions. First, if the cursor is in the first cell of the table, it adds a paragraph mark above the table. This is useful if you need to add text above the table quickly. Second, if you are in any other cell in the table, the action divides the table into two separate tables.

TIP

Keyboard users can press Ctrl+Shift+Enter to split the table. Rejoin the two tables by deleting the paragraph mark between the two tables.

AutoFit and Cell Options

By default, Word resizes table cells to accommodate information size. If you do not want the column width to change automatically, adjust the table properties.

Automatically Resize to Fit Contents

1. Create a blank new document.

2. Insert a 2-column, 2-row table.

3. Type your first name in the first table cell and press Tab to move to the next cell in the table.

4. Press and hold down the A key until the table cell expands to fit the contents.

5. Click the AutoFit command located in the Cell Size group on the Table Tools Layout tab (see Figure 9.29). Choose AutoFit Contents.

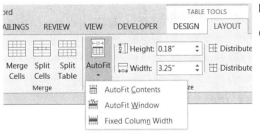

Figure 9.29

Control the format of tables.

6. Change the AutoFit option to AutoFit Window.

7. Close the document without saving.

Cell Size Group Options

You can set the row and column sizes, and thus the cell size, by changing the Height and Width options in the Cell Size group on the Table Tools Layout tab. Just type a number in the appropriate box or use the arrows to change the measurements.

Distribute Rows and Columns

The Distribute Rows option is great for unevenly created (especially hand-drawn) rows within a table. Select two or more rows, click Distribute Rows and all selected rows are resized to equal their largest row.

The Distribute Columns option treats the width to be equal for selected columns.

Alignment Options

When text is entered into a cell, by default, it is aligned in the top-left quadrant. With the commands in the Alignment group of the Table Tools Layout tab, you can change this behavior and specify the alignment of cell text and even rotate it (see Figure 9.30).

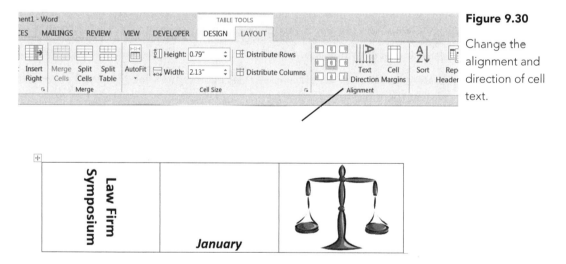

Figure 9.30

Change the alignment and direction of cell text.

SORTING IN A TABLE

In tables, you can sort by Column, Text, Number, Date, and more just by clicking the Sort command in the Data group on the Table Tools Layout tab. You can sort in ascending or descending order, and you can even include options that increase the sorting capabilities.

Sort Information in a Table

1. Open the exercise file entitled Table Sort.docx. You'll find this file, and all exercises referenced in the book in the following location: www.thepayne group.com/downloads/word2013forlawfirms/.

2. Click within the first table and click the Table Tools Layout tab, and then Sort in the Data group.

3. At the bottom of the Sort dialog box, note that under My List Has, Word identifies that you have a Header Row (see Figure 9.31).

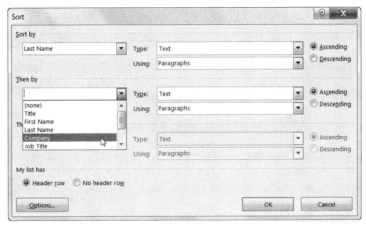

Figure 9.31

Choose what field to sort by and whether it should be reordered in ascending or descending order.

4. Under Sort By, select Last Name and click OK.

5. Try sorting by First Name or by City.

6. Keep this document open for the next exercise.

Advanced Sorting Options

The Options button in the Sort dialog box offers additional options for more advanced sorting. By default, Word will sort an entire cell at a time; however, if there is a lot of information in one cell, it is important to tell Word where to separate the text. This is especially useful for sorting by last name when both the first name and last name are in one cell.

Sort Table by Last Name

1. The document from the previous exercise should still be open.

2. In the second table (Table Sorting Challenge), click just before the name Samuel Adams located in the second row.

3. In the Merge group on the Table Tools Layout tab, click Split Table.

4. Click within the bottom table. Click Sort in the Data group on the Table Tools Layout tab, which displays the Sort dialog box.

5. Click Options, and under Separate Fields At, select Other, and press the Spacebar in the Other box, as shown in Figure 9.32. Click OK.

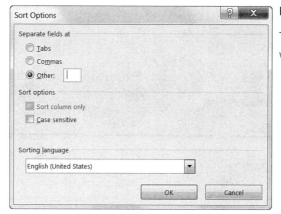

Figure 9.32

Tell Word what separates the words within the cell.

6. In Sort By, select Column 1. From the Using list, select Word 2. This instructs Word to sort by the second word in each cell in Column 1. The Sort Text dialog box is shown in Figure 9.33.

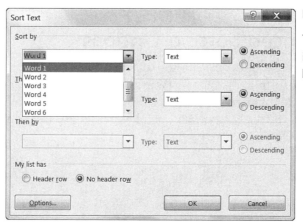

Figure 9.33

The Sort Text dialog box includes options to sort by words or fields.

7. Select Column 1 from the Then By list and select Word 1 from the Using list.

8. Click OK. Word sorts the list by the last name, which is the second word in the cell.

9. Now delete the paragraph mark above the sorted table to merge the table with the header row.

10. Close the document without saving.

NOTE

Note that in two of the names in the preceding exercise (James J. Jackson and Andrew R. Taylor), there is a middle initial. These two names sorted properly because a Nonbreaking Space was used to separate the first name from the middle initial. If a regular space had been used, these two names would have sorted by the middle initial rather than the last name.

TABLE MATH

You can perform simple math in tables, which comes in handy most often for summing rows or columns of numbers.

Simple Addition Formula

Adding numbers in Word tables is not quite as easy to do as it is in Excel; however, Word does include a Formula button in the Data group of the Table Tools Layout tab. First, type the numbers to be summed and then click the Formula option to display the Formula dialog box (see Figure 9.34).

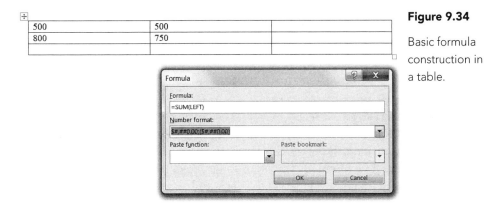

Figure 9.34

Basic formula construction in a table.

Use Formulas in Table

1. Create a new blank document.

2. Create a 3-column, 3-row table.

3. Type number values in the first two columns, rows 1 and 2.

4. Click in the third column of row 1. You will create a formula here that adds the numbers to the left of the column. In the Data group on the Table Tools Layout tab, click Formula. Note that Word identifies that you want to add the numbers to the left.

5. Click the down arrow next to Number Format and choose the option with the currency symbol.

6. Click OK to create the formula and return to the document.

7. Click in the first column, third row. Click Formula in the Data group and note that Word automatically is attempting to create a formula for you with =SUM(ABOVE). Since this is what you want, click OK to accept the formula. Note that since you did not specify a format for the number, it inserts without the currency symbol or other formatting.

8. Click in the second row, third column. Click Formula in the Data group and notice how Word defaulted to creating a formula with =SUM(ABOVE). If you wanted to add the numbers to the left instead, just replace the word ABOVE with the word LEFT. Click OK.

9. Close the document without saving.

NOTE

Word adds the cells above or to the left of the formula until it reaches the end of the table or a blank cell. That makes blank cells a great way to use subtotals in a table. However, if you want to add all the cells in a row or column whether they have values in them or not, type a zero in each blank cell.

Updating a Formula

As numbers in the table change, you might expect the calculation to update as well. Unfortunately, this is not the case in Word. Table results go into fields, which must be manually updated. To update a field, you must first click within the field and then press F9 (or right-click and choose Update Field).

Use Decimals in Tables

You can use tabs in cells in a table, but you will need to press Ctrl+Tab to move to the tab stop in a cell since the default behavior in a table is for Tab to move you to the next cell.

When working with numbers that have decimals in cells, first select the cells and then set the decimal tab stop. Make certain that you choose only to align numbers with decimal tabs, as opposed to text.

NOTE

Do not set a decimal tab in a column that has been centered or right-aligned. If you do so, the numbers may not align correctly on the decimal tab. Select the numbers and press Ctrl+L to left-align the cells before setting the decimal tab.

COMPUSAVVY

Jan Berinstein of CompuSavvy Computer Training & Consulting on Tables in Legal Documents
Tables work well for pleadings that require side-by-side columns, such as Separate Statements of Disputed and Undisputed Material Facts. Typically, Separate Statements use a header row to identify the material facts (listed in one column) and the supporting evidence (listed in another column). But setting up a header row can be confusing. Don't be misled by the Header Row check box on the Design portion of the Table Tools tab. That feature doesn't set up repeating text in tables that span multiple pages. Rather, it affects the *appearance* of the header row if you use one of the multicolored tables in the Table Styles gallery—which are seldom used in legal documents.

To create a header row with repeating text, click anywhere within the first row of the table, go to the Layout portion of the Table Tools tab, and click Repeat Header Rows. As the table expands onto additional pages, the header row will appear at the top of each page. (Another quick tip: It's easy to number both columns separately. Click in the first column below the header row, press the Shift key—and keep it pressed—and then click in the last row in the first column. Then go to the Home tab, Paragraph group, and click the Numbering button. Perform the same steps in the second column. Voilà! Both columns contain automatic numbers, starting with 1. And when you add a row, numbers appear in that row—in both columns—and the numbering in all the other rows automatically increments.)

CREATING AND DISTRIBUTING TEMPLATES

INTRODUCTION TO TEMPLATES

Templates are the foundation for every document that you create. A template stores information such as formatting, including page layout, styles, macros, and even boilerplate text. You can create your own templates, use the templates installed with Microsoft Office, or purchase a third-party product such as the Forms Assistant from PayneGroup. Templates are shortcuts for creating similar types of documents, and they are a real time-saver. For instance, instead of having to create a fax cover sheet document from scratch each time you want to send a fax, you can create a template that includes all of the requisite formatting. All future fax cover sheets then can be created using that fax cover sheet template. The same is true for pleadings where formatting and adherence to court rules are critical. Other types of templates prevalent in law firms are those for agreements, letters of intent, liability disclaimers, trademark assignments, and more. With templates, you create the file once, save it, and then use it whenever you need to create one of these document types.

NOTE

Word documents are saved with either a .docx (document) or .docm (macro-enabled document) file extension, whereas Word templates are saved with a .dotx (template) or .dotm (macro-enabled template) file extension. If you accidentally saved a file intended as a template as a regular Word document, you can easily solve the problem by opening the document, clicking File, Save As, and changing the file type to a template.

TEMPLATE TYPES

Three types of templates are used in Word: Normal, attached, and global. Understanding how each type works will provide a good foundation for working with templates.

Normal Template

The Normal template (Normal.dotm) is Word's all-encompassing, ever-present master template. There is only one Normal template, and it is so vital to Word that if you delete it, Word will automatically re-create it for you. The Normal template includes settings that control everything from margins, styles, macros, keyboard shortcuts, and much more. The Normal template is the template used by default when creating a blank Word document.

Even if you don't have a blank document open, the Normal template is still running in the background, giving you access to all of its settings. Here are just a few of the default settings you can change in the Normal template:

- Margins
- Font style
- Font size
- Header and footer parameters
- Keyboard shortcuts
- Macros
- Styles

When you make changes to the Normal template, each new blank document created thereafter will use those new settings.

EXPERT TIP

The Normal template is sometimes the target of malicious macro viruses due to Word's reliance on it and its predictable location. For this reason, Normal.dotm can become infected and even corrupt. If the Normal template is corrupt, it can cause Word to crash upon opening. If this happens, try renaming the Normal template to something else, for instance, OldNormal, and have Word re-create a new one for you. By renaming instead of deleting it, you may be able to copy some of the customizations from the OldNormal into the new Normal template using the Organizer.

If you delete the Normal template, any changes or customizations that are stored in the Normal template will be lost. It is preferable to store firm customizations in either an attached or global template, discussed later in this chapter. It is also a good idea to back up the Normal template to prevent the loss of individual customizations.

CAUTION

Since many customizations are stored in the Normal template, firm-wide customizations are best stored in an attached or global template. This way when updates are made to the firm-wide customizations and the relevant template replaced, others will not lose their own personal customizations.

Attached Template

Every document created in Word is based on a template and remains attached to that template. The document created from a template inherits settings from the attached template such as margins, styles, macros, and more. Examples of an attached template would be a Letter, Pleading, or Memo.

To find out which template is attached to your current document, do the following—from the File tab, click Options, and then select Add-Ins. Click the drop-down arrow for Manage, select Templates, and click Go. The Templates and Add-Ins dialog box displays, as shown in Figure 10.1. If you decide to attach a different template to the current document, click Attach and select a different template file.

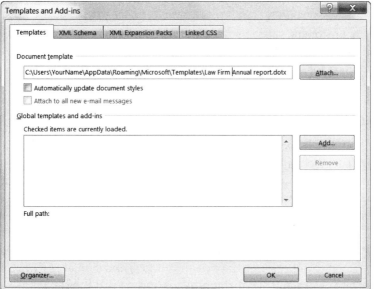

Figure 10.1

View the attached templates from the Templates and Add-Ins dialog box.

NOTE

A setting in an attached template takes precedence over the same setting in the Normal template. For this reason, if you have a style in both the Normal and attached template with the same name, the attached template's style is used.

Global Template

Global templates are templates that contain settings that are available to all files, independent of the attached template. Global templates are the place to store customizations you want to have access to when working with all documents. These customizations can include custom building-block entries, macros, ribbon customizations, and Quick Access Toolbar. Global templates are saved in Word's Startup folder location, which lets them load each time Word opens, giving you access to its customizations.

EXPERT TIP

If you prefer to specify a global template for the current session only, in the Templates and Add-Ins dialog box, click Add to browse and select the file to be included in the global template list.

NOTE

You can have multiple global templates. Stored in the Startup folder, each global template loads when you start Word. Be careful with having too many global templates, however, because it could slow down your system and use up system memory unnecessarily.

CAUTION

It is not recommended to store style customizations in global templates for the mere fact that the styles will not be available globally. Instead, you will want to store style customizations in attached templates.

Add-Ins

Although not technically a template, add-ins are included in this discussion of templates because they fit in the template layer and perform many of the same functions as templates. Add-ins are programs written in a programming language and compiled by a C compiler. They also are known as WLL (Word Link Libraries) files. They function similarly to global templates. More importantly, add-ins are typically software that add functionality that doesn't exist in the software. Some examples of add-ins widely used in the legal industry are numbering tools, document comparison, tables of authorities, and similar software programs. Their function is similar to global templates and extend the capabilities of the software being used.

To view all add-ins installed in Word, from the File tab, click Options, and then select Add-Ins, as shown in Figure 10.2.

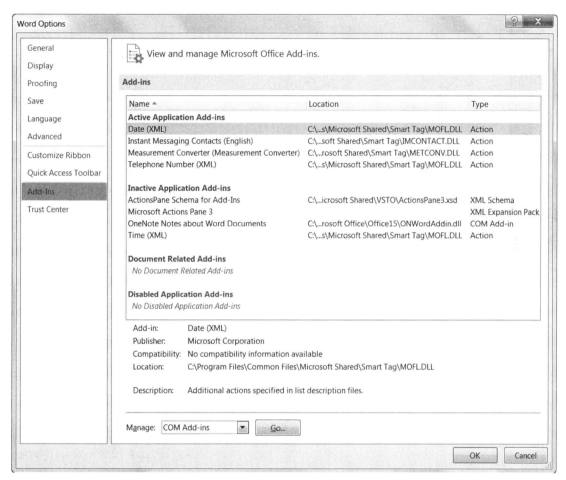

Figure 10.2 View a list of add-ins installed in Word.

SAVING AND ACCESSING TEMPLATES

In Word 2013, templates are available as follows:

- **Word's Built-In Templates.** Click File, New and select from Word's built-in templates listed, or click in the Search for Online Templates box and search for a template online. Preset searches are also available to access online templates (see Figure 10.3). Select from Letters, Resume, Fax, Labels, Cards, Calendar, or Blank.

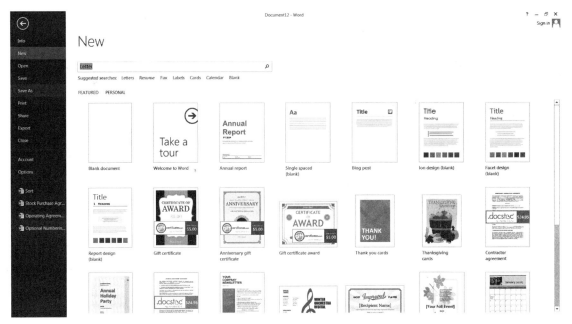

Figure 10.3 Access online templates in Backstage view.

NOTE

If you used Microsoft's fax templates in previous versions of Word, you will find these templates are no longer installed when you install Microsoft Office 2013. If you want to access these templates, click File, New, and then type fax in the Search for Online Templates box to search online.

- **Personal Templates.** Click File, New, and if you have already saved a template to the default location, you will have a Personal tab available. The Personal tab contains templates saved to the default Personal Templates Location, by default c:\Users\%UserName%\Documents\Custom Office Templates. When a template is created and the Save As Type selection is either .dotx or .dotm, the default save folder is changed to this location.

- **Legacy File | New Dialog Box.** This is the dialog box used in previous versions of Word. Add this command to your Quick Access Toolbar by clicking File, Options and then selecting Quick Access Toolbar. Change the Choose Command From list to All Commands. Locate New Document or Template and click Add. Templates listed here are those saved in the File Locations dialog box under the User Templates and Workgroup Templates options. See "File Locations" later in this chapter.

NOTE

The Default Personal Templates Location is set in Word Options. Click File, Options, and then click the Save tab. The Default Personal Templates Location is found in the Save Documents section.

EXPERT TIP

When you click File, New, and select the Personal tab, you see those templates saved in the default personal templates location (C:\Users\%UserName%\Documents\Custom Office Templates).

When you click the New Document or Template command added to the Quick Access Toolbar (see Legacy File|New Dialog Box), you see those templates saved to the User Templates folder indicated in File Locations.

To view a complete list of personal templates—those saved in the Custom Office Templates folder as well as the User Templates folder—in both Backstage view (File, New, Personal) or the Legacy File|New dialog box, set both the Default Personal Templates Location and the User Templates folder to the same location.

File Locations

The File Locations dialog box allows you to view or edit the default file locations for documents, images, templates and add-ins, AutoRecover files, tools, and the Startup folder. Click the File tab and then Options. Select Advanced, and at the bottom of the dialog box under General, click File Locations.

NOTE

Templates stored in the User Templates folder will only display in the New Document or Template dialog box (accessed only by adding the command to the Quick Access Toolbar—see the "Legacy File|New Dialog Box" bullet earlier) (and not File, New, Personal) unless the Default Personal Templates Location (File, Options, Save, Save Document section) and File Locations, User Templates indicate the same location.

TRUSTED LOCATIONS

In order for Word 2013 to recognize a template as "trustworthy," the location of the template needs to be set as a trusted location. By default, when Microsoft Office 2013 is installed, the locations for user templates, Microsoft advertised templates, and the startup templates are set automatically as trusted locations. When a location is defined as trusted, all of the content stored within the file (including macros) is enabled, and you won't see any warnings of potential risks that might exist within the file.

To view the trusted locations on your computer, on the File tab, click Options, and then select Trust Center. Click Trust Center Settings, select the Trusted Locations tab, and the Trust Center dialog box will display similar to what is shown in Figure 10.4.

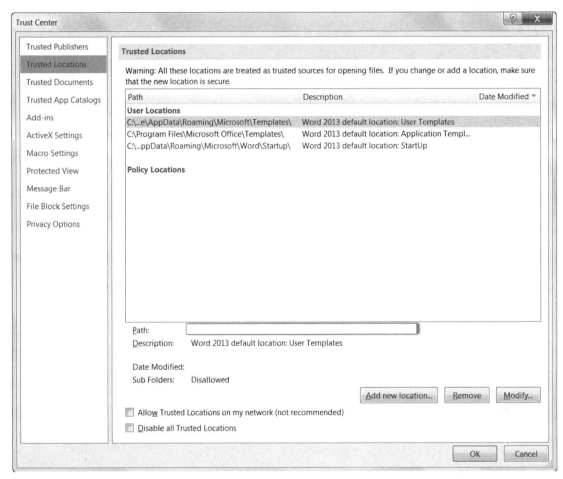

Figure 10.4 Set trusted locations to ensure that your templates can be accessed and are fully functional.

NOTE

Modify an existing trusted location or create a new trusted location by clicking Modify or Add New Location in the Trust Center dialog box.

When creating a document from a template that is not in a trusted location, the document will be opened in Protected View, and a security alert will display indicating the document was opened from an unsafe location. Placing your templates in a trusted location allows easy access to your templates and full functionality without the interruption of a security alert.

CREATE A TEMPLATE

There are several ways to create your own template: Create a document with the necessary formatting and save it as a template or open one of Microsoft's online templates, customize it, and then save it as one of your templates.

Create a Pleading Template from an Online Template

Microsoft provides many templates that can be customized for firm use. One example are its pleading templates. Choose from several options including Legal Pleading Paper (32 lines), Legal Pleading Paper (28 lines), Legal Pleading Paper (25 lines), Legal Pleading Paper (26 lines), and Pleading Paper With 28 Lines.

Create a Pleading Template with Line Numbering from an Online Template

1. Click the File tab and then select New.

2. In the Search for Online Templates box, type **pleading** and press Enter.

3. Select the template that best matches the court's requirements. The pleading templates are basically the same; the main difference is the number of lines per page.

4. Click Create. A pleading document is created.

5. From the File tab, choose Save As or press F12 to display the Save As dialog box.

6. Click Browse, and in the Save As dialog box, choose Word Template (*.dotx) from the Save As Type drop-down list. Word will automatically find your user template location: C:\Users\%UserName%\Documents\Custom Office Templates.

7. Type **My Firm Pleading** for the File Name and click Save.

8. Make any needed modifications to the template.

9. Click Save and close the template.

10. A new custom template has been created. To create a document based on this template, see the "Create a Document Based on a Custom Template" section.

**THE SACKETT
GROUP**

Linda Sackett of The Sackett Group on Pleadings

For anyone who's prepared a pleading or brief for filing in a court that requires lined and numbered pleading paper, one can truly appreciate the benefit of a well-formatted pleading template. Many courts in several Western U.S. states—including Alaska, Arizona, California, Nevada, Oregon, and Washington—require special layout and formatting so that the first line of every paragraph in the body of the document must align at a numbered line. In addition, the last line of text on each page must align with the last numbered pleading paper line, such as line 28. Some court clerks have been known to reject a filing when a pleading doesn't adhere to these formatting rules.

Several Word formatting "tricks" can be used to accommodate court requirements. Line spacing can be set at exactly 12 or 24 points, space before can be added or removed from paragraphs that don't align properly with the numbered pleading paper, and the top and bottom margins can be set to allow for footer information required by some courts.

If footer information such as a document title and case number is too lengthy, the body text may not align with the last numbered line of the pleading paper. In that instance, the simplest and most obvious solution is to abbreviate the document title in the footer. If that is not an option, you can decrease the font point size of the footer style (be mindful of any court rules specific to footers and footnotes). For courts such as California Superior that specify a border line must separate page numbering from the footer information, using a table in the footer is a solution. The table height can be adjusted as needed to accommodate longer footer text.

Create a Template from a Document

To create your own template, take any customized document and then save it as a template. Documents created from that template will contain all of the same formatting and other customizations found in the template.

Create a Template from a Document

1. Create a blank document.
2. From the File tab, choose Save As.

NOTE

In this example, the type of template being created is a Word Template with a file extension of .dotx. If a new template is going to contain macros, you would select Word Macro-Enabled Template (*.dotm); otherwise, the macros will be disabled.

3.   Type **My Firm Template** for the File Name and click Save.

4.   Make any needed modifications to the template.

5.   Click Save and close the template.

6.   A new custom template has been created. You will use the new template in the next exercise.

NOTE

If your firm is in the process of moving from Office 2003 or an earlier version but hasn't made the upgrade yet, it's important to note that Word 2003 cannot open .dotx and .dotm files.

CREATE A DOCUMENT BASED ON A CUSTOM TEMPLATE

Now that you've created the template, let's create a document based on that template.

Create a Document Based on a Custom Template

1.   From the File tab, click New.

2.   Below the search box, click Personal just above the Blank document.

3.   Select the template you created in the previous exercise.

4.   You now have a document based on the template you created.

CUSTOMIZE A TEMPLATE

Depending on the function of the template, whether it is an attached or global template will determine the kind of customizations you'll want to include in that custom template. An attached template will contain the formatting you want in the documents you create from the template, such as margins, styles, headers and footers, etc. A global template will have customizations that you can access from every document, such as macros, ribbon customizations, Quick Access Toolbar customizations, keyboard shortcuts, etc.

Add Styles to a Template

A lot of work goes into creating firm-specific styles. Once created, styles make applying consistent formatting a breeze. Since the template is the basis for all documents, firm styles should be added to each custom attached template as needed.

In essence, when you create a template, you are creating a document and then saving it as a template. Create styles in the template as you would in any document. For instance, styles in your firm pleading templates might include Body Text formatted to be double-space with a first-line indent. Quote style is often indented on both sides and single-spaced, and citations have their own format and style. When you do the advance work and save this into your pleading templates, they will be available to you, and you can be assured that they adhere to court-specified rules.

Manage Styles in a Template

When creating a template, you'll want to decide which styles in the template should take priority, which styles will be used most often, and which styles should show up only when needed. The Manage Styles dialog box, shown in Figure 10.5, has four tabs with options to modify and create styles, set a style's priority level, and specify whether a style should be hidden or visible. You also can set style restrictions and permissions as well as establish defaults for font and paragraph settings.

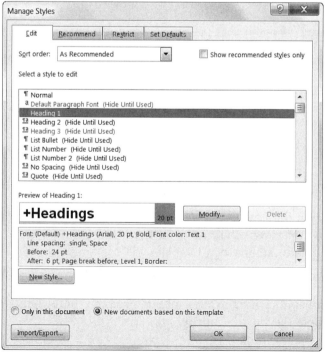

Figure 10.5

Use the Manage Styles dialog box to create and edit styles, set a style's priority level, or indicate whether a style should be hidden or visible in a template.

Edit Tab

To modify a style, select one from the list and click Modify. You can change how the style list is sorted by clicking the drop-down arrow next to Sort Order and selecting Alphabetical, for example. Select the Show Recommended Styles Only check box to hide all of the dimmed styles in the list.

NOTE

Changing the sort order on the Edit tab does not change it in the Styles task pane. Click Options on the Styles task pane to set the sort order for the task pane.

Recommend Tab

The Recommend tab is where you want to go to change how styles are sorted, to show styles that are hidden, hide styles until they are used, or always hide styles so they never show. By assigning a value between 1 and 100 (or Last) to the style, you establish its priority relative to the other styles in the template.

Set the Visibility and List Priority of Styles

1. Create a blank new document.

2. Open the Styles task pane (Ctrl+Alt+Shift+S).

3. Click Manage Styles.

4. In the Manage Styles dialog box, select the Recommend tab.

5. Select Alphabetical from the Sort Order list.

6. Select the No Spacing style and under Set Whether Style Shows When Viewing Recommended Styles, click the Hide button.

7. Select all of the Body Text styles and click the Assign Value button. The priority value will display 1. Click OK.

8. With the Body Text styles still selected, click the Show button.

9. Select the Heading 2 through Heading 9 styles and click Show.

10. Select the Intense Reference and Subtle Reference styles, click the Make Last button, and then click the Hide Until Used button.

11. Click OK to close the Manage Styles dialog box.

12. Notice how the styles display in the Styles task pane.

NOTE

Setting the visibility and priority levels for styles is performed in a template so these changes will be there for all documents created based on that template. You can further customize the styles in the template to show or not show in the Style gallery as well.

Restrict Tab

It is possible to lock down a document so that only permitted styles can be used. When this feature is enabled, it also will prevent the use of any direct formatting in the document. This can be ideal if you are collaborating with someone and the document is in near final format and should only be edited, and not have the formatting changed. If you do choose to restrict formatting in the document, make sure you either don't set a password or write it down. Passwords are case sensitive and cannot be recovered.

NOTE

Restricting styles and formatting may seem like a great idea at first glance; however, most law firms find it too restrictive since most legal documents still need to have direct formatting applied to text.

Set Defaults Tab

You can set font and paragraph defaults for the Normal style in the Manage Styles dialog box. Click the Set Defaults tab and modify the options as needed. You can choose to save the settings for the current document only or for all new documents based on the attached template.

CAUTION

If you're looking to make changes to the Normal style, it is recommended you modify the Normal style directly (right-click the Normal style in the Style gallery or Styles task pane and select Modify) rather than changing it through the Set Defaults tab since that method may produce inconsistent results. If you don't want to modify the Normal style, an alternate method is to change the defaults by going to the Font and Paragraph dialog boxes and clicking the Set As Default button.

Add Building Blocks to a Template

By default, building blocks are stored in the Building Blocks.dotx file, which you can tell from the file extension is a template. The entries within the template can be accessed from any document. However, there may be some instances where building blocks are specific to a certain type of document only. For example, a signature block in a pleading is different than in a letter. Word allows you to store building blocks in templates other than the building blocks template. This can offer many benefits to a law firm, including the following:

- **Easy Distribution of Firm Building Blocks.** All the firm's general building blocks such as office address, logo, etc., can be stored in a global template and made available to others without overwriting their personal entries stored in the Building Blocks.dotx file.

- **Streamline Building Block Names.** You could create multiple building blocks named Signature and each will have a different format and will be stored in separate templates. When you insert the Signature building block into your document, it will insert the entry associated with that particular template/document type.

Add a Building Block to a Template

1. The My Firm Template file should still be open from the previous exercise.

2. Type your firm's address.

3. Select the text and click the Insert tab; then from the Text group, click Quick Parts, and click Save Selection to Quick Part Gallery.

4. In the Name box, type **Firm Address**.

5. Click the Gallery drop-down arrow and select Custom 1.

NOTE

Saving the building block to the Custom 1 gallery will allow you to add the building block to a custom ribbon that you will create in a later exercise in this chapter. By default, the gallery selected is Quick Parts, which adds the building block to the Quick Part gallery on the Insert tab in the Text group.

6. Notice the Save In box is defaulted to Building Blocks.dotx. Select My Firm Template.dotx from the Save In drop-down list.

7. Click OK.

8. Delete the firm address that was typed.

9. Save My Firm Template and keep this template open for the next exercise.

Add a Ribbon Tab to a Template

When creating a global template for the firm, you will want to consider creating a firm tab and ribbon that includes an organized set of commands specific to your firm. To create a custom tab and ribbon, perform the following exercise steps.

Create a Custom Ribbon Tab

1. The My Firm Template should still be open from the previous exercise.

2. From the File tab, click Options, and then click Customize Ribbon.

3. Under the Customize the Ribbon section, click New Tab (see Figure 10.6).

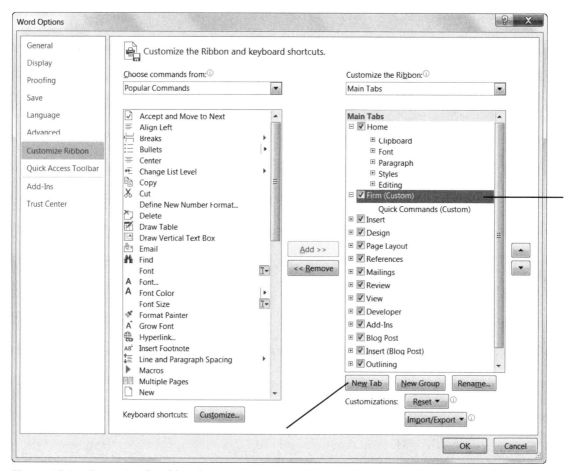

Figure 10.6 Customize the ribbon by creating a new tab that can be renamed to your specifications.

4. Select the newly created tab (New Tab (Custom)) and click Rename. Rename the custom tab Display name to **Firm** and click OK.

5. Select the newly created group (New Group (Custom)) below the Firm tab. Click Rename, rename the custom group to **Quick Commands**, select any icon, and then click OK.

6. With the filter in the Choose Commands From list set to Popular Commands, select and add each of the commands you want to appear in the Quick Commands group on the ribbon.

7. After adding the commands, click the Move Up or Move Down arrows to reorder the commands.

8. Leave the Word Options dialog box open for the next exercise.

Add Building Blocks to a Custom Ribbon Tab

1. The Word Options dialog box should still be open from the previous exercise.

2. Select the newly created Firm tab.

3. Click New Group again.

4. Select the newly created group (New Group (Custom)). Click Rename, rename the custom group Display name to **Building Blocks**, select any icon, and click OK.

5. Click the Choose Commands From drop-down arrow and change the filter from Popular Commands to Commands Not in the Ribbon. Select Custom Gallery 1 in the list and add it to the Building Blocks group.

NOTE

Using a custom gallery allows you to populate it with custom building block entries.

6. Rename Custom Gallery 1 to **Office Addresses**, select an icon, and click OK.

7. Click OK to save the changes and exit the dialog box.

8. Close the Word Options dialog box and leave the template open for the next exercise.

Add Macros to a Template

In order to save macros to a template, when saving the template you must select Word Macro-Enabled Template (*.dotm) as the File Type. If you select Word Template (*.dotx), any macros saved in the template would be disabled.

For detailed information on creating macros, see Chapter 15, "When You Need (or Want) Automation in Word."

Macro Security

There is always an element of risk involved with using macros in Word, and that is the purpose of having trusted locations to tell Word where you are saving approved templates. However, when you open a document or template containing macros, say from an e-mail attachment, the default setting is that all macros will be disabled and a Message Bar notification will display alerting you that macros are disabled. The Message Bar notification does allow you to enable the macros.

NOTE

Only enable macros when you know it is from a trusted source.

To access macro security settings, click the File tab, Options, Trust Center, and Trust Center Settings.

Being notified of the presence of macros and being able to indicate that the document or template is from a trustworthy source will allow you to run macros, if necessary. Another way to accomplish this is to save the document or template in a trusted location, which will bypass any security warning.

CAUTION

The Enable All Macros option is available, but not recommended. When viewing the option, the selection itself comes with the warning, "not recommended; potentially dangerous code can run."

EXPERT TIP

You might say to yourself, "I'm careful and check for macro viruses and would know if they exist in my templates or macros." Actually, this is not always possible, which is why you don't want to disable macro security. Persons with malicious intent could use one of Word's special names for their macro and have it execute in certain circumstances. For instance, AutoExec macros run every time you start Word or load a global template. AutoOpen and AutoClose run the macro on open or close. If you are unsure of the history of a template and want to prevent AutoOpen macros from running, you can always hold the Shift key when you open the file to prevent this; however, the best practice is to keep security on and take advantage of Word's extra protection to warn you of potential dangers.

Add a Quick Access Toolbar Command to a Template

When you add a command to the Quick Access Toolbar in Word, by default the addition is stored in the Word.OfficeUI file. Alternatively, commands on the Quick Access Toolbar can be saved in a global or attached template. Saving the commands to a global or attached template gives the firm the ability to maintain firmwide commands on the Quick Access Toolbar without affecting any of the individual user's changes.

Add a Quick Access Toolbar Command to a Template

1. The template from the previous exercise should still be open.

2. From the File tab, click Options, and then click Customize Quick Access Toolbar.

3. Notice the Customize Quick Access Toolbar box is defaulted to For All Document (Default). Select My Firm Template.dotx from the Customize Quick Access Toolbar drop-down list.

4. With the filter in the Choose Commands From list set to Popular Commands, select and add the commands you want to appear in the Quick Access Toolbar.

5. Click OK.

6. Save My Firm Template and keep this document open for the next exercise.

Add Custom Keyboard Shortcut Assignments to a Template

A great way to distribute custom keyboard assignments is to store them in a global or attached template. Keyboard shortcuts can be added to any command, style, or macro.

Add a Custom Keyboard Shortcut Assignment to a Template

1. The template from the previous exercise should still be open.

2. From the Style gallery, right-click on the Quote style.

3. Select Modify and then select Format, Shortcut Key.

4. In the Press New Shortcut Key box, press Alt+Ctrl+Q. Note that under Currently Assigned To, it indicates the keyboard shortcut is unassigned.

CAUTION

When assigning a keyboard shortcut, pressing Alt with most alpha keys will indicate the keystroke is unassigned. However, many of the Alt/alpha key combinations are used with KeyTips. For instance, if you press Alt+S, the References ribbon tab will display, and yet this keystroke is considered unassigned. To see some of the Alt key combinations in use, press Alt, and the KeyTips will display.

5. Click Assign to assign the keyboard shortcut.

6. Note the default location for saving keyboard shortcut is Normal.dotm. Select My Firm Template.dotx from the Save Changes In drop-down list.

7. Click Close and OK.

8. Click File and then select Options.

9. Select Customize Ribbon.

10. Click Customize next to Keyboard Shortcuts.

11. From the Customize Keyboard dialog box, select All Commands from the Categories list, as shown in Figure 10.7.

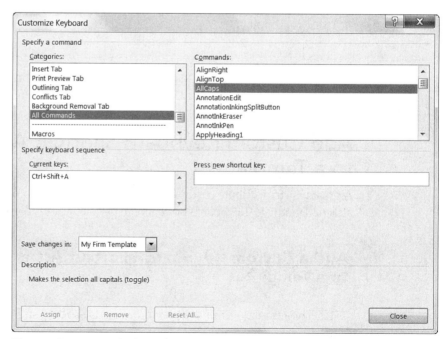

Figure 10.7 From the Customize Keyboard dialog box, select from a list of all commands available in Word.

12. From the Commands list, select AllCaps. Note under Current Keys, it indicates Ctrl+Shift+A has already been assigned to this command.

13. From the Commands list select BorderAll.

14. In the Press New Shortcut Key box, press Alt+Ctrl+B and click Assign.

15. Select My Firm Template.dotx from the Save Changes In drop-down list and click Close.

16. Click OK and then save and close the file.

EXPERT TIP

Macros can also be assigned keyboard shortcuts from the Customize Keyboard dialog box. Click File, Options, Customize Ribbon, and then select Customize under Keyboard Shortcuts. From the Categories list, select Macros. A list of macros available on all active templates will display.

DISTRIBUTE A CUSTOM TEMPLATE

When your custom template is ready to distribute to the firm, the template file can be included as part of the initial packaging of your Office 2013 build or can be pushed out to everyone via login script or other deployment method. If you need to make changes to the template later, you easily can edit the template and then push out the updated file to everyone.

TIKIT

Clare Waller of Tikit on International Template Considerations

Global harmonization of the complex document, through the provision of a consistent and rationalized set of templates, has become critical for law firms seeking to regulate their brand and image across an international branch network. This is more than an issue of style and layout. It is a challenge to disentangle legal requirements, where partners' names appear on the letterhead, national cultural standards regarding accepted layout of a document, and local idiosyncrasies—"that's just the way we do it here." Furthermore, deeper document structural issues arise from other factors, such as variations in the use of numbering schemes or different uses of the same functionality (e.g., track changes) or the use of different third-party products. Establishment of a common standard across global offices must be handled delicately, or the standards imposed by foreign IT departments potentially lead to further diversity and challenges to rationalization.

A number of steps can be taken to help harmonize the process, such as the following:

1. **Leadership.** There needs to be clear communication from the top partners about the business need for the change that filters down through fee earners to support staff.
2. **Training.** Ensure that the same messages and materials are used globally throughout all offices.
3. **Styles.** Use the same style names globally, even if the layout differs from office to office. This simplifies training and the exchange of documents between jurisdictions.
4. **Third-Party Product Assessment.** A critical assessment of all add-ins to the Office suite, such as document comparison, is essential when delivering a rationalized template set.

Taken together, these steps can help achieve the firm's goal of establishment of a common brand and image across all its global offices.

WHEN YOUR TEMPLATE IS A FORM

A form is generally used to collect information from others in an easy-to-use fill-in format. Examples of forms used in the legal industry might include new client intake, conflict checks, or even general business and administrative forms such as vacation requests, expense reports, supply requisitions, and FedEx airbills.

Steps for Creating a Form

Here are the steps for creating a form:

1. Create a new document and save it as a template or open an existing template.

2. Consider what information needs to be gathered from the people using the form, what controls you can add to make it easier (such as check boxes or drop-down lists), and how to best organize the form so it's logical and user-friendly.

3. Display the Developer tab, which holds all of the form fields, properties, and protection features commands.

4. Create a user-friendly and visually appealing form by adding fields and content controls.

5. Protect the form. Add a password if you want to prevent others from altering your work.

6. Test the form and then reset and protect it before deploying it to others.

Developer Tab

The Developer tab gives you access to all of the form fields, properties, and protection features for developing a form template, as shown in Figure 10.8. By default, however, the Developer tab is not visible. To display the Developer tab, from the File tab, choose Options, and then Customize Ribbon. Select the Developer tab check box and click OK.

Figure 10.8 The Developer tab offers many options for developing forms.

When you have displayed the Developer tab, it will stay visible until you hide it. When creating templates, be sure to hide the Developer tab before making your final save of the template, or the Developer tab will be visible to everyone using the template.

Form Fields and Tools

The form fields used for developing a form are found in the Controls group of the Developer tab. Each of the content controls and legacy form fields is described in this section.

When the form has been completed, the Restrict Editing command found in the Protect group is used to "lock" the form and prepare it for user input.

Content Controls

There are nine types of content controls in Word 2013 that can be added to forms (see Tables 10.1 and 10.2). You also can access legacy form fields and ActiveX Controls used in previous versions of Word.

TABLE 10.1—CONTENT CONTROLS

FORM CONTROL		DESCRIPTION
Aa	Rich Text	Inserts a Rich Text content control, which allows for any formatting and can include graphics and hard returns.
Aa	Plain Text	Inserts a Plain Text content control that does not allow any formatting and cannot include graphics
	Picture	Inserts a Picture content control that can contain a single drawing, shape, chart, table, ClipArt, or SmartArt.
	Building Block Gallery	Inserts the Quick Parts gallery containing building block entries that have already been created, if any.
☑	Check Box	Inserts a Check Box content control that allows the user to select the check box.
	Combo Box	Inserts a Combo Box content control that contains an editable list.
	Drop-Down List	Inserts a Drop-Down List content control in which the list is restricted.
	Date Picker	Inserts a Date Picker content control, which displays an interactive calendar from which to choose the date.
	Repeating Section	Inserts a content control that contains other controls and repeats the contents of the control as needed.
	Legacy Tools	Access form fields found in earlier versions of Word, including ActiveX controls.

Also included in the Controls group of the Developer tab are the following commands:

TABLE 10.2—FORM CONTROL TOOLS

FORM CONTROL TOOL		DESCRIPTION
Design Mode	Design Mode	Toggles on and off XML tags when designing forms.
Properties	Properties	View or modify properties for the selected control.
Group	Group	Group or ungroup a selected range of text.

Legacy Form Controls

Although there are nine content controls from which to choose, you can also access the legacy form fields and ActiveX controls. Click the Legacy Tools command in the Controls group of the Developer tab to access these commands.

NOTE

If you do not see all of the content controls enabled, check to see if the document is in Compatibility Mode. The document must be a Word 2013 document for you to use all of the available content controls.

Create the Form

In addition to the ease of use and rapid fill-in benefits of forms, another primary benefit is the ability to restrict where text is placed onto the form as well as the type of information input. This is accomplished through the use of various content controls and legacy form controls, as described in Table 10.1 and Table 10.2. For example, insert a Drop-Down List content control in your form and then limit the list to specific entries from which to choose.

Create a Form and Insert Content Controls

1. Create a blank new document.

2. Save the document as a Word Template (*dotx) in the user template location and name it **My Form**.

NOTE

If you plan to add macros to the template, save the template as a Word Macro-Enabled Template (*.dotm).

For detailed information on adding macro code to a form template, see Chapter 15.

3. From the Insert tab, choose Table and then Insert Table.

4. Change Number of Columns to **2** and Number of Rows to **3**.

5. Click OK.

6. In the first cell, type **Name** and press Tab.

7. From the Controls group on the Developer tab, select Rich Text content control.

8. Click Properties in the Controls group and the Content Control Properties dialog box appears, as shown in Figure 10.9.

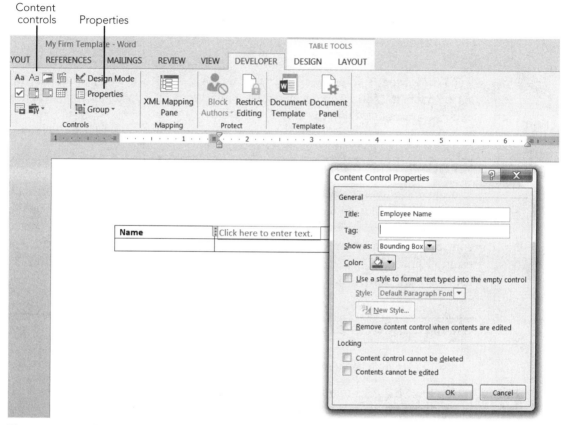

Figure 10.9   Additional options can be set in the Content Control Properties dialog box.

9. In the Content Control Properties dialog box, type **Employee Name** in the Title box and click OK.

10. Press Tab and type **Date** and press Tab.

11. From the Developer tab, click Date Picker Content Control in the Controls group.

12. In the Controls group, click Properties.

13. In the Content Control Properties dialog box, type **Select Date** in the Title box and click OK.

14. Note the Title information you entered appears above the content control. To view the XML tag information, click Design Mode in the Controls group, as shown in Figure 10.10.

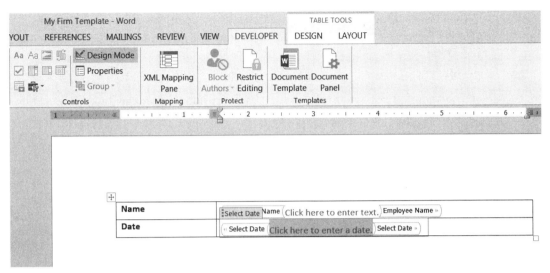

Figure 10.10   View XML tags in Design Mode.

15. Click Design Mode again in the Controls group to toggle off showing XML tags.

16. Press Tab and type **Status**.

17. Press Tab and select Drop-Down List content control in the Controls group.

18. Click Properties in the Controls group.

19. In the Content Control Properties dialog box, type **Employment Status** in the Title box.

20. In the Drop-Down List Properties section, click Add.

21. In the Display Name box, type **Full-time**. Note the Value box copies the text you type. Click OK.

22. Click Add and type **Part-time** in the Display Name box. Click OK.

23. Click Add and type **Contractor** in the Display Name box. Click OK.

24. Click Add and type **Temporary** in the Display Name box. Click OK.

25. Click OK to close the Content Control Properties dialog box.

26. Save the form and keep it open for the next exercise.

TIP

If the content controls are disabled in the Controls group, toggle off Design Mode.

CAUTION

When Design Mode is selected in the Controls group on the Developer tab, the Undo list is cleared. This means that you cannot undo any edits after toggling on or off Design Mode.

NOTE

If you need to delete a content control in a form, right-click within the content control and select Remove Content Control.

Forms Protection

Once a form has been completed and is ready for use, the final step is to set the protection. Once the form is protected, the content controls can be filled in without deleting the fields or affecting the original form template. To turn protection on, click Restrict Editing in the Protect group on the Developer tab.

A protected form is different from a regular document in several ways:

- The user cannot edit the text or formatting of a protected form.

- The entire document cannot be selected.

- Many commands will not be available when working in forms.

- The spelling checker will ignore protected sections of the document.

- Undo does not work for changes made to a form before it was protected.

Protect and Unprotect Your Form

1. My Form.dotx should still be open from the previous exercise.

2. On the Developer tab, click Restrict Editing in the Protect group. The Restrict Editing task pane opens, as shown in Figure 10.11.

3. Under 2. Editing Restrictions, select the option Allow Only this Type of Editing in the Document, click the drop-down arrow under the option, and select Filling in Forms.

4. Under 3. Start Enforcement, click Yes, Start Enforcing Protection.

5. In the Start Enforcing Protection dialog box, leave the password blank and click OK.

6. Try out the content controls and try to edit any area outside of the content controls.

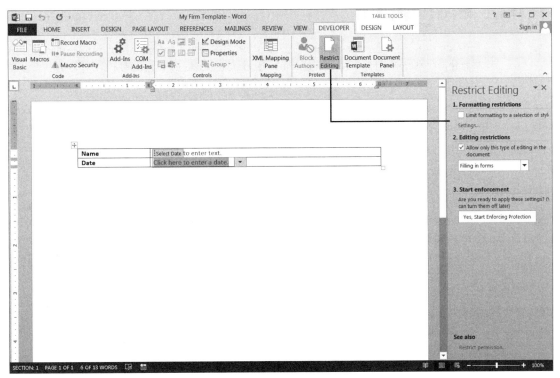

Figure 10.11   Protect the document for filling in forms.

7.   In the Restrict Editing task pane, click Stop Protection.

8.   Save the form and close it.

NOTE

To protect the form and prevent anyone from making edits by simply unprotecting the form, add a password in the Start Enforcing Protection dialog box. Keep in mind passwords are case sensitive.

NOTE

You can protect specific areas of a form by inserting a section break between the protected and unprotected areas of the form. Protect specific sections of the document using the Restrict Editing task pane. Click Select Sections to choose which sections to protect.

TIP

It's important to test the entire form before distributing it to others. Start by protecting the form and entering data into each of the fields. You can press the down arrow key to move to the next content control and the up arrow key to move to the previous content control. If you need to make a change, unprotect the form, modify the form as needed, and then protect the form again.

USING FIELDS

Fields are special codes that instruct Word to insert information into a document or template. With fields, you can add and automatically update text, graphics, page numbers, and other information in a document.

There are more than 75 fields in Word, which can be divided into three categories: Result fields, Marker fields, and Action fields.

Result Field

One type of field used frequently is a result field (see Figure 10.12). A good example of a result field is the Date field. The Date field retrieves the current date from your computer's system clock and inserts that date at the field position. Similarly, the Filename field retrieves the name of the document upon save and places that information at the field position.

Several Date Field Formats and Field Codes

11/20/2013	{ DATE \@ "M/d/yyyy" }
Wednesday, November 20, 2013	{ DATE \@ "dddd, MMMM dd, yyyy" }
November 20, 2013	{ DATE \@ "MMMM d, yyyy" }
11/20/13	{ DATE \@ "M/d/yy" }
20 November 2013	{ DATE \@ "d MMMM yyyy" }
11/20/2013 1:08 PM	{ DATE \@ "M/d/yyyy h:mm am/pm" }

Several File Information Fields and Format

Sort	{ FILENAME * MERGEFORMAT }
SORT	{ FILENAME * Upper * MERGEFORMAT }

Figure 10.12

Side-by-side example of a Result field, showing the results and the field code itself.

Marker Field

A marker field does not return a result; instead, it supplies information to Word. For example, the XE (Index Entry) field is used to mark entries for an index, which are used to compile an index (see Figure 10.13). Another good example of a Marker field used in legal is a table of authorities and marking citations.

Table·of·Authorities·Marked·Citations·Marker·Field¶

On·July·1,·2002,·ABC·filed·a·motion·for·summary·judgment·on·ABC's·
federal·and·state·antitrust·claims·under·Sections·One·and·Two·of·the·Filter·Act·(3·
U.S.C.·§§·1,·2){**·TA·\l·"Filter·Act·(3·U.S.C.·§§·1,·2)"·\s·"Filter·Act·(3·
U.S.C.·§§·1,·2)"·\c·2·}** and·Section·Three·of·the·Press·Act·(3·U.S.C.·§·11){**·
TA·\l·"Press·Act·(3·U.S.C.·§·11)"·\s·"Press·Act·(3·U.S.C.·§·
11)"·\c·2·}** ··III·E.R.·738.··¶

Generated·Table·of·Authorities·Sample¶

Cases¶
Java·Jitters,·Inc.·v.·United·States,·123·F.2d·703·(9th·Cir.·2002)............·............ 1,·4¶

Statutes¶
Filter·Act·(3·U.S.C.·§§·1,·2)....................................·....................3¶
Press·Act·(3·U.S.C.·§·11) ....·....................3¶
¶

Index·Field·¶

The·superior·court{**·XE·"superior·court:jurisdication"·}**·
granted·summary·judgment·and·defendants'·motion·to·dismiss·against·ABC,·but·
did·not·make·clear·¶

Index¶

{·INDEX·\c·"2"·\z·"1033"·}¶

Figure 10.13

Example of an index field.

Action Field

Unlike Result and Marker fields, Action fields perform an action. For example, the Fill-in field prompts the user for information. Once the information is provided, the Fill-in field will insert that data into the document as many times as needed (see Figure 10.14). Some Action fields perform the action only when you update fields, others perform the action automatically. The general syntax for a Fill-in field is { FILLIN ["Prompt "] [Optional switches] }.

Figure 10.14 A Fill-in field is a good example of an Action field.

Insert a Field

To insert a field, in the Text group on the Insert tab, click Quick Parts and then Field. The Field dialog box displays, listing the available fields in alphabetical order. Click the drop-down arrow under Categories to filter the list by category. To insert the field you want, select from the list and click OK (see Figure 10.15).

NOTE

If you do not want to use the ribbon, fields can also be inserted manually if you know the name of the field and are familiar with the available parameters. Press Ctrl+F9 (Insert Field), type the name of the field, and then press F9 again. For instance, after pressing Ctrl+F9, type Filename. Similarly, you can even type a simple equation by pressing Ctrl+F9 and typing an equal sign and then the formulas (i.e., =9+99). Press F9 to update the field, and you have the result without having to display the Field dialog box.

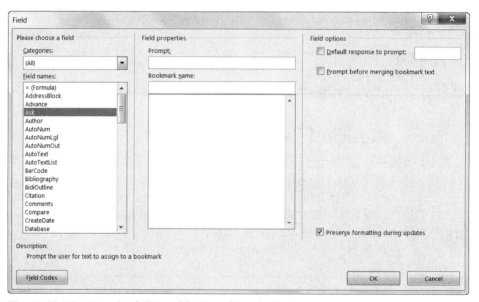

Figure 10.15 View the full list of fields or filter the list by category.

NOTE

If (All) is selected in the Categories list, all available fields are shown in the Field Names list.

EXPERT TIP

If you want to insert your response in more than one location within the document, use the Ask field. The Ask syntax looks like this: { ASK Bookmark "Prompt" [Optional switches] }.

Field Properties

Each of the fields listed has properties associated with that particular field. Click on a field from the list of fields and that field's properties will display in the Field Properties area of the Field dialog box. These properties will vary depending on the nature of the field. For instance, the Date field displays several date formats to refine how the field will display in the document.

Click Field Codes in the bottom-left corner to see the actual code and access any advanced field properties and switches available for the field. Click Hide Codes to return to Field Properties.

Field Options

Each of the fields listed also has various options available for formatting the field. Using the example of the Date field, the available options pertain to calendar formats. Field options can greatly simplify a field's formatting. To apply more complex options, click Field Codes and then Options.

View Fields

You can view the field code instead of the field result within the document by using a keyboard shortcut or the shortcut menu. You also can change your field view options in the Word Options dialog box (File tab, Advanced, Show Document Content).

Insert Fields and View Field Codes

1. Create a new document.

2. In the Text group on the Insert tab, click Quick Parts and then Field.

3. In the Categories list, select Date and Time. Under Field Names, select Date, and then under Date Formats, select a format for the date and click OK. The date will appear in your document.

4. Press Alt+F9 to toggle between the field code and the result.

5. Press Alt+F9 again to toggle the field code back to the result.

6. Right-click on the field and choose Toggle Field Codes to display the field code. Repeat this step to toggle the field code back to the result.

NOTE

Alt+F9 toggles all field codes in the document. To toggle a single field code, place your insertion point in the field code and press Shift+F9. Repeat the keyboard shortcut to toggle the field code back to the field result.

Field Code Shading

By default, field codes appear in the document as normal text. When your insertion point is within the field code, gray shading will appear around the text indicating it's a field code. You can change a setting to always have field codes display with gray shading or to never have them display. Click File, Options, and then Advanced. In the Show Document Content section, click the Field Shading down arrow and select from Never, Always, or When Selected (see Figure 10.16).

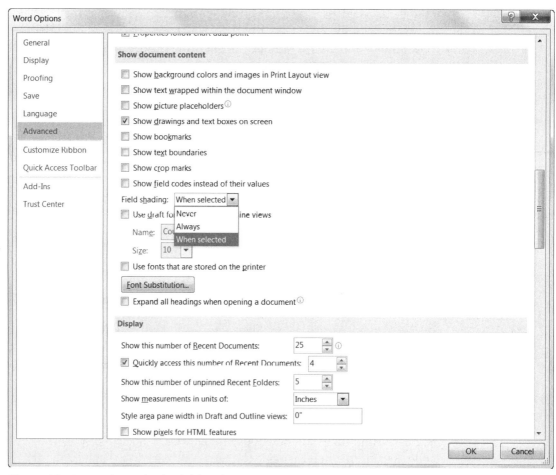

Figure 10.16 To always display field codes with gray shading, set Field Shading to Always.

Update Fields

Updating a field produces the most current result for a field code. For example, updating a TOC field (table of contents) will include any newly added headings to the table of contents as well as update the page numbers. Some fields automatically update and some have to be updated manually. You can update fields one at a time, or you can select and update all fields at once. There is also an option to automatically update all fields when printing a document.

Methods for Updating a Field

- Place the insertion point within the field and press F9. This updates a single field.

- Select the entire document (Ctrl+A) and press F9. This updates all fields in the document.

- Right-click within the field and choose Update Field from the shortcut menu. This updates a single field.

- When available, click the Update command on the content control when the field is selected (see Figure 10.17).

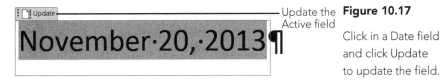

Update the Active field **Figure 10.17**

Click in a Date field and click Update to update the field.

- Activate the Update Fields Before Printing option. Select File, Options, and then select Update Fields Before Printing in the Display section.

Prevent a Field from Being Updated

To prevent a field from updating, you can lock the field using the Lock Field command. Click in the field and press Ctrl+F11. To unlock a field, click in the field and press Ctrl+Shift+F11.

CAUTION

Use the Lock Field command sparingly! Lock Field and Unlock Field can be accomplished using only the keyboard shortcuts (Ctrl+F11 and Ctrl+Shift+F11, respectively). When you right-click in the field, the Update Field option will be grayed out, indicating the field is locked, but unless the document editor is familiar with the keystrokes for locking and unlocking a field, he or she will not be able to update the field.

One example of when you may want to lock a field is with a TOC field (table of contents) and you have the Update Fields Before Printing option enabled (File, Options, Display, under Printing Options). If a manual change was made to the table of contents in a rush situation, and you do not want the field to update when you print the document, locking the field prevents the update from happening. Select the field and press Ctrl+F11 to lock the field; then print the document. Later when you have time to properly update the table of contents without the manual changes, you can unlock the field by selecting the field and pressing Ctrl+Shift+F11; then press F9 to update the field.

Unlink a Field

Unlinking a field permanently converts the field to text. To unlink a field, click in the field and press Ctrl+Shift+F9. If you need to unlink all the fields in a document simultaneously, press Ctrl+A to select the entire document and then press Ctrl+Shift+F9; however, before doing this, make sure that there are no fields that need to remain fields.

One final note on fields: You can use a combination of fields and building blocks to provide sequential numbering in your documents. These certainly come in handy when adding Interrogatories and Answers. The process for creating these is to press Ctrl+F9. Within the bracket, type **SEQ** and press the Spacebar, followed by ROG. Press F9 to update the field and you'll see the number 1 (since it's the only one in the document). Select both the text and the number. From the Insert tab, in the Text group, click Quick Parts, Save Selection to Quick Part Gallery. In the Name box, type **ROG** and accept all other defaults. Back within the document, type **ROG** and press F3. The next number in the sequence is inserted. Now you can add an Answer SEQ field option as well.

COMPLEX DOCUMENTS

While some legal documents contain only simple text and formatting, a majority of them are more complex, utilizing more advanced features such as a table of contents, footnotes and endnotes, a table of authorities, indexes, and cross-references. This chapter covers how to work with these advanced features.

TABLE OF CONTENTS

Two examples of legal documents that may require a table of contents are agreements and briefs. There are two basic methods of creating a Table of Contents: using Word's styles or manually marking entries using field codes and keystroke combinations. The styles method, and in particular using heading styles, is much easier and can be more efficient, preventing mistakes such as forgetting to mark or remove marks from specific entries.

Preparing a Document for a Table of Contents

Documents that require a table of contents typically have multiple sections, such as a cover page at the beginning, followed by a table of contents, and then the main body of the document. You might even have exhibits or schedules at the very end. Building each section of the document will require inserting section breaks between each segment of the document.

Insert an Isolated Section to Contain the Table of Contents

1. Create a new document.

2. Save the document as **Complex Document Practice**.

3. On the first page of the document, type the words **Cover Page** and press Enter.

4. Select the typed text and center-align the text (Ctrl+E), and then apply bold (Ctrl+B) and single underlining (Ctrl+U).

5. Press Ctrl+Shift+S to display the Apply Styles task pane. In the Style Name box, type **Cover Page** and press Enter to create a new style. This style will be used in a later exercise.

6. Press Ctrl+End to move to the paragraph below the text and insert a Next Page section break by selecting Breaks from the Page Setup group on the Page Layout tab and then choosing Next Page.

7. On the new page, press Enter two times to insert a few blank paragraphs. This is where the table of contents will be inserted later.

8. Insert another Next Page section break. This is where the body of the document will be placed. Note that the area that will eventually hold the Table of Contents is now isolated in its own section, Section 2.

9. Keep this document open for the next exercise.

TIP

When working on a document with multiple sections, it's helpful to know which section you're currently working on. By default, the Status bar in Word 2013 doesn't display the section number, but that's easy to remedy. Just right-click on the Status bar and choose Section. You will now be able to easily determine which section your cursor is in by looking at the far left of the Status bar.

Using Multilevel Numbering to Create a Table of Contents

If you studied Chapter 8, "Bullets and Numbering," you will have discovered that the ultimate numbering system in Word is to use multilevel numbering linked to heading styles. Using this method not only keeps the formatting consistent, but allows for easy creation of a table of contents and cross-references, among other benefits.

Apply a Multilevel List and Insert a Table of Contents

1. The Complex Document Practice document should still be open from the previous exercise.

2. Place your insertion point in Section 3 and type **Introduction to Complex Documents** and apply the Title style to the paragraph and press Enter.

3. On the Home tab, in the Paragraph group, click Multilevel List, and choose I., A., 1. The Heading 1 applies the top level number.

4. Type **Introduction** and press Enter.

5. On the Home tab, in the Styles group, select **Heading 2**, type **Statement of Facts**, and press Enter.

6. Press Alt+Ctrl+3 to apply Heading 3, type **Argument**, and press Enter.

7. Apply Heading 1 again, type **Conclusion**, and press Enter.

8. Save the document.

9. Place your insertion point in the first blank paragraph on the second page (Section 2) where the table of contents will be placed.

10. On the References tab, in the Table of Contents group, click Table of Contents. A variety of table of content layouts is available from which to choose. Select Automatic Table 2. The table of contents is inserted at the cursor location.

TIP

As shown in Figure 11.1, additional options are available if you right-click the selected table of contents building block before inserting it. These options allow you to choose a location for the table of contents or edit the properties of the table of contents before inserting it. The Organize and Delete option opens the Building Blocks Organizer.

Figure 11.1 Location options are available when inserting a table of contents building block.

11. If you click within the Table of Contents, you will notice a border surrounding the entire table of contents, as shown in Figure 11.2. This indicates that the table of contents is contained in a content control.

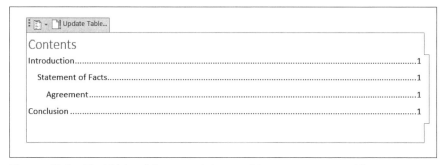

Figure 11.2 The Table of Contents is inserted in a content control for easy updating, deleting, or modifying.

12. Click the Table of Contents button on the top left of the content control to view the available options. You can change the table of contents to another format or even remove the table of contents. A command is also available to update the table of contents.

13. Keep this document open for the next exercise.

NOTE

The content control for the table of contents will display only while in Print Layout or Web Layout view.

Table of Contents Field Codes

When the table of contents is inserted, it displays the results of the TOC field code. If your table of contents does not display as expected, and instead, you see something that displays as {TOC \o"1-3"}, what you are seeing is the field code and not the actual results of the field code. To view the table of contents results, press Alt+F9, which will toggle on and off all field codes in the document.

EXPERT TIP

When working with a table of contents field or other fields, it is recommended that you always show field shading to distinguish between field codes and typed text. To show field shading all the time, choose Options from the File tab and click on Advanced. In the Show Document Content section, click the drop-down box next to Field Shading and select Always. The gray shading to indicate fields is displayed on-screen only, but will not print.

Updating a Table of Contents

The Table of Contents field is a type of field that doesn't automatically update. In other words, if you add another paragraph with a heading style applied to it, the table of contents does not automatically update to include that change. Fortunately, Word provides five ways to update a table of contents.

1. **Select Update Table.** If you inserted the table of contents using one of the built-in or saved building blocks, choose the Update Table button at the top of the content control, as shown in Figure 11.3 or click on the Update Table command in the Table of Contents group on the References tab.

Figure 11.3

An Update Table button is available at the top of the Table of Contents content control.

2. **Keyboard.** Click anywhere within the Table of Contents and press the F9 key on the keyboard.

3. **Shortcut Menu.** Right-click anywhere in the table of contents and choose Update Field from the shortcut menu, as shown in Figure 11.4.

Figure 11.4   The shortcut menu can be used to update any field in Word.

4. **Update the Entire Document.** Press Ctrl+A to select the entire document, and then press F9 to update all the fields in the document at the same time. This method works well, especially when you have other fields in the document, such as cross-references or an index.

5. **Update When Printing.** Enable the option Update Fields Before Printing (File tab, Options, Display). This will update the table of contents as well as all other fields in the document every time you print.

Whichever method you choose to update the table of contents, Word displays an Update Table of Contents dialog box with two options, as shown in Figure 11.5.

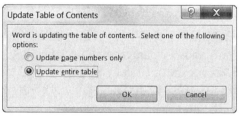

Figure 11.5

You can choose to just update the page numbers or the entire table when updating the table of contents.

- **Update Page Numbers Only.** Word will repaginate the document and update any page numbers that have changed during editing. Any manual editing or formatting in the table of contents is preserved.

- **Update Entire Table.** Word will update the table of contents headings and the page numbers. Any manual edits or formatting changes will be lost.

Your insertion point can be anywhere in your document when you use the Update Table button in the Table of Contents group on the References tab. Select Update Entire Table from the Update Table of Contents dialog box, and the Table of Contents will update to include any new headings applied.

TIP

Modifying Table of Content Styles

If you find yourself constantly reformatting the table of contents by adjusting tab settings, left indents, hanging indents, and spacing after, you'll find that you can save a great deal of time by modifying the table of content styles. Changing the styles will preserve the formatting changes whenever you update or replace the table of contents.

Word uses nine table of content styles named TOC 1 through TOC 9, and they correspond to each heading style level (e.g., Heading 1 through Heading 9). TOC styles are set to automatically update, which means that any formatting changes you apply to a paragraph formatted with a TOC style will automatically change the underlying style to match. TOC styles are also hidden until used , which means they will not display in the Styles task pane by default.

After you have modified TOC styles, you may want to save it as a custom table of contents building block for later use. TOC styles can be saved to the document template, so every time you create a document based on that template, the TOC styles will retain your changes.

The horizontal ruler is often used to manually change the tabs and indents for TOC styles; however, the ruler is not visible by default. Turn on the ruler from the View tab, and in the Show group, select the Ruler check box.

TIP

Modify a Table of Contents

1. The file from the previous exercise should still be open.

2. Place your insertion point after the Table of Contents heading and press Enter.

3. Verify that the Normal style is applied to that paragraph. Type **PAGE** and then right-align the paragraph.

4. Press Ctrl+Shift+S to display the Apply Styles task pane.

5. In the Style Name box of the Apply Styles task pane, type **TOC Page** and click New. A new style named TOC Page is created.

6. Place your insertion point in any of the level 1 table of contents paragraphs.

7. Using the ruler, set the hanging indent to .5", and set the tab stop to .5" to match the hanging indent. Notice all other TOC level 1 paragraphs are also changed. The style has been modified.

NOTE

At the time of this writing, although Word 2013 will allow you to set a tab stop beyond the right margin, it will ignore it, and the page numbers will align no further than the right margin. If the right indent marker is set to the inside of the right margin, then it will align to the tab. Additionally, if the tab marker is to the right of the right indent marker and you click on the tab marker on the ruler, it will unexpectedly jump to the same position as the right indent marker.

8. Place your insertion point in the level 2 table of contents paragraph.

9. Using the ruler, set the tab stop to 1", set the left indent to .5", and set the hanging indent to 1".

10. Click Format and select Paragraph.

11. Place your insertion point in the level 3 table of contents paragraph.

12. Using the ruler, set the tab stop to 1.5", set the left indent to 1", and set the hanging indent to 1.5". Leave this file open for the next exercise.

NOTE

At the time of this writing, although Word 2013 will allow you to set a tab stop beyond the right indent marker, it will ignore it, and the page numbers will align no further than the right indent marker. In previous versions of Word, the right tab with the dot leader controlled the placement of the page number in the table of contents. This is a common practice in legal documents for proper placement of the page number.

Saving a Table of Contents as a Building Block

After you have modified the table of contents styles with the proper formats, you might find that you would like to save these modifications for use in other documents. You can save this custom work as a building block in the Table of Contents gallery.

Save a Table of Contents Building Block

1. The document used in the previous exercise should still be open.

2. Select the table of contents.

TIP

A quick way to select the table of contents is to click the three dots on the left side of the content control, as shown in Figure 11.6.

Figure 11.6

The entire table of contents can be quickly selected by clicking the left side of the content control.

3. On the References tab, click Table of Contents in the Table of Contents Group, and then select Save Selection to Table of Contents Gallery. The Create New Building Block dialog box displays, as shown in Figure 11.7.

Figure 11.7 Save the table of contents for use in other documents.

4. In the Name box, type **Agreement**.

5. The description field is optional. In the Description box, type **For agreements**.

6. Click OK.

Your saved building block will appear in the list of available Table of Contents building blocks in the General category. To view the building block, click Table of Contents on the References tab.

Customizing a Table of Contents

If you prefer to insert a table of contents without a content control, use the Custom Table of Contents command. The Table of Contents dialog box will display offering additional options for the table of contents. The drawback of using this method is that a table of contents heading is not automatically inserted as occurs when using the building block method.

Insert a Custom Table of Contents

1. The document from the previous exercise should still be open.

2. On the References tab, click Table of Contents in the Table of Contents Group, and then select Remove Table of Contents.

3. Apply the Title style to the first paragraph of Section 2, type **Table of Contents** and press Enter.

4. On the References tab, click Table of Contents in the Table of Contents group and choose Custom Table of Contents. This opens the familiar dialog box used in previous versions of Word.

5. Among other things, the Table of Contents dialog box provides options affecting page number alignment, type of tab leaders to use, the format of the entire table of contents, and the number of levels to display, as shown in Figure 11.8.

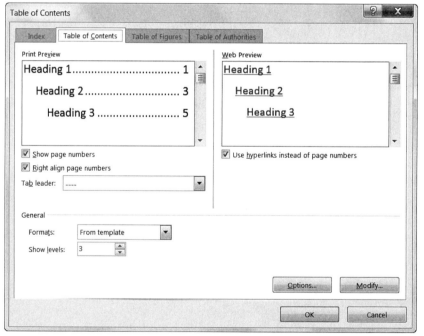

Figure 11.8 The Table of Contents dialog box allows you to customize formatting and what's included in the table of contents.

6. Accept the defaults and click OK to generate a table of contents.

7. Keep the document open for the next exercise.

Include Non-Heading Styles in the Table of Contents

Heading styles are automatically marked for inclusion in the table of contents; however, you can choose additional built-in or custom styles for inclusion as well. In this exercise, you will include the Cover Page style created earlier in this chapter.

Use the Options Dialog Box to Include Non-Heading Styles in the Table of Contents

1. Click within the table of contents inserted in the previous exercise.

2. On the References tab, click Table of Contents in the Table of Contents group. Choose Custom Table of Contents.

3. Click Options.

4. Under the TOC level column in the box next to Cover Page, type **1**. As shown in Figure 11.9, a check mark appears to the left of the Cover Page style indicating that the Cover Page style will be included in the table of contents. The "1" indicates that the TOC 1 style will be applied just like for the Heading 1 style.

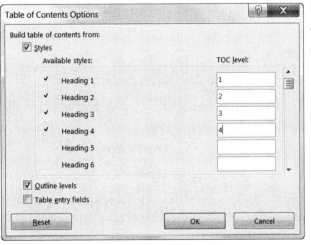

Figure 11.9

The Table of Contents Options dialog box allows you to choose which styles you want included in the table of contents.

5. Click OK to close the Table of Contents Options dialog box.

6. Click OK again to close the Table of Contents dialog box.

7. A message appears asking whether you want to replace the selected table of contents. Click OK.

8. The table of contents now contains the Cover Page heading and page number.

9. Keep this file open for the next exercise.

If you created a table of contents by assigning the levels in the Table of Contents Options dialog box, and the table of contents is deleted, you would need to reassign the levels to the styles again to re-create the same table of contents. Another method to create the table of contents without losing the outline level assignment is to modify the style. Then, if the table of contents gets deleted, it will retain the setting because it is in the style.

Modify Styles to Include Non-Heading Styles in the Table of Contents

1. The document from the previous exercise should still be open.

2. On the References tab, click Table of Contents in the Table of Contents Group, and then select Remove Table of Contents.

3. Press Ctrl+Home to move the insertion point to the beginning of the document. You should be in the Cover Page paragraph.

4. Open the Apply Styles task pane (Ctrl+Shift+S). The Cover Page style should appear in the Style Name box.

5. Click Modify.

6. Click Format and then select Paragraph.

7. On the Indents and Spacing tab of the Paragraph dialog box, select Level 1 from the Outline Level list.

8. Click OK twice to return to the document.

9. Click directly below the Table of Contents heading on page 2.

10. On the References tab, click Table of Contents in the Table of Contents group. Choose Custom Table of Contents.

11. Click OK.

12. The paragraph styled with the Cover Page style is included in the table of contents.

13. Save and close the document.

CAUTION

The Add Text command in the Table of Contents group on the References tab (as shown in Figure 11.10) will allow you to include or exclude specific paragraphs in the table of contents by assigning an outline level to the paragraph. Take care when using this feature as the results vary depending on the style applied to the paragraph. If the paragraph has the Normal style or a Heading style applied, this option will apply a Heading style corresponding to the level you select. If a style other than a Heading or Normal style (e.g., Body Text) is applied, it will apply the outline level as a direct format.

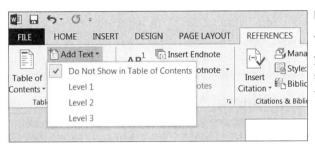

Figure 11.10

The Add Text feature allows you to exclude or include specific paragraphs in the table of contents.

Manually Marking Entries for a Table of Contents

There may be occasions where you will want specific text to appear in the table of contents. To mark an entry for inclusion in the table of contents, select the text, press Alt+Shift+O to open the Mark Table of Contents Entry dialog box, select a level, and click Mark.

In most cases, using manually marked table of contents fields to generate a table of contents is the least desirable method for the following reasons:

1. **Paragraph numbering is not included.** Word's mark table of contents entry feature only picks up text, not the automatic paragraph numbering. If the paragraph you are marking contains an automatic paragraph number, you will need to manually type the paragraph number to include it.

2. **Manually marked entries do not update.** Table Entry fields do not update to reflect changes in the document. For example, if you marked the paragraph "Introduction" and later changed the text to "Overview," you also would need to modify the field code with the same change.

Manually marking entries creates a TC field, which is formatted as hidden text and uses the following syntax: {TC "Text" [Switches]}. The text between the quotation marks is what will appear in the Table of Contents. The Mark Table of Contents Entry dialog box has options for how you want the entry to appear in the Table of Contents, as shown in Figure 11.11.

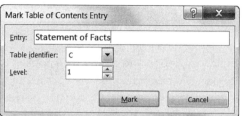

Figure 11.11

The Mark Table of Contents Entry dialog box allows you to enter or modify the entry, and choose a table identifier and a level.

The Entry Box

The text selected when invoking the Mark Table of Contents command is placed in the Entry box and can be modified. This is useful if the text appearing in the table of contents needs to be different than it appears in the body of the document.

The Table Identifier

The Table Identifier drop-down list box controls the \f switch, which identifies the TOC entry as a specific type. In a TOC field, you refer to the one-letter entry identifier to build tables of specific entries. For example, to build a table of illustrations in a document, you mark each entry with a field such as {TC "Illustration 1" \f i}, where "i" identifies only illustration entries.

The Level Box

This box controls the \l switch, which identifies the entry level of the TOC entry. In a TOC field, you refer to the one-letter level identifier to designate the level of specific entries. For example, a TOC entry similar to a level two heading might be marked with {TC "Entering Data" \l 2}. This makes it possible to create a table of contents composed only of entries for specific levels.

After you have completed manually marking entries for insertion in a table of contents, you have to tell Word to include these entries by enabling Table Entry Fields in the Table of Contents Options dialog box. These marked entries can be generated along with heading and non-heading styles, as well as outline levels.

Manually Mark Table of Contents Entries

1. Create a new blank document.

2. Type **=rand()** and press Enter to create five paragraphs of random text.

3. Select the first sentence of the first paragraph and press Alt+Shift+O to open the Mark Table of Contents Entry dialog box.

4. Accept the default Table Identifier and Level.

5. Click Mark to mark the entry. Leave the dialog box open for the next step.

6. Select the first sentence of text in the second paragraph.

7. Click on the Mark Table of Contents Entry dialog box to activate it or press Alt+Shift+O to redisplay it if closed. The Entry text again reflects the selected text.

8. In the Level box, click the arrow to increment the level to 2.

9. Click Mark to mark the entry.

10. Move the insertion point to the beginning of the third paragraph.

11. Select the first sentence of text in the third paragraph.

12. Click on the Mark Table of Contents Entry dialog box to activate it.

13. Click Mark.

TIP

If you're marking a new entry for the same level, after the text is selected, just click Mark even though it appears that the Mark button is not available. It will mark the selected entry without activating the dialog box first.

14. Mark the first sentence of the next two paragraphs following the same steps and mark each paragraph as Level 1.

15. Close the Mark Table of Contents Entry dialog box.

16. Leave this document open for the next exercise.

CAUTION

Table of Contents entry fields are formatted as hidden text. It is possible for these entries to affect the pagination of the document if hidden text displays on the screen. Before generating a table of contents with manually marked fields, be sure to turn off the display of hidden text by clicking Show/Hide in the Paragraph group on the Home tab.

Now that the entries are marked, you are ready to generate the table of contents.

Generate a Table of Contents from Manually Marked Fields

1. Press Ctrl+End to move your insertion point to the end of the document and add a page break by pressing Ctrl+Enter.

2. On the References tab, click Table of Contents in the Table of Contents group and click Custom Table of Contents.

3. Click Options.

4. On the Table of Contents Options dialog box, select the Table entry fields check box.

5. Click OK twice to insert the Table of Contents.

6. Close the document without saving.

TABLE 11.1—SHORTCUT KEYS FOR TABLE OF CONTENTS

SHORTCUT KEY	RESULTS
Alt+Shift+O	Mark Table of Contents entry
F9	Update selected Table of Contents field
Shift+F9	Toggle selected Table of Contents field

Using the Style Separator

The style separator is used to separate heading text from the rest of the paragraph's text. When the table of contents is generated, it will include only the heading text and not the entire paragraph. The style separator's function creates the separation of the heading and the body text by allowing two styles to be applied in the same paragraph.

The style separator does not appear by default on the ribbon; however, it can be added to the Quick Access Toolbar.

Add the Style Separator Button to the Quick Access Toolbar

1. Click the down arrow to the right of the Quick Access Toolbar.

2. Choose More Commands.

3. In the Choose Commands From drop-down list, choose All Commands.

4. Scroll down until you locate the style separator and select it.

5. Click Add.

6. Click OK.

If you prefer not to add the style separator to the Quick Access Toolbar, alternatively you can use the keyboard shortcut Alt+Ctrl+Enter.

Use the Style Separator

1. Create a new blank document.

2. Type **Agreement** and apply the Heading 1 style to the text by pressing Alt+Ctrl+1.

3. With the insertion point at the end of the text, click the Style Separator button that you added to the Quick Access Toolbar in the previous exercise. Word automatically inserts something that looks like a hidden paragraph mark.

4. After the style separator, type a period followed by a space and then type **This text will not appear in the Table of Contents.** Notice the Normal style is applied to this text. Press Enter.

5. Type **Definitions** and apply the Heading 2 style by pressing Alt+Ctrl+2.

6. Click the Style Separator button, type a period followed by a space, and then type **My text will appear here but not in the Table of Contents.** Press Enter.

7. On the References tab, click Table of Contents in the Table of Contents group, and then right-click Automatic Table 2 and choose Insert at Beginning of Document.

8. Notice that text formatted with heading styles is inserted into the Table of Contents field, but the text following the style separator is not included.

9. Close the document without saving.

By default, when you insert the style separator into an existing paragraph, it automatically places it at the end of the paragraph, not at the cursor position. If you want to add the style separator at a specific point in an existing paragraph, you will need to separate the heading text from the body text of the paragraph first and then apply the style separator.

Insert a Style Separator into an Existing Paragraph

1. Create a new blank document.

2. Apply the Heading 1 style by pressing Alt+Ctrl+1 and type **Defined Terms. For the purposes of this Agreement, the following words shall have the following meanings:**

3. Press Enter.

4. Apply the Heading 2 style by pressing Alt+Ctrl+2 and type **Affiliate. An Affiliate of any Person means any Person that controls, is controlled by, or is under common control with such Person.**

5. Press Enter.

6. Place your insertion point after Terms and before the period and press Enter.

7. Place your insertion point after Terms again and click the Style Separator button on the Quick Access Toolbar.

8. Delete the paragraph mark inserted in Step 6. If an extra space is inserted after the style separator, but before the period, delete it.

9. Press Ctrl+Shift+S to open the Apply Styles task pane, type **Body Text**, and press Enter to apply the Body Text style.

10. Repeat the same steps to insert the style separator to the second paragraph.

11. Insert a Table of Contents at the beginning of the document.

12. Close the document without saving.

If you completed the preceding steps to insert the style separator, you are probably asking yourself if there's an easier way to do this. Fortunately, PayneGroup's Numbering Assistant product not only assists with multilevel numbering linked to heading styles, but it has an automatic generation of style separators right where you want them. You can even tell the Numbering Assistant to insert multiple style separators throughout the entire document.

FOOTNOTES AND ENDNOTES

Footnotes and endnotes are prevalent in legal documents and serve four primary purposes.

- Reference an authority supporting a position made in the document.

- Furnish a source for a quotation.

- Make an argument where you paraphrase others' thoughts.

- Provide additional information about a topic that is not included in the main body of text.

Inserting footnotes and endnotes into legal documents is fairly simple. You also can edit and format the footnotes and endnotes; in fact, they will automatically renumber if you have to add, move, or delete the notes. Even better, you can quickly view footnotes and endnotes by hovering the mouse directly over the reference number in the document.

The footnote number in the document is called the footnote reference; likewise, the endnote number in the document is called the endnote reference. The formatting of the footnote reference number and the footnote text is controlled by styles. The Footnote Reference style is applied to footnote marks, and the Footnote Text style is applied to the text of the footnote. Similarly, the styles for endnotes are Endnote Reference and Endnote Text.

Footnote text appears at the bottom of a page, while endnote text appears at the end of a document or section. In Print Layout view, the footnotes appear at the bottom of the page while endnotes appear after the conclusion of the section or document. In Draft view, footnotes and endnotes appear in a separate Notes pane.

Footnote and endnote features are described in Table 11.2.

TABLE 11.2—ELEMENTS OF A FOOTNOTE OR ENDNOTE	
FEATURE	**DESCRIPTION**
Footnote or endnote reference marks	These are usually numbers, but they also can be symbols, or a combination of symbols and numbers, which indicate additional information is contained in a footnote or endnote. The reference marks automatically are superscripted and formatted with the Footnote Reference or Endnote Reference style.
Separator line	Also referred to as the Note Separator, this is the short horizontal line, which separates the body text of the document from the footnotes and endnotes.
Footnote text	The text of the footnote, which appears at the bottom of the page. By default, all footnote text is formatted with the Footnote Text style.
Endnote text	The text of the endnote, which appears at the end of the section or document. By default, all endnote text is formatted with the Endnote Text style.

Inserting Footnotes and Endnotes

You can use ribbon commands to insert notes, or you can insert them using keyboard shortcuts. To use the ribbon to insert a footnote, on the References tab, choose Insert Footnote or Insert Endnote in the Footnotes group. The keyboard combination to insert a footnote is Alt+Ctrl+F. The keyboard shortcut for inserting an endnote is Alt+Ctrl+D.

Inserting Basic Endnotes and Footnotes

1. Create a new blank document. Switch to Print Layout view (in the Views group on the View tab, select Print Layout).

2. Type **This report explains the rationale for the primary legal documents required to establish and operate a cooperative.** Press Enter.

3. Place your insertion point immediately following the word "establish," but before the space.

4. In the Footnotes group on the References tab, click Insert Footnote. The cursor automatically moves to the bottom of the page.

5. Type **Terminating on December 31, 2015.**

6. Place your insertion point back into the main body text of the document, immediately after the word "cooperative."

7. Use the keyboard shortcut Alt+Ctrl+F to insert another footnote.

8. Type **Commencing on January 2, 2014.** Double-click the footnote reference number 2. This moves you back to the main body text near the second footnote.

9. Place your insertion point immediately after the word "rationale."

10. On the References tab in the Footnote group, click Insert Endnote or press Alt+Ctrl+D.

11. Type **This is an endnote.**

12. Keep this document open for the next exercise.

NOTE

When inserting both footnotes and endnotes into the same document, the Number Format automatically changes so the type of reference marks used is different.

Change Footnote or Endnote Options

When using either a keyboard shortcut or ribbon command to insert a footnote or endnote, as described in the previous exercise, the Footnote and Endnote dialog box does not open. If the default formatting of the footnote and endnote is adequate, you can continue to use this method to add notes to your document. However, if you need to include custom marks that differ from the default, the best method is to open the Footnote and Endnote dialog box, as shown in Figure 11.12.

To display the Footnote and Endnote dialog box, on the References tab, click the dialog box launcher in the Footnotes group. When using the dialog box to insert notes, you can specify what formatting to use. In legal documents, numbers are commonly used; however, you can also use custom marks.

Figure 11.12

Modify existing notes or use a custom footnote or endnote.

Viewing and Editing Footnotes and Endnotes

For the previous exercise, the document was in Print Layout view. Since footnotes and endnotes appear differently in Draft view, the next exercise will explore the benefits of using Draft view when viewing and editing footnotes and endnotes.

Modifying a Footnote

1. The document from the previous exercise should still be open. Switch to Draft view (in the Views group on the View tab, select Draft).

2. On the References tab, click Show Notes in the Footnotes group (see Figure 11.13), and the Show Notes dialog box appears.

Show Notes

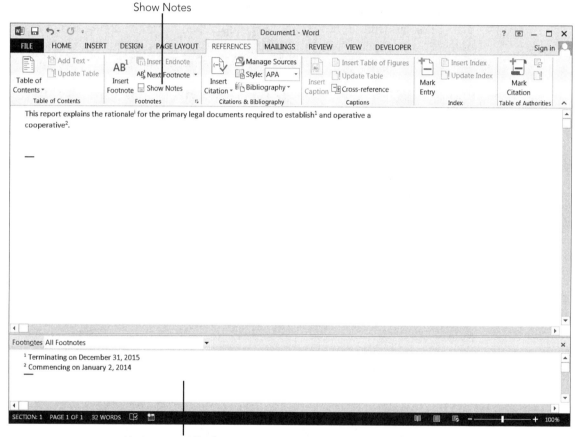

Notes pane in Draft view

Figure 11.13 For documents containing both footnotes and endnotes, the Show Notes prompt allows you to choose which notes area to view.

3. From the Show Notes dialog box, select View Footnote Area and click OK. The Notes pane opens displaying the footnotes text area.

TIP

A quick way to move to the footnotes or endnotes area is to double-click on a foot-note or endnote reference mark.

4. Change the first footnote date to **December 31, 2016.**

5. Keep this document open for the next exercise.

TIP

To easily switch between the footnote area and the endnote area while in the Notes pane, click the drop-down arrow next to Footnotes and select All Endnotes.

Modifying the Note Separators

In order to separate the main body text of the document from the footnotes or endnotes, Word offers three separator options.

- **Footnote or Endnote Separator.** A two-inch line that appears between the main document text and the note text.

- **Footnote or Endnote Continuation Separator.** The horizontal line that appears between the main document text and the note text when the note splits and continues onto the next page.

- **Footnote or Endnote Continuation Notice.** The text that appears when a note splits across pages. No text appears by default.

On occasion, and especially with lengthy footnotes, you may want to change how the continuation notice appears in the footnote area of the document. The next exercise will show you how to modify the footnote continuation separator.

Modifying the Footnote Continuation Separator

1. The document from the previous exercise should still be open.

2. Switch to Draft view (in the Views group on the View tab, select Draft).

3. On the References tab, click Show Notes in the Footnotes group, select View Footnote Area and then click OK.

NOTE

Legal documents typically do not contain both footnotes and endnotes. If you have just footnotes in your document, you will not receive the Show Notes dialog box.

4. In the Notes pane, click the drop-down arrow next to Footnotes and choose Footnote Continuation Notice.

5. Type **(continued)**. Close the Notes pane by clicking the "x" in the upper-right corner of the Notes pane.

6. Close the document without saving.

A graphic line or other text can be used in lieu of the Footnote Separator or Footnote Continuation Separator. Similar options are also available for endnotes.

CAUTION

At the time of this writing, when modifying the Footnote Separator, Footnote Continuation Separator, and Footnote Continuation Notice in a new Word 2013 document, only the customized Footnote Separator displays for all three notices at the bottom of the page in Print Layout view. The only workaround to this missing Footnote Continuation Separator and Notice issue is to keep the document in the previous file format (anything prior to Word 2013 will work) or if the document is already saved in Word 2013, you could save it as a Word 97-2003 (*.doc) document until this issue is fixed. Customizations to the Endnote Separator, Endnote Continuation Separator, and Endnote Continuation Notice all work properly in Word 2013.

Deleting or Moving Footnotes or Endnotes

To delete a footnote or endnote, select and delete the reference mark located in the main body of text of the document. This will simultaneously remove both the reference mark and the note text. Similarly, to move a footnote or endnote, select and cut the reference mark in the main body text of the document (Ctrl+X) and paste it (Ctrl+V) to the new location. When you delete or move a footnote or endnote reference mark, all other notes in the document automatically renumber.

CAUTION

When deleting a footnote or endnote, do not delete the footnote or endnote text. If you do this, the reference mark will remain in the document, and the footnote or endnote text area will be empty.

HYPERLINKS

Anyone who uses the Internet on a regular basis is probably familiar with the term hyperlink. Hyperlinks typically appear as colored, underlined text that when clicked take you to a location, such as an Internet website. When used in Word documents, a hyperlink can perform many functions, such as directing the reader to another part of the same document, a different document, a website, or even create a new e-mail message or a new document.

NOTE

You may be limited to what you can do with hyperlinks in your environment if your firm has a document management system.

Insert a Hyperlink

1. Choose Hyperlink located in the Links group on the Insert tab, or alternatively, you can press Ctrl+K to display the Insert Hyperlink dialog box.

2. The Link To bar on the left lists the different types of hyperlinks that can be created. They include Existing File Or Web Page, Place In This Document, Create New Document, and E-Mail Address. Select Existing File or Web Page.

3. In the Text To Display box, type **RSVP**. This is the text that displays in the document for the hyperlink. By specifying information here, you can have specific text appear in the document (such as RSVP), rather than showing a long path with a filename to a hyperlinked document.

4. Click ScreenTip and the Set Hyperlink ScreenTip dialog box opens.

5. Type **Click here to respond to the invitation** as the ScreenTip text and click OK.

6. In the Address box, specify the location where the hyperlink should direct the reader. Select any document from the current folder location and click OK. The hyperlink is inserted into the document.

7. Hover your mouse over the hyperlink, and if the mouse pointer changes to a pointing hand, click to activate the hyperlink. If the mouse pointer does not change to a pointing hand while hovering the mouse over the hyperlink, hold down the Ctrl key and click the hyperlink. This transports you to the hyperlinked location.

8. Close the document without saving.

Once the hyperlink has been activated, the default color of the hyperlink changes from blue to purple. This color change is controlled by the Hyperlink and Followed Hyperlink styles.

Other Hyperlink Choices

The following options are also available in the Insert Hyperlink dialog box:

- **Place In This Document.** Select a location within the current document for the hyperlink. This can be bookmarked text or a heading.

- **Create New Document.** If you are planning to create a new document when the hyperlink is clicked, select this option.

- **E-Mail Address.** Insert an e-mail address hyperlink, which will create a new message to the addressee when the hyperlink is activated.

TIP

Some firms use a list of hyperlinks to help temporary staff easily locate important documents when they are covering for someone during an absence. For example, the regular secretary can create a document that includes hyperlinks to each file used in a closing, along with pertinent instructions on what to do with each file. This eliminates the necessity for temporary personnel to rummage through and view numerous documents before finding exactly what they need.

Editing and Removing a Hyperlink

To edit a hyperlink, you can always delete and re-create it; however, an easier way to edit the hyperlink is to right-click the hyperlink and choose Edit Hyperlink from the shortcut menu.

The Edit Hyperlink command displays the Edit Hyperlink dialog box, Open Hyperlinks acts as if the hyperlink was clicked and performs the predefined action, Copy Hyperlink copies the link, and Remove Hyperlink strips the link and removes the hyperlink formatting, leaving only the text.

BOOKMARKS

Bookmarks are useful for a variety of tasks in Word. First and most obvious, you can use a bookmark to mark your place in a document. For example, when reviewing a contract, you can insert a bookmark named "ReturnHere." Bookmarks are sometimes used for calculations where you need to add two or more values. To illustrate this use, suppose that you have two tables, each with a total. By selecting each total and creating a bookmark, you can reference each to create a grand total equation (e.g., =Cost+Expense). Bookmarks can also be used for cross-reference purposes, and they can be used as placeholders for values when writing macros as well.

Making Bookmarks Visible

By default, bookmarks are invisible, meaning that at first glance, you will not be aware that bookmarks exist in a document. When working with bookmarks, you will want to see the bookmark locations by configuring an option. Choose Options from the File tab and click the Advanced tab. Check the option Show Bookmarks in the Show Document Content section. When bookmarks are visible, they appear as square brackets if they surround text, or they appear as an I-Bar next to the bookmarked text.

Insert a Bookmark

To insert a bookmark, select the text or click where the bookmark should go, and then choose Bookmark from the Insert tab in the Links group, or alternatively, use the keyboard shortcut Ctrl+Shift+F5 to display the Bookmark dialog box, as shown in Figure 11.14. Type a name that does not start with a numeric value or include any spaces (you can use an underscore character to separate words) and click Add.

NOTE

Bookmark names are limited to 40 characters.

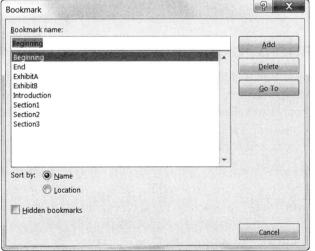

Figure 11.14

Insert the name of the bookmark in the Bookmark dialog box.

TIP

Bookmarks also can be sorted by name or by location within the document.

Redefine a Bookmark

If you need to change the location of an existing bookmark, you can display the Bookmark dialog box and overwrite the original. Place your insertion point where the bookmark should be moved to and select Bookmark from the Links group on the Insert tab. Select the bookmark name from the list and click Add. This moves the bookmark to the new location.

After you create a bookmark, its name cannot be changed. If you need to change the name of a bookmark, you must first delete the original bookmark and then re-create it. To delete a bookmark, display the Bookmark dialog box, select the bookmark to be removed, and then click Delete.

Navigate to Bookmarks

After a bookmark has been added to a document, you can navigate to a bookmark location by pressing Ctrl+G. By default, the Go To dialog box assumes that you want to go to a specific page number in the document. However, you also can type in a bookmark name instead of a page number, click Go To, and you're taken directly to the bookmark. There's no need to change the Go To What list selection first.

Another way to navigate to a bookmark location is to display the Bookmark dialog box by clicking Bookmark in the Links group on the Insert tab, selecting the bookmark, and then clicking the Go To button.

Automatic Bookmark

Word 2013 has a new automatic bookmark feature that will take you to the last location visited in your document. This bookmark does not appear in the Bookmark dialog box. If you close and reopen your document, a Welcome back! message appears, and when clicked, it returns you to the location where you last left off editing, as shown in Figure 11.15.

In Print Layout view, if you don't immediately click the message, it will change to a bookmark flag near the vertical scroll bar, as shown in Figure 11.16. If you hover your mouse over the bookmark flag, the Welcome back! message will reappear. In Print Layout view, the bookmark flag appears near the vertical scroll bar. In Read Mode, the bookmark flag appears near the status bar.

TIP

If you ignore the automatic bookmark and start editing the document, the bookmark flag goes away. Press Shift+F5 to return to the last edited area of the document.

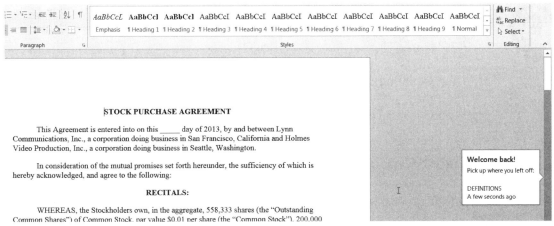

Figure 11.15   Click the new Welcome Back! message to quickly return to your last editing location.

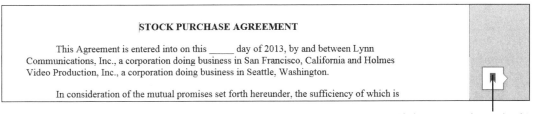

Click to see Welcome back!
Message bookmark

Figure 11.16   In Print Layout view, the bookmark flag appears near the vertical scroll bar.

CROSS-REFERENCES

In legal documents, cross-references are used most often in contracts when you refer a reader to another location in the document for additional information. For example, you might cross-reference a numbered heading or paragraph where the cross-reference reads "See Paragraph VI.A.3" and you can include the words "above"or"below"to point the reader to the location of the associated text. Other types of cross-references might refer the reader to a specific page, or even a specific footnote.

NOTE

Cross-reference fields do not update automatically while the document is being edited. To update a cross-reference, select it and press F9. Better yet, you can update all fields in the document at the same time by pressing Ctrl+A to select the entire document and then press F9 to update. Alternatively, you can right-click on the selected field and choose Update Field from the shortcut menu.

EXPERT TIP

You might consider enabling the option Update Fields Before Printing to force all fields to update each time the document is printed (File, Options, Display, Printing Options section).

When exploring the cross-referencing feature, you may find additional uses for this feature. Perhaps cross-referencing bookmarks, equations, figures, or tables may be essential in certain documents.

Insert Cross-References

1. Open a new blank document, type **=rand(5)**, and press Enter to insert text.

2. Select all text in the document (Ctrl+A), and from the Paragraph group on the Home tab, click on the Numbering button to add automatic paragraph numbering to each paragraph.

3. Place your insertion point at the end of the last paragraph where we will insert a cross-reference.

4. Type **For more information, see paragraph** and press the Spacebar.

5. On the References tab, choose Cross-reference in the Captions group. The Cross-reference dialog box opens, as shown in Figure 11.17.

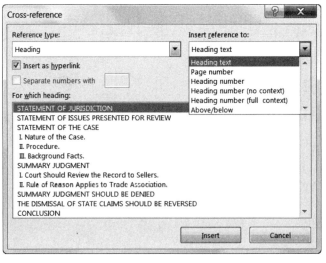

Figure 11.17

Choose the type of reference and how it should appear in the document.

TIP

Cross-references can be formatted as a hyperlink.

6. Under Reference Type, select Numbered Item from the drop-down list.

7. From the Insert Reference To list, choose Paragraph Number.

8. Select the Include Above/Below check box.

9. Under the For Which Number Item, select the first numbered paragraph from the list.

10. Click Insert.

NOTE

If you have multiple cross-references to insert, after inserting the first cross-reference, keep the dialog box open. Then click in the main document area to navigate to the next place you want to insert a cross-reference. When you're ready to insert the next cross-reference item, click in the dialog box and make the next cross-reference selection.

11. Click Close.

12. Close the document without saving.

NOTE

When you select the option Paragraph Number (Full Context) from the Insert Reference To list, the option Separate Numbers With is enabled. This option allows you to add a character, space, or hyphen between paragraph numbers so they are easier to read; for example, Article I-Section 1.1. Click in the box and type a dash to separate the paragraph level indicators.

TIP

By default, the cross-reference is inserted as a hyperlink. Ctrl+click on the cross-referenced item to be directed to the referenced location.

There are three choices for paragraph number in the Insert Reference To list. Table 11.3 describes each option.

TABLE 11.3—PARAGRAPH NUMBER CROSS-REFERENCE OPTIONS	
REFERENCE TYPE	**DESCRIPTION**
Paragraph Number	Inserts the cross-reference relative to its location. If your insertion point is in paragraph IV, and you insert a cross-reference to IV.B, Word will insert the B only. If your insertion point is in paragraph II, and you insert a cross-reference to IV.B, Word will insert IV.B.
Paragraph Number (No Context)	Inserts the lowest level of the paragraph number. If you insert a reference to paragraph IV.A.1, Word will insert the 1 only.
Paragraph Number (Full Context)	Inserts the full paragraph number at all times.

View and Update Cross-References

If you have inserted cross-references as hyperlinks, you can use Ctrl+click on a cross-reference to jump to the referenced location in the document. By default, the option Ctrl+click to follow hyperlink (File tab, Options, Advanced, Editing Options) is turned on.

Cross-references are fields and may appear on the screen with gray shading. The gray shading is determined by the Field Shading setting (File tab, Options, Advanced, Show Document Content). Field shading will not print.

When a paragraph or heading changes, the cross-reference will not automatically update to reflect the change. To update a single cross-reference, right-click on the reference and select Update Field from the shortcut menu. To update all cross-references, press Ctrl+A to select the entire document and press F9.

EXPERT TIP

When using cross-references with automatic numbering, when the cross-reference is inserted, it places a hidden bookmark that starts before the automatic number and ends at the end of the paragraph. You cannot see these hidden bookmarks even if the Show Bookmarks option is enabled (File tab, Options, Advanced, Show Document Content section). Be careful to not create a new numbered paragraph by pressing Enter just after the automatic number, but before the text that follows the number. Even though it will give you a new automatic number, you've just broken the bookmarked cross-reference. Rather, insert a new number by going above the numbered paragraph, create an empty paragraph and apply the style (e.g., Heading 1).

TABLE OF AUTHORITIES

Certain court rules require that briefs and other similar types of documents contain a table of authorities. *The Bluebook: A Uniform System of Citation* is one of the popular reference manuals commonly referred to when formatting legal citations in the United States. Some states have specific standards for which they even created their own style manuals. In addition to the reference manuals available, some courts may have their own approved criteria and rules.

Word's Table of Authorities feature is similar to marking Table of Contents entries—you find the text you want to mark and when all citations are marked, you generate the table. Depending on the requirements, you can mark and generate a list of cases, statutes, rules, and other items, including custom categories.

Marking Citations

Before you can generate a table of authorities, you need to mark the items you want to include in the table. The Mark Citation dialog box helps find citations in the document. When you start marking the citations Word finds, you can mark a single citation or have Word automatically mark the long and short forms of the citations.

There are certain terms that Word looks for when searching for a citation:

- in re
- v.
- Id.
- , Supra
- Ibid
- , Infra
- Cong. (for Congress)
- Sess. (for Session)
- § (section symbol)
- (19xx) (to find dates in parentheses where x is any number)

NOTE

Long and Short Form Citations:

A long form citation, also known as a long cite, contains the full case name and the location of the case within the publication. The long form must be included when marking the citation for the first time. A short form citation, or short cite, is similar to a nickname and is used when subsequently referring to the same long form citation within the same document.

Although there are as many variations as there are jurisdictions, if you are new to working in litigation, Table 11.4 lists some examples of case citations to help understand the basic syntax of a citation.

TABLE 11.4—SAMPLE CASE CITATIONS FOR COURTS

COURT	CASE CITATION	DESCRIPTION
United States Supreme Court	*Brown v. Board of Education,* 347 U.S. 483 (1954)	Case name, volume number for the United States Reports, starting page number, date when decision was issued.
Lower federal court	*Favre v. Muir,* 249 F. Supp. 2d 1150 (M.D. Ala. 2003)	Case name, volume number for Federal Supplement, second series, starting page number, date when decision was issued in the U.S. District Court for the Middle District of Alabama.
State court	*Smith v. Jones,* 319 Wn.2d 480 (1999)	Case name, volume number for Washington Reports, second series, starting page number, date decision was issued (note: abbreviations for courts vary by state).

When marking citations, you will want to mark both long and short form citations at the same time to expedite the process. The long form citation will appear in the table of authorities, along with the page number where it is initially referenced as well as the page numbers for each of its corresponding short form citations.

After the long form citation has been provided, subsequent references can be shorter or less complete. This short form citation must easily identify the long form citation reference. Table 11.5 provides samples of how short form citations may appear in the document when referencing a long citation.

TABLE 11.5—SAMPLE LONG AND SHORT CITATIONS

LONG CITATION	SHORT CITATIONS
Smith's Jeans Ass'n v. Jones PC, 460 F.2d 267 (3d Cir. 1991)	Smith's Jeans Ass'n, 460 F.2d 267; or Smith's Jeans Ass'n
29 U.S.C. § 185(b)(2)(C) (2013)	29 U.S.C. § 185(b)(2)(C); or § 185(b)(2)(C)

NOTE

There are many more examples of acceptable long and short form citations, which may differ from court to court. Some states may even have their own rules for acceptable long and short form citations.

TIP

Since a short form citation can contain either all or part of the case name as the nickname, make sure you are consistent in the use of the short form citation name throughout the document. After you've selected a short form citation's nickname, you must consistently use that same nickname every time you use the short citation to reference the long form citation.

Mark Citations

1. Open the exercise file Pleading for TOA.docx , which can be found at www. thepaynegroup.com/downloads/word2013forlawfirms/.

2. To display the Mark Citation dialog box, as shown in Figure 11.18, click Mark Citation in the Table of Authorities group on the References tab or use the keyboard shortcut Alt+Shift+I.

3. Click Next Citation to search for citations. It finds the"v."in the caption.

NOTE

Word may stop on the wrong text during the search for citations. This is common when a title is listed in the document that includes a stand-alone "v.". If this happens, click Next Citation until you find a valid citation to mark.

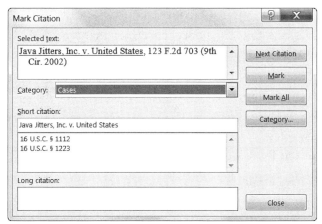

Figure 11.18

Click Next Citation to have Word search for citation-type terms.

4. Click Next Citation again and the search process stops on the § (Section symbol) of the citation 16 U.S.C. § 1112. Click in the document and select the entire citation.

5. Click back in the Mark Citation dialog box and the selected text automatically appears in the Selected Text box.

6. Select Statutes from the Category list.

NOTE

The Short Citation will automatically display 16 U.S.C. § 1112. When Word automatically marks all of the citations in the document, it will only look for and find 16 U.S.C. § 1112.

7. Click Mark All to mark all of the statutes that refer to 16 U.S.C. § 1112 within the document.

8. Click Next Citation. Word stops on the § (Section symbol) of the citation 16 U.S.C. § 1123(a). Click in the document and select the entire citation.

NOTE

You may or may not want to include the subparagraph number (a) in the preceding citation. Refer to the relevant court rules of procedure or check with the author of the brief for direction.

9. Click back in the Mark Citation dialog box. The selected text will appear in the Selected Text box.

NOTE

The Statutes category displays by default since Word remembers the last category selected.

10. Click Mark All to mark all of the statutes that refer to 16 U.S.C. § 1123(a) within the document.

11. Click Next Citation and Word stops on the "v." of the case *Easy v. Peasy*. Click in the document and select the entire citation: Easy v. Peasy, 811 F.2d 35 (3rd Cir. 1917).

12. Click back in the Mark Citation dialog box. The selected text will appear in the Selected Text box.

13. Select Cases from the Category list.

TIP

Use keyboard shortcuts to apply formatting to text in the Selected Text box. For example, select the case name, press Ctrl+U to add underlining or press Ctrl+I to add italics. Be careful when applying formatting to citations because certain courts may limit typefaces and formatting allowed in citations.

TIP

If you know ahead of time that the citation should appear directly beneath the case name in the table of authorities, press Enter after the comma following the case name to separate them onto two lines.

14. In the Short Citation box, edit the text to match the short form cites used in your document (e.g., Easy v. Peasy).

NOTE

Short citations generally include all or part of the case name; however, various forms of the short citations can appear in the document. It's important to review the document and consult with the brief's author to ensure the correct short form is used consistently throughout the document. This will make using Mark All to find short citations easier and more reliable.

15. Click Mark All to mark the long citation and all of the corresponding short form citations within the document.

16. Click Next Citation and continue marking the remaining citations.

17. Leave this document open for the next exercise.

CAUTION

If the long citation is in the body of the document and you choose Mark All, it will mark all subsequent short citations, even if they reside in a footnote or endnote. However, if the long citation is in the footnote or endnote, the Next Citation button in the Mark Citation dialog box will not find the long citation in the footnote or endnote. To alleviate this problem, click Show Notes from the Footnotes group on the References tab, and then use the Mark Citation feature.

Generating a Table of Authorities

Word provides a variety of options for inserting a table of authorities into your document. After you have marked the entries in the document, you can quickly generate the table of authorities.

Insert the Table of Authorities

1. The document from the previous exercise should still be open.

2. Place your insertion point below the Table of Authorities heading in the document.

3. Go to the Paragraph group on the Home tab and turn off Show/Hide.

CAUTION

Hidden text must be turned off so the document paginates properly; otherwise, the page numbers may not be accurate in the table of authorities.

4. On the References tab in the Table of Authorities group, click Insert Table of Authorities to display the Table of Authorities dialog box, as shown in Figure 11.19.

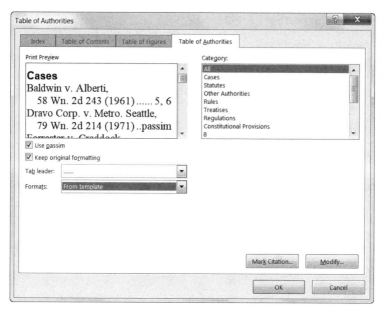

Figure 11.19

Select which categories you want to include in the table of authorities.

CAUTION

Custom categories that you create are saved with the computer, not the document. If you create custom categories and send the document to someone else to work on, the custom categories will not be available. Custom categories for tables of authorities are stored in the registry.

NOTE

If you enable the Use Passim option, any table of authorities entry with five or more page numbers will be listed with the word "passim." If you turn off the Use Passim option, all page numbers will be listed.

5. Uncheck Use Passim.

6. Click All from the Category list.

7. Click OK to generate the table of authorities.

8. Leave this document open for the next exercise.

Updating the Table of Authorities

The table of authorities, like the table of contents, is a field that needs updating after the document has been edited. You can use any one of the following methods to update a table of authorities:

- Click within the table and press F9.
- Right-click in the table and choose Update Field from the shortcut menu.
- On the References tab in the Table of Authorities group, click Update Table.
- On the File tab, choose Options and select the Display tab. Turn on the option to Update Fields Before Printing and then print the document.

Inserting Additional Citations

As you continue to edit the document, you may need to insert new citations and delete others. To add new citations to the table of authorities, mark the citation as described in the preceding exercise. If new short citations are added, select the short form citation and press Alt+Shift+I. As long as the short citation matches a previously marked long citation, the corresponding short citation will automatically be selected in the Short Citation list. Click Mark All.

When marking short citations, if you do not select the short citation in the Mark Citation dialog box, you will create another long citation marking. This will cause duplicate entries in the generated table of authorities.

Deleting Citations

To delete an entry from the table of authorities, turn on Show/Hide, find the TA fields in the document and delete them (long and short forms). The changes will be reflected when you update the table of authorities.

Modifying the Table of Authorities

Rather than manually changing the formatting of the generated table of authorities, you can save some time by modifying the table of authorities styles. On the References tab, click Insert Table of Authorities in the Table of Authorities group. In the Table of Authorities dialog box, click Modify. You can then access the TOA Heading style, which controls the formatting of the category title, and the Table of Authorities style, which controls how the entries appear in the table. For more information on modifying styles, refer to Chapter 7, "Styles."

You may have specific changes to how the case name appears in the table of authorities, such as adding italics or underline. Rather than modify the generated table of authorities, which would be a temporary change, a better practice is to make manual changes to each case name within the TA field code. To make this change manually, turn on Show/Hide (Home tab, Paragraph group) so the TA codes are visible, find each long citation TA code, and select the case name and manually change the formatting within the field code. Then, update the table of authorities.

CAUTION

Just like the table of contents, the table of authorities is a field. If you apply manual formatting to the table of authorities, each time you update the table, your changes will be lost. If you want to permanently change the format of the table of authorities, modify the styles used in the table of authorities (Table of Authorities and TOA Heading), or make changes to the text within the TA field codes of the document.

TIP

Separating the case name from the citation after the citations have been marked can still be done. Add a manual line break (Shift+Enter) after the case name and comma in the TA field code. When you update the table of authorities, the case name and citation appear on separate lines.

CREATING AN INDEX

An index is a set of words, phrases, or topics that you want to reference in a document. After the index entries have been marked, you can maintain the index much like a table of contents or table of authorities, updating it whenever changes are made to the document.

Marking Index Entries

Creating an Index is similar to marking entries for a table of contents or table of authorities. Indices make use of two fields: the XE field for marking the text and the Index field after generating the Index. Index entries can be marked in one of two ways: manually or by using a concordance file. An index entry will appear in one of three formats:

- A word or phrase and the corresponding page number.

- A subject matter and the corresponding page range in which it appears.

- A word or phrase referencing another index entry.

To mark an index entry, select the text to mark and press Alt+Shift+X to open the Mark Index Entry dialog box, or alternatively, in the Index group of the References tab, click Mark Entry.

Mark Index Entries

1. The document from the preceding exercise should still be open.

2. Select the words "Michael W. Johnson" in the caption of the pleading.

3. On the References tab in the Index group, click Mark Entry or press Alt+Shift+X. The selected text appears in the Mark Index Entry dialog box, as shown in Figure 11.20.

Figure 11.20

The index entry can reference a page number, another index entry, or a range of pages.

4. Choose Current Page under Options.

5. If desired, set the Page Number Format to be Bold or Italic.

6. Click Mark All to mark all the entries in the document.

7. Click in the document and select ACME AGENCY.

TIP

You can leave the Mark Index Entry dialog box open as you mark entries. Just click outside the dialog box, select the text, and click back in the dialog box to mark the entry. Notice the selected text will appear in the Main Entry box.

8. Click back on the Mark Index Entry dialog box, or press Alt+Shift+X to open the dialog box if closed.

9. Choose Current Page under Options. Click Mark All.

NOTE

Index entries appear as fields in the document that look like this: {XE "entry"}. The text within the quotation marks is what will appear in the generated Index as well as the page numbers where the text appears. If you do not see the fields, click Show/Hide (Home tab, Paragraph group) to view nonprinting characters.

10. Mark a few more entries and leave the document open for the next exercise.

CAUTION

Index entries are case sensitive. If you click Mark All, the text in the document must match exactly in order for the index entry to be created. For example, if the Main Entry is "Style," Word will skip the text "style" and "STYLE" and will not mark "Styles" because it is not an exact match.

Index Options

In most cases, an index will reference the page number; however, there are other options available, as described in Table 11.6.

TABLE 11.6—INDEX OPTIONS	
OPTION	**RESULT**
Cross-reference	Refers to another indexed entry in the document. For example, an entry marked "Extra Hours" might read "See Overtime Policies."
Current Page	Refers to the page number of the marked index entry.
Page Range	Refers to a range of pages spanned by a bookmark. For example, Pages 5–10.

Generating the Index

After index entries are marked, you are ready to generate the index. Place your insertion point at the point in the document where you want to insert the index, and from the Index group on the References tab, click Insert Index and click OK.

Inserting an Index

1. The document from the preceding exercise should still be open.

2. Turn off Show/Hide.

3. Press Ctrl+End to move to the end of the document, and you'll be on the Index page.

4. On the References tab in the Index group, choose Insert Index to display the Index dialog box, as shown in Figure 11.21.

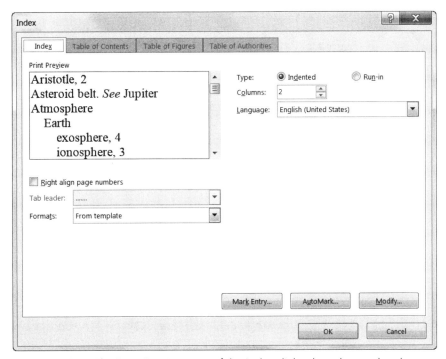

Figure 11.21   The Print Preview area of the Index dialog box shows what the index will look like with the selected options applied.

5. Choose a desired format from the Formats list. Select the preferred page number alignment, number of columns, and template format.

6. Click OK. Word inserts the index into the document.

7. Close the document without saving.

Updating the Index

If additional index entries are marked, update the index by right-clicking within the index and choose Update Field, or press F9 to update the field, or click within the index and choose Update Index in the Index group on the References tab. If the Update Index command appears disabled, make sure your cursor is within the index field.

NOTE

Tab leaders are available only with indented indexes and with certain formats, such as Formal.

NOTE

If you mark text that contains a colon or quotation marks, Word inserts a backslash before the colon or each quotation mark in the resulting index entry. This tells Word to print the colon or quotation marks as part of the index entry.

Concordance Files

A concordance file is a document that contains a Word table with a list of words and corresponding index field codes that need to be marked throughout a document. Concordance files are useful when there are multiple documents that have the same list of words that need to be marked.

To create a concordance file, insert a two-column table into a new document. The first column will contain the words and phrases Word should search for and mark. The second column will contain the corresponding index field codes.

After the concordance file has been created, open the document that needs to be marked, and on the References tab, in the Index group, click Insert Index. In the Index dialog box, click AutoMark. Navigate to the document that contains the table with index field codes and click Open. Word will automatically mark the index entries in the entire document.

TIP

Because index entries are case sensitive, you may want to turn off the feature that automatically capitalizes the first letter of table cells while you are creating the concordance file; otherwise, every entry you type in the concordance file will start with a capital letter. To access this option, click the File tab, Word Options, Proofing, and click the AutoCorrect Options button. On the AutoCorrect tab, clear the Capitalize First Letter of Table Cells check box.

COLLABORATION

As the practice of law has evolved over the years, the need to communicate with others has increased dramatically. As a result, the ability to share files and work collaboratively has become a necessity, whether it be with co-counsel, clients, opposing counsel, courts, or others domestically and globally.

With the introduction of cloud computing into Office 2013 and Office 365, attorneys are faced with the additional obligation of exercising due diligence to ensure that client confidential data is not inadvertently disclosed to third parties.

And if that wasn't enough, attorneys are now being vetted by prospective clients regarding the firm's use of state-of-the-art technology, even dictating technology requirements prior to engagement. As a result, attorneys now have a responsibility to keep up with technology that is relevant to the client's representation. To help address this need, Microsoft Word continues to offer new and improved tools for sharing documents. Understanding how to properly share a document is crucial, particularly with regard to metadata and where multiple editors are involved. This chapter covers using Track Changes, Comments, Compare, collaborating in SharePoint, and more.

WHO MADE THE REVISIONS?

Word's most commonly used collaborative tools to date are Track Changes and Comments. Although this chapter will dig deeper into these features, it's important to understand how each person will be identified when collaborating with others on documents. There is an option setting in Word in which you can personalize how you want your user name to appear alongside any tracked changes or comments you make. Word can identify who added comments or who inserted and deleted text by the User Name setting in Word Options, General, Personalize Your Copy of Microsoft Office section, as shown in Figure 12.1.

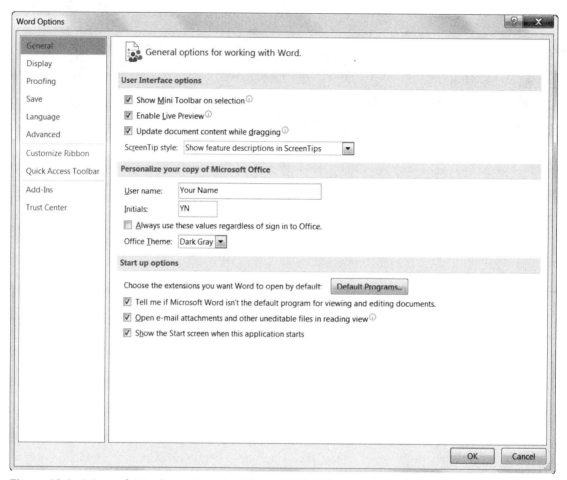

Figure 12.1   Microsoft Word populates the information for who is making changes or adding comments with the specified User Name and Initials.

NOTE

The reviewer's initials will display next to the comment when the balloon setting is off. When you hover your mouse over the comment, the user name also displays along with the comment and All Markup is set in the Display for Review list.

By default, Word will populate the user name with the credentials of the person who logged into the computer; however, you can change that data in the User Name field to reflect another person's name. Let's say, for example, that a legal secretary will be editing a document for an attorney and has a marked-up hard copy of the document as a guideline. If the attorney's name must appear as a reviewer, the User Name and Initials fields would need to be changed to the attorney's name on the legal secretary's computer before making the edits to the document. In addition, when changing the user name and initials, select the Always Use These Values Regardless of Sign In to Office check box. This option allows the user name and initials specified to be identified as the reviewer and not the person signed onto the computer.

Change Reviewer Information

1. From the File tab, choose Options.

2. On the General tab in the Personalize Your Copy of Microsoft Office section, type the reviewer's name in the User Name box.

3. Type the reviewer's initials in the Initials box.

4. Select the Always Use These Values Regardless of Sign In to Office check box.

5. Click OK.

NOTE

You can also change the reviewer information from the Review tab, in the Tracking group, click the dialog box launcher. In the Track Changes Options dialog box, click Change User Name.

OFFICE 365

Track Changes is automatically accepted and incorporated into the document when opening a file in Microsoft Word Web App (Office 365). The Comments will migrate to the Word Web app, although the functionality is limited to New, Reply, Mark as Done, and Delete.

Other Methods of Identifying the Origin of a Document

Sometimes people are concerned with Track Changes and Comments identifying the reviewer, but don't realize there is much more information (metadata) in a document that can cause a document recipient to question the origin of a document. From a client confidentiality breach perspective, the most potentially incriminating metadata is found in documents that have been inherited or reused from other organizations. Reusing documents received from outside the firm is not considered a best practice and may even have ethical implications. Unfortunately, it is also common practice among law firms that attorneys take their documents and work product with them when changing firms. The following are some of the tell-tale identifiers to watch out for:

- **Styles**. Some firms will use custom named styles that could identify the originating firm. For instance, you may work at ABC Law Firm, but the style names reflect XYZ Heading 1, XYZ Body Text, etc. (XYZ being another firm's name or initials). This is problematic because the document prepared by you or your firm could appear as though it were created by someone else.

- **Document Properties Summary**. The following properties may contain information about the origination of the document: Reviewer/Author, Manager, Company, and Template.

- **Document Statistics**. The Last Saved By property indicates the author's name who last saved the file.

- **Custom Document Properties**. Some template developers add Custom Document Properties that contain identifying information about the originating law firm, such as firm initials or even properties from their template package or document management system.

- **Leftover information in the header or footer**. When repurposing old documents, sometimes people neglect to look at headers and footers. Also, if the setting Different First Page is enabled in the header or footer, you might not even see all of the information that exists in these locations.

TIP

All organizations should purchase and use a metadata cleaner. You'll want one that gives you the ability to both analyze and clean files as long as you don't work in a jurisdiction that prevents the routine analysis of received files from other parties (certain federal and state rules can dictate if you can or should analyze files in some states). More importantly, choose a cleaner that integrates with your e-mail application, so e-mail attachments can be cleaned prior to sending them outside the firm.

PayneGroup's product Metadata Assistant is the most mature and robust on the market and has millions of users of the product worldwide. Figure 12.2 shows the PayneGroup Metadata Assistant. Not only will it clean Word documents, it will also take care of Excel, PowerPoint, PDF, graphic, and audio and video files, too (along with other file types).

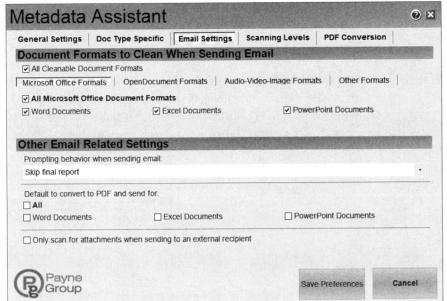

Figure 12.2

You can customize the Metadata Assistant to run in the background without prompting, or to allow the user control over all functionality.

COMMENTS

Word 2013 includes some noteworthy changes to the Comments feature. For instance, not only do you have the option to be identified in a comment with your picture, but comments can also be replied to, marked as "done," and spell checked. See Figure 12.3 for a sample comment thread.

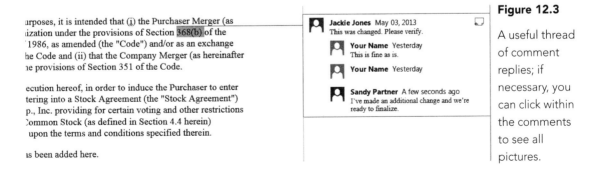

Figure 12.3

A useful thread of comment replies; if necessary, you can click within the comments to see all pictures.

Inserting Comments

You can insert a comment by clicking where you want to insert it, and in the Comments group on the Review tab, click New Comment. Alternatively, in the Comments group on the Insert tab, click Comment.

TIP

You can also right-click where you want to insert the comment and choose New Comment from the shortcut menu. The keyboard shortcut for inserting a new comment is Alt+R, C.

With Display for Review set to All Markup, when you insert a comment, you will type the new comment in a balloon that displays in the markup area located in the right margin, as shown in Figure 12.4. Microsoft calls these balloons; however, they are not balloon shaped. They are rectangles that by default are placed in the right side of the document.

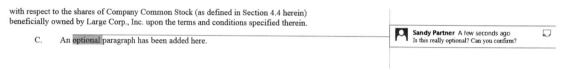

Figure 12.4 Type a comment in the balloon.

NOTE

When Track Changes is turned on and Display for Review is set to All Markup, comments and formatting changes both display in balloons by default.

With Display for Review set to Simple Markup, if the balloons are set to display and the comments are set to be hidden (Review tab, Comments group, Show Comments is toggled off), when you insert a new comment, a Comments pane will appear on the right, as shown in Figure 12.5.

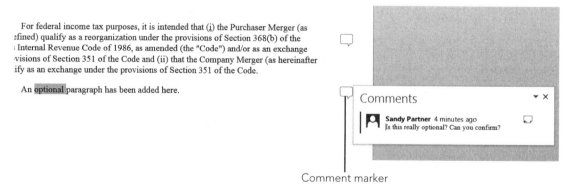

Comment marker

Figure 12.5 The Comments pane will display if comments are set to hidden.

If your balloons are off (in the Tracking group, click Show Markup, point to Balloons, and click Show All Revisions Inline), when you insert a new comment, the Reviewing pane opens on the left side for you to type the new comment, as shown in Figure 12.6.

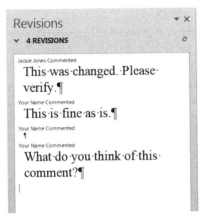

Figure 12.6

Type the comment in the Reviewing pane if the balloons are disabled.

Insert a Comment

1. Create a blank new document.

2. Type **=rand()** and press Enter.

3. Click to the right of the period at the end of the first paragraph and on the Review tab, in the Comments group, click New Comment.

4. Type **Has the client approved the final edits?**

5. In the second paragraph, select the first sentence.

6. Right-click the selected text and choose New Comment.

7. Type **Have you followed up with Joe on this yet?**

8. Keep this document open for the next exercise.

Viewing Comments

If you find the display of comments distracting, you can always hide them temporarily. Or let's say the document contains many comments and tracked changes that clutter up the window and make it hard to see them all; you could turn on the Reviewing pane (Review tab, Tracking group), which allows you to see all changes and comments in one place.

Show/Hide Comments

When balloons are enabled and Display for Review is set to All Markup, comments automatically display in the markup area on the right side just as they did in previous versions of Word. When working with comments, there is a new option that allows you to hide the comment details so they do not appear in the balloon and markup area. First, change Display for Review (Review tab, Tracking group) to Simple Markup. Then, on the Review tab, in the Comments group, click Show Comments to hide the comment details. When the comment is hidden, a comment marker displays as a visual clue that a comment or multiple comments exist in the adjacent paragraph. Hover your mouse over a comment marker, and the ScreenTip instructs you to Click to See Comments, as shown in Figure 12.7. When clicked, this expands the comment showing the existing comment or comment thread.

Figure 12.7

The comment marker indicates one or more comments exist in the adjacent paragraph.

When you click the comment marker, the comment(s) display in a Comments pane, as shown in Figure 12.8.

Figure 12.8 Click the comment marker to show the detailed comment text.

NOTE

If there are multiple comments within a single paragraph, only one comment marker displays. When the comment marker is clicked, it expands to show all of the comments that exist within the paragraph.

When you have finished reading the details in the Comments pane, click back into the document, or press the Esc key, to close the Comments pane.

If you would rather have comments always display, click Show Comments in the Comments group on the Review tab to toggle them back on, or change the Display for Review setting to All Markup.

NOTE

The Show Comments feature is available only when in Simple Markup view, as shown in Figure 12.9. In the Tracking group on the Review tab, select Simple Markup from the Display for Review drop-down list.

The Bill of Rights

I - Congress shall make no law respecting an establishment of religion, or prohibiting exercise thereof; or abridging the freedom of speech, or of the press; or the right of peaceably to assemble, and to petition the Government for a redress of grievances.

Figure 12.9   Simple Markup collapses the changes and shows only the change lines next to the affected areas instead of displaying the actual change.

Collaborate with Someone Else

If you are collaborating with others on a document and they have inserted a comment in the document, you can use Word to facilitate your collaboration.

When you and another reviewer are signed in via a Microsoft account or Active Directory, you can contact people directly from within your Word document to assist with the collaboration process. Hover your mouse over the person's picture in the comment balloon, and a pop-up displays allowing you to start an instant message, place a call, start a video, or e-mail the person directly from the comment. Double-clicking the person's picture instantly opens the detailed contact information.

Picture Display in Comments

Word will attempt to display a picture, by default, when a comment is inserted into the document. This makes it easy to quickly identify which comments come from which reviewer and to respond accordingly. Of course, not everyone will find this feature useful, so fortunately, it can be turned off on a case-by-case basis. To turn off the display of pictures, on the Review tab, in the Tracking group, click the Tracking dialog box launcher. Clear the Pictures by Comments check box and click OK.

TIP

Another method for turning off the picture display is to right-click a comment and choose Hide Pictures by Comments from the shortcut menu.

Reviewing Pane

When the Reviewing pane is enabled, it will display all revisions in a document, which include comments and tracked changes. The Reviewing pane can display vertically on the left side of the window or horizontally at the bottom of the window. Depending on the view chosen, the Reviewing pane can include the comment text, insertions and deletions, formatting changes, author, date and time the revisions were made, and a summary of the revisions. The default vertical Reviewing pane is shown in Figure 12.10.

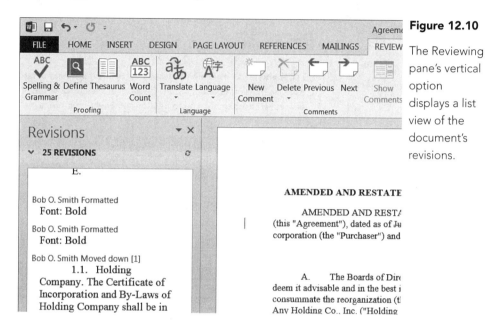

Figure 12.10

The Reviewing pane's vertical option displays a list view of the document's revisions.

TIP

Double-click the author's name in the Reviewing pane to move to that location within the document.

Using the Reviewing Pane

1. The document from the previous exercise should still be open.

2. On the Review tab, in the Tracking group, click Show Markup, and from the drop-down list, point to Balloons and then choose Show All Revisions Inline.

3. Click the Next button in the Comments group. At this point, the Reviewing pane should appear.

4. Click on a few of the comments in the Reviewing pane to review the comments. As you click on each comment in the Reviewing pane, your insertion point is moved to that location in the document.

5. At the top of the Reviewing pane, click the down arrow to the left of Revisions to show a detailed summary of the revisions.

TIP

The Reviewing pane helps to quickly identify the number of revisions made in the document. It's similar to what third-party revision tools call the change summary. The Refresh control to the right in the pane refreshes the revisions list with any new changes so the list continues to be up to date.

6. In the Tracking group on the Review tab, click the down arrow next to Reviewing Pane and select Reviewing Pane Horizontal.

7. Click Reviewing Pane again to toggle off the pane.

8. Leave this document open for the next exercise.

Editing Comments

You can edit pre-existing comments that you or someone else has inserted. If the comments are showing in the markup area, just click inside the balloon and edit the comment directly. If comments are not showing in the markup area and you only see the comment marker, click the comment marker to show the comment(s) for that paragraph and then make the edits. You also can edit comments in the Reviewing pane. The Reviewing pane looks similar to the Navigation pane discussed earlier in this book; however, unlike the Navigation pane, you are able to click in and type directly into the pane.

Replying to a Comment

When collaborating with other authors and comments are being used, you may want to reply directly to a specific author's comment rather than create a new one. This feature combines the original comment and the reply to that comment in an easy-to-follow thread. To reply to a comment, if Show Comments is enabled and the comment balloons are showing, click the Reply button in the upper-right corner of the comment, as shown in Figure 12.11, or right-click on the comment and choose Reply to Comment.

Reply button   **Figure 12.11**

Comment replies in the balloon are indented below the original comment, which makes them easy to read and follow.

If comments are not showing, click the comment marker to activate the Comments pane and then click the Reply button in the upper-right corner of the Comments pane, or right-click in the Comments pane and select Reply to Comment, as shown in Figure 12.12.

Figure 12.12

Reply to a comment even when balloons are not showing.

NOTE From the Reviewing pane, you can also right-click on a comment and choose Reply to Comment. Alternatively, look within the document and if you can see the comment shading that surrounds the text, right-click within that shaded area and choose Reply to Comment.

Marking a Comment as Done

When you've finished reading or replying to a comment, you can mark it as completed or done, which indicates that no further action is required. When you do this, it's easier to distinguish between comments you have already reviewed and possibly replied to, but do not want to delete, against comments that are still pending. Marking a comment as done dims the comment so that it is less distinguishable. Right-click either the comment balloon, the comment text, or the comment in the Reviewing pane, and choose Mark Comment Done. If you change your mind, you can right-click on the comment and choose Mark Comment Done again. The command works as a toggle.

Working with Existing Comments

1. The document from the previous exercise should still be open.

2. On the Review tab, in the Tracking group, select Simple Markup from the Display for Review list.

3. In the Comments group on the Review tab, be sure Show Comments is toggled off.

4. Click the first comment marker that is to the right of the first paragraph.

5. Click the Reply to Comment button and type **The client has asked for an additional week to review**.

6. In the Comments group on the Review tab, click Show Comments.

7. Right-click the balloon comment, "Have you followed up with Joe on this yet?" and choose Reply to Comment.

8. Type **Yes, I have the information we need.**

9. Right-click the balloon or the highlighted text in the document and choose Mark Comment Done.

10. Close the document without saving.

Deleting Comments

As you get close to finalizing the document, you'll want to delete comments that are no longer needed. Comments can be deleted one at a time, all at once, or by a specific reviewer. For instance, delete all of the comments inserted by a paralegal or associate before the partner sends the document to a client.

Deleting a Comment One at a Time

You can delete a comment as you review the document using a variety of methods:

- If comment balloons are showing, right-click on a comment balloon and choose Delete Comment from the shortcut menu.

- In the Reviewing pane, right-click on the comment and choose Delete Comment from the shortcut menu.

- If the Display for Review setting is set to All Markup (Review tab, Tracking group), right-click the comment in the document and choose Delete Comment from the shortcut menu.

- If the Display for Review setting is set to All Markup (Review tab, Tracking group), place the insertion point in the highlighted area of the comment in the document, and from the ribbon, click the upper half of the Delete button (Review tab, Comments group).

Delete Individual Comments

1. Change these settings to experience deleting comments when working in Simple Markup view, with balloons enabled for comments and formatting only, and with no comments showing (only comment markers display): In the Tracking group on the Review tab, select Simple Markup from the Display for Review list; in the Tracking group, click Show Markup, point to Balloons, and select Show Only Comments and Formatting in Balloons; and in the Comments group, ensure that Show Comments is toggled off.

NOTE

There are as many display settings for comments as there are methods to delete them. If you do not change your settings exactly as the previous step describes, it's okay—you just won't have the same options available in this exercise to delete comments. Look for the methods to delete that are available to you.

2. Open the exercise file Settlement Agreement Comments.docx. You'll find this file, and all exercises referenced in the book in the following location: www.thepayne group.com/downloads/word2013forlawfirms/.

3. Click Next in the Comments group on the Review tab.

4. Click the upper half of Delete in the Comments group.

5. Click Next in the Comments group on the Review tab.

6. Right-click the Comments pane and choose Delete Comment.

7. Change this setting to experience deleting comments when working in All Markup view: On the Review tab, in the Tracking group, select All Markup from the Display for Review list.

8. Click Next in the Comments group on the Review tab.

9. Notice the comments display in the balloon and the text "2" is highlighted where the comment was inserted.

10. Right-click the "2" in the document and choose Delete Comment.

11. Undo all of the deletions and keep the document open for the next exercise.

NOTE

When balloons are enabled for comments, you will notice that when the last comment has been deleted, the markup area that displays the balloons on the right side of the page disappears.

Deleting Specific Reviewer Comments

Sometimes it may be necessary to delete all the comments made by a specific reviewer. The steps here provide a quick method of deleting reviewer-specific comments while leaving other comments in the document.

1. The exercise file Settlement Agreement Comments.docx should still be open from the previous exercise.

2. In the Tracking group on the Review tab, select All Markup from the Display for Review list.

3. In the Tracking group on the Review tab, click Show Markup, point to Specific People, and select Fred Jones to remove the check mark next to this reviewer. Fred Jones is the reviewer whose comments you want to retain in the document.

4. In the Comments group on the Review tab, click the arrow beneath the Delete button and select Delete All Comments Shown.

5. In the Tracking group on the Review tab, click Show Markup, point to Specific People, and choose All Reviewers to see the remaining comments.

6. Keep this document open for the next exercise.

CAUTION

If the reviewer has replied within an existing comment, those responses will not be deleted using the steps listed in the previous exercise. To delete his or her response to the comment, you will need to right-click the response inside the comment, and choose Delete Comment.

Deleting All Comments

If you want to delete all the comments in the document simultaneously, there is a specific option you can use to streamline the comment deletion process.

Delete All Comments in a Document

1. The exercise file Settlement Agreement Comments.docx should still be open.

2. In the Comments group on the Review tab, click the arrow beneath the Delete button and select Delete All Comments in Document.

3. Close the document without saving.

TIP

You can identify when all comments have been removed from a document by looking in the Comments group on the Review tab. If the Previous and Next buttons are not available, there are no residual comments in the document.

Printing Comments and Revisions

When printing a document that contains comments and revisions, Word automatically prints the document with the comments and revisions showing. There may be instances in which you will want to print the document without the comments and revisions or maybe even print the comments and revisions in a separate list.

Print a List of Comments and Revisions

1. Open a document containing comments and tracked changes.

2. Click the File tab and choose Print.

3. Directly under Settings, click the drop-down arrow and choose List of Markup.

4. Click Print.

5. Close the document without saving.

In addition to the comment or revision text, the printed list of markup will also include the page number, author, and date and time the comment or revision was made.

TRACK CHANGES

Back in the days before computers with word processing software, Track Changes was actually known as Redlining or Blacklining. This involved taking a ruler or other straight-edge object and drawing a line through the text on the printed document that should be deleted. The proofer also had to manage to insert hand-written text into the document in or near the location where the new text belonged.

Later, but before the introduction of Word's Track Changes feature, text in a document would need to have direct formatting applied to identify the modified text. That formatting would come in the form of the Strikethrough and Underline font properties. Both of these earlier methods were time and labor intensive, so Microsoft's addition of the Track Changes feature has been a much-lauded improvement for anyone having to notate changes in documents.

When the Track Changes feature is enabled, as text and other content is inserted, moved, and deleted in the document, Word keeps track of each change. Although you can change the look of these revisions, the default display will mark deleted text with a strikethrough and mark new text with an underline. Additional properties are also added during the normal editing process while Track Changes is on, such as including the author's name and a distinct colored highlighting for each author, to name just a few.

NOTE

Whether you're using Word's Compare feature or a third-party program to compare two separate files that produces a third output file, this feature is very different from using Track Changes. Track Changes is a drafting tool used when collaborating that contains all of the changes in the same document. On the other hand, Compare feature and third-party comparison programs rely on three documents: the original document, the revised document, and the output document containing the comparisons.

The Track Changes feature and options can be found on the Review tab, in the Tracking group and Changes group. The Tracking group includes the option to turn on Track Changes and designate how those changes are displayed in the document, while the Changes group is used to review each revision as well as finalize the document.

Methods of Turning Track Changes On and Off

There are multiple ways to enable Track Changes in Word:

- **Track Changes button**. On the Review tab, in the Tracking group, click the upper portion of the Track Changes button to toggle the feature on and off. When Track Changes is on, the button will turn a blue color. When Track Changes is off, the blue color toggles off and the button color returns to normal.

- **Keyboard shortcut**. Press Ctrl+Shift+E to toggle on and off Track Changes. Watch the button color to identify if the feature is on or off.

- **Status Bar**. Single click Track Changes in the Status Bar to toggle Track Changes on or off. This indicator is a helpful tool to detect if Track Changes is activated.

NOTE

If you do not see Track Changes in the Status bar, right-click the Status bar and choose Track Changes.

CAUTION

In earlier versions of Word, to enable Track Changes from the Status bar, you would have double-clicked the TRK command. It is now just a single click to toggle on or off Track Changes using the Status bar.

Using Track Changes

1. Create a blank new document and save the document as **Track Changes.docx**.

2. In the Tracking group on the Review tab, click Show Markup, point to Balloons, and choose Show All Revisions Inline. Also, in the Tracking group, select All Markup from the Display for Review list.

3. Type **=rand(6),** press Enter, and save the document again.

4. In the Tracking group on the Review tab, click the upper portion of the Track Changes button to turn on Track Changes.

5. Select the last paragraph and press Delete.

6. In the Tracking group on the Review tab, click the Reviewing Pane down arrow and choose Reviewing Pane Vertical.

7. Press Ctrl+Home to return to the top of the document and press Enter twice.

8. Press Ctrl+Home again and type **Document Title**.

9. Press Ctrl+E to center align the text of the title.

10. Press Enter and type **Subtitle**.

11. In the first paragraph of the document text, select the text "way to help you prove" and type **method of proving** to replace the original text.

12. Place your insertion point at the beginning of the last paragraph that begins with "Reading is easier" and press Ctrl+Enter to create a page break.

13. On the Status bar, click Track Changes to toggle off the feature.

14. Save the document and keep it open for the next exercise.

NOTE

If the document is saved with Track Changes on, this setting will remain on in the document.

Display Options

When working with documents in Word, it's always important to know if Track Changes has been turned on in the document you are editing. It's just as important to know what Track Changes view display setting is used in the document as well. It's actually possible to change the view so you only see the original text in the document or change the view so you only see the finalized version without any of the markup showing. Let's say one of these views is used in the document, and you forget there are Track Changes that have not been accepted or rejected, and then you send that document to an adverse party. All the recipient of that document needs to do is change the view display to All Markup and the results can be catastrophic as a confidentiality breach.

Table 12.1 provides detail on the different displays from which to choose. These views are found in the Display for Review list in the Tracking group on the Review tab.

NOTE

The Display for Review settings do not travel with the document, but rather is a computer setting. The same setting will be used on any documents you open from this point forward until you change it again.

If you are editing a document containing a table of contents and want to update that table to reflect the page numbers of the finalized version (after all Track Changes have been accepted), change the Display for Review setting to No Markup before generating or updating the table of contents.

TABLE 12.1—DISPLAY FOR REVIEW OPTIONS		
BUTTON	**DESCRIPTION**	**COMMENT**
Simple Markup	Shows only where the revisions and comments are located by displaying a revision line near the left margin. Click the line to toggle on the display of revisions and comments.	A red line lets you know there are revisions and/or comments not shown. A gray line indicates that all revisions and/or comments are shown.
All Markup	Shows all revisions and comments.	The display may be inline or in balloons, depending on the Show Markup/Balloons setting.
No Markup	Shows the document as though all revisions were accepted and all comments were deleted.	Use caution with this display, as you may not realize the document contains revisions and comments. Only use this view for a quick look at how the final document will appear, and then change the view back to either Simple Markup or All Markup.
Original	Shows the document as though the document had not yet been edited.	Use caution with this display, as you may not realize the document contains revisions and comments. Only use this view for a quick look at how the original text appeared, and then change the view back to either Simple Markup or All Markup.

Changing the Markup Display

When working with Track Changes and Comments, the best views to become most familiar with are the Simple Markup and the All Markup views. The Simple Markup setting clearly displays the document text with a visual reminder in the left margin where revisions are located. The All Markup setting will act as a reminder to address all revisions prior to sending the document to an adverse party.

Changing Views and Navigating Track Changes in a Document

1. Open the exercise file Settlement Agreement Views.docx . You'll find this file, and all exercises referenced in the book in the following location: www. thepaynegroup.com/downloads/word2013forlawfirms/.

2. Turn Track Changes off. Note that when Track Changes is on when you open a document, it's because the previous editor had turned it on.

3. In the Tracking group on the Review tab, select All Markup from the Display for Review list.

4. In the Tracking group on the Review tab, click Show Markup and Point to Balloons, and choose Show Revisions in Balloons.

5. Scroll through the document to see the revisions and comments.

6. Press Ctrl+Home to return to the top of the document.

7. In the Tracking group on the Review tab, select Simple Markup from the Display for Review list.

8. In the Changes group on the Review tab, click Next until you have moved your insertion point to the Reimbursement section of the document. This is the first instance of an insertion or deletion.

9. Click the red revision line in the left margin. Note that the Display for Review setting has changed to All Markup, the revision line is gray, and the deletions appear in the balloons in the right margin.

10. Locate and click on one of the gray revision lines in the left margin. Note the Display for Review setting has changed back to Simple Markup, the revision line is red, and the deletions no longer appear in the balloons in the right margin.

11. Change the display setting to Original. This shows how the document looked prior to any edits.

12. Change the Display for Review setting to No Markup. This shows how the document would look if all revisions were accepted and comments deleted.

13. In the Tracking group, click Reviewing Pane. This is another way to check if a document contains revisions that have not been addressed.

14. Change the Display for Review setting to All Markup.

15. Change the Show Markup setting to Balloons, and Show All Revisions Inline.

16. Close the Reviewing pane.

17. Leave the document open for the next exercise.

Additional Markup Display Options

The markup displayed in a document can be further customized to display only revisions by specific editors. There are also options to display only specific types of revisions. A description of the markup options is found in Table 12.2.

TABLE 12.2—ADDITIONAL MARKUP FEATURES	
OPTION	**DESCRIPTION**
Comments	Toggle to show/hide Comments.
Ink	Toggle to show/hide Ink markups that were added using a touch-screen tablet.
Insertions and Deletions	Toggle to show/hide insertions and deletions.
Formatting	Toggle to show/hide formatting changes.
Balloons	Choose whether revisions should show in balloons or inline.
Specific People	Choose to display all or only specific reviewer changes.
Highlight updates	Available when working in a document saved to SharePoint and the document contains tracked changes.
Other Authors	Available when working in a document saved to SharePoint and the document contains Track Changes.

Track Changes Options

One of the advantages of Track Changes is that you can customize the feature to best suit your needs. To see all of the customization options, click the Tracking dialog box launcher from the Review tab to view the Track Change option settings. For additional settings, click the Advanced Options button to display the Advanced Track Changes Options dialog box, as shown in Figure 12.13.

In the Advanced Track Changes Options dialog box, you can designate how changes display in the document when inserting, deleting, or moving text. You can also set specific colors for these changes, including changes to a table. Tracking moves and formatting may be useful in some cases, but for the most part, these two options are not used as extensively as the other options. The reason for this is that tracking moves and formatting may cause excessive clutter on the screen when reviewing revisions in a document. See Table 12.3 for a description of each advanced option.

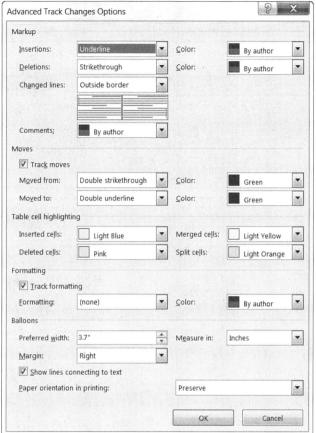

Figure 12.13

Another place that controls Track Changes display.

TABLE 12.3—ADVANCED OPTIONS DESCRIBED	
OPTION	**DESCRIPTION**
Insertions	Choose how Word displays inserted text whenever markup is displayed.
Color	Allows users to choose the color to identify their inserted text. By default, a different color is used for each reviewer.
Deletions	Choose how Word displays deleted text.
Color	Allows users to choose the color to identify their deleted text. By default, a different color is used for each reviewer.
Changed Lines	Sets the position of the vertical line that indicates changed text.
Comments	Choose the color for inserted comments.
Track Moves	Choose whether to mark cut/pasted text as a move.
Moved from	Indicates where the moved text was originally located.

continues

TABLE 12.3—*(CONTINUED)*	
OPTION	**DESCRIPTION**
Color	Allows user to choose the color to identify where the moved text was originally located.
Moved to	Indicates the new location where the moved text was pasted.
Color	Allows user to choose the color to identify where the moved text was pasted.
Inserted cells	Shows where cells were inserted.
Deleted cells	Shows cells that were deleted.
Merged cells	Shows where cells were merged.
Split cells	Shows where cells were split.
Track Formatting	Shows markup when formatting changes are made.
Formatting	Choose the formatting for formatting changes.
Color	Allows user to choose the color to identify the formatted text.
Use Balloons In Print And Web Layout	Choose when to use balloons to show markup elements in margin of the document.
Preferred Width	Sets the width of the margin that contains the balloons.
Measure In	Select the measurement type for the balloon width (typically inches).
Margin	Pick which margin (right or left) to display balloons.
Show Lines Connecting To Text	Shows a line connecting each balloon to the location in the document where a change occurred or a comment inserted.
Paper Orientation in Printing	Choose orientation in which the marked-up document should print. Auto lets Word pick the best layout. Preserve uses the orientation from Page Setup. Force Landscape is used to give the most room for the balloons.

NOTE

If the printed document has a large gray margin area on the right side of the page, it is because the Show Markup has Balloons set to Show all Revisions in Balloons. This setting should be the choice of the person printing the document with any intended recipients in mind.

Accept and Reject Changes

When you are finished collaborating on a document with others, it's time to either accept or reject each revision. While there's an option to Accept All Changes or Reject All Changes, most of the time you'll want to review each change individually before accepting or rejecting. After revisions have been accepted or rejected and the document has been saved, there is no way to determine what text has been added or deleted unless you use the Compare feature, as discussed later in this chapter, to compare the original document to the revised document.

Accept and Reject Changes in a Document

1. The exercise file Settlement AgreementViews.docx should still be open.

2. Verify that Track Changes is turned off.

3. Press Ctrl+Home to move to the top of the document.

4. In the Tracking group on the Review tab, verify that the Display for Review option is set to display All Markup.

5. In the Tracking group on the Review tab, click Show Markup and confirm that the first four items are checked, point to Balloons and choose Show Revisions in Balloons, point to Specific People, and confirm that both reviewers are selected.

6. In the Changes group on the Review tab, click Next. This should take you to the first comment group located in the Preamble paragraph.

7. In the Comments group, click Delete. This deletes all the comments in the group.

8. In the Changes group on the Review tab, click Next. This should take you to the first set of revisions located in the Reimbursement Amount paragraph.

9. In the Changes group on the Review tab, click the upper portion of the Reject button until the comments are deleted and the dollar values are restored to $5,500.

NOTE

Clicking the upper portion of the Accept or Reject buttons will Accept and move to the next change or Reject and move to the next change, respectively. If you want to accept or reject and have your insertion point remain in the same location, click the down arrow of the Accept or the Reject button and choose Accept this Change or Reject Change.

10. Rejecting the last change in the Reimbursement Amount paragraph automatically moves you to the next change in the Compensatory Educational Services Provided by District Staff paragraph.

11. In the Changes group, click Accept to change the ratio from 1:2 to 1:1.

12. Continue to click Accept for the ratios until you are at the dollar value change in the Compensatory Educational Services to be Funded by District paragraph.

13. Click to Reject all dollar values until they are restored back to $5,500.

14. Click Accept for all ratio values of 1:1 and reject the dollar values of $8,000.

15. In the RELEASES paragraph, Reject the deletion of the word Mutual and the deletion of the following paragraph.

16. When all Track Changes are accepted or rejected, click OK in the message box indicating that all revisions have been processed.

TIP

When finalizing a document that has Track Changes, it's important to confirm that all markup in the document has either been accepted or rejected. The quickest way to check is to turn on the Reviewing pane. If the Revision statistics at the top of the pane reports zero, all markup in the document has been addressed.

17. Save the file as **Settlement Agreement Final.docx**.

18. Close all open documents.

DOCUMENT PROTECTION

Most Word users are aware of the ability to password protect a file for opening and modifying; however, some may not realize there is an additional password-protection feature that can be used on documents that contain Track Changes.

Lock Track Changes

When collaborating with others on a document's revisions, it may be important to ensure that all modifications are documented with the use of Track Changes. When sharing documents with opposing parties during transactional work, it is possible to ensure that every change made by the opposing party is recorded as a tracked change. Locking the changes will enable Track Changes to remain on and will not allow existing changes to be accepted or rejected. Although a password is optional when using the Lock Tracking feature, it is recommended to add a password. That way, if recipients try to turn off Lock Tracking, they would need to supply the password.

Lock Tracking

1. Open a document that contains tracked changes.

2. On the Review tab, click the Track Changes down arrow and choose Lock Tracking. The Lock Tracking dialog box displays, as shown in Figure 12.14.

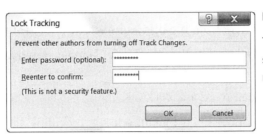

Figure 12.14

The password is optional, case sensitive, and cannot be recovered if forgotten.

CAUTION

As indicated on the Lock Tracking dialog box, this feature is not considered a security feature.

3. Type a password you will not forget and re-enter to confirm the password.

4. Click OK.

NOTE

The Lock Tracking feature turns on Track Changes and disables the ability to toggle Track Changes off unless it is unlocked and the password is provided. The Accept and Reject buttons are also unavailable.

5. Delete and add a sentence in the document. All revisions will be tracked.

6. Keep this document open for the next exercise.

NOTE

Word's Undo button will undo your revisions, but you cannot accept or reject revisions. Once the file has been saved and reopened, the Undo history is gone and the revisions remain until the file is unlocked.

Unlock Changes

Anyone who knows the password can unlock the Lock Tracking feature. More importantly, do not forget the password or you won't be able to unlock the file.

Unlock the Lock Tracking Feature

1. The document from the previous exercise should still be open.

2. On the Review tab, click the Track Changes down arrow and choose Lock Tracking.

3. Type the password and click OK.

4. The file is now open for full editing, including the ability to accept and reject changes.

5. Close the document without saving.

Restrict Editing

The Restrict Editing feature includes options to restrict what other reviewers can do when working in a document. This feature is located in the Protect group on the Review tab. Click Restrict Editing after you have finished revising the document, and the Restrict Editing task pane opens. Table 12.4 describes the restriction options.

TABLE 12.4—RESTRICT EDITING OPTIONS	
OPTION	**DESCRIPTION**
Formatting Restrictions	Restricts formatting options to a selection of styles in order to preserve the look or branding of a document. Click Settings to select which style areas are allowed to be edited.
Editing Restrictions	Control what can be edited in the document. When Comments or No Changes (Read Only) is selected, exceptions can be set to make certain parts of the document editable by certain people or groups.
Exceptions	Available when Comments or No Changes (Read Only) is selected. Select specific parts of the document to open for editing by certain people or groups.
Start Enforcement	Enter a password to turn on or off the restrictions. This button toggles between Yes, Start Enforcing Protection, and Stop Protection.

Additional Methods of Document Protection

Word provides some additional methods of protecting a document. Some of the methods require a Digital Signature or a connection to a Rights Management Server. Find these additional methods in the File tab, Info, and click the Protect Document button. Table 12.5 describes each of the protection options.

TABLE 12.5—ADDITIONAL PROTECTION OPTIONS	
OPTION	DESCRIPTION
Mark as Final	This features does not lock the document nor does it require a password. When Mark as Final is selected, the document is read only as shown in the Title bar. An icon in the Status bar also indicates the file is marked as final. Mark as Final is toggled off by selecting Mark as Final again or by clicking the Edit Anyway button on the notification bar that will display below the ribbon.
Encrypt with Password	Displays a prompt to add a password. This is the equivalent of a File Open password.
Restrict Editing	Launches the Restrict Editing task pane.
Restrict Access	This feature requires setup by a Systems Administrator.
Add a Digital Signature	A digital ID helps to validate your identity when signing electronic documents. When a digital signature is added to a document, Mark as Final is automatically set. If the Mark as Final designation gets toggled off, the digital signature automatically gets removed.

OPTIONS THAT AFFECT TRACK CHANGES

There are other options in Word to be aware of that either work with or affect Track Changes, such as the following:

Document Inspector. On the File tab, Info, Check for Issues, Inspect Document. If the Document Inspector finds comments and track changes, you have a choice to remove not only comments and tracked changes, but the Remove All command will remove versions and annotations as well.

NOTE

The Versions feature existed prior to Word 2007 and allowed you to have multiple versions of a file within one document. This feature no longer exists in the later versions of Word. If you open a document containing Versions in Word 2013, an automatic message prompt will display letting you know that previous versions of the document will be removed and the latest version retained. Note that this feature is not the same as the versioning feature found in document management systems.

The Trust Center has four privacy options to be aware of. To access these options, click the File tab, Options. Select Trust Center, click Trust Center Settings, and select the Privacy Options tab.

- **Warn Before Printing, Saving or Sending a File that Contains Tracked Changes or Comments**. Provides a warning when you attempt to save, print, or send a document that includes these elements—even if they are not visible on-screen.

CAUTION

If you are sending the document as an attachment to an e-mail message, the warning will not display. However, the warning option will display when you are sending a document from within Word using the Share feature found on the File tab.

- **Store Random Number to Improve Combine Accuracy**. Allows for greater accuracy when merging document together from different reviewers. This option is required to be enabled when using the co-reviewing feature.

- **Make Hidden Markup Visible When Opening or Saving**. If tracked changes or comments are detected in a document and this option is enabled, the markup is automatically displayed when a document is opened or saved.

TIP

The Make Hidden Markup Visible When Opening or Saving option is on by default and can help expose tracked changes or comments that may have appeared hidden. When this option is enabled, revisions will always display when opening or saving the file.

- **Remove Personal Information (RPI) From File Properties on Save**. This option will remove several pieces of information: (1) Author/Reviewer, (2) Manager, and (3) Company. This option becomes available only when the document is in Compatibility Mode.

NOTE

Metadata cleaners such as PayneGroup's Metadata Assistant provide options to programmatically handle leaving tracked changes and comments untouched in the document, but still remove the author/reviewer names from those revisions and comments. Manager and company information will be removed as well. This is often preferred when document collaboration is ongoing.

COMPARE AND COMBINE

Microsoft has made substantial improvements to Word's comparison feature, which has changed dramatically from earlier versions. The improved functionality offers many of the same features you find when purchasing third-party comparison software such as those from Workshare, Litera, GroupDocs, Microsystems, Esquire Innovations, and DocsCorp. The Compare feature splits the screen into three sections, showing the original document, the revised document, and a markup comparison of the two. The Combine feature compares two documents and creates a new document containing tracked changes to show the differences between the documents.

Compare Two Documents

1. From the Review tab, click Compare and then choose Compare.

2. Use the Browse button (folder) to select the original AssignmentV1.docx and the revised AssignmentV2.docx documents, as shown in Figure 12.15. These exercise files are part of the downloadable companion files for this book and are available at www.thepaynegroup.com/downloads/word2013forlawfirms/.

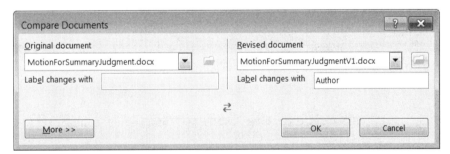

Figure 12.15   The two arrows represent the Swap button; click the button in case you need to switch the original and modified documents.

3. Click the More button to review the Comparison settings without making changes.

4. In the Show Changes section, directly under Show Changes At, select Character Level.

5. Click OK to compare the documents.

6. Keep the comparison window open for the next exercise.

Navigating the Comparison Screen

While you can manipulate the Comparison Screen, Figure 12.16 shows the default screen after initially clicking OK to compare the two documents.

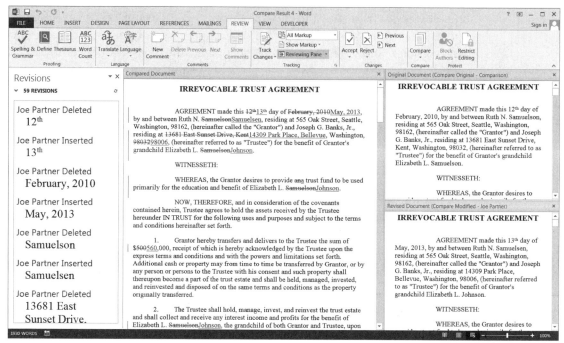

Figure 12.16 View the original and modified files as well as the compared document.

Navigate the Comparison

1. The comparison window should still be open from the previous exercise.

2. Click in the Compared Document window that contains the display of additions and deletions.

3. Using the scroll wheel on the mouse, or the Page Down key on the keyboard, scroll down through the document. Note that the documents showing in the Original and Revised Document panes scroll in synchronization with the Compared Document pane.

TIP

You can also use the Next and Previous buttons located in the Changes group on the Review tab to scroll through the text.

If the Reviewing pane is displayed, note that when scrolling through the Compared Document that the Reviewing pane does not scroll in synchronization with the other panes; however, clicking on a revision in the Reviewing pane will move the focus in the other panes to that revision.

4. Keep the comparison window open for the next exercise.

Manipulating the Document Panes

Afer you have compared two documents, an additional command becomes available in the Compare drop-down list. The Show Source Documents option allows you to turn the various panes on and off for your viewing convenience.

Showing the Source Documents

1. The comparison window should still be open from the previous exercise.

2. Click Compare, point to Show Source Documents, and select Hide Source Documents.

3. Click Compare, point to Show Source Documents, and select Show Original.

4. Click the Close button in the upper-right corner of the Original Document pane.

5. Save the file as **Assignment Compared.docx**.

6. Close all documents.

When a compared document has been saved, closed, and then reopened, the Source Documents are no longer available for viewing.

Using the Combine Feature

The Combine feature allows you to combine revisions from several authors into a single document, but only two at a time, and therefore, this feature is very similar to the Compare feature. Click Compare in the Compare group on the Review tab and select Combine. Much like the Compare option, you choose the two comparison documents; however, you do this from within the Combine Documents dialog box.

Indicate how to label unmarked changes in the Label Unmarked Changes With box. All of the Comparison options found in the Combine Document dialog box are the same as in the Comparison options found in the Compare Document dialog box.

Combine Two Documents

1. On the Review tab, click Compare and select Combine.

2. Select the same original and revised documents that were used in the Compare exercise (Original: AssignmentV1.docx, Revised: AssignmentV2.docx).

3. Click the More button, if needed, to review the Comparison settings.

4. Click OK. Note that Word does not show the source documents when using the Combine feature.

5. Close the Combined document without saving.

COLLABORATION IN SHAREPOINT

If your firm is using SharePoint, you can save and retrieve documents to SharePoint directly from within Word. Documents saved to a SharePoint library can be designated as view only or as editable. Although your firm will most likely have a customized SharePoint environment, this section provides examples from a standard SharePoint installation.

Files saved to SharePoint allow for multiple reviewers to work on a document simultaneously. When one reviewer clicks Save, the revision is automatically shown in the other reviewer's document with colored shading. That shading will go away and never prints.

NOTE

This section will not include hands-on exercises since you must have at least two reviewers editing a SharePoint document. SharePoint is a robust and highly customizable application, and this section will provide some basic information to get you started and possibly answer some of your existing questions when sharing files saved to SharePoint.

Communication Between Reviewers

Communication between reviewers is critical to successful collaboration with Word documents saved and accessed from within SharePoint. Here are a few questions to consider before beginning the collaboration:

- Do all reviewers have access to the document?

- Does one reviewer need to take the lead in accepting or rejecting revisions?

- Do all reviewers understand Track Changes?

- Will all reviewers agree to save their revisions frequently? This is the only way others will see the revisions.

Checked Out

If a document is checked out from SharePoint, only one reviewer is able to work on the file at a time. When another reviewer tries to open a checked-out document, a ToolTip displays when the reviewer hovers over the document letting that person know who has the document checked out, as shown in Figure 12.17. You can still open a checked-out document and will be prompted with a File in Use dialog box offering options to view or edit the file, as shown in Figure 12.18. The original reviewer must check the document back in to release the file for other reviewers.

Figure 12.17

You may need to contact the user who has the file checked out if you need to revise it.

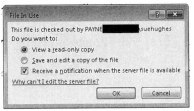

Figure 12.18

Open a read-only copy of a checked-out file and receive a notification when the file is available.

Co-authoring

Multiple reviewers can open the same document and simultaneously edit the file. This is known as co-authoring. Figure 12.19 shows how the main reviewer can determine how many reviewers are currently editing the file.

NOTE

It is important to save the document frequently. Saving is the only way the other reviewers will see the revisions made.

OFFICE 365

At the time of this writing, Microsoft had just updated co-authoring in Office Web Apps where co-authors do not need to save/refresh to see changes made in real time.

You are included in the
number of reviewers

Figure 12.19

Indicates how many reviewers currently have the document open; this only shows in the Status bar of the first person opening the file.

CAUTION

Two reviewers cannot work on the same block of text at the same time.

Indicators You Are Working with a Shared Document

When a document is being shared in SharePoint, the standard Save button is modified by Word, as shown in Figure 12.20.

 Figure 12.20

The modified Save button indicates the file is saved to SharePoint and may be shared.

As shown in Figure 12.21, Word alerts you when saving a document to SharePoint that your changes will be seen with green highlighting by the other reviewers.

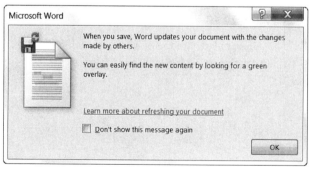

Figure 12.21

When saving, you will be alerted that other reviewers' revisions will be shown.

Collaboration with Co-authors

Let's take a look at some features that will come into play when co-authoring a document in SharePoint. We'll start with using Track Changes.

TIP

Communication between reviewers is critical for successful collaboration in SharePoint.

Track Changes On

If all reviewers have Track Changes turned on, the revisions will be tracked after the original reviewer clicks Save and then the other reviewers click Save as well.

Track Changes Off

If all reviewers do not have Track Changes turned on, the other reviewers will see a callout when another reviewer makes a change, as shown in Figure 12.22.

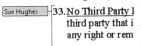

Figure 12.22

The callout displays the name of the editing reviewer next to the text being revised.

Word highlights the changes of other reviewers with green shading. Figure 12.23 shows a sample of the shaded text.

Figure 12.23

33. No Third Party Beneficiaries.
third party that is not referred
any right or remedy to any suc

Shading occurs after the original reviewer clicks Save; the shading is not permanent and will not print.

NOTE

Unless a reviewer locks a block of text, any reviewer may accept or reject changes.

Reviewer Conflict

Only one reviewer may edit a paragraph of text at any given time. If two or more reviewers are trying to edit the same text, Word will show a conflict warning, as shown in Figure 12.24. At this point, the reviewer should click the Resolve button.

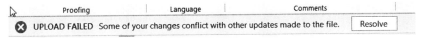

Figure 12.24   A conflict alert displays after the second reviewer saves recent edits.

Resolving the Conflict

Once the conflict warning displays, the reviewer should click the Resolve button, and the Revisions pane displays a listing of the conflicts found.

NOTE

To avoid conflicts, communicating with fellow reviewers ahead of time is important. Perhaps assigning the areas in which to edit is a great start before jumping in. Also, designating a lead review person is essential.

The reviewer can use the Revisions pane to accept or reject his or her change. By clicking Accept My Change, both revisions will appear in the document. Reviewers will need to edit further to resolve which text should remain. By clicking Reject My Change, the other reviewer's revisions will be saved. Figure 12.25 shows the choices for accepting or rejecting the changes when a conflict has occurred.

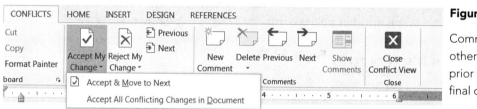

Figure 12.25

Communicate with other reviewers prior to making the final decision.

Blocking Authors

After communicating with other reviewers and you have agreed on the best method of collaboration, it may be determined that reviewers should only work on their own specific areas of the document. If this is the case, the Block Authors feature is for you, as shown in Figure 12.26. Either click in the paragraph or select multiple paragraphs and click Block Authors. Other users are not allowed to edit the blocked area.

Figure 12.26

Select one or more paragraphs, click Block Authors, and then click Save.

When you block other authors from making changes, you will see a callout when you place your mouse pointer on the blocked author icon in the document, as shown in Figure 12.27.

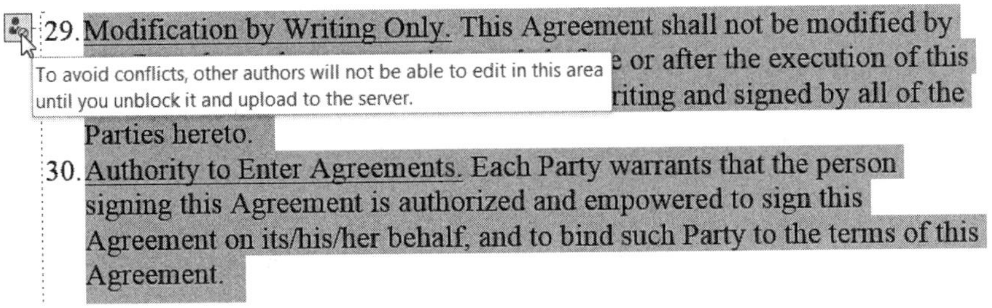
29. Modification by Writing Only. This Agreement shall not be modified by
To avoid conflicts, other authors will not be able to edit in this area until you unblock it and upload to the server.
e or after the execution of this
riting and signed by all of the
Parties hereto.
30. Authority to Enter Agreements. Each Party warrants that the person signing this Agreement is authorized and empowered to sign this Agreement on its/his/her behalf, and to bind such Party to the terms of this Agreement.

Figure 12.27

The icon and dotted lines indicate you have blocked this area from other reviewers' edits.

Reviewers who have been blocked from revising a section of text will see who blocked that section from the callout, as shown in Figure 12.28.

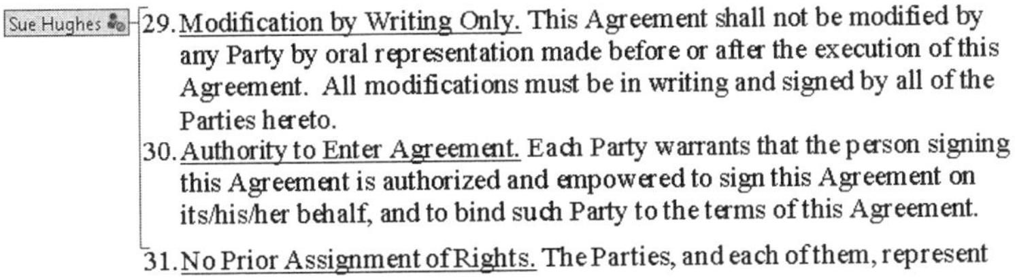
Sue Hughes
29. Modification by Writing Only. This Agreement shall not be modified by any Party by oral representation made before or after the execution of this Agreement. All modifications must be in writing and signed by all of the Parties hereto.
30. Authority to Enter Agreement. Each Party warrants that the person signing this Agreement is authorized and empowered to sign this Agreement on its/his/her behalf, and to bind such Party to the terms of this Agreement.
31. No Prior Assignment of Rights. The Parties, and each of them, represent

Figure 12.28

The name and solid line indicate who blocked this area and the size of the blocked area.

Releasing Blocked Areas for Further Review

When you have finished editing, you will want to release the blocked areas for other reviewers. From the Block Authors button, choose Release All of My Blocked Areas. Save the document so other reviewers are no longer blocked.

Final Tip on Collaborating

We have tried to stress the importance of communication among reviewers and saving the file frequently so that all collaborators' edits update in a timely manner. Many collaborators also take advantage of Word's Comment feature to facilitate this communication.

When the document is finalized, you can delete all of the comments.

Potential Issues when Collaborating in SharePoint

As described previously in this section, we have offered several pointers when co-authoring documents, such as getting familiar with and understanding the process of co-authoring a document, staying in active communication with the other reviewers, and saving often, just to name a few. If you run into problems using this feature, take a look at Table 12.6 for a possible cause and solution.

TABLE 12.6—TROUBLESHOOTING THE CO-AUTHORING FEATURE	
ISSUE	RESOLUTION
You cannot access a file and find that the file is using Information Rights Management (IRM) or Digital Rights Management (DRM).	Contact the author of the file or the systems administrator for access to the document.
The file is checked out.	SharePoint should indicate who has checked the file out.
The file is encrypted.	Contact the author of the file who may have encrypted the file.
The file format is not supported. Only .docx formats are supported.	In most cases, you can save the document into the supported format.
The file is marked as final. The file owner has decided to stop the process of editing or co-authoring the file and the file is now read-only.	Contact the author of the file who may have marked the document as final.
Certain Microsoft Office group policy settings prevent co-authoring to include the following: Disable Automerge Client Policy, Disable Co-Authoring Server Policy, and Disable Co-Authoring Client Policy.	Contact the Systems Administrator.
The file contains ActiveX controls.	Contact the template developer or author of the file.
The file contains certain objects that cannot be uniquely identified, such as an OLE object, a SmartArt graphic, chart, or Ink object.	Contact the template developer or author of the file.
The Word document uses master documents with subdocuments, contains HTML Framesets, or is being published as a blog.	Contact the template developer or author of the file.
The Word document does not have the Store Random Numbers to Improve Combine Accuracy check box selected.	Go to the File tab, Options, Trust Center, Trust Center Settings to display the Trust Center dialog box. Select Privacy Options, and under the Document-specific Settings section, select the Store Random Numbers to Improve Combine Accuracy check box.

COLLABORATING ON DOCUMENTS WITH SKYDRIVE

If you aren't prohibited from sharing the document to the cloud, and you have a SkyDrive account, you can choose to Share the document to SkyDrive to enable collaboration directly from inside of Word.

To prepare a document for sharing, click File, and then Share. There are several options available for sharing; the first is Invite Others. When this is selected in the left side, as shown in Figure 12.29, any recent folders on your SkyDrive account display along with a Browse button that, when clicked, displays the Save As dialog box associated with your SkyDrive account. Double-click the Documents folder and click New folder to create subfolders categorized by your document type. When you've chosen a location folder in which to save the document, click Save. The document is saved to the cloud.

Document2 - Word

Figure 12.29

The difference between saving to SkyDrive versus locally is documents are saved to the cloud and available from anywhere you log in.

Now that the document is saved to your SkyDrive account, you can invite others to share the file by clicking File, Share, and Invite People. Type the name or e-mail address of the person with whom to share the document in the Invite People box. To the right of the Type names or e-mail addresses box, choose what the reviewer is able to do, for instance, instance, whether the file can be edited or just viewed. Click in the text box below to type a message to the recipient(s).

If you prefer to share a link to the document instead of typing multiple names into the Invite People box, on the left side of the pane, click Get a Sharing Link, as shown in Figure 12.30. This is sometimes useful if you have large groups of people to edit the file, or if you don't have the e-mail addresses of the reviewers handy. There is a separate link to send for those with edit privileges and for those who have permissions to just view the document as Read Only. Select and copy the appropriate link and paste it into an e-mail message.

Figure 12.30 Sharing a link is useful when you are collaborating with a large group or when you don't have all of the e-mail addresses.

At any time, you can go back to the Share tab, right-click on the person's name who has been given permission, and either remove the user, or change the permission, as shown in Figure 12.31. This is useful when the file is no longer in need of collaboration and is for your eyes only.

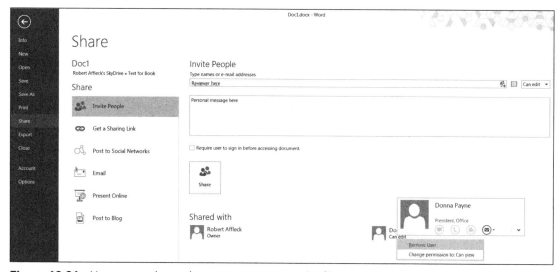

Figure 12.31 You can revoke or change permissions to the file at any time.

One final thing about working in files saved to SkyDrive: Take a look at the Save button on the Quick Access Toolbar and note that it looks just a little different from the normal appearance of the Save button. That's because when files are saved to the cloud, an arrow appears above the button, which indicates that when clicked, the file will be saved and refreshed in the cloud and all changes will be reflected to be up to date.

Law Firms and Mobility

Since the introduction of laptops, tablets, smartphones, and other mobile devices, it's become commonplace for lawyers and others to require access to files remotely. Surveys are showing that more and more lawyers are going mobile, and at an accelerated pace. It's not only convenient to be able to access work product from anywhere, but some clients insist upon being able to touch base with their attorney or share documents in real time. To help facilitate mobile computing in the practice of law, most firms are constantly evaluating current hardware and software options.

HOLLAND & KNIGHT LLP

D. Dean Leung, CIO, Holland & Knight LLP
Surface Pro 2 with Office 2013—Better Together
Before the Surface Pro 2 was released, there was a functionality void between the iPad and traditional notebook. While the iPad has great portability and battery life, the support for legal vertical applications, while growing, is in its infancy, which makes it better suited as an information consumption device. It is great for reading, but ineffective for drafting legal documents. Notebooks provide the full functionality of a desktop computer, but weight and size make travel and use on the road cumbersome. Requiring both information consumption and document drafting necessitates the road warrior to carry both an iPad and notebook while out of the office, resulting in even more weight to carry while mobile.

The Microsoft Surface Pro 2 with Office 2013 fills the gap between the notebook and iPad. Splitting the difference in terms of weight, screen size, and battery life and the ability to run all applications on a standard desktop has generated considerable interest at our firm. Notebook users are requesting the Surface Pro, and many are noting they are able to leave their iPads behind after the switch. Even if the iPad is still necessary, the combined weight of the iPad and Surface Pro is on par with a notebook.

The initial positive feedback on the Surface Pro was gathered while piloting Office 2007. As we deploy Office 2013, the new ability to switch between touch and mouse-optimized interfaces further enhances the productivity of the attorneys. This functionality allows the best of both worlds, whether the device is docked and used with dual monitors and a mouse, or whether it's being used while flying in a cramped economy seat managing e-mail by touch. A final accolade for the Surface is the ability to use the stylus rather than the keyboard for note taking, which resonates with a demographic of attorneys whom prefer the pen-and-paper approach for work product development.

Time will tell if Microsoft can be successful as a "devices and services" company, but the current generation Surface Pro 2 and Office 2013 is a powerful combination for mobile users in the legal arena.

WORKSHARE

Barrie Hadfield from Workshare on Secure File Transfer

Thanks to developments in technology, people are no longer constrained to working in the office and can work anywhere, using any mobile device. This has completely transformed the way people collaborate. People are now able to work with multiple teams across the world on a document to ensure absolute accuracy. This means that teams are now extended and can rely on expertise throughout the company. As you can imagine, this is a real competitive advantage for many.

On the flipside, there are a number of data security threats that people open themselves up to when sending sensitive documents using unsecure methods. This threat is on the rise with the majority of employees using unsecure e-mail and consumer-grade file-sharing applications to send high-value and sensitive documents to different teams. Firms need to ensure that their documents and Intellectual Property remain safe. Implementing an enterprise file-sharing application like Workshare provides businesses with control over how employees are collaborating and sharing files outside of the organization. It also allows IT administrators and document owners to set policies around how documents are used, giving them full visibility over what documents are being shared and with whom.

Capabilities that provide control will be integral to the future of collaboration, as organizations seek ways to comply with local and international legislation requirements while meeting their users' needs.

LITÉRA

Norm Thomas, Chief Commercial Officer (CCO) Litéra, on Cloud Capabilities and Word

Typically, every Windows and Xbox Live user has a Microsoft Account with a Windows Live ID e-mail address using one of these domains: @hotmail.com, @outlook.com, @msn.com, @passport.com, and @live.com. Along with this e-mail account comes access to a free online 25GB storage and collaboration service called SkyDrive (skydrive.com). SkyDrive is for consumers to sync, share, and co-author their personal files across their devices and the cloud in a SharePoint environment.

SkyDrive Pro is a feature in SharePoint 2013 that allows organizations to provision and manage personal cloud storage for their employees. SkyDrive Pro comes as part of Office 365 Small Business, Office 365 Enterprise, and SharePoint 2013.

SkyDrive Pro is for employees to sync their work files across devices and to their enterprise cloud. Your SkyDrive Pro library is managed by your law firm IT administrator and allows you to share and collaborate on documents with coworkers. Your SharePoint site collection administrator controls how you use the library. People can access personal and work files from both places together in Windows Explorer and in their Microsoft Office 2013 applications, desktop or mobile.

Office files can be created and edited from within any SkyDrive, SkyDrive Pro, or SharePoint library as well. To create a new Microsoft Office file, just click the Create link. Just by double-clicking, users can also edit these types of Microsoft Office files stored in SharePoint libraries no matter where they've been created. Users remain within a browser and begin editing in Microsoft Office Web Apps, even if they do not have Microsoft Office installed on their desktop or mobile device.

There are, however, some significant functional differences between the Microsoft Office Web Apps and the desktop versions of Microsoft Office.

Some notable features used in legal document editing that are not present in Microsoft Word Web Apps are: Insert Header or Footer, Page and Section Breaks, Table of Contents, Table of Authorities, Index, Cross-references, Comments, Symbols, Fields, Mail Merge, Envelopes and Labels, and Columns.

Only the Editing and Reading views are available in Microsoft Word Web Apps, with no rulers, guidelines, zooming, and multiple window or macro capabilities. Review Table 12.7 for details what is available on each of the standard tabs in Word Web Apps.

TABLE 12.7—WORD WEB APPS TABS

DESKTOP MICROSOFT WORD 2013 TABS	BROWSER MICROSOFT WORD WEB APPS
File	Info option allows only switching to the desktop version or displaying prior versions of the document in the library. No New, Open, or Export options
Home	No Format Painter, SmartArt, Multilevel lists, Sorting, Paragraph formatting (shading or borders), Find, Replace, Select functions. The Review tab's Spelling (and Grammar) Check function is moved to the Home tab but no Grammar checking functionality is available.
Insert	Only Table, Picture, ClipArt, and HyperLink capabilities
Design	None
Page Layout	Only Margin, Page Orientation and Size, Paragraph Spacing, and Indentation functions are available
References	None
Mailings	None
View	Only Editing and Reading Views offered.

Browser-based editing and file creation using Microsoft Office Web Apps is a significant advancement in the power and freedom users have to manage their document authoring and collaboration. However, because these new tools are designed for consumer-grade purposes, attorneys should remember that they are not compliant with ABA Ethics Codes pertaining to client privacy and content security. Law firms should be careful to include third-party capabilities for content risk management that are both professional-grade in nature and that work in harmony with how attorneys work, while maintaining close integrations with Microsoft technology.

ENCORETECH

Jeffrey Roach, President at EncoreTech, on Collaboration and the Cloud

Over the last few years it's become clear that Microsoft's strategy around document collaboration and the cloud is organizing around SkyDrive. Unfortunately for Office users, the connection between SkyDrive and applications like Word and Excel has been tenuous at best, and downright painful at worst.

All of that changes with Office 2013. SkyDrive integration is not only robust, but incredibly easy to use. You'll find links to SkyDrive when saving and opening files or browsing recently edited documents. You'll also find a much improved Share feature that allows your Invite People to your file by saving it to the cloud. Recipients will need a Microsoft Account (Live, Outlook, et al.) or an Organizational Account (Office 365) to access the file. Once shared, you can collaborate in real time using the improved co-authoring features of Office. Best of all, Office 365 users can use web-based versions of their favorite apps to collaborate on their shared documents when they are away from the office.

It sounds like a lot of moving parts to keep track of, but Microsoft has done an admirable job combining several key pieces of its technology arsenal into a useable and useful set of features that have the potential to dramatically change the way we work with others.

MAIL MERGE FOR THE LEGAL COMMUNITY

Microsoft Word provides a robust yet intuitive method for producing mass mailings. Regardless of whether you need to create merge letters, envelopes, labels, announcements, directories, or even e-mail messages, Mail Merge is the simplest way to create personalized mass mailings. Create your own Data Source "on the fly" or merge the main document with an existing firm database, Excel file, Word table, or Outlook Contact List.

WHY USE MAIL MERGE?

Mail Merge is an often under-utilized and misunderstood tool; however, when used to its fullest, it is one of the biggest time-savers imaginable. The goal of this chapter is to take the mystery out of Mail Merge, so you can focus your efforts on the more important legal matters of your practice.

While the initial setup of the merge document may take a bit more time, the payoff when having to edit the main document or modify the recipient list and then remerge is well worth the effort. Data sources, which contain the variable information for the merge process, may be reused for other purposes and even filtered for use with other merge projects later.

If you are migrating from Microsoft Office 2003 or an earlier version, you will find that Microsoft has completely redesigned Mail Merge.

Microsoft Word Web App provides no mail merge functionality. Any merge fields that were inserted via the standard installation copy of Microsoft Word will be locked in the Web App, where they cannot be modified or deleted.

UNDERSTANDING THE BASIC MAIL MERGE TERMS AND FEATURES

There are some unique terms used in Word's Mail Merge feature that aren't used in other parts of the software. For instance, there is a Main Document, a Data Source file, and a resulting Final Document. Table 13.1 describes the features associated with a mail merge, while Table 13.2 explains the Mailings tab.

TABLE 13.1—MAIL MERGE TERMS		
TERM	**DESCRIPTION**	**COMMENT**
Main Document	The Word file, envelope, label, or e-mail containing common text and mail merge fields.	The Data Source populates the merge fields in the Main Document.
Data Source	File, database, or Outlook Contacts containing the merge recipients' information records.	Labeled "Recipients/Lists" in the Mailings tab. After you've opened a Main Document that is connected to the Data Source file, the Data Source is considered open, and you will not be able to perform some common commands on that file such as Cut, Rename, etc.
Records	Each recipient's set of information is known as a record or entry.	Each record contains columns of unique fields (e.g., Last Name, First Name, Phone Number, etc.).
Merge Field	The column containing unique information for each record (e.g., Last Name, First Name, Phone Number, etc.).	Merge fields are inserted into the Main Document and may be used in multiple locations in the Main Document. Only use the category of fields applicable for a mail merge.
Final Document	The resultant Word document, label sheet, or e-mail message where the merge has been completed between the Main Document and the Data Source. All of the merge fields will be populated from the Data Source.	Creates a new document combining the data with the main document text. This document can be saved or just used for printing.

Figure 13.1 Many of the commands on the Mailings tab become available only when performing a mail merge.

TABLE 13.2—MAILING TAB OVERVIEW		
BUTTON	**DESCRIPTION**	**COMMENTS**
Envelopes	Create an envelope based on an address selected in the active document or just type the name and address into the Delivery Address box.	Add the envelope to the beginning of the document or simply print the envelope. This function is not used with the Mail Merge function.
Labels	Create a single label or a full page of labels.	Save the document created from the label sheet for future use or simply print the label(s). This function is not used with the Mail Merge function.
Start Mail Merge	Choose the type of Main Document to create.	Choose from Letters, E-mail Messages, Envelopes, Labels, Directory, a blank document, or use the handy Step-by-Step Mail Merge Wizard.
Select Recipient List	Choose the Data Source with the variable information.	You can either use an existing Data Source or create a new Data Source.
Edit Recipient List	Choose which recipients to merge.	Options include Sort, Filter, Find Duplicates, Find Recipients, Validate Addresses.
Highlight Merge Fields	Identify (by shading) where the merge fields are located in the Main Document.	Non-mail merge fields will not be highlighted. The shading does not print.
Address Block	Choose from several address block formats to place in the Main Document.	Optional, but efficient, feature.
Greeting Line	Choose from several greeting lines to use for the Main Document's salutation.	Optional, but efficient, feature.
Insert Merge Field	Insert commonly used merge fields in the appropriate locations of the Main Document.	Individual merge fields may be used in multiple locations of the Main Document or not used at all.
Rules	Set custom conditions for merging records.	Setting rules or conditions is optional, but well worth learning.

continues

TABLE 13.2—*(CONTINUED)*

BUTTON	DESCRIPTION	COMMENTS
Match Fields	Used to match field names in the Main Document with field names from the Data Source, if they do not match.	Used with the Address Block feature. Confirm the Data Source fields match up to populate the Main Document fields.
Update Labels	Updates the rest of the labels in the Main Document with the fields that were inserted into the first label.	Used with a Labels Main Document.
Preview Results	Show the merged data in the Main Document prior to completing the merge.	Use this feature to determine if any editing needs to be done prior to completing the merge.
Find Recipient	Quickly locate a recipient from within the Preview.	Only works in Preview Results view or the Mail Merge Recipients List. Useful when the Data Source has many records.
Check for Errors	Tell Word how to report any errors that may occur while merging the Data Source and the Main Document.	Optional, but informative, feature.
Finish & Merge	Complete the mail merge. Merge the Data Source information into the Main Document.	Results in a final Word document, label sheet, or e-mail message.

NOTE

As with any Microsoft Office feature, commands on the Mailings tab will not be active if you are not using the process required for use with that feature.

METHODS OF MAIL MERGE

There are several methods for starting mail merge projects. Use the Step-by-Step Mail Merge Wizard if you are new to Mail Merge, or if you are new to the redesigned Mail Merge in Microsoft Word 2013. If you are already comfortable with mail merge, you can skip the Wizard and start from scratch, using the various commands mentioned in Table 13.2.

Opening a Main Document

If a Word document is set as a main document *with* a data source attached, you'll see the dialog box shown in Figure 13.2 when opening that main document. Answering Yes will connect the document to the data source. Answering No will not connect the main Document to the data source (for this Word session only), thus, you will not be able to do any merging or recipient record editing.

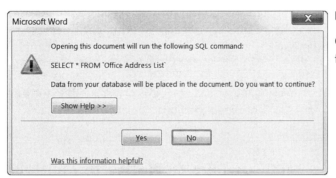

Figure 13.2

Click Yes to connect for full merge functionality.

Step-by-Step Mail Merge Wizard

The Step-by-Step Mail Merge wizard opens the Mail Merge task pane. The task pane logically progresses through the process, so no steps are missed. The Wizard may automatically create a new Word document, depending on what is currently open in the Word application window.

Overview—Six Steps in the Mail Merge Wizard

Step 1—Select Document Type. Choose which type of mail merge document to create.

Step 2—Select Starting Document. Create the file from the current document, from a template, or from an existing document that can be converted to a Main Document.

Step 3—Select Recipients. Choose your Data Source. You may choose from an existing list, select the list from Outlook contacts, or create a new list.

Step 4—Write Your Letter. Here you add both the standard text to the Main Document as well as the merge fields. The Mail Merge task pane includes handy consolidated fields such as Address block, Greeting Line, or select the More Items link for more merge field options.

Step 5—**Preview Your Letters.** See how your mail merge document will appear with the merged data. Click the Next Record and Previous Record buttons to scroll through the merged records. Click the Exclude This Recipient link in the Mail Merge task pane to remove a person from the merge. (This does not delete the recipient from the Data Source.) Click Edit Recipient List link in the task pane to make any changes, remove, or add someone to the Data Source list.

Step 6—Complete the Merge. You can either print the final mail merge document or edit individual letters within the resultant mail merge document. The merged document consists of multiple sections, with each section representing one merged document.

NOTE

At any point while using the wizard, you may click Previous at the bottom of the Mail Merge task pane to go back to a previous step and make changes or corrections.

Create a Past Due Invoice Notice to Multiple Recipients Using the Wizard

1. Create a new blank document.
2. Save the file as **JanuaryInvoice2014.docx.**
3. Click the Mailings tab.
4. In the Start Mail Merge group, click Start Mail Merge.
5. Choose Step-by-Step Mail Merge Wizard.

Step through the Wizard

Step 1 of 6: In the Mail Merge task pane, choose Letters. Click Next: Starting Document located at the bottom of the task pane.

Step 2 of 6: Because the document has just been saved, choose Use the Current Document. Click Next: Select Recipients located at the bottom of the task pane.

Step 3 of 6: Choose Type a New List. Click the Create link below the Type a New List section of the Mail Merge task pane.

Modify the New Address List

1. Click the Customize Columns button.

2. Click the Add button and type a new field name titled **Due Date.**

3. Click OK or press Enter.

4. Add another field name called **Amount Due.**

5. For ease of typing the data, select the First Name and Last Name fields and click the Move Up button to move those fields. Delete the fields as needed so your list looks similar to what is shown in Figure 13.3.

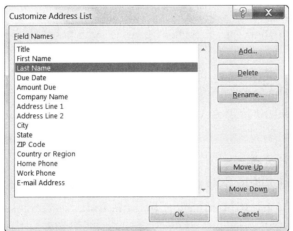

Figure 13.3

Customize Address List provides many edit options for the new Data Source when creating a new list.

NOTE

The Customize Address List dialog box provides the ability to not only add new fields, but to delete unnecessary fields as well as arrange the fields in a logical manner to make it easier to insert data using the Tab key when inputting recipient data.

6. Click OK to close the Customize Address List dialog box.

TIP

Use the mouse to resize the New Address List dialog box. This allows you to see all (or most) of the fields to which you'll be adding data.

7. Type the information, as shown in Figure 13.4.

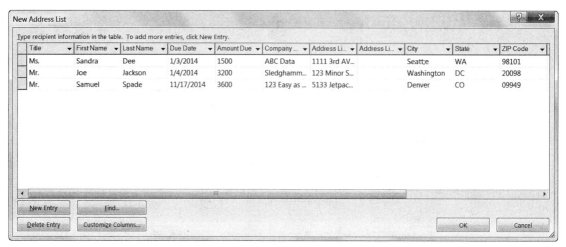

Figure 13.4 When creating a new entry, press the Tab key to move from field to field. Alt+N also creates a new entry (record).

8. Click OK when you are finished typing the records.

9. Save the file as **PastDueClients.mdb** to the default My Data Sources folder.

10. Click Save.

11. Click OK to close the Mail Merge Recipients dialog box.

Step 3 of 6 (continued): Now that the Data Source is saved, click Next: Write Your Letter located at the bottom of the Mail Merge task pane.

Write the Letter

1. Press Ctrl+Home to move your insertion point to the top of the document.

2. Click the Address block link in the Mail Merge task pane.

3. Accept all defaults and click OK.

4. Press Enter twice and type **Dear** : and then press Enter twice.

5. Type **Please remit payment of $ by the following date.**

Insert the Merge Fields

1. Place your insertion point between the space and the colon after Dear.

2. On the Mailings tab, in the Write & Insert Fields group, click the upper portion of the Insert Merge Field split button.

3. Double-click each on Title, First Name, and then Last Name to quickly insert these fields into the Main Document and then click Close.

4. Insert a space between the Title and First Name and between the First Name and Last Name fields. Be careful to insert the space between the chevrons of the different fields.

TIP

You can also use the Insert Merge Fields drop-down list to insert one merge feld at a time.

5. Click the mouse directly after the dollar sign in the body of the letter.

6. On the Mailings tab, in the Write & Insert fields group, click the Insert Merge Field drop-down list.

7. Choose Amount Due.

8. Repeat steps 6 and 7 to insert the Due Date merge field before the period at the end of the sentence.

Preview the Results

1. On the Mailings tab, in the Preview Results group, click Preview Results.

2. In the Preview Results group, click the Next Record and Previous Record arrows to view each recipient.

TIP

To view the underlying merge fields, press Alt+F9. Press Alt+F9 again to hide the fields. Alt+F9 is a field display toggle.

Step 4 of 6: Now that the Data Source is saved, click Next: Preview Your Letters at the bottom of the Mail Merge task pane.

Step 5 of 6: Review the merged letters using the Next Record and Previous Record buttons. If you see a mistake, you can edit "on the fly;" however, this is not the preferred method for editing. We'll discuss proper editing methods next.

3. Click Next: Complete the Merge at the bottom of the task pane.

   Step 6 of 6: At this point you can print your letters or save the merged Final Document.

4. Close all files without saving.

NOTE

Saving a Final Document is particularly useful for printing purposes. For example, if the printer runs out of paper or jams, it's nice to have the saved file so you can continue the print job from that point forward without having to remerge the Main Document and Data Source. Other than for purposes of printing, saving the final merged file is not a good idea as it may result in outdated information if the Data Source has been edited after the final merge.

Manual Mail Merge

If you're comfortable with the mail merge process, you can skip the wizard and go straight into creation of your Main Document as the first step in the merge project.

Use an Existing Word Document and Data Source

1. Open the exercise file AddressUpdate.docx available for download at www.thepaynegroup.com/downloads/word2013forlawfirms/. This document will be used as the Main Document.

2. Click the Mailings tab to display the ribbon.

3. In the Start Mail Merge group, click Select Recipients and choose Use an Existing List.

4. Open the exercise file ClientList.xlsx.

5. Click OK.

6. Click in the second line beneath the Customer Relations information and click the Address Block button in the Write & Insert Fields group on the Mailings tab.

7. Click OK.

8. Click to the left of the colon in the Salutation block.

9. In the Write & Insert Fields group, click the Insert Merge Field drop-down list, select Title, and press the Spacebar.

10. Click the Insert Merge Field Button drop-down list and select Last.

11. Save the Main Document.

12. In the Preview Results group, click Preview Results.

13. In the Preview Results group, click Next Record to view the next recipient and click Previous Record to view the previous recipient.

14. In the Finish group, click Finish & Merge and choose Edit Individual Documents.

15. In the Merge to New Document dialog box, select All and click OK.

16. Press the Page Down key on the keyboard to review the merged letters in the Final Document.

17. Close all open documents without saving.

E-mail Messages Mail Merge

Create a mass E-mail merge to selected recipients from Outlook Contacts or from a Data Source that has an e-mail address field. Using this feature requires a bit of planning, such as testing the end result with e-mail recipients who are in your test group (or just yourself). You may also want to let your Exchange Administrator know if you will be sending the message: (1) to a large number of recipients, (2) the message has a large attachment, or (3) the message includes a large-sized picture or ClipArt within the body of the e-mail message. The size of the attachments and pictures from the mass e-mail will quickly claim significant amounts of space both in your Sent Items folder as well as on the Exchange Server.

NOTE

You should open Outlook and then minimize it in the background while you complete the following exercise.

CAUTION

When conducting an e-mail merge as in the following exercise, you do not get to review the merged e-mail message before the e-mail is sent. The last step merges and sends the e-mail.

Create a Mass E-mail Merge

1. Create a new blank document.

2. Save the file as **EmailMergeText.docx.**

3. Click the Mailings tab.

4. In the Start Mail Merge group, click Start Mail Merge.

5. Choose E-mail Messages.

6. Using the Word document as the e-mail editor, type the desired text. This is the text that will appear in the body of the e-mail message.

7. Click Save.

8. In the Start Mail Merge group, click Select Recipients, and select Choose from Outlook Contacts or another Data Source containing e-mail addresses.

9. Uncheck any recipients, as necessary.

10. Insert the appropriate merge fields into the body of the message if you are personalizing the text with other data from the Data Source.

11. Click Save.

12. In the Finish group, click Finish & Merge.

13. Select Send E-mail Messages, and the Merge to E-mail dialog box displays.

14. Be sure the To box contains the E-mail_Address merge field.

15. Type the Subject Line.

Figure 13.5

Complete the Merge to E-mail dialog box before clicking OK.

16. Click OK. The e-mail messages are now being sent.

EDITING

While it's easy to edit your merged records after the final document has been created, this offers only a temporary fix. It's important to edit both your Main Document and your Data Source if any changes need to be made. This ensures that future merge projects using these same files will contain the correct information, so the next merge process with these files can be completed quickly and without modification.

NOTE

If the edits needed in the Final Document are extensive, it's a better practice to close the Final Document, edit the Main Document and Data Source, and then remerge those two files.

Edit the Main Document

Simply open the Main Document and make any necessary corrections. This includes text, spelling, grammar, punctuation, and anything else that would make this a solid Main Document moving forward. Be sure to save your changes.

Edit the Data Source

1. Open the Main Document.
2. On the Mailings tab, in the Start Mail Merge group, click Edit Recipient List.
3. Double-click the Data Source in the Data Source list.
4. Make the necessary changes.
5. Click Yes to update the recipient list and then click OK to close the recipient list.
6. Save the document.

REFINE RECIPIENT LIST OPTIONS

After you have the recipient list created and displayed, you can fine-tune it by sorting, filtering, removing duplicates, and much more. This section looks at these options.

Sort

Sorting is a useful feature when dealing with large lists. Sometimes it's helpful to have a list sort one way for one situation and then have it sorted another way in another situation. For example, you might want to sort the list in alphabetical order by Last Name, then First Name, when creating a Client Address Book. Next, you might want to sort it by Attorney so each attorney's letters will be generated and grouped together to make it easier to divide and distribute the printed documents for attorney signatures.

This is particularly useful when printing and where you need to have the documents printed in a specific order, such as by ZIP code.

Filter

One of the benefits of using Mail Merge is the ability to reuse Data Sources. Filter the list by one or more criteria to narrow down the number of records to be merged. Filtering a list can be as simple as excluding just one individual, or the list can be filtered to include only a subset of the records in the database that match specified criteria, such as all clients who live in the state of New York. Filtering a list of records does not delete their information; just remove the filter and all records are once again available.

Find Duplicates

This option prompts Word to locate and display duplicate records in the data source list. Duplicates are an exact match with no variation in the record's data.

Find Recipient

Use this option to search through a data source list more quickly than scrolling. Type the search criteria into the Find box. The Look In field provides a method for searching through all fields, or narrowing the search down to one specific field. Choosing the All Fields option would most likely return more results.

Validate Addresses

Additional software is needed for this feature to work. There are at least two companies that supply such functionality: CorrectAddress by Intelligent Search Technology and Stamps.com.

For more information on what services are available, click Yes to the prompt you receive when clicking the Validate Addresses button.

MERGE WITH AN EXISTING DATA SOURCE

Microsoft Word's Mail Merge feature is designed to merge with a number of different types of Data Source files. We'll list a few of the common file types here. Keep in mind that when using an external Data Source, you cannot edit the records from within Word; instead, open the native application, such as Access or Excel, to edit the records.

- Office Databases Connections—.odc

- Access Databases—.mdb, .mde

- Access 2007 Data Base—.accdb, .accde

- Microsoft Office Address Lists—.mdb

- Microsoft Office List Shortcuts—.ols

- Microsoft Data Links—.udl

- ODBC File DSNs—.dsn

- Excel Files—.xlsx, xslsm, .xlsb, .xls

- Web Pages—.htm, .html, .asp, .mht, .mhtml

- Rich Text Format—.rtf

- Word Documents—.docx, .doc, .docm

- Text Files—.txt, .prn, .csv, .tab, .acs

- Database Queries—.dqy, .rqy

- OpenDocument Text Files—.odt

Prepare to Use a Different Data Source

1. Open the Main Document or create a new blank document.

2. Click the Mailings tab.

3. In the Start Mail Merge group, click Select Recipients.

4. Click Use an Existing List.

5. Browse to the location containing the Data Source file.

Excel as a Data Source

Oftentimes the database administrator at a law firm will provide users with data in a more user-friendly format, such as an Excel spreadsheet. This format allows the recipient of the file to chart, sort, filter, create PivotTables, etc., and in this case, use that data as a Mail Merge Data Source.

Because worksheets often have more information than just the table of fields and records that contain the source data needed for the merge file, you may want to consider having the Data Source table in a separate worksheet, starting in cell A1, within the Excel file. In the separate worksheet, you could delete blank rows and remove any extraneous information not needed for the merge (e.g., PivotTables, etc.). The Data Source file can contain many fields that are not referenced in the Main Document's merge fields. As with any merge project, you only need to insert the needed fields into the Main Document.

We recommend that you name the worksheet something intuitive, so that it is easy to find the appropriate worksheet when prompted for the Data Source file.

After you've chosen the worksheet file, the Insert Merge Field button will be populated with the names of the fields in the Excel list.

NOTE

Word will try to parse through all the data in the worksheet in an attempt to determine where the Data Source (table) is located. If you have extraneous information outside the table of records, Word will pull the wrong information into the recipient list. Figure 13.6 shows the worksheets that are available when Excel is used as a Data Source for the merge.

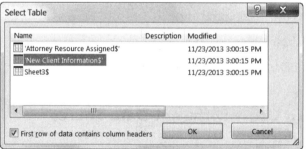

Figure 13.6

All of the worksheets in the Excel file will be listed, so it is best to rename the worksheet to make it easier to identify and choose the correct Data Source in the Excel file.

Word as a Data Source

When using a Word file as the Data Source, be sure the data is in a table format and that the table includes unique headings. There should be nothing else in the Word file besides the table.

After you've chosen the appropriate Word document, the Insert Merge Field button will be populated by those fields in the table (i.e., the headings).

If your Word document is not laid out properly, Word will attempt to inform you, as shown in Figure 13.7.

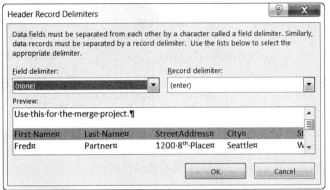

Figure 13.7

Note the text from the document as well as the first row of the table; Word cannot delimit nor parse through extraneous information in the Data Source.

Access as a Data Source

When using Access as a Data Source, you may need to contact your Database Administrator for the following information: (1) Access database filename and path to the database file, (2) name of the table, and (3) name of the query.

When opening the database, Access lists the available tables (Type – Table) and queries (Type – View). After you've chosen the table or query, the Insert Merge Field button will be populated with the fields in the table or query. Using Microsoft Access as a Data Source is shown in Figure 13.8.

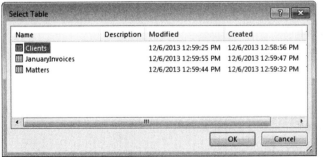

Figure 13.8

Access lists the available tables and queries that may be used as the Data Source.

Text Delimited File as a Data Source

In addition to exporting files to an Excel format, some administrators, as well as courts, will export data into what is known as a Text Delimited File. The delimiter is the character that tells the program where one field ends and another begins. Most commonly, the delimiter is a tab or comma character (tab or comma delimited). When using a Text Delimited File as the Data Source, Word generally will be able to identify the delimiter character. However, you may need to review the .txt file to verify that there are no extraneous tabs or commas present. A good example of an extraneous comma would be if one field contained both last and first name separated by a comma (last, first) and the delimiter between fields was also a comma. You'd need to remove those extraneous commas between the last and first name, or you'd need to replace the actual comma delimiters with tabs.

Outlook Contacts as a Data Source

If the Contacts folder list already exists in Outlook, there is no need to create a new list or export the data to another format. Word's Mail Merge can connect to any Contacts list in your personal Contacts folders. If you are using your primary Contacts folder for the merge, you do not need to do anything other than select Outlook Contacts as your source and then click OK (see Figure 13.9). If you need to use another person's Contacts folder, some extra steps are necessary.

Figure 13.9

Choose the Contacts list with which to merge.

If your mail merge project requires you to merge Contacts from your attorney's Contacts list, the attorney will need to make sure that you have permission to the Contacts folder first. After that, you must add that folder as a node to your main Outlook folder list.

To make the Contacts folder in Outlook available for a Mail Merge data source, first go to Outlook and display the Contacts folders. Right-click on the folder of choice and choose Properties. On the Outlook Address Book tab, check the option Show This Folder as an E-Mail Address Book and click OK. This Contacts folder should now display as being available for the merge. If necessary, ask your IT support to set up the permissions to add the attorney's Contacts to your Outlook folder.

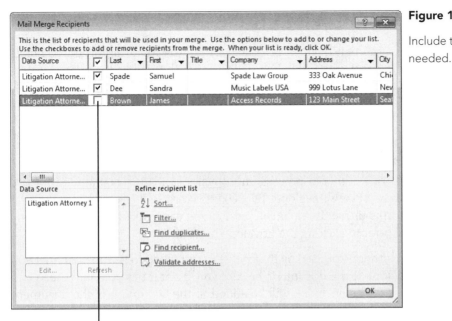

Figure 13.10

Include the recipients needed.

Uncheck to not include in merge

RETURN A MAIN DOCUMENT BACK TO A REGULAR WORD FILE

After you've set up a document as the Main Document, Word has made connections with the Data Source file in the background. This information contained in the Main Document may refer to a Data Source that either exists, has been deleted, has been moved to another location, or been renamed.

Follow these steps to remove the connections so this document is no longer considered a Main Document:

1. Open the Main Document.

2. Click the Mailings tab.

3. In the Start Mail Merge group, click Start Mail Merge.

4. Click Normal Word Document.

At this point, the document is no longer identified by Word as a Main (merge) Document.

ENVELOPES AND LABELS

The Envelopes command, which is located in the Create group on the Mailings tab, displays the Envelopes and Labels dialog box with the Envelopes tab selected. Conversely, clicking Labels will display the same dialog box; however, the Labels tab will be selected.

Creating Envelopes

Unless it's part of the merge process, the Envelopes feature is intended for use with the creation of one envelope. By default, Word will try to detect the first address block in your file. If it is unsuccessful, you can select the address (or any address block) prior to clicking the Envelope button.

Envelopes can either be printed by themselves or attached to the document. If you attach the envelope to the document, be sure your printer has both letterhead and envelopes loaded. The envelope will be added to the beginning of the document with a Next Page Section Break between the envelope and the letter.

Create an Envelope

1. Create a new blank document.
2. Type your name and full home address at the top of the page. This should be at least a three-line address block.
3. Press Enter twice.
4. Click the Mailings tab.
5. In the Create group, click Envelopes.
6. Click Add to Document.
7. Keep this document open for the next exercise.

Return Address

Many law firms use preprinted envelopes with the firm's return address already printed on the envelope. If you are using a plain envelope, you may either type your address into the Return Address field, or you can use the Outlook button to select a Contact along with that person's address.

Once you've chosen a contact for the return address, that name will be populated in the drop-down list next to the Outlook button.

Envelope Options

Click the Options button to select the proper envelope size, Delivery Address font and Return Address font, and printer feed method.

E-Postage Properties

This feature is only available if you have the electronic postage software installed.

NOTE

Word no longer supports delivery point bar codes on envelopes or labels.

Creating Labels

Unless you are merging, the Labels feature is intended for one label or an entire sheet of the same label. By default, Word will try to detect the first address block in your file.

The Labels tab of the dialog box is pretty straightforward and is slightly different from earlier versions of Word. You specify the address, choose what to print, and then see a preview of the label. The buttons at the bottom of the dialog box include Print, which sends the print job to your printer; New Document, which creates a new document of the labels; Options, which allows you to choose what type of label to use; and E-postage Properties, which allows you to print your postage from your computer if you have subscribed to this service.

Create a Sheet of Labels

1. The document from the previous exercise should still be open. If you are not in the same document, create a new blank document and type your name and address.

2. On the Mailings tab, in the Create group, click Labels.

3. Select the Options button.

4. Change Label Vendors to Avery A4/A5.

5. Change Product Number to EM88386V.

6. Click the Details button to review the size.

7. Click Cancel.

8. Click OK twice.

9. Click the New Document button.

10. Close the new labels sheet without saving.

11. Close the document without saving.

NOTE

If you're not using labels from any of the commercial products available in the Labels dialog box, you will need to define a new label specification, as shown in Figure 13.11. After a custom label has been created, it can be found on the Label Options dialog box's Label Vendors list as Other/Custom Label.

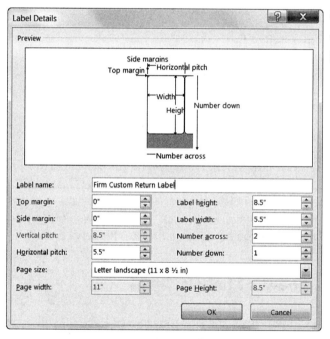

Figure 13.11

You can define the custom label specifications.

ADVANCED MAIL MERGE FEATURES

Some of the more advanced features available in Mail Merge are setting up rules that apply some type of basic logic in different lists or scenarios and checking for errors.

Rules

Not every mail merge is as straightforward as just adding an address block and greeting line. Some merge projects require built-in logic. When this occurs, you can use rules to apply logic to the merge process. Figure 13.12 shows how rules can be useful for your legal merge needs.

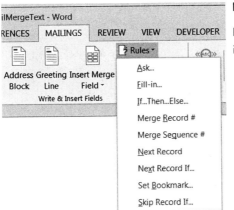

Figure 13.12

Rules allow you to build more complex logic into the merge process.

Word offers a number of fields to control how data is merged. A few commonly used fields are as follows:

- ASK and FILLIN fields display a prompt as Word merges each data record with the Main Document, as shown in Figures 13.13 and 13.14. The text will be inserted at the location of the merge rule field. Use this option when you may have variable information for a record during the merge process that is not intended to be part of the Data Source.

Figure 13.13

Define the Fill-in prompt; this example will ask only once and will insert the same text into all records.

Figure 13.14

Define the Fill-in prompt so that your text can be input once and automatically inserted into all records.

- If. . . Then. . . Else fields print information only if a condition you've specified is met. The text will be inserted at the location of the merge rule field. In the Step-by-Step Wizard exercise in this chapter, the Amount Due could trigger Word to put in a specific line of text, based on the criteria. Figure 13.15 shows the text to be inserted using the Insert Word Field dialog box.

- Merge Record # is used in a mail merge to print the number of the corresponding merged data record in each resultant merged document. The record number will be inserted at the location of the merge rule field. The number reflects the sequential order of the merged data records. It does not necessarily indicate the actual order of the records as they occur in the Data Source.

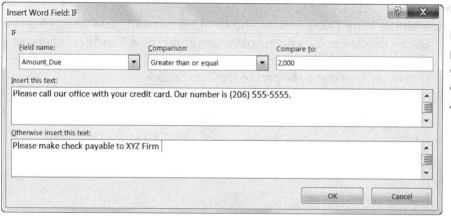

Figure 13.15

Define the IF prompt. This example bases criteria on the Amount Due.

- Merge Sequence # counts the number of data records successfully merged with the Main Document. Word starts numbering merged records starting with 1 each time you merge documents. The number may be different from the value inserted by the MERGEREC field.

- Next Record instructs Word to merge the next data record into the current resultant merged document, rather than starting a new merged document.

The NEXT field produces no printed result. Use this field when you set up a mailing label Main Document during a mail merge.

- Next Record If field may be used in documents created in previous versions of Word, but don't use the NEXTIF field in the current version of Word.

- Set Bookmark fields allows you to assign text, a number, or other information to a bookmark. You can use the information multiple times in the resultant merged documents. If the information changes, then you can edit the SET field once rather than searching through the main document and changing each occurrence. Bookmark names cannot contain spaces or start with a numeric value.

The SET Bookmark field, shown in Figures 13.16 (document) and 13.17 (Header), is generally placed in a safe location of the document, such as the Header of the document. You must then use the REF field to refer to the named bookmark. Place the REF field wherever you want the Bookmark information to display throughout the document.

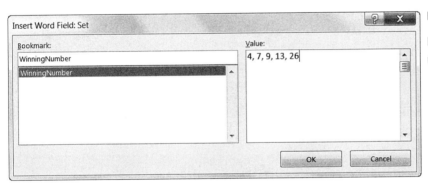

Figure 13.16

Define the SET Bookmark name and value.

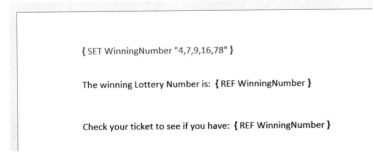

Figure 13.17

The SET field is typically placed in the Header, and the value of the bookmark is referenced in a REF field in the document.

Figure 13.18 shows the document results of using the SET field in several locations of a document.

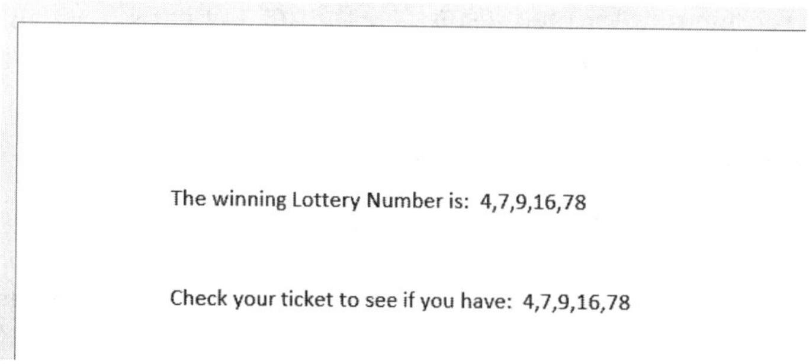

Figure 13.18

Document results of using the SET field.

The winning Lottery Number is: 4,7,9,16,78

Check your ticket to see if you have: 4,7,9,16,78

Using Advanced Features

The following exercise sets the stage for the following scenario:

Your law firm commonly hosts CLEs for other attorneys to attend. While the locations, dates, and times are known ahead of time and can be modified in the Main Document, the speaker, topic, and cost are often learned just prior to sending the invitations.

The following steps guide you through not only merging a document, but adding advanced fields that prompt for specific information about the speaker and topic. You will also add a field that inserts text based on the state in which the attorneys live.

The following advanced fields will be used in this exercise: Fill-in, Ask, Ref, and If-then.

Add the Data Source and Insert the Merge Fields

1. Open the exercise file CLE-Invitation.docx available for download at www.thepaynegroup.com/downloads/word2013forlawfirms/. This document will be used as the Main Document.

2. On the Mailings tab, in the Start Mail Merge group, click Select Recipients and choose Use an Existing List.

3. Open the exercise file CLE-Firms.mdb.

4. Place your insertion point two lines below the date at the top of the document.

5. On the Mailings tab, in the Write & Insert Fields group, click the Insert Merge Field down arrow, choose First Name, press the Spacebar once, and then insert the Last Name field.

6. Press Enter and insert the City and State fields with a comma and space in between.

7. Click Save.

Add Three Fill-in Fields

The Fill-in fields will be used to prompt for the seminar title, speaker's full name, and the speaker's first name.

1. Select the xxx title placeholder beneath the"Please join…"paragraph. Press Delete so the insertion point remains between the quotes.

2. On the Mailings tab, click Rules and choose Fill-in.

3. In the Prompt box, type **Enter seminar title here**.

4. In the Default Fill-in box, type **Seminar title**.

5. Select the Ask Once check box.

6. Click OK.

7. When the prompt is displayed, click Cancel. Clicking Cancel tells Word not to accept the default text, but to prompt during the merge process for the correct information.

8. Click Save.

9. Follow Steps 1–8 to prompt for the speaker's Full Name in the xxx place-holder prior to "partner at . . .". Be sure to check Ask Once.

10. Follow Steps 1–8 to prompt for the speaker's First Name in the xxx place-holder prior to"will present in person…". Be sure to check Ask Once.You may need to add a space just to the left of the word"will".

11. Click Save.

NOTE

When setting up the advanced fields, the text you type in the prompts should be intuitive. This way, anyone merging the document will know exactly what information should be inserted, as shown in Figure 13.19.

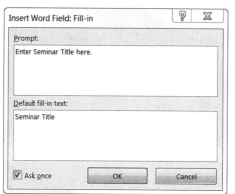

Figure 13.19

Prompts need to be intuitive so the user knows what type of information is required.

Add an Ask Field

The Ask field creates a bookmark to be used throughout a document. The Ask field will need to be modified each time the information changes. We are going to store the Ask field in the document's Header.

1. Press Ctrl+Home to move your insertion point to the top of the document.

2. Double-click at the very top edge of the document page to open the Header.

3. On the Mailings tab, in the Write & Insert Fields group, click Rules and choose Ask.

4. In the Bookmark box, type **cost**.

5. In the Prompt box, type **Enter seminar cost**.

6. In the Default Bookmark Text box, type a **zero (0)**.

7. Select the Ask Once check box.

8. Click OK twice.

9. Click Save.

Add Two Ref Fields

The Ref field will call and insert the bookmark information that was created with the Ask field. The information needs to be placed in two locations of this document.

1. Double-click anywhere in the document to move out of the Header.

2. Select the xxx placeholder in "The CLE fee is an. . ." and press Delete.

3. Press Ctrl+F9 to manually add a field. (Unfortunately, the Ref field is not in the Rules list.)

4. Between the curly braces of the new field, type **Ref cost**. This is going to reference the Set field value you placed in the Header.

5. Scroll down to the bottom of the document.

6. Right-click the RSVP Footer section.

7. Click Edit Footer.

8. Select the xxx placeholder in "…online by making your $…" and press Delete.

9. Press Ctrl+F9 to manually add a field.

10. Between the curly braces of the new field, type **Ref cost**.

11. Double-click anywhere in the document to move out of the Footer.

12. Click Save.

Add the If-Then Field

This field will check the state information from the recipient list in the Data Source. If the state is not equal to WA, then a specific line of text will be inserted into the document; otherwise, another line of text will be inserted if the state is WA. The IF field does not prompt the user. The logic is already built into the information you will enter into the If dialog box.

1. Place the cursor in the second blank line below the paragraph that starts with "This is a great way…"

2. On the Mailings tab, click Rules and choose If . . . Then . . . Else….

3. Change the Field name to State.

4. Change the Comparison to Not Equal To.

5. In the Compare box, type **WA**.

6. In the Insert This Text box, type **We hope you can join the webcast being broadcast from Milwaukee.**

7. In the Otherwise Insert This Text box, type **We look forward to seeing you in Kirkland.**

8. Click OK.

9. Click Save.

Review the Fields

Reviewing the fields placed in a document will ensure the merge process places the correct information in the appropriate locations within the file.

1. On the Mailings tab, in the Finish group, click Finish & Merge.

2. Press Alt+F9 to display the field codes.

3. Press Alt+F9 again to turn off the field display.

NOTE

Displaying the fields also provides the opportunity to edit the prompt text. Click within the quotes of a field and edit the prompt; however, do NOT edit the REF field, as it is referencing an explicitly named bookmark.

TIP

When entering text into a prompt, you can either click the OK button or press Tab and Enter to complete and close the prompt.

Perform the Merge

Not only will Word merge the records from the Data Source into the Main Document, but you will also be prompted for specific information.

1. Click the Mailings tab and click the Finish & Merge button.

2. Click Edit Individual Documents.

3. Choose All Records and click OK.

4. When prompted for the Seminar Title, type **E-Discovery, the Latest Information**.

5. Click OK.

6. When prompted for the Speaker's full name, type **Edward Anderson**.

7. Click OK.

8. When prompted for the Speaker's first name, type **Ed**.

9. Click OK.

10. When prompted for the seminar cost, type **80**.

11. Click OK.

12. Scroll through the merged document and check for:

    The Recipient's full name, city, and state information.

    Edward's full and first name.

    The $80 dollar value being placed in two locations.

    Based on the state, ensure the correct, final sentence was placed in the document.

TROUBLESHOOTING

Match Fields

If you find that some of your data is missing, you can click Match Fields to match up required fields in the Address Block field with what currently exists in your Data Source list. Use this if your Data Source is not using the exact same field names as the merge fields in the Address Block. Match Fields is also important when you are performing a mail merge with international recipients whose information might be in a different format, for instance, ZIP code in the U.S. and postal code in the United Kingdom. Figure 13.20 shows the Match Fields dialog box.

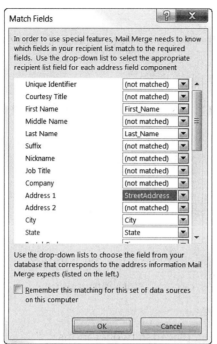

Figure 13.20

Use Match Fields when your data includes blank lines, different field names, or is missing fields.

Error Locating Data Source

When a Main Document is connected to a Data Source, Word is looking for the original Data Source in a specific location. If the Data Source has been moved, deleted, or renamed, you will see a series of prompts when opening the Main Document.

As referenced in Figure 13.21, this is an example of the prompt received when Word cannot find the Data Source when opening the Main Document.

Figure 13.21

The Data Source cannot be located.

Locating the Data Source

1. Open the Main document.

2. Click OK in the Error Has Occurred dialog box.

3. Click Cancel in the Data Link Properties dialog box.

4. Click OK in the prompt referenced in Figure 13.22.

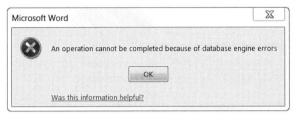

Figure 13.22

Word cannot complete the operation because it cannot locate the database (Data Source).

5. Click OK.

6. Click the Find Data Source button.

7. Browse to the location where the Data Source may have been moved or renamed.

8. Double-click the Data Source.

Data Source No Longer Exists

If you know the Data Source has been deleted, you will need to remove the Data Source from the Main Document.

Removing a Data Source

1. Open the Main document.

2. Click OK in the Error Has Occurred dialog box.

3. Click Cancel in the Data Link Properties dialog box.

4. Click OK in the An Operation Cannot Be Completed dialog box.

5. Click the Options button.

6. As shown in Figure 13.23, click the Remove Data/Header Source button.

Figure 13.23   The document opens as a Normal Word Document without a Data Source connected.

Check for Errors

Before completing the merge using the Finish & Merge button, you can check to see whether Word detects any errors. If errors are encountered, you can choose from one of three ways in which to handle them:

- Simulate the merge and report errors in a document.

- Complete the merge, pausing to report each error as it occurs.

- Complete the merge without pausing. Report errors in a new document.

As shown in Figure 13.24, Word provides a number of methods to identify errors.

Figure 13.24

Use the Checking and Reporting Errors feature to identify problems with the merge process.

Chapter

14

GRAPHICS, VIDEOS, AND ILLUSTRATIONS

It's tempting to skip writing a chapter on graphics since they don't carry the same importance as pleadings, section breaks, styles, and numbering. However, since corporate branding entered the picture, graphics now carry considerable weight and can greatly impact a document. Nowadays, IT and marketing departments work together to create a consistent and memorable presentation on all materials seen by clients, potential clients, and filed with the courts. Litigation attorneys may use video as demonstrative data in trials, and pictures, charts, and equations will always find their place in common correspondence and legal documents.

This chapter covers graphics used in most types of legal documents.

INSERTING AND DELETING PICTURES

Whether you are inserting a firm logo, picture of a senior partner, or an illustration to show a position to its best advantage, you will need to insert pictures into documents. Experienced Word users will notice that these simple tasks have changed in 2013.

There are three types of pictures that you can insert into documents: ClipArt, saved picture files, and pictures stored and available online.

Word makes it easy to browse and search for picture file formats stored in both local and network folders as well as on the Internet.

NOTE

The list of graphic file types that you can insert into Word are .emf, .wmf, .jpg, .jpeg, .jfif, .jpe, .png, .bmp, .dib, .rle, .gif, .emz, .wmz, .pcz, .tif, .tiff, .eps, .pct, .pict, .wpg.

Insert a Picture from a File

In order to add any picture to a document, you must first identify where the file is stored as well as where it should be placed in the document. The placement is less important because you can always move the picture around later.

Insert a Picture from a File

1. In the Illustrations group on the Insert tab, choose Pictures. The Insert Picture dialog box opens.

2. Navigate to the location where the picture is stored and select it.

3. Click Insert. The picture is inserted into the document at the cursor position.

Insert an Online Picture

Microsoft Word now includes the option to browse for graphics online. In order for this to work, you need to be connected to the Internet. Online pictures can be accessed from Office.com Clip Art, Bing Image Search, SkyDrive, Flickr, and Facebook, just to name a few sources. Not all are available without configuration, which makes sense since you don't want to offer the ability to search Flickr if you don't have a Flickr account.

To access online pictures, select the Insert tab, and in the Illustrations group of the ribbon, choose Online Pictures. Alternately, the keyboard shortcut combination is Alt+N, then F.

NOTE

If your goal is to insert an online picture into a header or footer, you'll find the equivalent command on the Header and Footer Tools ribbon when you are editing the header or footer. In the Insert group on the Design tab, click Online Pictures.

Inserting an Online Picture

1. Create a new document.

2. In the Illustrations group on the Insert tab, choose Online Pictures. This displays the Insert Pictures dialog box, as shown in Figure 14.1.

Figure 14.1   Use the Office.com Clip Art search box to search for Clip Art images or the Bing Image Search box to browse the Internet.

TIP

Sign into your Microsoft account to access Facebook, Flickr, SkyDrive, or similar locations if you want to expand the locations in which to search.

3. Type **Smart** in the Clip Art search box and press Enter. All Clip Art images with the associated keyword "Smart" display.

4. Click Back to Sites at the top of the dialog box.

5. Type **Smart** in the Bing Image Search box and press Enter. Now you're searching for all results on the web licensed under Creative Commons.

6. Click Show All Web Results and you will see all images, even those restricted by Copyright protection.

7. Select an image and click Insert. Close the Insert Pictures dialog box.

8. Close the document without saving.

TIP

You can insert multiple pictures into the document at the same time by holding down the Ctrl key and selecting each picture. Once you're ready to insert the images into the document, click Insert.

NOTE

The Clip Art Organizer from prior versions of Word has been removed and replaced with Online Pictures.

Insert a Screenshot

Creating documentation just got a whole lot easier, not to mention less expensive, because Microsoft Office now includes an option to take and insert screenshots into your documents. You'll find the Screenshot command in the Illustrations group on the Insert tab. When you have an open window running in the background and you click Screenshot, it will display the available windows. If you select one of the available windows, a picture of the entire window is inserted into the document.

If you want to create a picture of only a portion of the window, click on Screen Clipping at the bottom of the menu instead. The open window displayed changes to the most recent window running in the background. For instance, if you view an Excel workbook and then switch back to Word, when you choose Screen Clipping, the Excel window will display allowing you to select which area to use as a picture. You are not limited to Microsoft Office applications and can take a screen clipping of any open window, including content from the Internet.

Inserting a Screenshot

1. In the Illustrations group on the Insert tab, choose Screenshot.

2. Click any of the Available window options showing if you have other documents or applications open. This inserts a picture of that window into your document at the current insertion point location.

3. Click Screenshot again, and this time, choose Screen Clipping at the bottom of the menu. The previous window appears. Click and drag the mouse to select any area of the window. Release the mouse to insert a screenshot of the selection.

Deleting a Picture

If you no longer want to have a picture in your document, you can delete it. Select the picture and press Delete on your keyboard. You can tell when a picture is selected because it will have handles surrounding it, and the Picture Tools Format tab will be available.

ALIGNMENT AND LAYOUT OPTIONS

Word includes the ability to set the alignment of graphical objects as well as the layout. If you find yourself using the same, non-default layout repeatedly, you can change the default settings for how pictures are inserted.

Aligning Pictures on the Page

Once you have a picture in the document, you will want to position and size it so it works best with your other content. Moving a picture can be as simple as dragging it to the new location; however, understanding text wrap settings, alignment, and other options will alleviate common frustration, and the end result will be a more professional-looking document.

Changing the Picture Layout Options

The previously somewhat hidden layout options can now be found at your fingertips! When an image is selected, a Layout Options icon displays at the top-right corner of the picture. This button not only gives you easy access to the wrapping choices, but you can also select Move with Text or Fix Position on Page to control the location of the object. See Table 14.1 for details on the various Layout Options.

And for those of us who prefer the old Layout dialog box, just click See More....

NOTE

When a picture is selected, the Layout Options are different than when a shape or other type of object is active.

TABLE 14.1–LAYOUT OPTIONS	
In Line With Text	The picture is inserted into the text of the paragraph. It is not floating so it cannot be easily moved to a new location. This is the default setting in Word 2013.
Square	Text wraps around a rectangle or *bounding* box surrounding the image. You can select, rotate, and resize using elements on the box surrounding the image.
Tight	Instead of aligning to the box surrounding the image, Tight text wrapping means that the text will be wrapped around the shape of the image.
Through	Text can flow into the white or empty space of your image. This option is often used in conjunction with Edit Wrap Points to achieve the desired result.
Top and Bottom	The image will appear on a line by itself and text will be positioned above and below it.
Behind Text	Text appears in front of the image and the graphic is placed in a separate layer behind the text.
In Front of Text	The image is put into a different layer than the text and will appear in front of the text.
Move with Text	This option associates the image with text so when the accompanying text is moved, the image will move along with it.
Fix Position on Page	This option keeps the image in the exact same position on the page, regardless of where surrounding text may be relocated. The only exception is when the anchor moves to the next page, the image also moves.
See More	Displays the Layout dialog box where you have full options for positioning, layout, and sizing.

As with previous versions of Word, when pictures are added, the layout is set to "in line with text." Adding or deleting text that is on the same line as the picture will move the picture, similar to how text would move. You can change the layout by clicking the Layout Options icon and select a different layout.

Use Layout Options

1. Create a document with three paragraphs of text.

2. After the first paragraph, press Enter and insert a picture.

3. With the image selected, click Layout Options at the top-right corner of the picture.

4. Notice the In Line with Text option is selected. There is no text wrapping around the image.

5. With the image still selected, click Layout Options and choose Square. Drag the image inside of the text area to see how the text now wraps squarely around the bounding box that holds the image.

6. Change the Layout Option to Tight. If your image is square or rectangular, you may not see much of a difference.

7. Select the Behind Text option to see how text can be wrapped on top of the image. Behind and in front of text produces an interesting and useful effect; however, if the image is small, it can be hard to see.

NOTE

If more than one image is selected, the Layout Options button will not appear. However, you can set the alignment for multiple images simultaneously by selecting them using the Ctrl key, and then on the Picture Tools Format contextual tab, in the Arrange group, click Wrap Text. The Wrap Text option will be applied to all selected images.

Line up Images Using Alignment Guides

When you insert a picture, it's placed at the insertion point in the document. More often than not, you may need to adjust its position on the page. If you just want to move it to a new location, you can use cut and paste; however, you can also drag the image to the new location and use Word 2013's new alignment guides. These alignment guides provide visual cues that you can use to easily line up and snap charts, photos, and diagrams into place. Alignment guides automatically appear as horizontal or vertical lines that pop up when the image is aligned with key page locations, such as the edge of the page and the left and right margins.

Use Alignment Guides

1. Click on the image you want to align.

2. Drag the image until an alignment guide pops up (close to the top or side margins of a paragraph, or even the center of the paragraph).

3. Release the image.

TIP

If the Layout or Alignment option you are looking for is grayed out and unavailable, the image is probably set to be In Line with Text. Change this to Tight, Square, or another alignment to access other layout and text wrapping options.

FORMATTING A PICTURE

There are times when you need to adjust a picture to improve its appearance. The Picture Tools Format tab offers a number of Formatting options to apply styles, choose color variations, crop, rotate the object, compress, remove the background, and apply special effects.

The Format Picture task pane is new to 2013 and is very handy when making modifications to pictures. There are many commands on the Picture Tools Format tab that will activate the task pane automatically or you can choose Format Picture when you right-click on a selected image.

Figure 14.2

The Format Picture Task Pane has many different formatting options.

Adjusting the Picture

Use the Adjust group of the Picture Tools Format tab to change the color, remove the background, add artistic effects, compress the picture, insert a different picture in its place, reset the picture to its original format, and more.

The Compress Picture command offers great benefits for quickly changing the size for your target document or permanently removing cropped areas to prevent reverse cropping, which can be a potential metadata exposure risk. In addition, while the rest of these formatting options will not be applicable to most legal documents the majority of the time, they are being used more frequently with the introduction of more pictures and graphical items.

Remove Background

If you would like to remove the background of a picture in order to keep only certain portions of the picture, select the picture, and then click Remove Background in the Adjust group on the Picture Tools Format tab. The Background Removal contextual tab displays, as shown in Figure 14.3.

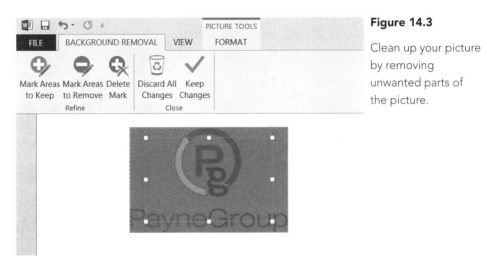

Figure 14.3

Clean up your picture by removing unwanted parts of the picture.

Word tries to guess what parts of the image are the background. Notice what areas are still in color and what areas are marked as background (in pink). Click either Mark Areas to Keep or Mark Areas to Remove, and your pointer will turn into a pencil. Draw a line through any areas that are no longer in color that you want to keep. Experiment with the position and size of the marquee lines to obtain the desired results. When finished marking, click Keep Changes.

TIP

If you mark an area and it's not what you wanted, just click the Undo button and try again.

Corrections

Like many of the commands in Word, the Corrections command offers Live Preview. Once a picture has been inserted into your document, select it and click the Corrections drop-down arrow. Hover your mouse over the various preformatted options to see changes in brightness or sharpness. Click on one of the formats to change the picture.

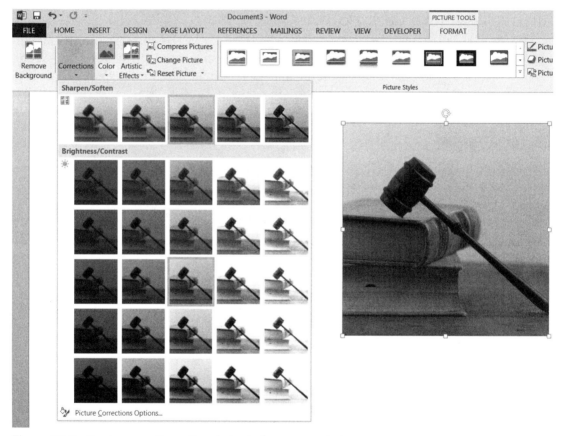

Figure 14.4 Preview your Correction choice before you apply it.

Color

The Color button in the Adjust group on the Picture Tools Format tab provides you with preset and custom choices to change the color saturation, tone, or recolor the picture.

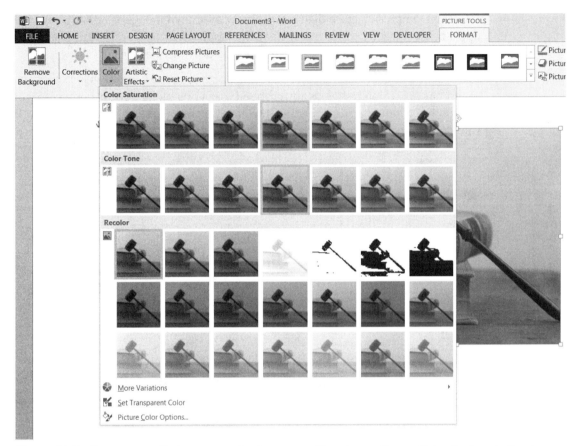

Figure 14.5 If you cannot find a preset color format you like, choose Picture Color Options to fine-tune the picture color.

Artistic Effects

Artistic Effects allow you to make the picture look more like a sketch or painting. From the Adjust group of the Picture Tools Format tab, click Artistic Effects and hover your mouse over the various options to see a live preview. Click on an option to select it.

Compress Pictures

With the fancy new digital cameras available now for taking high-resolution pictures, it is common for picture file sizes to be quite large. Adding one or more of these pictures to a firm's marketing brochure can greatly increase the file size of the document. You can compress one or all pictures in a document to reduce the file size of the picture(s). Select any of the pictures in your document and click the Compress Pictures button in the Adjust group on the Picture Tools Format tab. The Compress Picture dialog box opens, as shown in Figure 14.6. Choose the appropriate Target Output. Also, clear the Apply Only to This Picture check box to apply the compression to all pictures in the document and click OK.

Besides reducing the size of a picture in the document, the Compress Picture command has an option to delete any cropped areas of a picture. Most people do not realize that when you crop a picture, the cropped areas are just hidden and can be revealed by reverse cropping or resetting the picture.

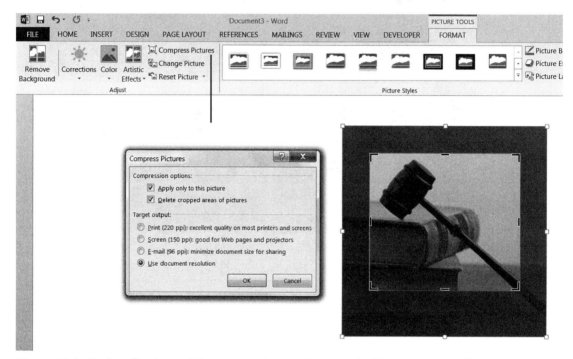

Figure 14.6   Reduce file size or delete cropped areas of one or all of the pictures in a document.

Change Picture

Changing a picture may seem as easy as deleting the existing one and inserting a new one; however, if you want to keep all of the same formatting and size of the current picture when replacing the original picture, use the Change Picture button in the Adjust group on the Picture Tools Format tab.

Reset Picture

To discard all of the formatting changes you have made to a picture and reset the picture to its original format, click the Reset Picture button in the Adjust group on the Picture Tools Format tab.

Adjust and Reset a Picture

1. Create a new document and insert a picture.

2. In the Adjust group on the Picture Tools Format tab, click Corrections. Select one of the Brightness and Contrast options.

3. In the Adjust group, click Color. Hover your mouse over each of the variations. Click More Variations and apply a color from the Theme or Standard Color palettes.

4. In the Adjust group, click Artistic Effects and try one of the options.

5. Also in the Adjust group, click Reset Picture. This takes the picture back to the original format.

Picture Styles

To assist with the corporate branding process, you can apply styles to pictures, which standardizes the look of all pictures, making them look more polished and professional. As with any style in Word, you can hover your mouse over each style to see how it will look if applied to the picture.

The Picture Styles group includes sample styles that you can apply. Click the More button to expand the gallery to show all styles in the gallery. The Picture Shape, Picture Border, and Picture Effects commands help you further format the picture.

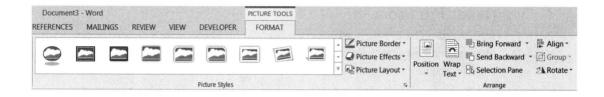

Figure 14.7 The Picture Styles group contains tools that help format the picture.

NOTE

Available picture styles include many shapes, frames, effects, and rotations.

Picture Effects

Picture Effects applies different visual effects including Preset, Shadow, Reflection, Glow, Soft Edges, Bevel, and 3-D Rotation. In the Picture Styles group of the Picture Tools Format tab, click the Picture Effects button and select from the list of options.

Picture Layout

Picture Layout allows you to convert pictures into one of the SmartArt layouts. Select the picture, and in the Pictures Styles group, click Picture Layout.

TIP

To select multiple pictures, click the first picture and then hold down the Ctrl key while you click on the next picture, and so on.

If you are having difficulty selecting more than one picture, try changing the Wrap Text option to Square or Tight.

Other Picture Format Tools

Rotate and Flip

Found in the Arrange group, the Rotate button offers preset Rotate and Flip options as well as custom options under More Rotation Options. Alternatively, you can select the picture and use the Rotate handle to free-form rotate the picture, as shown in Figure 14.8.

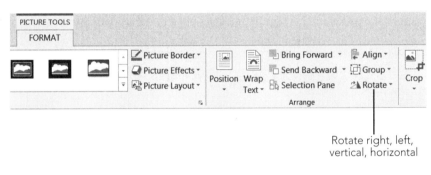

Figure 14.8

Click and drag the rotate handle to manually rotate your image.

Rotate right, left, vertical, horizontal

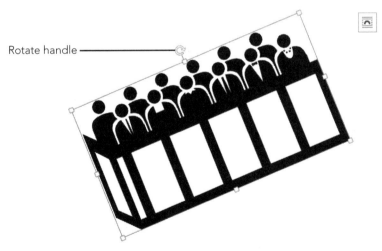

Rotate handle

Crop

More times than not, you will want to crop (remove) parts of the picture to show only certain areas of the picture. Cropping removes the unwanted edges of a picture. You can crop from the top, bottom, left, or right sides of the picture. In the Crop drop-down list, you can also crop to a specific shape or Aspect Ratio.

Crop Portions of a Picture

1. Create a new document.

2. Insert a picture that has multiple people or excess background images.

3. Select the picture and click the upper half of the Crop button in the Size group of the Picture Tools Format tab. You will notice cropping handles around the border of the picture, and when you place your mouse near a handle, the cursor changes to a cropping tool.

TIP

New in Word 2013, you can right-click on the picture and choose Crop from the Mini toolbar.

4. Click and drag the middle-left or right handle to reduce the area on the sides of the picture.

5. Crop the upper-left corner to reduce the area on the top and the left of the picture at the same time.

6. When done cropping the picture, click the Crop button again or just press Esc.

CAUTION

Since cropped areas of a picture are only hidden and not removed from the image, be sure to use the Compress Picture option to delete any cropped areas of a picture in client documents since not doing so could result in a confidentiality breach.

Selection Pane

For the longer, more complex document that contains multiple graphical items such as text boxes, pictures, and shapes, the Selection Pane can be helpful. It displays all of the objects found on a page and makes it easy to select multiple objects, reorganize, hide/show, and navigate to objects. Click the Selection Pane button found on the Picture Tools Format tab in the Arrange group to open the pane, as shown in Figure 14.9.

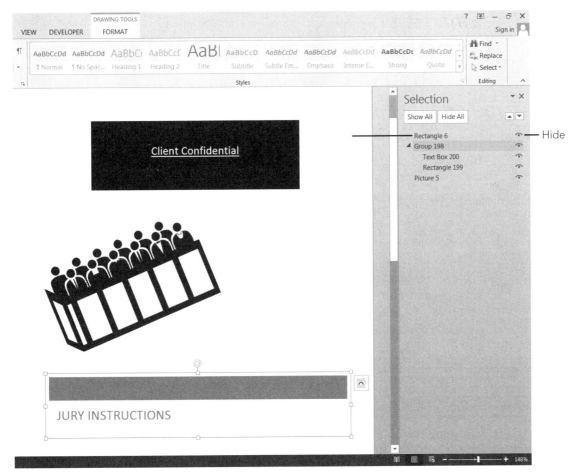

Figure 14.9 Click on the various options to select an object, reorganize, or show/hide.

OTHER ILLUSTRATION TYPES

In the constantly evolving world of the law firm, the need to include artistic and creative elements in legal documents has increased over the years. Presenting data in interesting and creative ways is becoming more prominent and can be quite powerful. While it is understandable that this type of creativity is limited to only certain types of documents and not others (e.g., pleadings, briefs, etc.), Word offers a variety of innovative choices for illustrating important points through the use of charts, shapes, and even online video.

SmartArt

SmartArt is a visual representation of information—like a diagram—that makes concepts and lists more visually appealing. It has been available in several of the Office applications since Office 2007.

To insert a SmartArt graphic, click the SmartArt button in the Illustrations group on the Insert tab. Click on one of the categories on the left to navigate to the desired category, or scroll down the list to see the various options grouped by function. Select the layout that you want and click OK.

TIP

If you are unsure which SmartArt will best represent your data, click on one of the options in the list and Word will display a short description of how that type of SmartArt is used in the pane on the right.

Once the SmartArt is inserted into the document, you can type directly into each shape or add your text using the Text pane that opens on the left. To open/close the Text pane, click the control located on the left edge of the SmartArt graphic. Since this control is sometimes difficult to see, Figure 14.10 shows where it is located.

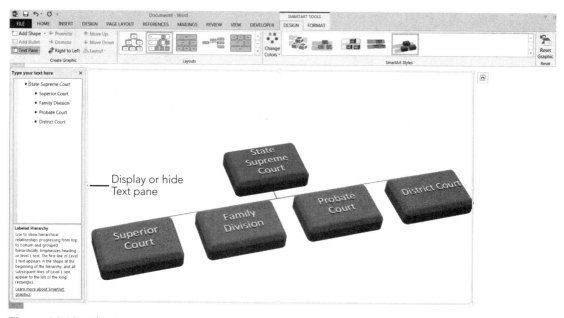

Figure 14.10 The SmartArt Text pane makes it easy to add, remove, or edit text from the graphic.

Shapes

In some documents, you may not need a true picture, but rather more of a shape, to draw attention to a particular comment, quote, or idea. For instance, in certain pleadings, a Line shape is used to add a vertical line to the right or left sides of the margin. Besides lines, the Shapes command offers basic shapes (circles, squares, etc.), callouts, stars, flowchart items, and much more, as shown in Figure 14.11.

Figure 14.11

Word offers many different shapes.

There are nine groupings of shapes as well as the New Drawing Canvas command from which to choose. Click on the shape that you want, click anywhere in the document, and then drag your mouse to insert the shape in the location and size desired.

TIP

When drawing or resizing a shape, click and drag the corner of the shape to resize it while preserving its proportion. Hold the Ctrl key and use the handles to resize the graphic while retaining the center of the object in the same location.

Select the shape and press Ctrl+Right Arrow or Ctrl+Left Arrow to move the shape to the right or left in small increments. Likewise, press Shift+Right Arrow or Shift+Left Arrow to rotate the shape to the right or left.

Drawing Canvas

The primary purpose of a Drawing Canvas is to store multiple objects in one location along with the ability to manipulate all the objects at the same time, such as moving or resizing a group of objects.

Click the Shapes button in the Illustrations group on the Insert tab and select New Drawing Canvas. Click Insert again and select an object to add to the canvas. Repeat this for as many objects as you want in the canvas.

You can resize the canvas by clicking and dragging the braced edges of the Drawing Canvas. Right-click on the edge of the Drawing Canvas and choose Format Drawing Canvas to open the Format Shape task pane to access additional formatting options.

Formatting a Shape

When a shape has been selected, the Drawing Tools Format tab displays, as shown in Figure 14.12.

Figure 14.12   The Drawing Tools Format tab is very similar to the Picture Tools Format tab.

Charts

While SmartArt offers a good method for visually representing textual elements, the Chart feature is great for displaying numerical data. If you are familiar with Excel, you should be quite comfortable with the Chart feature. If Excel intimidates you, the Chart feature in Word allows you to access the charting capabilities without leaving the comfort of Word. Charts are embedded in Word, and the chart data is stored in an Excel worksheet that becomes incorporated into the Word document.

When you need a chart in your document, click Chart in the Illustrations group on the Insert tab. The Insert Chart dialog box presents a gallery of chart types and layouts from which to choose. Simply select the type of chart you want and click OK.

Once a chart is added to the document, a small Excel window opens to help you customize and populate the chart with data.

A chart object can be modified using the Chart Tools Design and Format tabs. The Chart Tools Format tab is very similar to the Picture Tools Format tab described earlier. The Design tab allows you to easily change the style of the object as well as access the data and chart type.

When you insert a chart, four small buttons appear in the upper-right corner of the chart. The Layout Options button allows you to choose how the object relates to the text around it. Use the Chart Elements button to add, remove, or change chart elements such as the title, legend, gridlines, and data labels. The Chart Styles button allows you to quickly change the color scheme or style of the chart. Use the Chart Filters button to edit what data points and names are visible in your chart. There are a variety of chart styles available in Word, as shown in Figure 14.13.

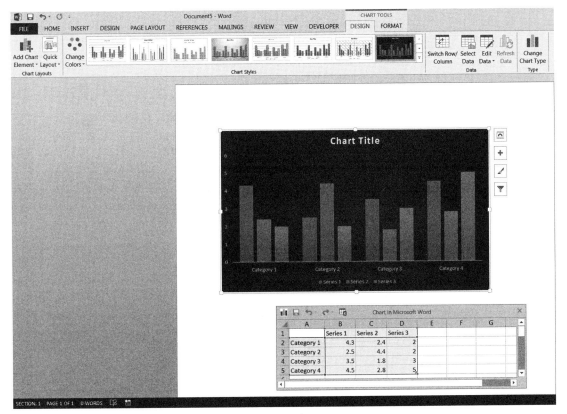

Figure 14.13   Select the best chart to represent your data.

Double-click the chart border to display the Format Chart Area task pane for additional formatting options. Once the task pane is open, click on different elements within the chart and notice the task pane changes to offer formatting options for the element you selected. You also can right-click on various chart elements and use the Mini toolbar to change certain formats.

Online Video

You can insert an online video into your document and then watch the video right in Word without leaving the document. In the Insert Video dialog box, choose either Bing Video Search or YouTube to perform a search.

Hover over the thumbnail of a search result to show the title of the video, the provider, and its length.

To preview the video before inserting it, click the View Larger icon in the bottom-right corner of the thumbnail.

The video is inserted into the document as a picture with a link to the original online source, and as a result, you must have Internet access to run the video. The picture can be positioned and resized using any of the picture formatting tools.

GRAPHICAL TEXT COMPONENTS

When you think of graphics, most people think of pictures and Clip Art, but there are many other graphical elements found in Word. While these elements have more integration with text as opposed to pictures, they still use similar layout options and have numerous formatting choices.

Text Box

Text boxes hold data or information that you want to place outside of normal document margins. They actually float on top of the document layer; so unlike standard text, text boxes can be placed in locations not otherwise available for adding text. Text boxes are sometimes used in pleading documents to place the firm name and address inside the left margin area or in the lower-right corner of the page.

To insert a default text box, click Text Box located in the Text group of the Insert tab. Select from one of the displayed Text Box samples, or choose Draw Text Box.

If you have an existing text box you use frequently, you can save it to the gallery of available text boxes for future use.

WordArt

WordArt adds decorative impact to the text in your document. In the Text group on the Insert tab, click WordArt. Select the preferred format, add the text and that's all there is to it.

TIP

Most of Word's built-in Watermarks are using WordArt, so if you choose to manually edit the Watermark, you will have access to the WordArt styles and formatting commands.

Drop Cap

This feature allows you to create a large initial, or dropped capital letter, at the beginning of a paragraph or in the margin next to a paragraph.

Equation

Looking back to the old WordPerfect days, there were many power secretaries that were impressive in their ability to create complex equations in Intellectual Property documents and the early versions of Word definitely fell short by comparison. As new Word versions were introduced, the Equation functionality continued to improve. In this latest version, Microsoft is using TeX standards and a new Math Font to produce equations that look better than ever before.

In the Symbols group on the Insert tab are built-in equations you can drop into your document—no formatting required. You can modify any of the built-in equations to meet your needs, or you can build your own sophisticated equations from scratch.

Once you have created an equation, you can save it to the Equation building block gallery for future use. To save an equation to the Equation building block gallery, select the equation, click the Insert tab, and then click the lower half of the Equation split button in the Symbols group. Select Save Selection to Equation Gallery. Give a name to your building block and click OK.

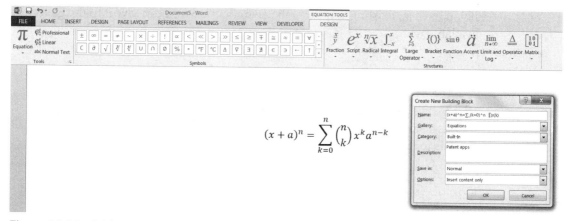

$$(x + a)^n = \sum_{k=0}^{n} \binom{n}{k} x^k a^{n-k}$$

Figure 14.14 Add your own custom equations to the gallery for future use.

Watermark

The most common watermark used in legal documents is the word DRAFT inserted behind the text in a light-gray, large font. This watermark, as well as others, is available in Word's Watermark gallery. If you prefer your firm's logo or a picture, these images can also be used as watermarks.

The Watermark command has been moved to the Design tab in this version of Word, located in the Page Background group. When you click the Watermark, the gallery opens with some preset choices as well as the ability to look up watermarks from Office.com or create a custom one. Likewise, you can remove an applied watermark from the document or save a selection as a new watermark in the Watermark building blocks gallery.

TIP

The Watermark text or graphic is inserted into the Header of the document. If you want to reposition, rotate, or add custom formatting to the watermark, you'll need to access the Header first and then select the Watermark.

WHEN YOU NEED (OR WANT) AUTOMATION IN WORD

Microsoft Word in and of itself is very powerful. You can use Building Blocks to store reusable text or graphics and access them whenever needed. You can insert fields, apply styles that standardize the look and feel of a document, link and update data, and of course, apply even complex bullets and numbering—all without having to write a single macro.

While Word is a robust and very capable software application, there will come a time when you will want to enhance functionality, simplify repetitive tasks, or make the program easier to use.

This chapter covers getting started with automation and Visual Basic for Applications.

OVERVIEW OF VBA AND AUTOMATION

The macro language inside of Office 2013 is Visual Basic for Applications, or VBA for short. VBA is based on the Visual Basic programming language; however, unlike Visual Basic, VBA needs an application from which to run. VBA is the programming language for Microsoft Office, and as such, is available from within Word, Excel, PowerPoint, and the other applications of Office.

The best thing about VBA is that you don't have to be a programmer or even a Word expert to get started. The most efficient way to learn Word automation, including VBA, is to jump in with both feet and practice. Chances are, it won't be easy right away; however, with practice and experience, you will find that it's a fairly logical programming language and more user friendly than most.

Not all solutions in this chapter involve writing a macro. Generally, the purpose of automation is to streamline a process, fix a deficiency, or to extract information from a different location or source. Take a look at the following list of potential motivations for automation and see if anything looks like what you've wanted to do.

1. Streamline a process.

2. Automate features that are too advanced for most people who need to use it.

2. Perform repetitive tasks.

3. Prevent user error by providing lists and input forms.

4. Edit locked (forms) or hidden data (variables or properties).

5. Automate editing nonvisible areas of a document (e.g., second-page header or footer on a single-page template).

6. Apply a change to multiple documents.

7. Connect to other add-ins or databases.

Automation in Word is available, accessible, and can help with all of the aforementioned scenarios as well as others that may be unique to you or the needs of your firm.

GETTING YOUR ENVIRONMENT READY

Before you can do any customizations with macros and automation, you'll need to display the Developer tab, which is hidden by default. It's hidden in large part because not everyone who uses Word will create macros or forms. From the File tab, select Options, and then Customize Ribbon. Under Customize the Ribbon, select the Developer check box from the Main Tabs list and click OK. This ribbon includes commands for working with macros, templates, and a whole lot more.

Figure 15.1 shows how to enable the Developer tab, and Figure 15.2 shows the resulting Developer ribbon.

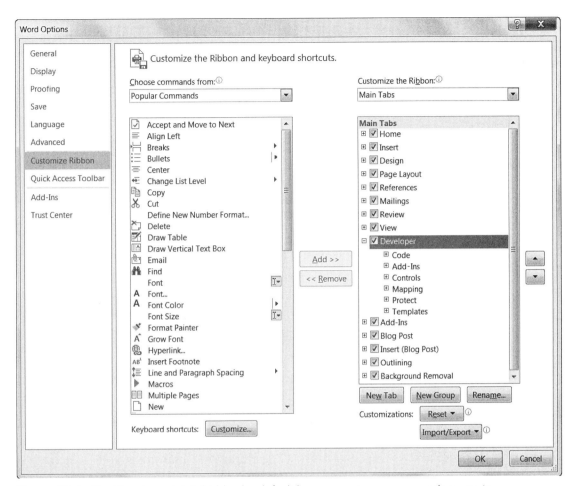

Figure 15.1   The Developer tab is hidden by default because not everyone needs to use it.

Figure 15.2   Among other things, the Developer tab contains useful commands for working with macros, add-ins, and content controls.

INTRODUCTION TO THE WORD OBJECT MODEL

When creating and editing macros in Word, you will be working closely with the Word object model using VBA programming language.

Think of the Word object model as a hierarchy of all of the items you can name in Word. For example, documents, paragraphs, fonts, margins, headers and footers, building blocks, and a lot more. In fact, there are hundreds of objects in Word and almost everything you can name in Word is an object that can be manipulated programmatically. Each object has a set of members, which comprise various properties and methods. You might think of properties as adjectives that describe the characteristics of an object, while methods are verbs, or actions that the object can be asked to programmatically perform.

Many objects are also part of collections. A collection is a group of all objects of a specific type. For example, each document is part of the documents collection—even if only one document is open. In a situation where you would like to make a change to every open document, you would write code to iterate through each document in the collection. Or maybe you would like to make a change to every paragraph that meets certain criteria within a document. For example, if any paragraph in the document begins with the word "Whereas," make the word bold and all caps.

To explore the Word object model in more detail, you can go to the VBA Editor by pressing Alt+F11, or click Visual Basic on the Developer tab, and then select View, Object Browser, or press F2. The Object Browser window is a great resource for learning about Word's very robust object model and to see what objects are available.

In the Object Browser window, you can find any object available in the Word object model. For example, in Figure 15.3, we searched Documents and drilled down to view the members of the Documents collection. Once you have located the object that you're looking for, use the Help menu, or press F1, to see detailed information about that object and its members.

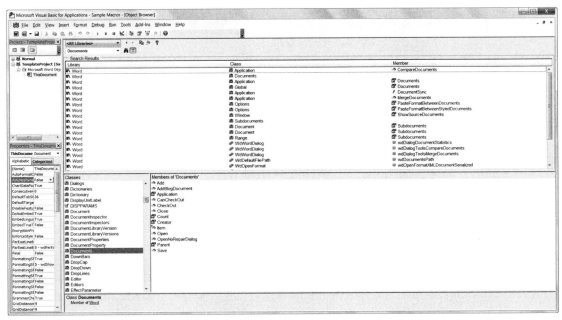

Figure 15.3 The Object Browser is a great resource for those new to Word who are not yet familiar with the object model, as well as experienced programmers alike.

STORING AND DISTRIBUTING MACROS

General-purpose macros that must be available whenever Word is open should be stored in a global macro-enabled template—but ideally, not the Normal template. Avoid storing any firm customizations in Normal because user-specific settings are saved there, and they won't be very happy when these settings are overwritten every time the firm needs to push out an update. User settings include default font, font size, keyboard shortcuts, and so much more. Firm customizations are better housed in a separate template or templates and saved in the Startup folder. By doing so, the firm is able to maintain control over macros in the future without overwriting any user customizations. Remember, macros stored in a template that is saved in the Startup folder will be available in all Word documents. Macros that should be available only to documents, such as those used for pleadings, should be saved in the attached document template. For more information on creating and distributing templates, see Chapter 10, "Creating and Distributing Templates."

Create a Global Macro Template

1. Create a new blank document.

2. Click File and then Save.

3. From the Computer tab, click Browse.

4. Change Save As Type to Word Macro-Enabled Template (*.dotm).

5. Navigate to the Startup folder (e.g., C:\Users\<username>\AppData\Roaming\Microsoft\Word\STARTUP).

NOTE By default, Windows hides certain files and folders, including the startup template folder. To display hidden folders, right-click the Start button and choose Open Windows Explorer. Click Organize and choose Folder and Search Options. Select the View tab, and select Show Hidden Files, Folders, and Drives. If you do not have the option available to show hidden files, this may have been disabled by your firm.

TIP While you are in the Folder Options dialog box, clear the Hide Extensions for Known File Types check box in the Advanced Settings list. As a result, all file extensions will display so you can see a clear distinction between .doc and .docx files. These file extensions will display in Word's Title bar and in the Open and Save As dialog boxes.

6. Change the File Name to **Sample Macros.dotm**, as shown in Figure 15.4 and click Save.

7. Leave the file open for the next exercise.

Figure 15.4 To create a global template with macros, select Word Macro-Enabled Template (*.dotm) as the Save As Type and save it to the Startup folder.

When creating a global template that contains macros, be sure to select the Save As Type (Word Macro-Enabled Template (*.dotm)) *before* selecting the Startup folder. Selecting a template Save As Type will automatically redirect the folder location to your default personal template folder location.

In order to save macros to this template, it must first be loaded when Word opens. Close Word, reopen Word, and then reopen this template. The best way to open the template for editing is to locate it in Windows Explorer, right-click, and select Open. Once the template is loaded, it will now be available when choosing where to save your macros.

Another way to load a newly created macro-enabled template instead of closing and reopening Word is to click Document Template in the Templates group on the Developer tab. Under Checked Items are Currently Loaded, activate the check box for the template and click OK.

When editing a template, be sure the Title bar in Word reflects the template name (*.dotm). If you see Document1 in the Title bar, you're working with a document based on the template, not the actual template itself.

RECORDING MACROS

The macro recorder is still available in this version of Word; however, there are many limitations when using it. Sometimes too much is recorded, sometimes too little, and sometimes nothing at all. Another limitation of the recorded code is that it uses the Selection object, which causes the cursor to move all around the document while performing the recorded steps. It is not considered best practice to rely on or distribute code created with the macro recorder. Modifying recorded code, however, can sometimes be helpful when getting started.

Starting the Macro Recorder

To start the macro recorder, on the View tab, select Macros, and then Record Macro. Alternatively, you can click Macro Recording from the Status bar. By default, Macro Recording is not on the Status bar. To add it, right-click the Status bar and choose Macro Recording. Once you have done this, the icon is placed on the Status bar, and when clicked, displays the Record Macro dialog box.

In the following exercise you are going to create a macro that will make the word "Whereas" found at the beginning of the paragraph formatted with bold and all caps.

First, you will record a macro to discover the necessary objects, then you will modify the macro to make it more streamlined and elegant.

Record a Macro

1. The Sample Macros.dotm template should still be open.

2. Add a few paragraphs of text to the document. Make sure several of the paragraphs begin with the word Whereas, including the first paragraph. Press Ctrl+Home to position the insertion point at the top of the document.

3. Start the macro recorder using one of the methods described previously.

4. In the Macro Name field of the Record Macro dialog box, type **ChangeWhereasToBoldCaps**. Macro names cannot contain spaces or special characters, nor can they exceed 80 characters. The Record Macro dialog box is shown in Figure 15.5.

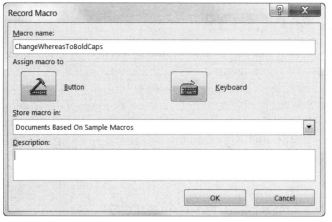

Figure 15.5

When naming a macro, be sure not to use spaces or special characters.

5. Change Store Macro In to Documents Based on Sample Macros.dotm.

6. Click OK to start the macro recorder.

7. With the macro recorder running, select the first Whereas and apply bold and all caps formatting.

NOTE

While the macro recorder is running, you cannot use the mouse to select text. Use keystrokes to select Whereas.

8. Select the Developer tab, and from the Code group, click Stop Recording, or from the Status bar, click the Macro Recording button to stop recording the macro.

9. Leave the file open for the next exercise.

EXPERT TIP

There are a few rules when naming macros. First, macro names must begin with a letter. If you attempt to name the macro 1abc, once you click OK to start recording the macro, an Invalid Procedure error message displays. Many characters cannot be used in macro names as well. For instance, -, &, *, ?, % and most other special characters are restricted; however, the exception is that you can use an underscore.

THE VISUAL BASIC FOR APPLICATIONS EDITOR

The macro recorder produces VBA code. To view the code, switch to the VBA Editor by pressing Alt+F11 and then navigate to the module containing your code. If you don't see the code that you recorded right away, look in the Project window on the left side of the window and find the template or document where the recorded macro was saved. For instance, if you saved it in the Normal template, look for the Modules folder and beneath that, in NewMacros or whichever sheet the macro was recorded in.

NOTE

The VBA Editor can also be opened by clicking Visual Basic in the Code group of the Developer tab.

Another way to view the code that you just recorded is to use the Macros dialog box. Make sure the Sample Macros template is active. From the View tab, choose Macros, and then select View Macros to display the Macros dialog box. If you have a lot of startup templates with various macros, you can narrow the list by selecting Sample Macros.dotm from the Macros In drop-down list. Select the macro, then click Edit.

A Tour of the Visual Basic Editor

The VBA Editor uses a legacy-style menu and toolbar user interface rather than ribbons. Below the toolbars, the VBA Editor shown in Figure 15.6 is divided into three sections: the Project window, the Properties window, and the Code window.

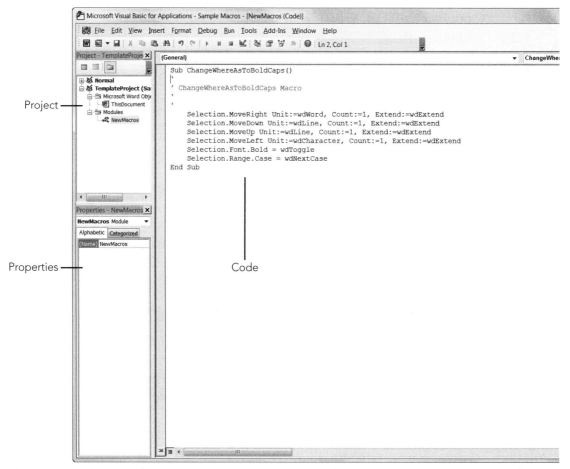

Figure 15.6 The VBA Editor gives you access to a macro's code.

The Project Window

The Project window displays a node for each open document or template. Documents are listed as either a Project or a TemplateProject. Documents and non-macro-enabled templates are named Project by default. Macro-enabled templates are named TemplateProject by default. These designations can be changed, as you will see in a moment. The Windows name of the document or template is displayed in parentheses after either the Project or TemplateProject designation.

Each document or template node contains the components of that document, such as ThisDocument, Forms, Modules, and Class modules, if any.

The Properties Window

The Properties window shows available properties for the object selected in the Project window. For example, if you select the TemplateProject (Sample Macros) in the Project window, the Properties window displays the Name property, which can now be changed. Figure 15.7 shows the Properties window where you can make changes to the project.

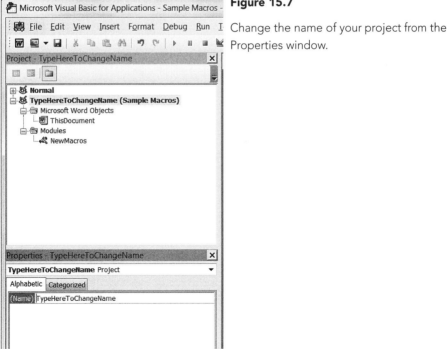

Figure 15.7

Change the name of your project from the Properties window.

User forms and other objects have many other properties, as shown in Figure 15.8.

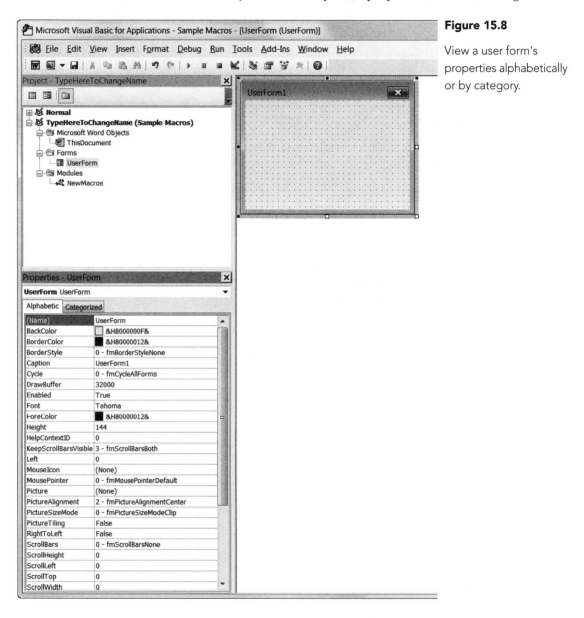

Figure 15.8

View a user form's properties alphabetically or by category.

The Code Window

The Code window displays the code in the selected module, form module, or class module. Procedures are visually separated by horizontal lines.

Let's examine the recorded macro created in the previous exercise.

Examine and Modify a Recorded Macro

1. The Sample Macros template created earlier should still be active.

2. Open the VBA Editor (Alt+F11).

3. From the Project window, click the plus sign (+) next to Project (Sample Macros).

4. Click the plus sign (+) next to Modules and double-click NewMacros.

5. Keep the VBA Editor open for the next exercise.

Here are additional items to note about the recorded macro:

- By default, recorded code is contained within a module called NewMacros. This module can be renamed in the Properties window. Also, additional modules can be added to the Project or TemplateProject as needed or to organize the code in a more orderly fashion.

- The code is within a block of text called a procedure. A procedure starts with Sub (sub name) and ends with End Sub.

- Right now the macro only works on the selected text. Code needs to be added, using the object model, which will iterate through each paragraph in the document. Using the Selection object would require the code to move through each paragraph in the document and select the relevant text, which would not make the macro run smoothly.

- The macro recorder provided the Font object to apply bold and all caps attributes to the selected text.

- The Selection and Font objects were used by the macro recorder.

- The Paragraph object will be needed to make the macro work on all paragraphs.

Declaring Variables

Although you are not always required to declare variables in by it is good practice to do so. To force variable declaration (so you don't forget), type the words Option Explicit at the very top of every code module. Doing this will prevent you from using an undeclared variable.

Variables can be declared at various levels, such as on a global level, module level, or procedure level. In our examples, we will be using procedure level variables.

That means the variables we use are only available within the current procedure and retain no value after the procedure runs.

Variables are identified by type. Some common variable types are integer (numbers), string (text), boolean (true or false), and various objects.

When writing code, variables are identified by using the keyword Dim. The following example creates a variable for the paragraph object. The code to create a paragraph object is as follows:

```
Dim oPara As Word.Paragraph
```

Another object that is commonly used to prevent the cursor from moving around the document is the Range object. The Range object can be used in most instances to replace the Selection object in recorded code.

In order to iterate through each paragraph in the document, you can use a For Each loop. Other looping techniques are also available in VBA. The loop contains opening and closing text. In a For Each loop, the loop starts with For Each and ends with Next. The Next object can be specifically identified, if desired. The code to iterate through each paragraph below the variable declarations is as follows:

```
For Each oPara In ActiveDocument.Paragraphs

Next oPara
```

Next, you need to determine if the paragraph starts with the word "Whereas." If it does, that text will be formatted with bold and all caps, and then move on to the next paragraph. To do this, we will use an If/Then statement in conjunction with the Range object to look at the first word in the paragraph, as follows.

```
For Each oPara In ActiveDocument.Paragraphs

        If oPara.Range.Words(1).Text = "Whereas" Then

                oPara.Range.Words(1).Font.Bold = True

                oPara.Range.Words(1).Font.AllCaps = True

        End If

Next oPara
```

A good practice when typing code is to type in all lowercase. If your spelling is correct, Word will automatically change the code to proper case. If the case isn't changing, Word is not recognizing the code you're entering.

Further Modify the Recorded Macro

1. The Sample Macros template created earlier should still be active and the VBA Editor open.

2. Place the insertion point at the beginning of the ChangeWhereasToBold-Caps procedure to the left of the first Selection line.

3. Press Enter and move the insertion point back up to the blank line.

4. Type the following text, pressing Tab to indent the lines:

```
Dim oPara As Word.Paragraph

For Each oPara In ActiveDocument.Paragraphs

Next oPara

For Each oPara In ActiveDocument.Paragraphs

        If oPara.Range.Words(1).Text = "Whereas" Then

                oPara.Range.Words(1).Font.Bold = True

                oPara.Range.Words(1).Font.AllCaps = True

        End If

Next oPara
```

5. Select the rest of the recorded code, except for End Sub, and press Delete.

6. Save your changes by selecting File and then Save Sample Macros.

7. Press Alt+F11 to return to the Word window and then navigate to your Sample Macros template in Word.

NOTE

Before running a new macro, you'll want to make sure there are no errors in the code. Within the VBA Editor, from the Menu bar, select Debug, and then select Compile TemplateProject. Correct any errors. Debug is shown in Figure 15.9.

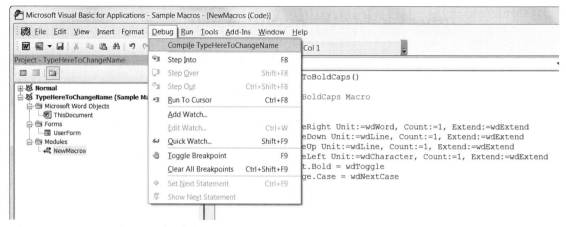

Figure 15.9 Run Debug to check for errors in your macro.

Test the Macro

1. The Sample Macros template created earlier should still be open and the Word window active.

2. Remove the bold and all caps formatting applied to the first Whereas.

3. Click the Developer tab, and from the Code group, select Macros.

4. Select ChangeWhereasToBoldCaps and click Run.

TIP

If you don't see the ChangeWhereasToBoldCaps macro in the list, click Document Template on the Developer tab in the Templates group. Make sure the Sample Macros.dotm check box is selected.

5. Examine the document to make sure the macro worked. Note the cursor does not need to start at the top of the document and will remain in place after the macro runs.

6. Delete the sample text and save the template.

7. Leave the template open for the next exercise.

Getting Fancier

You can make your macro more flexible in several ways. Perhaps you want to offer users the ability to select their own word or phrase to format with bold and all caps. One way to do this is with an input box. An input box is a built-in object that will display a form to users where they can insert text. That text can then be used within your code. You can even prefill the input box with default text.

An input box example is shown in Figure 15.10.

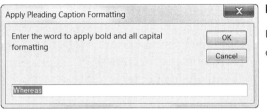

Figure 15.10

Use the input box to allow users to enter their own text.

Perhaps you want to allow the changes to be made only within a particular portion of the document. You can accomplish this by using the Range object again to identify where the changes should be applied. You can make this automatic (only apply the changes to selected text) or ask the user with a message box.

A message box that returns a Yes/No response would look something like the example shown in Figure 15.11.

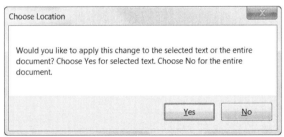

Figure 15.11

A message box can return a Yes/ No response.

Input boxes and message boxes are examples of built-in functions that accept arguments.

The InputBox function, shown in Figure 15.12, accepts arguments for Prompt, Title, Default, XPos, YPos, HelpFile, and Context, but only the Prompt is required; the rest of the arguments are optional. Optional arguments are surrounded by brackets. Arguments are separated by commas.

```
InputBox "Enter the word or phrase to make bold and all caps.", "Bold and Caps", "Whereas"
InputBox(Prompt, [Title], [Default], [XPos], [YPos], [HelpFile], [Context]) As String
```

Figure 15.12   The InputBox function lists arguments that are required as well as those that are optional (in brackets).

The MessageBox function, as shown in Figure 15.13, accepts arguments for Prompt, Buttons, Title, HelpFile, and Context, but only Prompt is required.

MsgBox
| MsgBox(***Prompt***, [*Buttons As* VbMsgBoxStyle = vbOKOnly], [*Title*], [*HelpFile*], [*Context*]) As VbMsgBoxResult |

Figure 15.13   For the MessageBox function, only Prompt is a required argument.

Input Forms

Creating input forms in Word makes macros even more flexible. Input forms allow data to be saved for reuse, allow default values to be displayed or enforced, allow integration with third-party add-ins, document management systems, other Office programs, and for a multitude of other purposes.

An input form may offer more choices, allowing users to select the type of formatting they want to apply. Figure 15.14 shows an example of an input form.

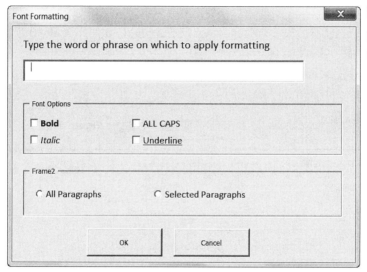

Figure 15.14

Example of an input form.

ADD A MACRO TO THE QUICK ACCESS TOOLBAR

An easy way for users to access your macro would be to place a button on the Quick Access Toolbar that calls the macro.

NOTE

Macros can also be assigned keyboard shortcuts from the Customize Keyboard dialog box. Click File, Options, Customize Ribbon, and then select Customize under Keyboard Shortcuts. From the Categories list, select Macros. A list of macros available on all active templates will display.

To add the macro to the Quick Access Toolbar, open the template containing the macro:

Add a Macro Command to the Quick Access Toolbar

1. Click the down arrow to the right of the existing Quick Access Toolbar.

2. Select More Commands.

3. From the Choose Commands From drop-down list, select Macros, as shown in Figure 15.15.

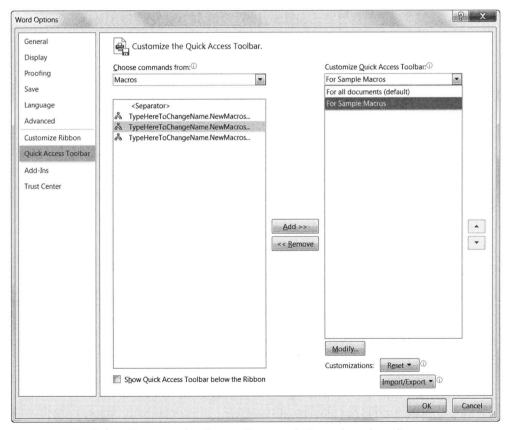

Figure 15.15 Select Macros in the Choose Commands From drop-down list.

4. From the Customize Quick Access Toolbar drop-down list, select Sample Macros.

5. Select the macro that you created, then click Add. Select an icon and change the Display Name, as desired. Some icon choices are shown in Figure 15.16.

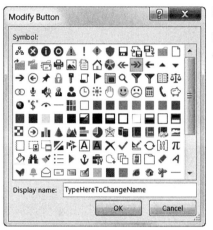

Figure 15.16

Select from several icons for your macro command.

6. Click OK to close the Word Options dialog box. The icon now appears on the Quick Access Toolbar and will be available in all documents.

NOTE

Saving the command to Sample Macros.dotm gives users access to the macro command on the Quick Access Toolbar when they are in any document. This is because Sample Macros.dotm is a global template saved in the Startup folder and will load every time Word is opened.

ADDING AUTOMATION TO A FORM

In the previous example, we created a utility macro to manipulate the text in a document. While that macro was saved as part of a global, or startup, template, the template itself is not used as the basis for a new document. Macros can also be used to automate a form containing content, such as the Delivery Request Form shown in Figure 15.17.

Here are the basic steps for creating a macro-enabled template that contains macro automation:

NOTE

For specific steps in creating a form and adding content controls, see the "Create the Form" section in Chapter 10, "Creating and Distributing Templates."

EXPERT TIP

As mentioned in Chapter 3, "Compatibility and Conversion," if you are in charge of creating templates for the firm and have had to set certain compatibility settings within the template, you will find that you no longer have these same options available in Word 2013 (File, Options, Advanced, Layout Options For section). The only way to select the layout options is to create the template on a machine that has Office 2007 or Office 2010 installed and save the template in that format. When saving the template, in the Save As dialog box, be sure to select the Maintain Compatibility with Previous Versions of Word check box. This will allow the template to be used in Word 2013 and maintain the layout settings.

- Create a new document and save it as a macro-enabled template named Delivery Form.dotm.

- Next, create the body of the template. It's often preferable to use a table in the template because the table cells provide a nice structure for the various placeholder fields. Table borders also serve as helpful visual guides when setting up a template.

- The next step is to create the placeholders, such as form fields, bookmarks, or content controls, for inserting the information dynamically. You will make use of both content controls and bookmarks when automating this template, just for fun.

- In this example, there is an updating field for the date and Rich Text content controls for Deliver To, Client/Matter #, and From. Bookmarks have been added for the Comments and Delivery Confirmation Telephone fields. The check boxes for Confirm and Signature were created using the Check Box content control. To easily modify the content control's placeholder text, you can toggle on Design Mode from the Developer Tab. When in Design Mode, the content controls appear to be surrounded in tags, as shown in Figure 15.17. Don't forget to give your content controls and bookmarks meaningful names so you can programmatically insert information into them later. The Delivery Request form example is shown in Figure 15.17.

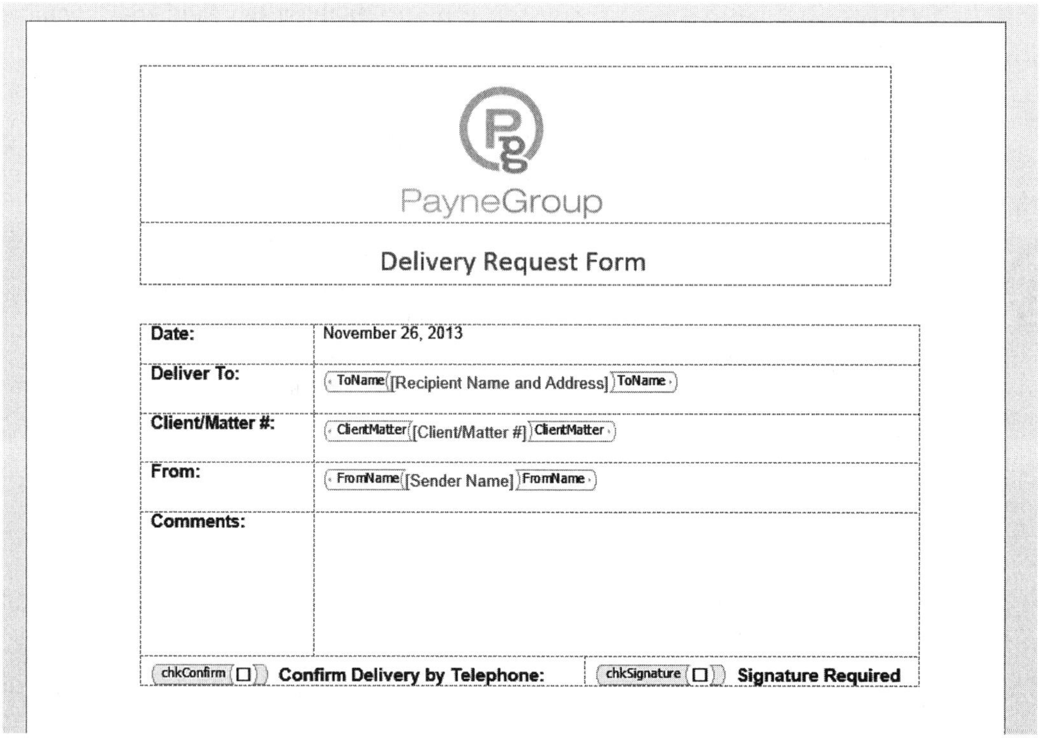
PayneGroup

Delivery Request Form

Date:	November 26, 2013
Deliver To:	ToName [Recipient Name and Address] ToName
Client/Matter #:	ClientMatter [Client/Matter #] ClientMatter
From:	FromName [Sender Name] FromName
Comments:	
chkConfirm ☐ **Confirm Delivery by Telephone:**	chkSignature ☐ **Signature Required**

Figure 15.17 Delivery Request form.

- After creating the template, you're ready to design the input form and code the related logic to show the form and insert the information into the placeholders. In the VBA editor window (Alt+F11), select the template in the Project window. Using the Insert menu, add a new UserForm and a new Module to the Template Project. Name them frmDeliveryForm and modDeliveryForm, respectively.
- Design the input form, adding controls as needed from the Toolbox (View, Toolbox). Make sure to supply unique names for the controls on the form, along with captions and accelerator (shortcut key) assignments for the labels, buttons, and check boxes. A well-thought-out design always makes the input form more usable, as shown in Figure 15.18.

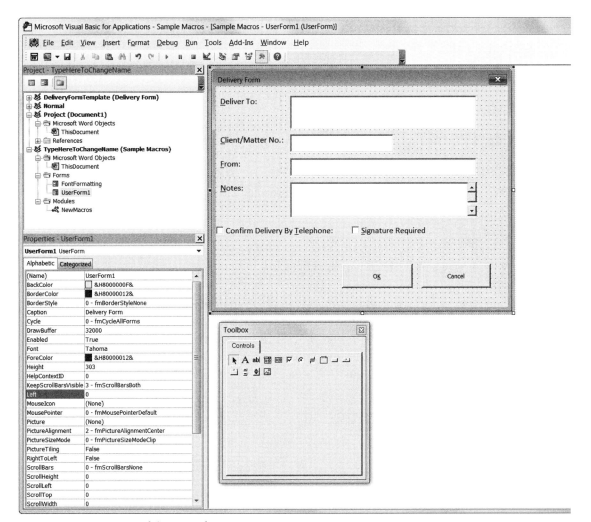

Figure 15.18 Design of the input form in progress.

- Behind the VBA form, add logic to handle what should happen when the various command buttons on the form are clicked, as well as a QueryClose event handler, which will run when the user clicks Close (X) in the upper-right corner of the form. The Cancelled variable will allow us to return a result to the calling subroutine. To keep this example short, the code shown in Figure 15.19 has intentionally been kept very basic.

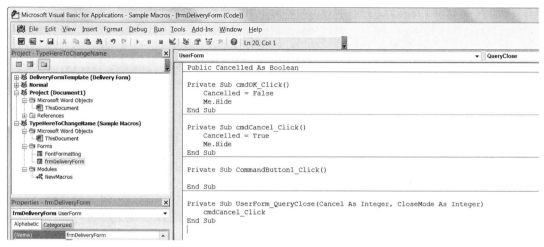

Figure 15.19 The logic behind the command buttons.

- Next, write the macro to create an instance of the Delivery Method form (frmDeliveryForm). The code will be added to show the form using a Public Sub, as shown in Figure 15.20, in the module called modDeliveryForm. By making it a Public (as opposed to Private) subroutine, it will be made available to other code modules.

Figure 15.20

Make a subroutine Public, and it will be available to other code modules.

- To automatically display the input form when a new document is created based on the Delivery Request form, use the Document_New event that is built into the ThisDocument object. The Document_New event is shown in Figure 15.21.

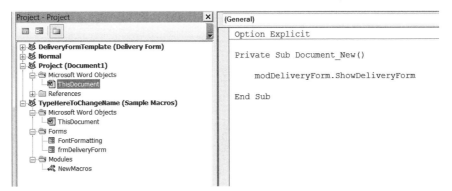

Figure 15.21　Use the Document_New event to automatically display the input form when a new document is created.

- Finally, let's add the remaining VBA code to get the information from the input form's controls and insert the text into the document after the form is displayed, as shown in Figure 15.22.

There are a few important things to notice about the code that inserts the information into the document. The Word object model provides several ways to reference a content control in order to assign text to its range. However, you cannot directly reference a content control by its title or name, as you can with a bookmark. For instance, `ActiveDocument.Range.ContentControls("ToName").Range.Text = mstrRecipientName` will result in an error. This is because a document can contain multiple content controls with the same title. You can, however, use the content control's index, or item number (e.g., `ActiveDocument.Range.ContentControls(1).Range.Text = mstrRecipientName`).

While we could have identified the content controls by index, we chose to use a For Each loop along with a Select Case statement. This allows us to iterate through all the content controls in the document and perform the appropriate handling based on the content control's title.

NOTE

Each content control has a unique ID assigned by Word, but you need to use the Word object model to find out the ID.

Also, notice that we used the Range object when writing text to the document. Using the Range object is more efficient than the Selection object and doesn't result in the cursor moving about on the screen as your code is running.

```
Option Explicit

Private mstrRecipientName As String
Private mstrClientMatter As String
Private mstrSenderName As String
Private mstrNotes As String
Private mblnConfirm As Boolean
Private mstrConfirmTelephone As String
Private mblnSignature As Boolean

Public Sub ShowDeliveryForm()

    Dim oFormInstance As frmDeliveryForm

    Set oFormInstance = New frmDeliveryForm

    With oFormInstance
        .Show

        If Not .Cancelled Then
            mstrRecipientName = .txtTo.Text
            mstrClientMatter = .txtClientNumber.Text
            mstrSenderName = .txtFrom.Text
            mstrNotes = .txtNotes.Text
            mblnConfirm = .chkConfirm.Value
            mstrConfirmTelephone = .txtTelephone.Text
            mblnSignature = .chkSignature.Value

            WriteInformationToDocument
        End If
    End With

    Unload oFormInstance
    Set oFormInstance = Nothing

End Sub

Function WriteInformationToDocument() As Boolean

    Dim oContentCtrl As Word.ContentControl

    For Each oContentCtrl In ActiveDocument.ContentControls
        Select Case oContentCtrl.Title
            Case "ToName"
                oContentCtrl.Range.Text = mstrRecipientName
            Case "ClientMatter"
                oContentCtrl.Range.Text = mstrRecipientName
            Case "FromName"
                oContentCtrl.Range.Text = mstrRecipientName
            Case "chkConfirm"
                oContentCtrl.Checked = mblnConfirm
            Case "chkSignature"
                oContentCtrl.Checked = mblnSignature
        End Select
    Next oContentCtrl

    ActiveDocument.Bookmarks("Comments").Range.Text = mstrNotes
    ActiveDocument.Bookmarks("Telephone").Range.Text = mstrConfirmTelephone

    WriteInformationToDocument = True

End Function
```

Figure 15.22 Code to transfer the information from the input form controls to text in the document. The complete code listing is available, along with the exercise files, at www. thepaynegroup.com/downloads/word2013forlawfirms/.

USE OBJECTS FROM OTHER PROGRAMS

We briefly looked at creating macros that automate the Word object model, but what if you want to use an object from another program from within Word? An example of this is sending an e-mail through Outlook. To use objects from another program, you can set a reference to the program, which uses Early Binding, or you can create objects on the fly, which is called Late Binding.

NOTE

Binding is a process used for matching function calls that you write to the actual code.

To see a list of available references, open the VBA Editor. From the Menu bar, select Tools, and then select References.

If the item you need is not listed in the Available References, such as a .Net project or a DLL, you can use the Browse button to find it.

Create an E-mail Message from within Word

1. In this example, you will use Early Binding. Open the Sample Macros template.

2. Press Alt+F11 to view the VBA Editor.

3. Within the VBA Editor, ensure that the correct module is selected in which to write your code. In this example, select the NewMacros module. The code you wrote earlier should be displayed in the code window. If the code window doesn't display, try double-clicking the NewMacros module.

NOTE

This type of macro can come in handy if you have a button on a form that sends the document to a certain person or department within the firm. For example, you may have new employees fill out information in a form and then have them click a button that automatically sends the document to the correct person in HR.

4. Place the insertion point below End Sub and press Enter. Type **Sub,** press the Spacebar, type **SendAnEmail,** and press Enter.

5. From the Menu bar, choose Tools, and then select References. Select Microsoft Outlook 15.0 Object Library, which is shown in Figure 15.23.

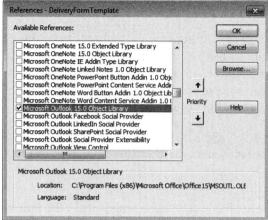

Figure 15.23

Set the reference to the Outlook 15.0 Object Library to include Outlook objects.

6. Click OK. You will now be able to use the Outlook objects in your code as if they were native Word objects.

7. Place the insertion point after `Sub SendAnEmail()` and press Enter twice. To declare an Outlook MailItem and set its value to a new Outlook Mail-Item, type the following:

```
Dim oOLEmail As Outlook.MailItem

Set oOLEmail = Outlook.CreateItem(olMailItem)
```

NOTE

This creates the MailItem (e-mail message), but it is not yet displayed. This allows us to manipulate the e-mail message in various ways before displaying it.

8. Type the following to add a subject, recipients, set the body of the message, add attachments, set the level of importance, display the e-mail for further editing by the user, and send the e-mail without having to show it first.

NOTE

Typing an apostrophe before text is used for adding comments to code. Notice the text turns green. While using the single apostrophe is by far the most commonly used method for adding comments to code in VBA, you can also type REM followed by a space before text that you want to be a comment. One final word on the subject; if your code will potentially be viewed or edited by anyone else, it's good practice to briefly intersperse comments throughout complex coding.

```
'Set the subject

oOLEmail.Subject = "Sample email"

'Set the recipients

oOLEmail.To = "lm@thePayneGroup.com"

oOleEmail.CC = "kw@thePayneGroup.com"

oOleEmail.BCC = "dp@thePayneGroup.com"

'Set the Body

oOLEmail.Body = Selection.Text

'Display the email

oOLEmail.Display

'Send the email

oOLEmail.Send
```

9. With the insertion point in the code, click Run, and select Run Sub/ UserForm to test the macro.

SOMETHING HAS GONE WRONG!

If you write any significant amount of code, errors are inevitable. There are three types of errors: syntax errors, runtime errors, and logical errors.

Syntax Errors

Syntax errors are usually discoverable before running the code. These errors include misspellings, using the wrong properties or arguments, and other items within code syntax.

If something is obviously wrong with the syntax as you're writing code, your code will turn red, and a helpful tip on how to correct the error will be displayed.

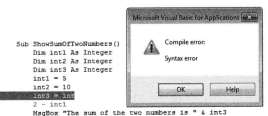

Figure 15.24

A compile error will help you identify what needs to be fixed.

To discover other syntax errors, use the method described previously to compile your code before running it (from the Menu bar, select Debug, and then select Compile TemplateProject). The compiler will stop at the offending line of code and allow you the opportunity to fix it. In the following example, the variable name is misspelled.

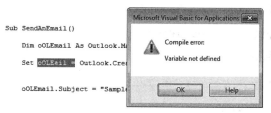

Figure 15.25

Compile error showing a misspelling in the variable name.

Continue to compile the project until no syntax errors are found or the Compile TemplateProject option appears disabled.

IntelliSense

When you type an object name in the code window and then a period, IntelliSense causes all of the object's members to display. This allows you to select an item from the list instead of trying to remember the correct spelling on your own. IntelliSense is also a nice way of discovering all of the members of any object.

For example, if you would like to see a list of all of the members of the Document object, type **ActiveDocument.** or **ThisDocument.** in the code window. Figure 15.26 shows IntelliSense in action and how it makes working in VBA easier.

Figure 15.26

Type ActiveDocument followed by a period to see a list of all of the members of the Document object.

Runtime Errors

Runtime errors, rather obviously, can only be discovered at runtime or while the code is running. Runtime errors are sometimes more difficult to track down because they may happen only in specific environments. For example, suppose you write a macro that opens a certain document from a mapped drive. On your development machine, you have the drive mapping as designated in your code. When the user runs your macro, they receive a runtime error if they do not have the correct drive mapping.

Other runtime errors can be discovered by the developer by running the code during the testing process. Runtime errors will not prevent the code from compiling.

Logic Errors

Logic errors are perhaps the most insidious of all types of errors. They do not prevent your code from compiling, and they do not cause errors to occur at runtime, but still something may be wrong or an incorrect result will occur.

An example of a logic error is shown in Figure 15.27.

```
Sub ShowSumOfTwoNumbers()
    Dim int1 As Integer
    Dim int2 As Integer
    Dim int3 As Integer
    int1 = 5
    int2 = 10
    int3 = int2 - int1
    MsgBox "The sum of the two numbers is " & int3
End Sub
```

Figure 15.27

An example of logic error. Can you see what the error is?

The result of running this procedure is obviously not the sum of the two numbers because the wrong mathematical symbol was used in the code shown in Figure 15.28.

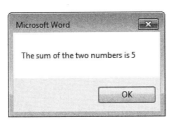

Figure 15.28

Either change the symbol in the code to a plus or change the message to read, "The difference between the two numbers is 5." .

BEYOND VBA...

Hopefully, in this chapter you have seen that VBA provides an accessible, powerful platform for automating almost every aspect of Word. However, as user friendly and powerful as VBA is, you may decide you want to explore using a more advanced programming environment to automate Word.

Visual Studio Tools for Office (VSTO) is a set of tools installed as part of Microsoft Visual Studio. VSTO is fully integrated with Microsoft Office, allowing automation not only of Word, but other applications including Excel, PowerPoint, Outlook, Project, InfoPath, and Visio. Using VSTO, you can create professional enterprise applications in the C# or VB.Net languages, which execute as managed code within the .Net Framework. The applications you develop in VSTO are typically compiled into DLL or EXE files and then deployed with a Windows installer package (MSI) or ClickOnce technology. You can create Word add-ins (similar to a global template containing macros), or even automated templates containing document content or boilerplate text.

OFFICE 365

You may also want to venture into the realm of developing Apps for Office 365. Office 365 Development Tools (Napa) offers a web-based development environment that supports web technologies and cloud services in Office 365 documents. PayneGroup and other organizations offer training and project consulting on automation along with robust template and macro solutions for organizations of all sizes.

Your understanding of VBA and the Word object model will come in handy as you begin developing more complex Microsoft Word add-ins using these other development tools. And even if you decide to hire a consultant, having a good foundational knowledge of VBA will allow you to communicate your needs and to know when a project is going down the wrong path. If timeline and budget on your project allow, instead of hiring a developer to do the work for your firm, consider having an external developer perform a code review (of your code) and provide expertise and feedback for optimization.

APPENDIX

NAVIGATION

Open Navigation pane	Ctrl+F
Next search result	Ctrl+Page Down
Previous search result	Ctrl+Page Up
Collapse heading	Alt+Shift+_
Expand heading	Alt+Shift+ +
Beginning of document	Ctrl+Home
End of document	Ctrl+End
Beginning of line	Home
End of line	End
One paragraph up	Ctrl+Up Arrow
One paragraph down	Ctrl+Down Arrow
One word to the left	Ctrl+Left Arrow
One word to the right	Ctrl+Right Arrow
Go to previous revision(s)	Shift+F5
Go To	Ctrl+G
Replace	Ctrl+H
Move between open Word documents	Ctrl+F6

QUICK EDITING

Undo	Ctrl+Z
Redo or Repeat	Ctrl+Y
Insert page break	Ctrl+Enter
Spell check	F7
Define a word	Ctrl+F7

2013 RIBBON

Hide or show the ribbon	Ctrl+F1
Show KeyTips	Alt + letter(s) or number(s)
Scroll tabs	Alt (or F10), then release and press the Left or Right Arrow
Scroll ribbon groups	Alt (or F10), then release and press Ctrl+ or Right Arrow
Scroll ribbon commands	Alt (or F10), then release and press Ctrl+ or Right Arrow
Select ribbon command	Enter or Spacebar
Move from ribbon to document, task pane, Status bar	F6

TASK PANES

Open Clipboard task pane	Select text, Ctrl+C, C
Open Reveal Formatting task pane	Shift+F1
Open Thesaurus task pane	Shift+F7
Open Styles task pane	Alt+Ctrl+Shift+S
Place focus on task pane	F6
Close task pane	F6, Ctrl+Spacebar, C
Open the Dictionary task pane	Ctrl+F7

BUILDING BLOCKS (QUICK PARTS)

Create a building block	Alt+F3
Insert a building block	Type building block name, F3

CHARACTER FORMATTING

Bold	Ctrl+B
Italic	Ctrl+I
Underline	Ctrl+U
Underline words only	Ctrl+Shift+W
Double underline	Ctrl+Shift+D
Toggle case	Shift+F3
All capitals	Ctrl+Shift+A
Small capitals	Ctrl+Shift+K
Increase font size by 1 pt	Ctrl+]
Decrease font size by 1 pt	Ctrl+[
Increase font size one value	Ctrl+Shift+.
Decrease font size one value	Ctrl+Shift+,
Display font dialog box	Ctrl+D
Hidden	Ctrl+Shift+H
Superscript	Ctrl+Shift+=
Subscript	Ctrl+=
Remove character formatting	Ctrl+Spacebar

PARAGRAPH FORMATTING

Align Left	Ctrl+L
Align Right	Ctrl+R
Center	Ctrl+E
Justify	Ctrl+J
Single space	Ctrl+1
Double space	Ctrl+2
Space and a half	Ctrl+5
Toggle 12 pts before	Ctrl+0
Increase left Indent .5"	Ctrl+M
Decrease left indent .5"	Ctrl+Shift+M
Increase hanging indent .5"	Ctrl+T
Decrease hanging indent .5"	Ctrl+Shift+T
Toggle Show/Hide	Ctrl+*
Remove paragraph formatting	Ctrl+Q

STYLES

Open Apply Styles task pane	Ctrl+Shift+S
Open Styles task pane	Alt +Ctrl+Shift+S
Apply Normal style	Ctrl+Shift+N
Heading 1	Alt+Ctrl+1
Heading 2	Alt+Ctrl+2
Heading 3	Alt+Ctrl+3
List Bullet	Ctrl+Shift+L
Insert style separator	Alt+Ctrl+Enter

TRACK CHANGES

Turn on/off revision marks	Ctrl+Shift+E
Insert comment	Alt+Ctrl+M
Close Reviewing pane	Alt+Shift+C

FILE & VIEW

New document	Ctrl+N
Open	Ctrl+O
Save	Ctrl+S
Save as	F12
Close	Ctrl+W
Close or Exit	Alt+F4
Print	Ctrl+P
Draft view	Alt+Ctrl+N
Print Layout view	Alt+Ctrl+P
Outline view	Alt+Ctrl+O
Maximize application	Alt+F10
Split document (toggle)	Alt+Ctrl+S
Display shortcut menu	Shift+F10

SELECTING TEXT

Select all	Ctrl+A
One word	F8 F8
One sentence	F8, F8, F8
One paragraph	F8, F8, F8, F8
To a specific character	F8+Character
Stop extend selection	Esc
One word right	Ctrl+Shift+Right Arrow
One word left	Ctrl+Shift+Left Arrow

Paragraph down	Ctrl+Shift+Down Arrow
Paragraph up	Ctrl+Shift+Up Arrow
Vertical selection	Ctrl+Shift+F8
Turn vertical selection off	Esc

COPYING, PASTING, MOVING TEXT

Copy	Ctrl+C
Copy formatting	Ctrl+Shift+C
Cut	Ctrl+X
Paste	Ctrl+V
Paste formatting	Ctrl+Shift+V
Paste special	Alt+Ctrl+V
Move selected paragraphs up	Alt+Shift+Up Arrow
Move selected paragraphs down	Alt+Shift+Down Arrow
Delete one character to the left	Backspace
Delete one word to the left	Ctrl+Backspace
Delete one character to the right	Delete
Delete one word to the right	Ctrl+Delete

SYMBOLS AND SPECIAL CHARACTERS

Nonbreaking space	Ctrl+Shift+Space
Nonbreaking hyphen	Ctrl+Shift+-
Insert cents symbol	Ctrl+/+C
Insert copyright symbol	Alt+Ctrl+C
Insert registered trademark symbol	Alt+Ctrl+R
Insert trademark symbol	Alt+Ctrl+T
Insert a character (<char>) with an accent	Ctrl+', <char>

COMPLEX DOCUMENTS

Insert a footnote	Alt+Ctrl+F
Insert an endnote	Alt+Ctrl+D
Insert a bookmark	Ctrl+Shift+F5
Insert a hyperlink	Ctrl+K
Mark entry for table of authorities	Alt+Shift+I

Mark entry for table of contents	Alt+Shift+O
Mark entry for index	Alt+Shift+X
Column break	Ctrl+Shift+Enter
Display macro dialog box	Alt+F8

TABLES

Move to the next cell	Tab
Tab within a cell	Ctrl+Tab
Move to the preceding cell	Shift+Tab
Move to the first cell in a row	Alt+Home
Move to the last cell in a row	Alt+End
Move to the first cell in a column	Alt+Page Up
Move to the last cell in a column	Alt+Page Down
Move selected row up one row	Alt+Shift+Up Arrow
Move selected row down one row	Alt+Shift+Down Arrow
Go to beginning of row	Alt+Home
Go to end of row	Alt+End
Go to top of column	Alt+Page Up
Go to end of column	Alt+Page Down

FIELDS

Insert Date field	Alt+Shift+D
Insert Time field	Alt+Shift+T
Insert Listnum field	Alt+Ctrl+L
Insert Page field	Alt+Shift+P
Update fields	F9
Insert field manually	Ctrl+F9
Go to next field	F11
Go to previous field	Shift+F11
Lock field from updating	Ctrl+F11
Unlock field	Ctrl+Shift+F11
Unlink field	Ctrl+Shift+F9
Toggle on/off selected field code	Shift+F9
Toggle on/off field codes in document	Alt+F9

Assign Custom Keyboard Shortcuts

1. **For existing Word commands:** File, Options, Customize Ribbon, Customize. Select command and assign new shortcut key.

2. **For styles:** Right-click a style in the Style gallery or task pane, Modify, Format, Shortcut Key. Assign new shortcut key.

3. **For symbols:** Insert, Symbol, More Symbols, Shortcut Key. Assign new shortcut key.

INDEX